Sustainable Peacebuilding and Social Justice in Times of Transition

Mieke T.A. Lopes Cardozo • Elizabeth J.T. Maber
Editors

Sustainable Peacebuilding and Social Justice in Times of Transition

Findings on the Role of Education in Myanmar

Springer

Editors
Mieke T.A. Lopes Cardozo
University of Amsterdam
Amsterdam, The Netherlands

Elizabeth J.T. Maber
University of Cambridge
Cambridge, UK

ISBN 978-3-030-06725-0 ISBN 978-3-319-93812-7 (eBook)
https://doi.org/10.1007/978-3-319-93812-7

This Springer imprint is published by the registered company Springer Nature Switzerland AG
The registered company address is: Gewerbestrasse 11, 6330 Cham, Switzerland

Foreword

This book marks an important contribution to the literature on education and peacebuilding. It is the result of extensive fieldwork in Myanmar and is an output of research undertaken as part of the UNICEF Peacebuilding, Education and Advocacy (PBEA) programme. The approach to the research and its findings are significant for a number of reasons.

At the time, the investment of $150 million in the PBEA programme by the Government of the Netherlands, Ministry of Foreign Affairs, represented the largest contribution to UNICEF by a single government donor. The programme operated from 2012–2016 across 14 conflict-affected countries (Burundi, Chad, Côte d'Ivoire, the Democratic Republic of the Congo, Ethiopia, Liberia, Myanmar, Sierra Leone, Somalia, South Sudan, the State of Palestine, Uganda, Pakistan and Yemen).

PBEA was innovative because it challenged the prevailing orthodoxy of 'liberal peacebuilding' which prioritizes security concerns, political reforms and economic development. These are all crucial areas for post-conflict reconstruction, but there is often an assumption that social development in areas such as education will follow at a later stage once these other issues have been resolved. This underestimates the crucial importance of social development in bringing about durable solutions as part of post-conflict peacebuilding. To be sustainable, peacebuilding processes must address the needs of local communities and marginalised groups as well as the concerns of political and economic elites – otherwise there is always the risk of a relapse into conflict.

In practice, the programme involved a 'conflict analysis' in each country which attempted to identify how education might contribute to conflict (for example, by creating and reproducing inequalities), as well as its potential role in addressing these underlying causes. As a consequence, there was an attempt to see the role of education as going beyond 'peace education', so that 'education for peacebuilding' meant an examination of how the structure and functions of education – in all their complexity – might be factors that need to be addressed as part of conflict transformation. This meant that it was important to consider the governance of education in various conflict-affected situations as well as technical aspects related to teaching and learning. Inevitably, this was a more politically sensitive endeavour.

PBEA was also unusual in that it included a strand to support learning from knowledge generated by the programme. One part of this was the creation of a Research Consortium on Education and Peacebuilding involving a partnership between UNICEF and the Universities of Amsterdam, Sussex and Ulster. Collectively, the partnership involved more than 40 researchers across a number of countries, and the fieldwork in Myanmar is a good example of a commitment to work closely with local research partners. Overall, the Research Consortium focused on three main issues: Policy (how is peacebuilding integrated into education policies and vice versa?); Teachers (what is the role of teachers in peacebuilding?); and Youth (how do formal and non-formal peacebuilding education programmes address youth agency?).

Perhaps, one of the most significant achievements of the Research Consortium was the development of a common theoretical framework (Novelli, Lopes Cardozo, Smith, 2015; 2017), which was used to guide the research across each of the countries. This drew on social justice dimensions of redistribution, recognition and representation, as defined by Nancy Fraser (2005), complimented by post-conflict issues of reconciliation (Lederach 1995, 1997; Hamber 2007, 2009). Together these represent the 4Rs framework, and this was developed as a way of examining the contribution of education systems, processes and programmes to peacebuilding in terms of Redistribution (equity and non-discrimination in education access, resources and outcomes for different groups in society); Recognition (respect for and affirmation of diversity and identities in education structures, processes and content, in terms of gender, language, politics, religion, ethnicity/race, culture and ability); Representation (participation, at all levels of the education system, in governance and decision-making related to the allocation, use and distribution of human and material resources); and Reconciliation (dealing with legacies of past events, injustices and the material and psychosocial effects of conflict, as well as developing new relationships of trust). The framework is presented and discussed in more detail in Chap. 2.

The work in Myanmar was led by Dr. Mieke Lopes Cardozo and colleagues at the University of Amsterdam in conjunction with Myanmar based researchers. Political sensitivities and tension related to the ongoing process of transition towards democracy meant that field based research was fraught with difficulties. The capacity of the research team to complete the fieldwork is a tribute to their collective tenacity and perseverance. As recent and horrifying news reports of the situation of the Rohingya demonstrate, there is a huge democratic deficit in Myanmar and ongoing human rights violations undermine Myanmar's democratic transition.

As the reader will note as they travel through the pages of this book, education and the education system really matter to people affected by conflict. The fieldwork was carried out in Mon state and Yangon, and the findings are specific to those particular contexts. The focus on policy highlights how the existence of multiple education systems can generate inequalities and how contentious decisions over language of instruction can fuel tensions about state recognition of different ethnic groups. Other chapters highlight the often neglected area of teachers and their role in peacebuilding, not just in terms of how teacher education and professional development can support the creation of more inclusive learning environments, but also how the representation of teachers in curriculum and other reform processes can reduce tension and develop a sense of ownership for much needed changes. Finally, the chapters dealing with youth agency highlight the importance of recognising the diversity of experience amongst youth and avoiding the tokenism that often characterises youth engagement programmes.

A pervading message is that education is a central pillar of social reproduction, social cohesion and social transformation and while education can contribute to positive change it also has the potential to aggravate the drivers of conflict and be an obstacle to long-term and sustainable peace. The need for a more equitable, culturally sensitive and humane education system that can build the human and social potential of Myanmar youth is clear, and this book makes a strong contribution in pointing us towards the necessary changes that need to take place across the country.

UNESCO Chair Alan Smith
Ulster University
Coleraine, Northern Ireland
Chair in the Political Economy of Education Mario Novelli
University of Sussex
Brighton, UK

References

Fraser, N. (2005). Reframing justice in a globalized world. *New Left Review, 36*, 79–88.

Hamber, B. (2007). Forgiveness and reconciliation: Paradise lost or pragmatism? *Peace and Conflict, 13*(1), 115–125.

Hamber, B. (2009). *Transforming societies after political violence: Truth, reconciliation, and mental health*. New York: Springer.

Lederach, J. P. (1995). *Preparing for peace: Conflict transformation across cultures*. Syracuse: Syracuse University Press.

Lederach, J. P. (1997). *Building peace: Sustainable reconciliation in divided societies*. Washington, DC: United States Institute of Peace Press.

Novelli, M., Lopes Cardozo, M.T.A. & Smith, A. (2015). *A Theoretical Framework for Analysing the Contribution of Education to Sustainable Peacebuilding: 4Rs in Conflict-Affected Contexts*. University of Amsterdam, Research Consortium on Education and Peacebuilding. Available online https://educationanddevelopment.files.wordpress.com/2014/11/theoretical-framework-jan15.pdf

Novelli, M., Lopes Cardozo, M. T. A., & Smith, A. (2017). The 4Rs framework: Analyzing education's contribution to sustainable peacebuilding with social justice in conflict-affected contexts. *Journal on Education in Emergencies, 3*(1), 14–43.

Acknowledgements

This edited volume is the result of a collaborative process between various members of a diverse research team, with researchers from Myanmar, the University of Amsterdam and the University of Auckland. As editors, and as the broader team of authors, we are grateful to the support of a wide range of colleagues. Firstly, the team is grateful to the generous time and support offered by the colleagues at the UNICEF Country Office in Yangon, the UNICEF Field Office in Mawlamyine, the UNICEF Regional Office and the PBEA team at UNICEF in New York. Their commitment and engagement throughout the research process has been crucial in facilitating the research in terms of access, feedback and validation. In addition to the support and collaboration with UNICEF, this report would not have been possible without the support of many people who participated in the study, and to whom we are very grateful. These include: the youth respondents; staff and participants of (non)formal education initiatives; teachers and educators from different levels and systems; policy-makers and those involved in the reform processes; staff of various civil society organisations in and beyond Myanmar; and colleague researchers based in and/or working on Myanmar. In addition to the authors of chapters in this collection, we extend our thanks to research team members Nandar Nwe Oo, Htet Yin Tun and Aung Thura Htun. The team would also like to thank representatives from Myanmar's Ministry of Education, the Department of Educational Planning and Training and the Ministry of Labour, Employment and Social Security for their contributions and willingness to give up their time to support the research.

We also thank all reviewers of the initial version of the unpublished report for their valuable contributions: Dr. Matthew Walton, Dr. Khin Mar Mar Kyi, Dr. Rose Metro, Dr. Ashley South, Prof. Marie Lall, Dr. Patrick McCormick, Matthew Sheader, Prof. Joseph Lo Bianco, Teija Vallandingham (UNICEF EAPRO), Devashish Dutta (UNICEP EAPRO), Fernando Balmaceda (UNICEF EAPRO), Jane Davies (UNICEF CO Myanmar), Mathias Kjear (UNICEF CO Myanmar), Cliff Meyers (UNICEF CO Myanmar), and colleagues at the University of Sussex, Ulster University and UNICEF's PBEA team. We are grateful for the overall support and collaborations with Prof. Novelli and Prof. Smith, and for providing a start to this book with a foreword. We thank Marielle Le Mat and Kiymet Schipper

(University of Amsterdam) for their research assistance in the period 2014–2016, and Melina Merdanovic, Cybele Atme and Hannah Sturm (all students in the Research Master International Development Studies at the University of Amsterdam) for their editorial support.

Finally, we sincerely hope the outcomes of this study will be of use at the various levels of engagement with processes of peacebuilding, and to all participants of the study – including youth, educators, (I)NGO staff, international organisations, policy-makers and other stakeholders – and we welcome a continued dialogue, to move these debates beyond a static output into support to a more dynamic, socially just and peaceful future.

University of Amsterdam
Amsterdam, The Netherlands
Mieke T. A. Lopes Cardozo

University of Cambridge
Cambridge, UK
Elizabeth J. T. Maber

Contents

About the Authors

Editors

Mieke T. A. Lopes Cardozo is Assistant Professor at the Amsterdam Institute for Social Science Research of the University of Amsterdam, where her work focuses on education in relation to social justice and peacebuilding. She co-directed the Research Consortium on Education and Peacebuilding (2014–2016), a partnership with UNICEF's Peacebuilding, Education and Advocacy (PBEA) programme, together with Prof. Mario Novelli (University of Sussex) and Prof. Alan Smith (University of Ulster) and coordinated the country study in Myanmar. She is appointed by the UN SG to work as part of an Advisory Committee of Experts for a UN mandated study on Resolution 2250 on Youth, Peace and Security. For more information on her work and publications visit: https://educationanddevelopment.wordpress.com/members/mieke-lopes-cardozo/

Elizabeth J.T. Maber is a Teaching Associate in the Faculty of Education at the University of Cambridge. She completed her doctorate in education and international development at the Amsterdam Institute for Social Science Research, University of Amsterdam, in 2017, specialising in gender and education in conflict. During this time, she also worked as a research consultant and Yangon fieldwork co-ordinator for the Research Consortium on Education and Peacebuilding. Since 2009 she has worked in Myanmar and Thailand as a trainer, curriculum writer and education consultant.

Contributors

Khin Mar Aung is Director of World Education in Myanmar, with more than 30 years experience in education and development research and practice in Myanmar and regionally. She is currently involved in policy analysis and policy development of education programmes at the national level in Myanmar.

Katharina Buske holds a Master of Science in International Development from the University of Amsterdam, where her studies focused on the nexus between education and peacebuilding. She is currently working for the United Network of Young Peacebuilders as the Fundraising and Outreach Officer.

Sean Higgins is a doctoral researcher at the University of Amsterdam where his work focuses on the agency of teachers as peacebuilders. His interest in education and social justice started while a secondary school teacher for 20 years in England before teaching in conflict affected Sierra Leone. He was a consultant for UNICEF and the IRC in Sierra Leone before becoming full time researcher and coordinator (Mon State) for the Research Consortium on Education and Peacebuilding.

Taru Niskanen holds a Master of Science in International Development Studies from the University of Amsterdam. She currently works as a Development Director at Architects for Society.

Mario Novelli is Professor of the Political Economy of Education and Director of the Centre for International Education (CIE) at the University of Sussex. He previously worked at the University of Amsterdam and the University of Bristol, working across the disciplines of Education, International development, Geography and Politics. He was Co-director of the Research Consortium on Education and Peacebuilding, together with Mieke Lopes Cardozo and Alan Smith.

Aye Aye Nyein works as an Outreach Coordinator at the US Embassy Rangoon and a researcher based in Yangon specialising in education and social development. She was Chevening Scholarship recipient (2013–2014) from the UK Foreign and Commonwealth Office and holds an M.Ed. in Educational Leadership, Policy and Development from the University of Bristol.

Hla Win May Oo is an ESL Teacher/Teacher Trainer at B.S.I Learning Academy and a Social Enterprise Consultant and 'Education for Entrepreneurs' Trainer with the British Council, Myanmar. She has also worked as a Lecturer for the MBA program at Temasek International College and was an In-country Research Partner/Research Assistant for the Research Consortium on Education and Peacebuilding.

Tabea Campbell Pauli is currently working in Myanmar, for a local NGO focused on supporting the formal peace process. After completing her master's degree at the University of Amsterdam, she has focused on issues of social justice, inclusion and peace education, in the context of conflict in Myanmar.

Naw Tha Ku Paul *(Mie Mie)* works with Point B, training local trainers to develop their techniques in visual-thinking, design and facilitation for community development. Now based in Mon, Naw Tha Ku has also spearheaded non-formal education and child protection networks for migrant communities in Thailand, having previously worked in education development on the Thai-Myanmar border.

Kiymet Schipper has a background in Child and Adolescent Development Psychology. After graduating from the Research Master International Development Studies at the University of Amsterdam, she worked as a research assistant for the Research Consortium Education and Peacebuilding.

Ritesh Shah is a Senior Lecturer of Comparative and International Education at the University of Auckland. His current research, teaching and consultancy work focusses on education provision in situations of conflict and spans several regions of the world.

Alan Smith is Professor and UNESCO Chair in Pluralism, Human Rights and Democracy, and the Director of the UNESCO Centre at the School of Education at the University of Ulster. Professor Smith's work includes research on education and conflict, young people's understanding of human rights and the development of social, civic and political education. He was Co-director of the Research Consortium on Education and Peacebuilding, together with Mario Novelli and Mieke Lopes Cardozo.

Abbreviations

ABFSU	All Burma Federation of Student Unions
ABSDF	All Burma Student Democratic Front
ADB	Asian Development Bank
ASEAN	Association of South East Asian Nations
BC	British Council
CBO	Community Based Organisation
CESR	Comprehensive Education Sector Review
CMOC	Context-Mechanism-Outcome Pattern Configuration
CPE	Cultural Political Economy
CSO	Civil Society Organisation
DEPT	Department of Education Planning and Training
DFAT	Department of Foreign Affairs and Trade
EAG	Ethnic Armed Group
ECCD	Early Childhood Care and Development
ECCE	Early Childhood Care and Education
EFA	Education for All
EfECT	English for Education College Trainers
EMIS	Education Management Information System
GEN	Gender Equality Network
GBV	Gender Based Violence
IDP	Internally Displaced People
ILO	International Labour Organisation
INGO	International Non-Governmental Organisation
IOM	International Organisation for Migration
JICA	Japan International Cooperation Agency
KIO	Kachin Independence Organisation
KNPP	Karenni National Progressive Party
KNU	Karen National Union
KWEG	Karen Women's Empowerment Group
KYO	Karen Youth Organisation
LGBT	Lesbian Gay Bisexual Transgender

MDGs	Millennium Development Goals
MEDG	Monastic Education Development Group
MNEC	Mon National Education Committee
MoE	Ministry of Education
MoRA	Ministry of Religious Affairs
MPC	Myanmar Peace Centre
MPSI	Myanmar Peace Support Initiative
MWO	Mon Women's Organisation
NCA	Nationwide Ceasefire Agreement
NCCT	National Ceasefire Coordination Team
NESP	National Education Strategic Plan
NFE	Non Formal Education
NLD	National League for Democracy
NMSP	New Mon State Party
NNER	National Network for Education Reform
NRPC	National Reconciliation and Peace Centre
NSAGs	Non-State Armed Groups
OECD	Organisation for Economic Cooperation and Development
PBEA	The UNICEF Peacebuilding Education and Advocacy Programme
QBEP	Quality Basic Education Programme
SD	Senior Delegation
SITE	School Based In Service Teacher Education
SLORC	State Law and Order Restoration Council
SPDC	State Peace and Development Council
SSA-N	Shan State Army North
SWAN	Shan Women's Action Network
Tatmadaw	The Myanmar military forces
TRCs	Truth and Reconciliation Commissions
TVET	Technical Vocational Education and Training
UNDP	United Nations Development Programme
UNCESCO	United Nations Educational, Scientific and Cultural Organization
UNFC	United Nationalities Federal Council
UN OCHA	United Nations Office for Coordination of Humanitarian Affairs
UNRCO	United Nations Resident Coordinator
UPE	Universal Primary Education
UPWC	Union Peacemaking Working Committee
USDA	The Union Solidarity and Development Association
USDP	Union Solidarity and Development Party
WLB	Women's League of Burma

List of Figures

List of Tables

Chapter 1
Introduction

Mieke T. A. Lopes Cardozo and Elizabeth J. T. Maber

Peacebuilding and Education – Why This Book on Myanmar, and Why Now?

Communities and nations around the world are faced with contemporary and multi-scalar challenges, ranging from huge social inequalities to conflicts over political autonomy, belief systems, citizenship rights or natural resources, to name a few. Myanmar plays a unique part in relation to such challenges, which not only feature within its national and state borders, but in many ways is connected to ongoing processes in the region and beyond. Conflicts within Myanmar are of a very diverse nature in terms of what drives these, while at the same time conflict-affected regions are covering various parts of the country's soil. Most notably is the enormous crisis in Rakhine state, where large parts of its Muslim Rohingya population have fled the country amid a highly insecure situation. While tensions that led to the current emergency in Rakhine have their historical roots (see Chap. 3), present-day media has painted a dire picture of the state of human rights due to the recent eruption of violence and displacements in this state. For reasons noted below, the findings in this book do not deal directly with the conflict in Rakhine state, yet touch upon a myriad of other dimensions of conflict and social injustices as experienced by students, teachers, trainers and policy or NGO officials included in the research. In such turbulent times, the schooling of a nation's younger generation lies close to the hearts of the various population groups, regardless of their socio-economic

M. T. A. Lopes Cardozo (✉)
University of Amsterdam, Amsterdam, The Netherlands
e-mail: mlopescardozo@fmg.uva.nl

E. J. T. Maber
University of Cambridge, Cambridge, UK

M. T. A. Lopes Cardozo, E. J. T. Maber (eds.), *Sustainable Peacebuilding and Social Justice in Times of Transition*,
https://doi.org/10.1007/978-3-319-93812-7_1

background, faith system or geographical location; parents desire the best possible education for their children and the possibility of a brighter future. In addition, education has gained the interest of policy-makers, international organisations and civil society alike, as its crucial role in relation to conflict and peacebuilding becomes increasingly pertinent. Nevertheless, there is still a gap of knowledge on the specific relations and interactions between education systems, actors and outcomes and broader societal processes of conflict or peacebuilding. This book is dedicated to further explore these themes in the context of Myanmar, and respond to the growing body of literature over the past two decades in the field of education, conflict and peacebuilding (see for instance Bush and Saltarelli 2000; Davies 2005; Smith 2005; Novelli and Lopes Cardozo 2008; UNESCO 2011).

This introductory chapter first highlights the specificities of the research location of Myanmar. Secondly, we briefly introduce the three key research areas that informed the structure of our data collection, analysis and its presentation in this book in three parts. Thirdly, we discuss the partnerships, scope and limitations of the study as well as the ethical and practical challenges faced. Finally, we invite the reader to explore this book further by outlining the structure of the book.

Research Context – Education in Myanmar in a Time of Transition

Although the book title is referring to *the role of education in Myanmar* the scope of this collection of works is not covering the whole of the country by any means. More specifically, while in the sections dealing with national (and regional) issues of peacebuilding and education policy and reform we do aim to speak to the national context, our data collection and analysis has focused on two specific geographical regions: the wider Yangon area and Mon State. We chose these regions in consultation with UNICEF, being one of the partners of the consortium that formed the major framework in which this work took place (see below). We based this regional selection on a range of practical (accessibility, prior networks) and ethical considerations (no clearance for research in more conflict-prone areas). The authors are mindful of the unique contexts of both Mon and Yangon in relation to peacebuilding within the broader national context, such that our findings are not generalizable to other areas of the country with specific conflict drivers, some of which are currently conflict-affected.

While initial data collection started in August 2014, most of the analysis of the data collected for this book was completed at the end of 2015. Considering Myanmar's period of constant transition, we have aimed to update our data concerning the political and peacebuilding situation as much as possible up to the time of writing this edited book (end of 2017). However, we would like to mention up front that the empirical findings of this report should be seen in the light of this specific time period. In addition, our analysis of the current policy environment has been characterised by a constantly developing approach, as documentation (of reforms) is of conditional nature and meant an engagement with 'latest' versions available to the research team. This 'developing' and 'emerging' nature of Myanmar's transition is reflected throughout the analysis presented in the book.

Research Themes and Transversal Topics

The chapters that form the body of this book were developed as part of the work of the Research Consortium on Education and Peacebuilding, which is a co-led research partnership between the Universities of Amsterdam, Sussex and Ulster, and supported by UNICEF's Peacebuilding, Education and Advocacy (PBEA) programme. This 2-year partnership with UNICEF (mid 2014–mid 2016) sought to build evidence on the relationship between education and peacebuilding in conflict-affected contexts. The consortium carried out research in five countries: Myanmar, Pakistan, South Africa, Uganda and Liberia. The research was carried out in partnership with colleagues in each of the participating countries and sought to contribute both to theory and practice in the field of education and peacebuilding, developing theoretically informed, policy relevant outputs. The report draws on the theoretical framework developed for this broader consortium (Novelli et al. 2017), which gives a distinctive focus on the role of education within cultural, political and economic processes of conflict and peacebuilding from a '4R's' perspective, including the analytical and strongly interconnected dimensions of redistribution, recognition, representation and reconciliation (further developed in Chap. 2). The consortium worked on three key thematic research areas, and two transversal themes, which are also present in the structure and contents of this book on Myanmar (Fig. 1.1):

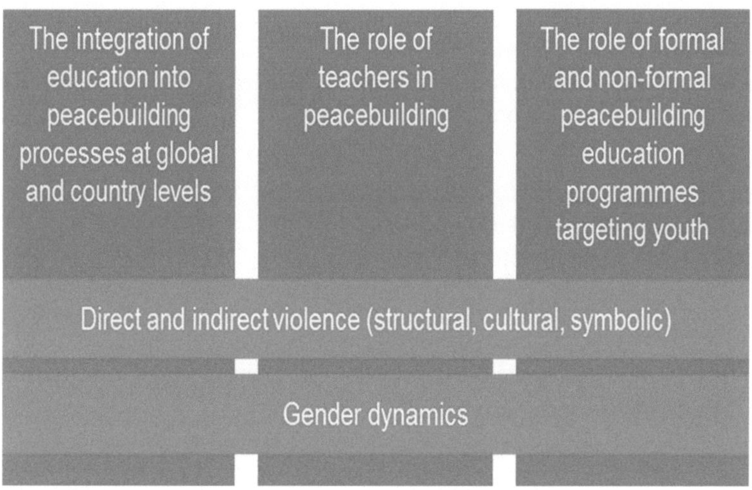

Fig. 1.1 Three thematic research areas and two cross-cutting themes

The Integration of Education and Peacebuilding at (Global/National) Policy Levels

Notwithstanding the growing recognition that education plays an important role in the context of a fragile state, the majority of education and peacebuilding interventions remain explicitly and implicitly framed in terms of service delivery and formal, or conventional, educational infrastructures. This research area therefore addressed two main questions:

1. *To what extent is education (as part of social service provision) integrated into broader peacebuilding policies and practices at the global and country levels?*
2. *What policies and programmes are being adopted to ensure the integration of education into peacebuilding at country level?*

In examining these questions, we pay particular attention to policies related to the following areas: equity, social cohesion, reconciliation and governance in education, recognising their inter-relations.

The Role of Teachers in Peacebuilding

This research area identifies education policy interventions that enable (or hinder) teachers to become active agents of peacebuilding and social cohesion in and outside the classroom contexts, exploring how such agency is both enabled and constrained. It specifically explores the governance of teachers, their training and professional development, their recruitment and deployment, their morale, terms and conditions and their role in promoting peace, reconciliation, social cohesion and violence mitigation. Hence, this area of research focused specifically on the conditions under which education interventions focused on teachers can promote or mitigate violence, focusing on:

1. Teacher training
2. Teacher recruitment, deployment and management
3. Teacher performance and practices
4. Curricula and textbook reform

The Role of Formal and Non-formal Peacebuilding Education Programmes Focusing on Youth

This third research area explores the ways in which the agency of youth – or their 'space for manoeuvre' – is impacted through a range of formal and non-formal education interventions, and how this enables or restricts young people to contribute to processes of peacebuilding and social cohesion, either in political, socio-cultural or economic ways. It combines a focus on youth agency, peacebuilding and education – an intersection that is often not addressed simultaneously. The report discusses the voices of youth respondents, including how youth see peace, (formal) education and their most pressing challenges in relation to gendered inequalities and violence. Our analysis aims to illustrate both the heterogeneity of 'youth' in the five countries, as well as highlight how often only a selection of youth constituencies are included in (formal and non-formal) education.

Research Collaborations and Scope of Work: Partnerships and Ethical Considerations

One month after the official start of the Research Consortium's work, in late July and early August 2014, a small team on behalf of the University of Amsterdam visited Myanmar to establish relationships with possible in-country partners and to inform multiple relevant organisations and actors about the project. Based on the responses that were received to an expression of interest (December 2014), the University of Amsterdam selected seven in-country researchers. Four of these in country researchers fall under institutional partnerships, with World Education and Point B.

The team, consisting of three researchers from the University of Amsterdam, one colleague from the University of Auckland and seven researchers in Myanmar (three individuals, one affiliated with World Education, and three affiliated with Point B) carried out the fieldwork between January and April 2015. The research team was extended with the inclusion of four (now graduated) Master students that were part of the International Development Studies Master programme at the University of Amsterdam, who were able to provide additional data beyond the timeframe and providing complementary analysis into topics not yet covered in detail by work of the Research Consortium on Education and Peacebuilding. All together, 72 RA1-related respondents (including policy-makers, peacebuilding actors, and experts), 115 RA2-related respondents (including head teachers, teachers, and teacher trainers), and 144 RA3-related participants (including youth and staff of micro-cases) participated in the research. Additional data collected by the four students added 127 youth respondents (58 through interviews and 69 through questionnaires/surveys) and 72 teacher respondents to this picture. The main research sites where we collected data were Yangon and Mon State, including two specific townships (kept anonymous in public outputs for ethical considerations).

The first training and workshops with the newly established research team were held in the last week of January 2015. In these workshops, the research team together with colleagues from UNICEF collectively adapted the methodological and theoretical framework developed by the Research Consortium to suit the context of Myanmar in collaboration with local researchers, and specifically focused on six data collection areas:

1. **Research Area 1 (RA1):** processes of reform development and competing perspectives; a unique peacebuilding moment and challenges of a situation in flux;
2. **Research Area 2 (RA2):** teacher training and teacher deployment; violence at school; gendered nature of the teaching profession;
3. **Research Area 3 (RA3):** 'post-secondary' youth leadership/voice; youth perspectives and responses (targeted focus on gender and general theme of violence); formal and non-formal education initiatives;
4. **Educational autonomy**, including the training of teachers and youth responses;
5. **Language of instruction** by inclusion of ethnic languages in policy discussion, teacher training and deployment, and youth experiences of this;
6. **History education**, as presented in policy reform, curriculum development, teacher training, and youth agency/perceptions for reconciliation.

On a more practical level, due to very limited internet access it proved to be difficult to engage in-country researchers in collective data analysis processes using online analysis software. However, we ensured that in-country researchers could have their input on initial coding and findings in the second data-analysis workshops in April 2015 in Myanmar. The members of the research team collectively developed and presented the initial insights drawn from the data collection period in an end-of-fieldwork dissemination seminar, hosted by UNICEF and visited by a range of participants in the study. Further validation of findings is ensured through continuous (online) communication between members of the various country teams and in meetings (in Myanmar and during collective team meetings connected to a conference in Oxford in September 2015).

As a result of the partnership, the UNICEF Country Office Myanmar and local researchers and civil society institutions have been engaged throughout this process. For instance, our interaction with UNICEF in Myanmar (Country and Field Office) was dialogic, involving the exchange of documents, methodological insights, literature and useful contacts. We have also shared and validated our research methodology, theoretical framework, literature review and findings of the study. The support of UNICEF has been indispensable with regard to facilitating contacts and meetings with key respondents in the international civil society networks, as well as with national and local government and non-government organisations.

We encountered a number of challenges during the research process that limited the scope and possibly the generalizability of the findings in this particular work. Firstly, while UNICEF and our other prior network has been crucial in the sampling of both case studies and respondents, we encountered difficulties in obtaining formal permissions to collect data within school settings. Our access to teachers and students was further hindered by the timing of school examination periods and the Thingyan (water festival and New Year) holidays. With support of UNICEF and our Myanmar research colleagues, we managed to have access to a number of teachers and students, mainly outside of school premises, yet we were not able to conduct observations of educational practices. As a creative solution, we asked youth respondents to enact classroom practices in role-plays, which obviously represent a certain interpretation of classroom realities. Furthermore, our partnership with UNICEF also meant we had to find consensus on the locations of our data collection, where we could build on existing networks and on-going relevant activities, while at the same time being aware of the safety of respondents and our research team. This resulted in the choice to focus on Mon State and the broader Yangon area, which considering the historical and present-day nature of these regions as relatively stable, obviously has implications for our findings in relation to peacebuilding. We therefore strongly support the idea that more research is needed, on thematic areas we have not covered in these contexts, as well as on similar thematic areas in other regions of the country.

Secondly, due to a legacy of restricted interaction with the academic research community, we were unable to establish partnerships with universities or other academic research institutes, as happened in the other country studies in the Research Consortium. This led us to select seven Myanmar researchers with very relevant (academic and/or practitioner) experience in conducting (qualitative) research. The set-up of the team, with members from different linguistic, ethnic and religious backgrounds, might have influenced the way we have selected certain (micro-)case studies, while for reasons of safety and (political) sensitivities we could not select others.

Thirdly, trust building with participants in the research and avoiding where possible a wholly extractive approach to data gathering was an important dimension of the process, especially in relation to engaging youth. Nevertheless, the relatively short time frame implies that the ethnographic nature of our research approach was somewhat limited, and would benefit from a continued research engagement, which is something we hope to be able to take on.

Finally, the actual status of a country in (political, economic and socio-cultural) transition means our study is both timely and time-bound, especially in light of the elections in November 2015 that followed immediately after the writing of the initial report. This also calls for further studies to document and understand the highly complex and rapidly changing nature of transition in Myanmar.

However, having clarified some of the main challenges and why we see these findings as reflecting a particular geographical as well as time-bound context within Myanmar, rather than representing the country as a whole, we do feel this book brings a unique and more ethnographic, while at the same time 'critical realist', understanding into the wider debate (see also Chap. 2). Our aim is to facilitate a better informed discussion on the possibilities as well as the limitations of the role of formal and non-formal education governance, policies, practices and experiences in the on-going and highly complex, and yet very much unresolved, processes of building a lasting peace. We welcome feedback to the findings shared in this book, as we consider knowledge building and sharing as a dialogical rather than 'final' or linear process. This book is also aimed to foster further debate on the potential opportunities and limitations that the various forms of education and learning covered here might play in the future, and hence does not provide clear-cut recommendations.

Structure of the Book

We begin the following chapters of this collection with Mieke Lopes Cardozo's in-depth presentation in Chap. 2 of the theoretical and methodological approaches employed in the work of the research consortium and across the studies presented here. The chapter defines the key concepts and terms that are applied throughout the book before going on to outline the '4R' framework and theoretical underpinnings which have informed the analysis of the studies. The framework builds on Fraser's (2005) dimensions of social justice to explore the contribution of education to building sustainable peace through combining the dimensions of Redistribution, Recognition and Representation with notions of Reconciliation. Lopes Cardozo also presents the methodologies and methods applied in gathering the data for this work, reflecting on the ethical considerations that have been imperative in conducting research in such a sensitive context. These ethical reflections underlie the nature of our work and partnerships, resurfacing in the subsequent chapters and the conclusions of this research. Likewise, across the chapters, attention is paid to the transversal themes of the research and recurrent areas of focus introduced here. So gender dynamics and diverse experiences of direct and indirect violence are prioritized throughout the three parts of this work, as are issues relating to educational autonomy, language of instruction and the teaching of history.

Following the three thematic research areas of the consortium the subsequent chapters are correspondingly divided into three parts. Part I draws together three chapters which serve to further introduce the context of conflict, peacebuilding and political transition in Myanmar, ultimately focusing attention on the processes of policy reform in the education sector initiated since 2012. Beginning by providing historical context in outlining the multiple nature of Myanmar's conflicts, in Chap. 3, "Conflict and Peacebuilding: Background, Challenges and Intersections with Education", Elizabeth Maber explores the interrelation between the conflicts and educational grievances, examining the renewal of peace processes and the potential role for education reforms. In seeking to locate education within the broader peacebuilding architecture, Maber sets up the policy landscape which forms a backdrop to the processes of education reform.

In Chap. 4, "Myanmar's Education System: Historical Roots, the Current Context, and New Opportunities", Ritesh Shah and Mieke Lopes Cardozo provide an overview of the education sector and the multiple school systems that operate within the country. In so doing they highlight challenges for the ongoing education sector reforms, drawing attention to inequalities within and between the education systems and the contentious issue of the language of instruction used in classrooms. Analysis of the education reforms is expanded on in Chap. 5, "Education and Policy Challenges of a Situation in Flux", by Ritesh Shah, Khin Mar Aung and Mieke Lopes Cardozo detailing the original drivers of the ongoing reform processes. Particular attention is given to the Comprehensive Education Sector Review (CESR) begun in 2012, the National Education Law (NEL) first passed in 2014 and later amended, and the development of the National Education Sector Plan (NESP) ultimately approved in 2017. Questions are raised over participation within the reform process and implications for peacebuilding revealed through the application of the ‘4R’ framework, setting up a dialogue with subsequent chapters which reflect responses from teachers and from youth.

The chapters collected in Part II shift the emphasis from policy development to the practices and experiences of teachers. In Chap. 6, “Understanding the Changing Roles of Teachers in Transitional Myanmar”, Elizabeth Maber, Hla Win May Oo and Sean Higgins draw attention to the position that teachers occupy within Myanmar society as well as how the traditional respect that teachers have received may have been eroded by underinvestment in the education sector. The authors explore varying perceptions of the roles of teaches, including within policy discourse, on the part of teacher educators and from the perspectives of teachers themselves, revealing the diverse ways in which teachers navigate conflicting influences. These influences and experiences are then related to the context of conflict and teachers’ agency for peacebuilding, examining opportunities for promoting peace and social justice that are emerging from the reform processes. In particular, ongoing revisions to the state curriculum and textbooks are presented as an opportunity to reduce the negative impact of unequal representations within textbooks and to support teachers in creating more inclusive classrooms.

Attempts to reform textbooks and teacher pedagogy evidently require complimentary attention to teacher education practices, and consequently Chap. 7, “Navigating Teacher Education Reform: Priorities, Possibilities and Pitfalls”, presents an examination by Sean Higgins and Naw Tha Ku Paul of teacher preparation and professional development. Situating their study within the context of teacher deployment, governance and accountability, the authors highlight four case studies of teacher education initiatives including three implemented nationally and one uniquely in Mon State. The challenges, opportunities and peacebuilding implications of such initiatives are discussed in relation to the ‘4R’ framework which reveals factors evident in the implementation of the teacher education reforms which may contribute to or conversely undermine broader processes of social justice.

The issues of teachers’ identities, motivations and experiences of inequalities are further explored in relation to education provision beyond the government school sector in Mon State by Taru Niskanen and Katharina Buske in Chap. 8, “Non-state Teachers in Mon State: Teacher Identity and a Struggle with Inequality”. The authors present two case studies conducted with teachers in monastic schools and in the ethnic Mon parallel system of schools run by the Mon National Education Committee (MNEC). Despite differences in the school contexts, the authors find similarities in the desires of teachers to serve their communities and the influence of (Buddhist) religion and cultural preservation as motivating factors for their work. Additionally, in both cases the effect of low salaries and inequalities in the distribution of resources between the non-state and state school sectors, as well as inadequate representation in the political sphere of reform processes, has resulted in tensions which undermine attempts to bridge divisions in the educational landscape. However, extending discussions raised in the previous chapters in this section, teachers are navigating different paths in negotiating their responses, with several monastic teachers expressing their intention to transition into work in the government schools, while MNEC teachers expressed greater inclination to move away from shared schooling or training initiatives that were perceived to reinforce their subordination. Together the studies presented in this section offer varying perspectives on the ways in which teachers are influenced by and respond to developments in the policy landscape, and the ways in which teachers' agency for peacebuilding may be constrained or enhanced by current reform efforts.

Reflecting the third thematic area of the research, the chapters of Part III each bring attention to the experiences and agency of youth in relation to education and to peacebuilding. The section begins with Sean Higgins and Mieke Lopes Cardozo's analysis in Chap. 9, "Youth Agency for Peacebuilding in and Beyond Education: Possibilities and Constraints". Varied young people are differently affected by conflict and are differently positioned within Myanmar's social, political and economic transitions, leading the authors to warn against a tendency to homogenise youth rather than seeking to understand the variety of young peoples' experiences. In addition to diverse experiences, the authors indicate the range of ways in which youth have been perceived and portrayed by others to form a variegated pattern of young peoples' agency for peacebuilding. The authors conclude by presenting a multiscalar conceptualisation of youth agency and strategic engagement for peacebuilding informed by the youth respondents participating in the research.

Building on this conceptualisation of youth agency for peacebuilding, Chap. 10, "Prioritising Education: Youth Experiences within Formal and Non-formal Education Contexts", explores the role that education experiences play in supporting or undermining agency. After positioning education as a priority amongst young people's concerns the authors, Elizabeth Maber, Naw Tha Ku Paul, Aye Aye Nyein and Sean Higgins, draw attention to the often negative prior experiences of youth respondents in formal education and their desires for changes. Subsequently the authors present three case studies of non-formal education initiatives which aim to empower and support young people to take action for positive transformation in their communities. In Chap. 11, "Youth Experiences of Non-formal Education for Peacebuilding", Tabea Campbell Pauli and Kiymet Schipper conclude this collection of chapters exploring youth agency with a discussion of two extended case studies undertaken with non-formal post-secondary initiatives in Yangon aiming to support students' political and social leadership. Campbell Pauli and Schipper find differences in the approaches of the two programmes, offering an exploration of the impacts, intended and unintended, of the application of political awareness training and peace education. Relating their findings to the 4R theoretical framework, the authors draw attention to the challenges that influence these non-formal learning sites including ensuring inclusion, the implications of instructional language and strategies for broaching sensitive topics.

Drawing the collection to a close, in the final chapter, "Drawing Conclusions: The Role of Education in Moving Towards Sustainable Peace in Myanmar", Elizabeth Maber, Mieke Lopes Cardozo and Sean Higgins reflect on the three strands of the research, presenting considerations and ways forward which resulted from discussion workshops held in Yangon and Mawlamyine. These workshops were undertaken at the end of the data gathering period with teachers, youth, policy makers and other stakeholders who had participated in the research to consolidate the findings of the study and collectively identify desired next steps. We then return to discuss the application of the 4R theoretical framework to the context of education and peace processes in Myanmar offering concluding reflections on the contributions of this approach.

Finally, a note should be made about the referencing of citations from respondents in the chapters. Chapters 3, 4, 5, 6, 7, 9, and 10 all draw from the data collected by the research team of national and international researchers, as described above, and further outlined in Chap. 2. Citations from these interviews and group discussions are referenced with an anonymised description of the respondent in the text and the inclusion of the interview number (e.g. int. 32). The data referenced in Chap. 8, "Non-state Teachers in Mon State: Teacher Identity and a Struggle with Inequality", and Chap. 10, "Prioritising Education: Youth Experiences within Formal and Non-formal Education Contexts", were collected independently by the authors and are referenced with anonymised descriptions in the text only.

References

Bush, K. D., & Saltarelli, D. (2000). *The two faces of education in ethnic conflict: Towards a peacebuilding education for children*. Florence: UNICEF Innocenti Research Centre.

Davies, L. (2005). Teaching about conflict through citizenship education. *International Journal of Citizenship and Teacher Education, 1*(2), 17–34.

Fraser, N. (2005). Reframing justice in a globalized world. *New Left Review, 36*, 79–88.

Novelli, M., & Lopes Cardozo, M. T. A. (2008). Conflict, education and the global south: New critical directions. *International Journal of Educational Development, 28*(4), 473–488.

Novelli, M., Lopes Cardozo, M. T. A., & Smith, A. (2017). The 4Rs framework: Analyzing education's contribution to sustainable peacebuilding with social justice in conflict-affected contexts. *Journal on Education in Emergencies, 3*(1), 14–43.

Smith, A. (2005). Education in the twenty-first century: Conflict, reconstruction and reconciliation. *Compare: A Journal of Comparative and International Education, 35*(4), 373–391.

UNESCO. (2011). *The hidden crisis: Armed conflict and education*. Paris: UNESCO.

Chapter 2
Analytical Framework and Methodological Approach to Research Education and Peacebuilding

Mieke T. A. Lopes Cardozo

Introduction

This chapter focuses on the main theoretical and methodological approaches that informed the design and analysis of the findings presented in this edited volume, and contextualises the consequent methodological insights and applies them to the context of Myanmar, and in doing so it highlights key ethical considerations. While acknowledging the wide variety and richness of the expertise and experience of the team of contributing authors, and the diversity of perspectives such a team brings to this volume, the book has an underlying coherence since all authors aligned their analysis to the overarching 4R analytical framework. The 4Rs framework (Novelli et al. 2017), with "4Rs" referring to the social justice dimensions (Fraser 2005) of Redistribution, Recognition, Representation and the additional "R" of Reconciliation, was developed at the start of the work of the broader Research Consortium on Education and Peacebuilding, to provide the various research teams with an overarching skeleton to collect, analyse and present empirical data. This chapter elaborates on this 4Rs model and discusses its relevance specifically in relation to the context of Myanmar.

The first section below features the key concepts and definitions used in the research, with specific attention to: *peacebuilding*, *social justice*, *governance,* the *agency of teachers* and *youth*, and *formal and non-formal education.* Moreover, it discusses the notions of gender, intersectionality and violence as transversal themes covered in the overall research project and chapters of this book. The second part of the chapter discusses the underlying analytical 4Rs framework as well as its relevance and operationalization for the research in Myanmar on education and peacebuilding. Thirdly, the chapter outlines how the methodological approaches applied

M. T. A. Lopes Cardozo (✉)
University of Amsterdam, Amsterdam, The Netherlands
e-mail: mlopescardozo@fmg.uva.nl

M. T. A. Lopes Cardozo, E. J. T. Maber (eds.), *Sustainable Peacebuilding and Social Justice in Times of Transition*,
https://doi.org/10.1007/978-3-319-93812-7_2

in the chapters in this volume were inspired by both the strategic relational approach (SRA, Sum and Jessop 2013) and a Critical Cultural Political Economy of Education approach (CCPEE, Roberston and Dale 2015). This section also outlines the rationale for a mostly qualitative and exploratory nature of our data collection processes. Finally, the chapter briefly outlines the key ethical considerations of anonymity and consent in the conflict-affected context of Myanmar.

Key Concepts and Definitions

A number of key conceptual tools are central to the research presented in this edited volume. While mindful of the need for context specificity in their application, and the differences even within and between the various states in Myanmar, this section lays out the working definitions of the key research concepts.

Peacebuilding from a Social Justice Perspective

Recognising that there are multiple interpretations of the term "peacebuilding," the 4Rs framework for *sustainable peacebuilding* (see below) draws on a conceptualisation that focuses on the need for core transformations in order for post-conflict societies to move towards sustainable peace. Key post-conflict transformations necessary to produce sustainable peace, or positive peace, as Galtung (1976) calls it, requires going beyond the mere cessation of violence (negative peace) in order to address the root causes of violent conflict. This involves addressing both drivers and legacies of conflict and the promotion of both social justice and cohesion, by addressing injustices and bringing people and communities together. This is in line with a range of contemporary theories of war and conflict (Stewart et al. 2005, 2010; Cramer 2005), which see horizontal and vertical inequalities as drivers of conflict. Addressing these inequalities in and through education (content and governance), in their different economic, cultural and political dimensions, supports the promotion of social cohesion, whereby trust, solidarity, and a sense of collectivity and common purpose are key aspects.

Social Cohesion

In the UNICEF PBEA programme, social cohesion has been used in several contexts, including Pakistan and South Africa, as a proxy for peacebuilding, due to local sensitivities related to peace or peacebuilding language in some of the countries in which the PBEA operates. In Myanmar, we are aware of similar sensitivities and varied understandings of the term social cohesion (as well as peacebuilding).

The way social cohesion is employed in this book connects it closely to issues of social justice and sustainable peace. It also acknowledges the various (community, state and national) scales where social cohesion plays out, and/or where it can be employed strategically by a range of (political) actors. The UNICEF Peacebuilding, Education and Advocacy Programme (PBEA) defines social cohesion as "the quality of coexistence between the multiple groups that operate within a society […] along the dimensions of mutual respect and trust, shared values and social participation, life satisfaction and happiness as well as structural equity and social justice" (UNICEF 2014). Within the Research Consortium on Education and Peacebuilding, we defined social cohesion as a societal rather than individual property, based on the promotion of positive relationships, trust, solidarity, inclusion, collectivity, and common purpose.

Education Governance and Policy

The way in which educational management functions and processes of education systems are laid out, and how stakeholders' participation is facilitated within them can foster constructive interactions and relationship building, or promote distrust and entrench intolerance. Decision-making power (Young 2006) and political representation (Fraser 2005) should ideally be fostered though fair representation (of all kinds and categories) at multiple (*supra and sub*) national scales of educational governance. Centrally controlled and managed educational provision can lead to a general lack of accountability and transparency between citizens and the state, particularly when educational resources and services are seen to be inequitably deployed. As a solution, mechanisms such as school-based management and decentralization of authority and control have the potential to promote citizenship, social inclusion, and cooperation, and also increase levels of accountability between educational service-providers and communities (Lopes Cardozo and Shah 2016). Moreover, when participation and cooperation between various educational actors enhance trust, this can become beneficial for broader aims of peacebuilding (Dupuy 2008). Nevertheless, they also hold the danger of exacerbating differential access to resources, to lead to partisan decision-making influenced by local politics and to carry the potential for dominant groups to force their views at the local level, limiting rather than enhancing levels of trust (Poppema 2009).

Generally speaking, governance refers to the sum of all concurrent forms of collective regulation of social issues: from the institutionalised self-regulation of civil society, through the diverse forms of cooperation among state and private actors, to the action of sovereign state agents (Mayntz 2003, 66, in: Smith et al. 2016). While governance is often most immediately related to political control of a system and the policy-making process (e.g. how the rules of a political regime provide the context for policy-making), it is also key to explore the technical capacity and the ability to implement such policies (Smith 2010, 2014). The research presented in this book concerns both of these aspects: the politics and the process of education sector governance. There is also a third aspect of governance, which is more analytical and considers "governance" as a concept of our time, reflecting a shift from government to governance, and for some towards "global governance" (Rosenau and Czempiel 1992, in: Smith et al. 2016, 25–26). This involves a shift from the idea of the government as the unitary source of educational governance (that funds, provides, regulates, and owns the education system) towards a more "coordinating" and facilitating role involving a range of actors operating at multiple geographical scales, which is very much the case in Myanmar as Chap. 4 will illustrate. This can be traced to the shift from Keynesian to neoliberal political economy approaches that have dominated international development debates since the 1980s (Robertson et al. 2006). Dale (2005) sees this as the scalar and functional division of education governance, which necessitates exploration of the supra-national or international, national, and sub-national levels. It also requires exploration of governance activities: funding, provision, regulation, and ownership, and the actors and institutions (state, market, community, household and so forth) responsible for carrying them out. Analysis of educational governance reflects on who is doing what, where, with what outcomes, and for whom (Smith et al. 2016).

Hence, education governance is closely intertwined with education policy. Consistent with the analysis by Rizvi and Lingard (2010) the focus of our research is not just on the normative view of policy (policy as it is written), but also on the process by which policy emerges (policy process) and how policy emerges in practice (policy as implemented). We therefore include in our analysis the policy-design, (national/sector level) reform plans, and implementation mechanisms (sometimes referred to as programmes or projects).

Teachers, Teacher Education and Teacher Agency

The ILO/UNESCO 1966 definition for teachers states: *All those persons in schools or other learning sites who are responsible for the education of children or young people in pre-primary, primary, lower-secondary and upper-secondary education* (UNESCO/ILO 2008). However, the definition for our work also looks at tertiary/higher education, and includes other learning sites than schools (non-formal education contexts, see below).

Teacher Education, Teacher Training and Teacher Professional Development are all associated with pre- and in-service teacher education. A distinction between education and training is illuminating here, where education is traditionally a learning process which requires the synthesis of knowledge, understanding principles and values while training is about practice and acquiring techniques and skills, usually applied to standards and criteria (and shorter term). While there is a great deal of overlap between the two and teachers require both technical skills and procedures (e.g. reading and writing) and knowledge and insight (e.g. appreciation of the beauty and understanding of the meaning of the poem they are skilfully reading) the choice of language can arguable reflect the emphasis framing the teacher. In our work we use 'teacher education' and only refer to 'training' in quotes from other sources (Sayed and Novelli 2016).

Integral to teachers' role as peacebuilders is their "agency" in peacebuilding (a more detailed theoretical discussion on "agency" is included below). A pervasive dualism within social sciences is structure and agency. For Emile Durkheim (e.g. 1912) structure took priority over agency meaning that social life is largely determined by social systems and conditions that regulate individual behaviour, whereas, in Weberian sociology this order is reversed. In this view, "social life is largely determined by those individuals "agents" without whom there would be no social structures" (Bullock and Trombley 2000, 835, in: Sayed and Novelli 2016). Teacher agency as peacebuilders is understood in relation to their capacity to influence their conflict-driven surroundings. It is their ability to think, feel and act in order to foster "values and attitudes that offer a basis for transforming conflict itself" (Novelli and Smith 2011, 7). Teachers' agency as peacebuilders can be seen as static, fixed and essentialised or as multidimensional, situated and dynamic. Teachers act as both the agents of change, for example, by promoting harmony between pupils including respect, justice and inclusiveness and the agents of conflict, for example, in the way teachers use pedagogy and curricula to perpetuate inequity and conflict between opposing ethnic, religious or socioeconomic groups. The lines between the two are not always clear and the same teacher may play out both roles simultaneously in different moments and contexts. This is because teachers do not exercise their peacebuilding agency in isolation from their surroundings and their agency both influences their surrounding and is influenced by it (O'Sullivan 2002; Vongalis-Macrow 2007; Weldon 2010; Welmond 2002). Teachers are selective, strategic and pragmatic actors in an often politically-charged context (Lopes Cardozo 2011; Lopes Cardozo and May 2009).

Youth and Youth Agency

There is a lack of consensus within the international community over the precise chronological definition of youth (see UNICEF 2009, 11). The UN (2007) and World Bank (2007) define youth as those between 15 and 25, while the African Union (2006) and many African nations define youth as those aged between 15 and 35 (UNICEF 2009, 11). Meanwhile, UNICEF defines adolescents as children between 10 and 19 years (UNICEF, 2009, 11). Considering these inconsistencies at the level of (age-driven) definitions of youth, it might seem an impossible task to contribute something meaningful into the debates about "youth" – in others words, to say something meaningful about a massive segment of Myanmar's population, while being such a diverse group at the same time. In addition, definitions of the term "youth" itself remain contested all over the globe, ranging from more technical age-ranges to a wide scope of social categorisations. Often, youth are portrayed as those that are 'in-between' childhood and adulthood, and that supposedly need protection, control, and social management to move from a state of dependency to one of independence and autonomy. Such mainstream ideas of youth have led in many contexts to a variety of deep-rooted fears, ambivalences, and unsettling anxieties around the implications of large and growing young populations (Sayed et al. 2016). For the purpose of this book, we have broadly defined youth as those within the second and third decade of life. We recognize that this is a culturally and contextually specific category of the population that needs an adapted working definition in each specific research location. Part three of the book will further elaborate on how in addition to this lack of a clear definition of whom we refer to when speaking of youth, there is also a dearth of information and data on youth related issues in Myanmar, hindering effective policy-making and programmes that would respond to the needs of the younger generation in the country today.

Building on the notion of 'agency' as set out above in relation to teachers, the concept of 'youth agency' is also key in this book. In moving beyond narrow perceptions of youth agency and a 'youth bulge' as mere threats to peace, and inspired by work of Jessop (2005) and Hay (2002a, b), for this edited volume youth agency is defined as the space for manoeuvre available to young people (in their second and third decade of life) in developing conscious or unconscious strategies that either support or hinder peacebuilding in relation to the broader cultural political economy context (see below for further elaboration).

Formal and Non-formal Education (for Peacebuilding)

We follow a broad understanding of education and *education initiatives related to peacebuilding*, which includes both, formal and non-formal forms of learning and schooling. Formal education refers to government-led, formal curricula following forms of schooling, often organised in so-called government-schools or state-schools. Since Myanmar's hybrid system of schooling also includes various parallel (non-)governmental systems of schooling, such as (I)NGO or Community Based Organisation (CBO) led learning activities, our analysis is also inclusive of these forms of learning. Chapter 4 will provide a more comprehensive overview of these various parallel systems and how they function and relate to one another. Finally, considering our specific interest in the relation between education and peacebuilding, yet the acknowledgement that many of such (both positive and restrictive) relations might not be directly labelled as such, we have selected both 'direct' peacebuilding education initiatives, while we also analyse more 'indirect' connections between education (governance, content and practices) and broader peacebuilding processes.

Gender and Intersectionality

We apply a comprehensive definition of gender, understanding this in the light of our broader 4Rs framework, and mostly building on the work of Nancy Fraser. Fraser, from a critical feminist perspective, asserts that in order to reach 'parity of participation' for all men and women in society, regardless of sex and sexual orientation, class, ethnicity, geographical location and so forth, it is not enough to only assume the economic solution of redistribution. Rather, equal importance should be given to socio-cultural remedies for better recognition and political representation in order to ensure "participation on par with others, as full partners in social interaction" (Fraser 2005, 73). In line with our 4Rs framework, and specifically the fourth R of reconciliation, we argue there needs to be an acknowledgment of the varying needs, societal positions, decision-making power and experiences of various forms of violence (further explained below) of women/girls and men/boys of all ages before, during and after conflict. In dealing with the legacies of a violent past, the victim-perpetrator binary which pervades the representation of youth in conflict settings reflects underlying assumptions of feminine and masculine characteristics and behaviours, which often reduce both women and men to limiting roles, reinforcing subordination, and denying the capacity of both to exercise agency (Becker 2012, in: Lopes Cardozo et al. 2015). Educational institutions and curricula, when dominated by patriarchal traditions, may perpetuate traditional gender roles and entrench patriarchal values in each generation of school-going children (Leach 2000; Kabeer 2005; Unterhalter 2005), a situation which extends from formal to non-formal forms of schooling. Finally, we emphasise how conceptualisations of gender (relations, notions) are context-dependent and often contested (e.g. gender relations might be perceived very differently by, to mention a few, women's rights organisations, labour movements or the military). In Appendix I we share a table that guided a gender-informed analysis of the various sections of the book.

Violence

Our definition of violence begins with a recognition that physical attack is but one dimension of violence:

> Violence can never be understood solely in terms of its physicality – force, assault or the infliction of pain – alone. Violence also includes assaults on the personhood, dignity, sense of worth or value of the victim. The social and cultural dimensions of violence are what gives violence its power and meaning. Focusing exclusively on the physical aspects of torture/terror/violence…. subverts the larger project of witnessing, critiquing, and writing against violence, injustice and suffering. (Scheper-Hughes and Bourgois 2004, 4)

Violence, then, should be understood in its many forms and dimensions. Galtung (1990) visualised a triangle with the more visible, direct forms of violence at the top, complemented by the less visible but equally damaging forms of structural (or indirect) and cultural violence at the other two corners of the pyramid. Cultural violence refers to the use of some aspects of the perpetrators culture to legitimize domination or direct violence (Galtung 1990). Cultural legitimacy can use religion, ideology, language, or any other belief, value, norm or general way of life of a dominant group. The longer-term harm, loss and death caused by cultural exclusion is often attributed to the victims. Symbolic violence (Bourdieu 1989) is a tacit mode of social and cultural domination, drawing on symbols, subliminal messages, and indirect discourses – the perpetrator exerts violence and the victim often accepts this and normalizes it. Discourses impact the public sphere through social and state structures such as the media, laws, policies, programs and institutions, politics and economic systems.

Finally, structural violence describes the social and institutional structures used to exclude groups from satisfying their basic needs (Galtung 1990). These can take the form of institutionalized elitism, racism, and sexism that can cause harm, loss and eventual death in marginalised communities. Unpacking some of these processes leads us to reflect on the way that narrow conceptualisations of violence, emphasising visible manifestations of overt violence and obscuring cultural, structural, symbolic and other forms of violence leads to international actors targeting symptoms (public expressions of violence) rather than the underpinning causes. While recognising the importance of understanding this multi-dimensional nature of violence in its overt and covert forms, we are also mindful of the relational nature of violence. In education, when we talk of violence, we refer to both overt and covert processes, from direct attacks on schools and teachers, gender-based violence, pupil on pupil and teacher on teacher violence to institutionalised modes of religious, class, ethnic and cultural modes of violence, including cultural and linguistic modes of violence. Butler nicely captures the complexity and nuance needed to uncover that 'violence and non-violence are not only strategies or tactics but form the subject and become its constitutive possibilities, and so, an ongoing struggle' (Butler 2010, 165). Appendix II includes a table on the key dimensions of violence that have guided our analysis for the three Research Areas.

Redistribution, Recognition, Representation and Reconciliation: Applying the 4Rs Analytical Framework to Myanmar

The 4 Rs Analytical Framework provides the overarching framework for all the research themes addressed in this book. This framework combines social justice and transitional justice thinking to develop a normative framework for the study of education and peacebuilding, which recognises the multiple dimensions of inequality and injustice that often underpin contemporary conflicts and the need to address the legacies of these conflicts in and through education. Crucial to this approach of researching education is that we consider it as being an inherent part and parcel of society and its conflict/peacebuilding dynamics, with 'education' meaning the education sector and its policy framework and mechanisms, education actors and stakeholders at multiple scales, and the practice of education as practiced in formal (school settings) and non-formal settings. Dale and Robertson (2014) have referred to this as the 'education ensemble', which has been an underlying inspiration to the framework as set out below. The framework is in line with broader and well-established peacebuilding thinking (c.f Galtung 1976; Lederach 1995, 1997) of the need to address both negative peace (the cessation of violence) and positive peace (the underlying structural and symbolic violence that often underpins the outbreak of conflict – the drivers of conflict). It also recognises the importance of addressing and redressing the 'legacies of conflict' in tandem with addressing the 'drivers of conflict'.

Within conflict studies, there has been a long and heated debate on the relationship between inequality, injustice and conflict. The debate is often framed in terms of "greed versus grievance" explanations, with the former suggesting that wars are driven less by justified "grievances" and more by personal and collective "greed" (Collier and Hoeffler 2004). Humans are viewed as engaged in conflict as "economic agents" making cost-benefit calculations and trying to maximize returns on engagement in violent conflict. For these thinkers, the route to peace and security is not through addressing injustice, inequality and structural exclusion, but through increasing the cost of access to resources for violent actors. A strong critique of this work argues that horizontal inequalities (between groups) are important indicators for outbreaks of conflict (Stewart et al. 2005; Stewart 2010), arguments supported by econometric evidence (Cederman et al. 2011). Horizontal inequalities, which often relate to ethnicity, tribe, or religion, involve a range of dimensions: economic (access to land, income, and employment), political (access to political power and representation), social (access to public services), and cultural (respect for difference and identity, language rights, etc.). In armed conflicts, real or perceived horizontal inequalities can provide a catalyst for group mobilisation and uprisings, and hence we have indicated those as part of the 'drivers of conflict' in the 4Rs model (see Fig. 2.1 below, Novelli et al. 2017).

There is limited research on the relationship between education and inequality in the outbreak of armed conflict. However, recent quantitative research drawing on two international education inequality and conflict datasets (FHI 360 2015) demonstrates a consistent statistical relationship, across five decades, between higher levels of inequality in educational attainment between ethnic and religious groups, and the likelihood that a country will experience violent conflict. However, this research is less able to identify causal mechanisms, or explain the complexities of understanding those. Therefore, the 4Rs framework works from the premise that there is a need to explore the multiple dimensions of inequality beyond just educational outcomes, as well as the different ways in which the education system might contribute to or alleviate conflict (Novelli et al. 2017).

The 4Rs framework presents a normative approach that seeks to capture the multiple economic, cultural, political, and social dimensions of inequality in education and the ways in which these might relate to conflict and peace. The framework

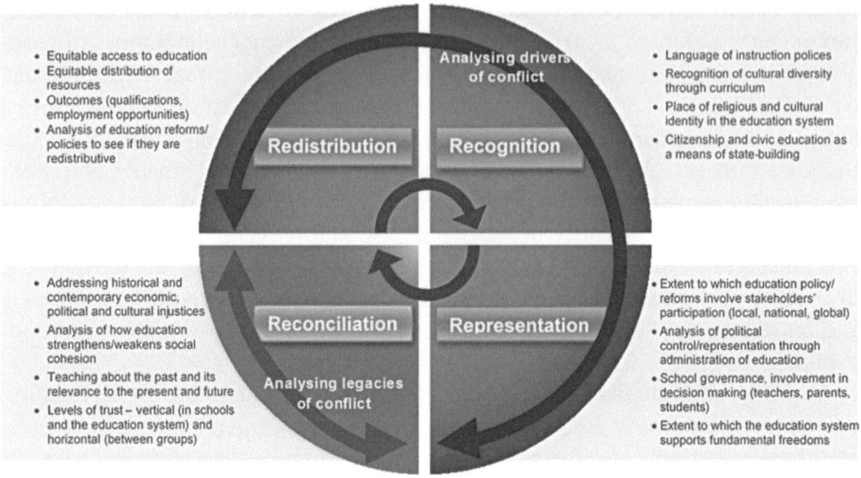

Fig. 2.1 Sustainable peacebuilding in education: the 4Rs analytical framework. (Novelli et al. 2017)

combines dimensions of recognition, redistribution, representation, and reconciliation, linking Fraser's (1995, 2005) work on social justice with the peacebuilding and reconciliation work of Galtung (1976), Lederach (1995, 1997), and others, to explore what sustainable peacebuilding might look like in post-conflict environments. The examination of inequalities within the education system seeks to capture the interconnected dimensions of the "4Rs" (visualised in Fig. 2.1):

- *Redistribution* concerns equity and non-discrimination in education access, resources, and outcomes for different groups in society, particularly marginalised and disadvantaged groups.
- *Recognition* concerns respect for and affirmation of diversity and identities in education structures, processes, and content, in terms of gender, language, politics, religion, ethnicity, culture, and ability.
- *Representation* concerns participation, at all levels of the education system, in governance and decision-making related to the allocation, use, and distribution of human and material resources.
- *Reconciliation* involves dealing with past events, injustices, and material and psychosocial effects of conflict, as well as developing relationships trust.

Based on multiple applications of the framework in a number of research projects over the past years, it seems to provide a useful tool to analyse the extent to which education is/can support cross-sectorial programming for conflict transformation in terms of redistribution, recognition, representation, and reconciliation and as an analytical tool within the education sector, as outlined in Table 2.1 (Novelli et al. 2017).

Addressing both the drivers of conflict (the first "3Rs") and the legacies of conflict and perspectives towards the future (reconciliation) is a complex process, but

Table 2.1 Analysing education systems using the 4Rs

Analysing education systems using the 4Rs: potential 'indicators'	
Redistribution (addressing inequalities)	Vertical and horizontal inequalities in education inputs, resources, and outcomes (quantitative data)
	Redistribution in macro education reforms or policies (e.g. impact of decentralisation and privatisation on different groups and conflict dynamics)
Recognition (respecting difference)	Policies on language of instruction
	Recognition of cultural diversity and religious identity in curriculum
	Citizenship and civic education as a means of state-building
Representation (encouraging participation)	Participation (local, national, global) in education policy and reforms
	Political control and representation through education administration
	School-based management and decision-making (teachers, parents, students)
	Support for fundamental freedoms in the education system
Reconciliation (dealing with injustices and the legacies of conflict)	Addressing historical and contemporary injustices linked to conflict
	Integration and segregation in education systems (e.g. common institutions)
	Teaching about the past and its relevance to the present and future
	Vertical trust in schools and education system, and horizontal trust between identity-based groups

Adapted from Novelli et al. (2017)

one that is crucial for the promotion of sustainable peace. Our analysis has illuminated how there can be significant tensions or trade-offs between the various "Rs", and the chapters that follow will highlight how the balance between policies that promote social justice (and therefore address the drivers of conflict) and those that promote reconciliation (and address the legacies of conflict and creatively design the future) is part of a political process of decision-making and prioritisation, often instigating considerable tensions and differences in opinion and approach. Hence, we refrain from a too deterministic and descriptive application of this 4Rs model, but rather highlight interrelations between the "Rs" where appropriate in our analysis presented in this volume. In that sense, the 4Rs might alternatively be visualised in a pyramid shape (Fig. 2.2), where the three drivers of inequalities/conflict are at the base of the pyramid, while the R of reconciliation becomes visible as an umbrella or overarching principle/process that has a quality of being 'lifted up'. This then signifies how the concept of reconciliation carries a potential quality of transformation, of a higher level of consciousness and interconnectedness in relation to processes of sustainable peacebuilding and a socially just society. This allows both research design, analysis and presentation of findings that are relevant to the field of practice, policy and academia to move away from a problem solving orientation,

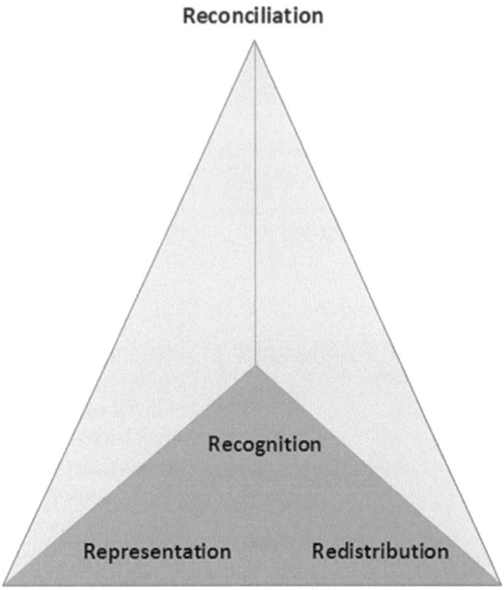

Fig. 2.2 Visualising the connected relations between the 4Rs

which "causes us to look backwards while the world evolves forward, [as] focusing on problems may eliminate what we *don't* want, at least for a while, but there's no guarantee that it will bring about the systemic changes required to sustain the quality of life we *do* want" (Mang and Haggard 2016, 114). The 4Rs model is designed to enable research to explore, and perhaps support, more systemic transformations.

A Further Note on Reconciliation

Honing in on the 'added' fourth R of reconciliation then, the framework draws on a "relational" (Hamber and Kelly 2004) understanding of reconciliation, or: "a process of addressing conflictual and fractured relationships" through "voluntary acts that cannot be imposed" (Ibid: 3–4). Similarly, Jean Paul Lederach (1995, 1997) builds a strong argumentation around the need to combine short-term as well as long-term approaches, supporting transformations in various dimensions of human life (political, economic, psychological and spiritual), ultimately to support processes of reconciliation. Reconciliation also should be considered as a paradoxical process, as it "promotes an encounter between the open expression of the painful past" on the one hand while it "seeks a long-term, interdependent future" on the other (Lederach 1997; cited in Hamber and Kelly 2004). In a sense, while reconciliation might start from a direct need to build trust and address people's trauma, despair and grief, on multiple sides of the conflict, at the same time reconciliation holds the potential of envisioning new, alternative ways of enactment and living together. In this sense, and similar to Fraser's view on the other 3Rs, conceptually reconciliation connects closely to the idea of *transformation*.

A concrete example of education's role in reconciliation processes and in dealing with a conflictive past is the teaching of history. We also recognize Hamber and Kelly's (2004) "warning" that the concept of reconciliation is always influenced by people's underlying assumptions or ideologies – religious, political, economic, or other. Applying the 4Rs framework therefore requires us to develop contextualized, locally defined, and historically informed understandings of what reconciliation means in the context of Myanmar. Furthermore, while it is important to bring people from different and even opposing social groups together, either through formal integrated schooling or non-formal programs, it is important to move beyond a narrow interpretation of Allport's Contact Hypothesis and allow for more meaningful long-term encounters and reflection. Simply getting together to shake hands and share food is to suggest that conflict is driven (only) by interpersonal animosities rather than (also) by structural grievances and inequalities (see also Novelli et al. 2017).

Finally, it is worth highlighting here that the term reconciliation is often politically charged, and comes with multiple interpretations and approaches depending on the rationale or interest that is driving it. In Myanmar, reconciliation is far from a unitary adopted concept, and we will highlight in the data analysis presented in the chapters to follow how the term is both embraced and rejected for multiple reasons, by multiple actors and at multiple scales of the peacebuilding-and-education arena. This is not dissimilar to the ways in which reconciliation has become a contested term, especially for those that have historically found themselves in a marginalised position, and especially when (new) governments seem to adopt the term in their political narrative (for instance also in Sri Lanka, see Duncan and Lopes Cardozo 2017).

Cultural Political Economy of Education and Strategic Relational Approach as Methodological Inspirations

Drawing on our earlier work by and together with colleagues in this area (Shah and Lopes Cardozo 2014; Lopes Cardozo and Shah 2016), this chapter presents a combination of insights from the Strategic Relational Approach (SRA, see Jessop 2005) and the Critical Cultural Political Economy of Education (CCPEE, see Robertson and Dale 2015) – both of which are rooted in Critical Realism. We argue that a critical realist ontological lens is best suited within the broader field of critical theory in doing so. Building on the critical realist recognition of the importance of identifying visible and invisible structures and mechanisms that lead to that which we empirically observe, the objective is to (retroductively) examine: (1) the ways in which the relationship between education and peacebuilding is articulated discursively and materially through social relations, experiences, and practices (the cultural); (2) the ways in which education and peacebuilding fit into relations of production, distribution and exchange in society (the economic); and finally (3), the fashion in which political agenda setting and decision-making deal with education's links to peacebuilding (the political) (Shah and Lopes Cardozo 2014). Motivated by a recognition that "orthodox political economy tends to offer impoverished accounts of how subjects and subjectivities are formed" (Jessop 2004, 3), the role of culture is brought into equal footing with political and economic structures and institutions, as a constitutive element and as a contingent factor in the actions of actors.[1] The thinking inspired by both CCPEE and SRA is also present in the design of the 4Rs theoretical framework introduced above.

CCPEE helps us to see "education as part of societies; it does not sit outside of it" – by not simply 'adding' education to a Cultural Political Economy approach (see Sum and Jessop 2013), but by *critically* viewing education as being both constituted by and connected to cultural, economic and political dynamics and processes (Robertson 2012, 4). The things we can empirically observe in educational settings are understood as connected to a particular conceptualisation and rationalisation of political, economic and social relationships in society at a particular time, space and place (Robertson 2000, 8–9). In the context of a conflict-affected and post-colonial society such as Myanmar, where meanings, purposes, and beliefs about the role of education are thrown into question, CCPEE can offer a powerful tool for retroductively unpacking how discursive claims on education's role and function in society might be reconsidered and reframed by both government and non-government actors. The types of claims, beliefs, and values made, and the material capabilities they enable/constrain, can have powerful resonance in terms of education's potential to serve productive means of building a more peaceful and socially just society (Lopes Cardozo and Shah 2016). Building on the CCPEE Robertson and Dale (2015) have developed a series of 'education moments' that can help to guide such exploration: (1) the **moment of educational practice** – where one looks into the questions of who is taught, what and the circumstances in which education takes place; (2) the **moment of educational politics** – where the relationship between policy and practice is analysed, acknowledging that not everything that happens in practice is a direct consequence of the decision and actions of policy-making; (3) the **moment of the politics of education** – where the rules of the games set limits to what is possible and desirable in education are analysed, and where education is understood in relation to the broader economic, political and cultural projects (i.e. the relationship between neoliberalism and education); and (4) the **moment of the outcomes of education** – where the consequences of educational practices, policies and politics are studied in relation to both immediate actions and wider social relations and processes. These moments have informed the

[1] Jessop (2004) originally interpreted culture in his proposition of *cultural political economy* as semiosis defined as the inter-subjective production of meaning, including narrativity, rhetoric, hermeneutics, identity, reflexivity, historicity and discourse. Robertson (2012) takes the notion of culture a step further by adding the materiality of social relations, and the constraints agents face to such analysis. According to her, in order to fully comprehend the complexities of the field of educational governance and practice, critical examination of meaning-making processes are vital for our understanding (Robertson 2012, 3).

focus of our multiscalar data collection and the analysis of our data as presented in the following chapters.

The SRA, then, allows seeing structures and agents as analytically separate entities, which simultaneously have a contingent and dialectal relationship (Hay 2002b; Jessop 2005). Specifically, structures are seen as *strategically selective*. They can reinforce the motivations, actions or strategies of particular individuals/groups, and work against others – thus creating both, opportunities and constraints for specific courses of action for specific actors and constituencies. Within the confines of particular temporal periods and spaces, specific structures and structural configurations can selectively reinforce the action, tactics, activities and strategies of actors (also defined as their *agency*) and discourage others. All *actors* have tendencies, or preferences for action, but the structural spaces they operate within may allow only certain tendencies to be realised. The social, economic and political spaces in which actors operate are "densely structured and highly contoured" which presents an "unevenly distributed configuration of opportunity and constraint to actors'"(Hay 2002b, 381). SRA acknowledges that different individuals and groups may have varying opportunities to do so and constraints due to their levels of access to particular strategic resources (social, political, cultural, economic capital). Actors may be differentially motivated in their desire to alter such structures, acting in ways that consciously and unconsciously serve to reproduce/transform existing conditions. Even if driven by a desire for transformation, actors often lack perfect information of their context. Imperfect information leads to false assumptions and actions that may appear unintentional, but are responding to a set of perceived structural constraints, which may not be perceived correctly (Hay 2002b, 381–383).

A noteworthy argument of SRA is that in any moment the way in which actors understand and respond to their environment can greatly vary, as can their motivations and intentions for action, leading to an assortment of potential outcomes. Thus, both the structured context within which action occurs, and the types of agency that actors exhibit, have a bearing on what role and function they might play in constructing a positive and sustainable peace. Hence, the SRA can help us in our understandings of *how* and *why* possibilities and limitations to education actors' agency as peacebuilders are shaped, and are both time and place-bound. Finally, from an SRA perspective it might be assumed that, over time, actors would come to better understand and respond in kind to their context through the routine monitoring of the consequences of their actions. However, very rarely do the environments in which these actors act remain static. This is particularly true in the changing environment of conflict-affected environments – such as Myanmar – where a density of existing institutions and practices, in combination with a proliferation of new strategic actors and new discourses lead to the possibility of changing strategic selectivities in short periods of time (Lopes Cardozo and Shah 2016). While the above insights from the SRA have been helpful in the research design, data collection and analysis, there is a need to move away from a somewhat functionalist tendency of the model. As such, the all too rationalist idea of actors' "strategic calculations" (Hay 2002b) was adapted, and instead CPE thinking and more semiotic and post-structuralist notions of identities, beliefs and motivations were brought in. The methodology applied in the chapters in this book hence applies an orientation to the *cultural* within recent formulations of cultural political economy (Robertson and Dale 2015), to unravel the agentic factors in relation to the education-peacebuilding nexus.

A Mostly Qualitative and Critical Ethnographic Methodological Approach

Engaging with a critical theoretical approach, as set out in the 4Rs framework and above, and while recognizing the relatively short time frame that was available to the fieldwork, our methodological approach draws from, yet does not do full justice to critical ethnographic research approaches and critical discourse analysis (of 'raw' collected data/texts/photographic material as well as transcriptions). Following from this rationale, and the both exploratory and sensitive nature of the research topic, the research methods applied were primarily qualitative in nature. Methods that supported the data collection for the analytical chapter that follow included semi-structured interviews (both individual and in small groups), document analysis, stakeholder mapping exercises, and a range of participatory methods particularly for the youth and teacher areas of study (e.g. focus group discussions, interactive workshops, collective drawing or theatre activities).

The methodology applied to study the programmatic and policy interventions included in our study, also drew on Pawson's (2006) realist approach (again rooted in critical realism), which views evaluation as a process that both identifies how the evaluated policies and programmes work and how they expect to achieve their objectives. In a realist evaluation, it is not enough merely to test whether an intervention achieves (or does not achieve) its objectives; what is required is an understanding of why the intervention does (or does not do) so as a way of drawing lessons that will contribute to improve future interventions. It recognises that programmes do not work 'generically' but work in particular ways in particular places and give rise to both intended and unintended outcomes.

Concluding Notes on Conducting Research in Myanmar

As a final note to this chapter and as a way to bridge to the more Myanmar specific chapters that will follow, I would like to highlight a few methodological and ethical considerations that have guided our collaborative team workshops that took place in Myanmar, as well as the consequent data collection, analysis and presentation of the findings here in this edited volume. While working from an agreed ethical guidelines document that went through numerous iterations at the three leading universities (Amsterdam, Sussex and Ulster), in the specific case of Myanmar we dealt with the issue of respondents consent in a context specific and conflict sensitive way. In close conversation with our Myanmar members of the team, we discussed how issues of trust and anonymity are incredibly important considering the country's conflictive past, as well as a present situation where mistrust and participant safety is still a major concern. For this reason, we only worked with verbal consent, which was asked to all respondents that participated in the research conducted for the chapters present in this volume. Consent was provided after an explanation of the purpose and focus of the study was given and the announcement that any respondent could stop the conversation (or activity) at any time, and was guaranteed anonymity. Hence, while we refer to interview numbers throughout the chapter (for example as "int. 1" or "ints. 44, 76"), we have not included a full overview of all collected data as we want to ensure respondents anonymity as best as possible.[2]

References

Bourdieu, P. (1989). Social space and symbolic power. *Sociological Theory, 7*(1), 14–25.

Butler, J. (2010). Performative agency. *Journal of Cultural Economy, 3*(2), 147–161.

Cederman, L. E., Weidmann, N. B., & Gleditsch, K. S. (2011). Horizontal inequalities and ethno-nationalist civil war: A global comparison. *American Political Science Review, 105*(3), 478–495.

Collier, P., & Hoeffler, A. (2004). Greed and grievance in civil war. *Oxford Economic Papers, 56*(4), 563–595.

Cramer, C. (2005). *Inequality and conflict: A review of an age-old concern, Identities, conflict and cohesion programme paper, 11*. Geneva: United Nations Research Institute for Social Development.

Dale, R. (2005). Globalisation, knowledge economy and comparative education. *Comparative Education, 41*(2), 117–149.

Dale, R., & Robertson, S. L. (2014). Global education policies. In N. Yeates (Ed.), *Understanding global social policy*. Bristol: Policy Press.

Duncan, R., & Lopes Cardozo, M. T. A. (2017). Reclaiming reconciliation through community education for the Muslims and Tamils of post-war Jaffna, Sri Lanka. *Research in Comparative and International Education, 12*(1), 76–94.

Dupuy, K. (2008). Education for peace: Building peace and transforming armed conflict through education systems. *International Peace Research Institute, Oslo, for Save the Children Norway*. http://toolkit.ineesite.org/toolkit/INEEcms/uploads/1050/Education_for_Peace_Building_Peace.pdf.

Durkheim, E. (1912). *The elementary forms of religious life*. New York: Free Press.

FHI 360. (2015). *Does horizontal education inequality lead to violent conflict? A global analysis*. Washington, DC: FHI 360 Education Policy and Data Center.

Fraser, N. (1995). From redistribution to recognition? Dilemmas of justice in a 'post-socialist' age. *New Left Review, 1*(212), 68–93.

Fraser, N. (2005). Reframing justice in a globalized world. *New Left Review, 36*, 79–88.

[2] Any specific questions on the source, validity or analysis of the presented data can be addressed, either directly to the authors of the chapters, or to the editors (Mieke Lopes Cardozo: mlopescardozo@fmg.uva.nl or Elizabeth Maber: ejtm2@cam.ac.uk).

Galtung, J. (1976). Three approaches to peace: Peacekeeping, peacemaking and peacebuilding. In J. Galtung (Ed.), *Peace, war and defence: Essays in peace research* (Vol. 2, pp. 282–304). Copenhagen: Christian Eljers.

Galtung, J. (1990). Cultural violence. *Journal of Peace Research, 27*(3), 291–305.

Hamber, B., & Kelly, G. (2004). *A working definition of reconciliation: SEUPB & democratic dialogue*. Belfast: PEACE II Funding Guidelines.

Hay, C. (2002a). *Political analysis: A critical introduction*. Balkingstoke: Palgrave.

Hay, C. (2002b). Globalisation as a problem of political analysis: Restoring agents to a 'process without subject' and politica to a logic of economic compulsion. *Cambridge Review of International Affairs, 15*(3), 379–392.

Jessop, B. (2004). Critical semiotic analysis and cultural political economy. *Critical Discourse Studies, 1*(2), 159–174.

Jessop, B. (2005). Critical realism and the strategic-relational approach. *New Formations, 56*, 40–53.

Kabeer, N. (2005). Gender equality and women's empowerment: A critical analysis of the third millennium development goal. *Gender and Development, 13*(1), 13–24.

Leach, M. (2000). Gender implications of development agency policies on education and training. *International Journal of Educational Development, 20*(4), 333–347.

Lederach, J. P. (1995). *Preparing for peace: Conflict transformation across cultures*. Syracuse: Syracuse University Press.

Lederach, J. P. (1997). *Building peace: Sustainable reconciliation in divided societies*. Washington, DC: United States Institute of Peace Press.

Lopes Cardozo, M. T. A. (2011). *Future teachers and social change in Bolivia: Between decolonisation and demonstration*. Delft: Uitgeverij Eburon.

Lopes Cardozo, M. T. A., & May, A. (2009). Teaching for peace – Overcoming division? Peace education in reconciliation processes in Sri Lanka and Uganda. In S. Nicolai (Ed.), *Opportunities for change. Education innovation and reform during and after conflict* (pp. 201–217). Paris: IIEP UNESCO.

Lopes Cardozo, M. T. A., & Shah, R. A. (2016). The fruit caught between two stones': The conflicted position of teachers within Aceh's independence struggle. *Globalisation, Societies and Education, 14*(3), 331–344.

Lopes Cardozo, M. T. A., Higgins, S., Maber, E., Brandt, C. O., Kusmallah, N., Le Mat, M. L. J. (2015). *Literature review: Youth agency, peacebuilding and education, research consortium education and peacebuilding*. University of Amsterdam. Available online: http://learningforpeace.unicef.org/partners/research-consortium/research-outputs/

Mang, P., Haggard, B., & Regenesis. (2016). *Evolution, in regenerative development: A framework for evolving sustainability*. Hoboken: Wiley. https://doi.org/10.1002/9781119149699.ch1.

Novelli, M., & Smith, A. (2011). *The role of education in peacebuilding: A synthesis report of findings from Lebanon, Nepal and Sierra Leone*. New York: UNICEF.

Novelli, M., Lopes Cardozo, M. T. A., & Smith, A. (2017). The 4Rs framework: Analyzing education's contribution to sustainable peacebuilding with social justice in conflict-affected contexts. *Journal on Education in Emergencies, 3*(1), 14–43.

O'Sullivan, M. C. (2002). Reform implementation and the realities within which teachers work: A Namibian case study. *Compare: A Journal of Comparative and International Education, 32*(2), 219–237.

Pawson, R. (2006). *Evidence-based policy: A realist perspective*. London: Sage Publications.

Poppema, M. F. (2009). Guatemala, the Peace Accords and education: A post-conflict struggle for equal opportunities, cultural recognition and participation in education. *Globalisation, Societies and Education, 7*(4), 383–408.

Rizvi, F., & Lingard, B. (2010). *Globalizing education policy*. London: Routledge.

Robertson, S. L. (2000). Teachers' labour, social class and change: Toward a new theoretical framework. *International Studies in the Sociology of Education, 10*(3), 285–302.

Robertson, S. L. (2012). Placing teachers in global governance agendas. *Comparative Education Review, 56*(4), 584–607.

Robertson, S. L., & Dale, R. (2015). Towards a 'critical cultural political economy' account of the globalising of education. *Globalisation, Societies and Education, 13*(1), 149–170.

Robertson, S., Novelli, M., Dale, R., Tikly, L., Dachi, H., & Ndibelema, A. (2006). *Globalisation, education and development: Ideas, actors, dynamics, Researching the Issues* (Vol. 68). London: DFID.

Sayed, Y., & Novelli, M. (2016). *The role of teachers in peacebuilding and social cohesion: A synthesis report of South Africa, Uganda, Pakistan and Myanmar case studies. Research Consortium Education and Peacebuilding*. University of Sussex.

Sayed, Y., Badroodien, A., McDonald, Z., Balie, L., De Kock, T., Garisch, C., Hanaya, A., Salmon, T., Sirkhotte-Kriel, W., Gaston, J., Foulds, K. (2016). *Teachers and youth as agents of social cohesion in South Africa*. Research Consortium Education and Peacebuilding. Available online at: http://learningforpeace.unicef.org/partners/researchconsortium/researchoutputs/

Scheper-Hughes, N., & Bourgois, P. (Eds.). (2004). *Violence in war and peace: An anthology*. London: Blackwell.

Shah, R., & Lopes Cardozo, M. T. A. (2014). Education and social change in post-conflict and post-disaster Aceh, Indonesia. *International Journal of Educational Development, 38*, 2–12.

Smith, A. (2010). *The influence of education on conflict and peace building, Paper prepared for the Education for All Global Monitoring Report 2011*. Paris: UNESCO.

Smith, A. (2014). Contemporary challenges for education in conflict affected countries. *Journal of International and Comparative Education, 3*(1), 113–125.

Smith, A., Datzberger, S., McCully, A. (2016). *The integration of education into peacebuilding processes at global and country levels. Global synthesis study: Myanmar, Pakistan, South Africa and Uganda*. Research Consortium Education and Peacebuilding. Ulster University.

Stewart, F. (2010). *Horizontal inequalities as a cause of conflict: A review of CRISE findings, World Development Report 2011 Background Paper*. Washington, DC: World Bank.

Stewart, F., Brown, G., & Mancini, L. (2005). *Why horizontal inequalities matter: Some implications for measurement, CRISE Working Paper No. 19*. Oxford: CRISE.

Sum, N., & Jessop, B. (2013). Competitiveness, the knowledge-based economy and higher education. *Journal of the Knowledge Economy, 4*(1), 24–44.

UNESCO/ILO. (2008). *Recommendation concerning the Status of Teachers, 1966*. ILO and UNESCO.

UNICEF. (2009). *Young people in West and Central Africa: Trends, priorities, investments and partners*. UNICEF West and Central Africa Regional Office.

UNICEF. (2014). *PBEA programme social cohesion definition*. UNICEF.

Unterhalter, E. (2005). Global inequality, capabilities, social justice: The millennium development goal for gender equality in education. *International Journal of Educational Development, 25*(2), 111–122.

Vongalis-Macrow, A. (2007). I, Teacher: Reterritorialization of teachers' multi-faceted agency in globalized education. *British Journal of Sociology of Education, 28*(4), 425–439.

Weldon, G. (2010). Post-conflict teacher development: Facing the past in South Africa. *Journal of Moral Education, 39*(3), 353–364.

Welmond, M. (2002). Globalization viewed from the periphery: The dynamics of teacher identity in the Republic of Benin. *Comparative Education Review, 46*(1), 37–66.

Young, I. M. (2006). Taking the basic structure seriously. *Perspectives in Politics, 4*(1), 91–97.

Part I
Myanmar's Policy Landscape

Chapter 3
Conflict and Peacebuilding: Background, Challenges and Intersections with Education

Elizabeth J. T. Maber

Introduction

The multiple, simultaneous nature of Myanmar's conflicts, stemming from long rooted historical grievances as well as more recent triggers, presents a pattern of complex issues and actors within which to situate the role of education. This chapter aims to introduce this context of the various conflicts and peace processes in Myanmar which provide a backdrop for the research conducted and is further explored in the subsequent chapters. In so doing, I draw on experiences in the context and existing literature, as well as data collected with those involved in the peace processes and education reforms.

The chapter starts with a brief summary of key historical events that informed Myanmar's independence transition, followed by an outline of the antecedents to the conflicts, covering the origins of the ethnic civil wars and the dominance of the military junta. Additional dimensions to the conflicts are also introduced including some of the historical political, economic and socio-cultural factors that have contributed to the current climate of a complex interplay between inter-religious, inter-community and inter-ethnic hostility. This is accompanied by a discussion of political transitions since 2010 and the resurfacing of religious tensions which have preceded current hostilities in Rakhine State.

I then outline the status of peace processes, providing some background on the nature of the peace negotiations to date and identifying some of the key actors involved in forging ceasefire agreements between ethnic armed groups and the state. The chapter concludes by exploring the location of education within the broader peacebuilding architecture of Myanmar, and the implications for current approaches to education reform efforts. A key point to make about the analysis in this chapter is

E. J. T. Maber (✉)
University of Cambridge, Cambridge, UK
e-mail: ejtm2@cam.ac.uk

M. T. A. Lopes Cardozo, E. J. T. Maber (eds.), *Sustainable Peacebuilding and Social Justice in Times of Transition*,
https://doi.org/10.1007/978-3-319-93812-7_3

that much of it explores the evolution of change, rather than its outcomes, as both the peace process and education (as well as broader socio-political and economic) reforms are in a state of transition.

Historical Context to Myanmar's Conflicts

Prior to the Anglo-Burmese wars of the mid-nineteenth century, the territory that became Myanmar was ruled by a series of powerful, and at times overlapping, kingdoms. Of particular relevance for the geographical orientation of this research, the Buddhist Mon kingdoms exerted substantial power in South East Asia and dominated the southeast territories that stretched from Bago (then Pegu) across Thailand until the eighteenth century (South 2008). The influence of these successive kingdoms has left a distinctive legacy in Mon State of pride in pre-colonial history and ethnic identity constructions, including language and religion (Lall and South 2013, 11). These legacies continue to hold influence and resurface in education settings, where much history teaching has focused on the pre-colonial kingdoms (Salem-Gervais and Metro 2012).

Following a piecemeal process of colonisation dating from the first Anglo-Burmese war of 1824, Myanmar, then known as Burma, was fully under British control by 1885 and largely remained so until independence in 1948. Yangon (then Rangoon) was established as the capital and colonial rule shaped the legal, administrative and education systems. This impact is enduring and is particularly evident in issues of language of instruction in the education systems, where English use remains prominent (British Academy and École française d'Extrême-Orient 2015, 5). Likewise, agreements made between the British administration and the varied ethnic groups over the extent of their autonomy continue to be a source of contestation and a driver of conflicts (TNI 2013). Dissent always accompanied imperialism and was commonly met with brutal suppression. Throughout the 1920s and 1930s nationalist movements gained traction, with monks, university students and workers organisations all leading protests (Holliday 2011, 36–7), fomenting a pattern of civil resistance to oppressive leadership which would become a recurrent feature of Myanmar's modern history. World War II brought further disruption to colonial rule and an unsettling of variant alliances during the Japanese occupation between 1942 and 1945. By the end of the war, General Aug San had emerged as a leading independence hero and was instrumental in negotiating the transferal of administrative powers back to a national government. However, conflicts were already beginning to surface amongst a climate of dissatisfaction in the ethnic territories as well as emerging political and ideological divisions.

The Panglong Conferences

The original *Panglong Conferences* of 1946 and 1947 were held with General Aung San and representatives of several ethnic minority states in Panglong, Shan State, to discuss the transition to independence and culminated in the signing of the *Panglong Agreement* by the Kachin, Shan and Chin (Holliday 2011, 39). The Agreement proposed uniting the so-called Frontier Areas, as they had been termed under colonial rule, under a federal union which offered autonomy and possibilities for succession to the ethnic States. However, after Gen. Aung San was assassinated immediately prior to the official handover of power, the Agreement was never fully enacted by the new incoming government and continues to be a point of contention behind the ethnic civil wars (Raw 2016; Metro 2013).

In 2016 the newly inaugurated NLD government relaunched the national political dialogue process, started under the previous USDP government, dubbing the biannual gatherings "21st Century Panglong Union Peace Conferences". The first of these large-scale national events, held in September 2016 this time in Nay Pyi Taw, was attended by 750 representatives from the government, political parties, state military and ethnic armed groups, who were given the opportunity to outline their positions and expectations for the peace processes (Nyein 2016). This was followed in May 2017 by a second 6-day conference to begin debating the process forward in earnest. Conclusions over progress have been decidedly mixed and are greatly overshadowed by ongoing military offensives in Kachin, Shan and Rakhine States. While the events have signalled a renewal of dialogue, there remain significant concerns about the willingness of all parties to reach compromises (Lynn and Slow 2017; TNI 2017).

On July 19th 1947, General Aung San was assassinated along with six of his cabinet colleagues. However, despite the event shattering the cohesion of the transitional government, preparations for the transferal of power, and the drafting of the new constitution, continued, with independence formally occurring on January 4th 1948 (Holliday 2011, 39). After this uneasy passage to independence, conflicts continued to intensify with the outbreak of civil wars lead by ethnic armed groups multiplying (TNI 2013). Largely on the pretext of this instability the military was able to dominate the political arena through successive military coups throughout the twentieth century, consolidating military control over all areas of public life and heavily restricting civil liberties.

Dimensions of Myanmar's Post-independence Conflicts

This section further introduces the multiple points of tension which have emerged through Myanmar's conflicts in the twentieth century, outlining additional dimensions, albeit briefly, to these conflicts and the factors that influence and sustain them. It is recognised that these dimensions are highly interdependent and intersect to form a web of influences, motivations and exacerbations that contribute to the historic and current climate of conflict in Myanmar. The emphasis here is on introducing the origins and implications of the conflicts, and an examination of the state of peacebuilding efforts will follow in the subsequent sections.

Military Control and Ethnic Conflicts

Multiple civil wars broke out in 1946 and 1948, initially with the fracturing of the communist movements and disillusionment on the part of Arakan Muslim groups, followed by claims for autonomous rule by Mon, Karen and Pa-Oh ethnic minorities. The 1950s and 1960s saw increasing numbers of ethnic armed groups engaging the central government in civil war, including the newly redefined New Mon State Party (NMSP), Karen National Union (KNU), Karenni National Progressive Party (KNPP) and Kayan New Land Party (KNLP), as well as Kachin, Shan, Palaung and Lahu military groups reacting against the new government's failure to respect the "*spirit of Panglong*" (Metro 2013). Central to these initial conflicts were claims to self-determination on the part of ethnic groups who did not see themselves as ever having been part of a fully unified Myanmar. A sense of injustice was further fuelled by the perceived backtracking of the newly independent central government which rejected the forming of a federal union, instead stressing an agenda of unification and centralised control (BNI 2014). The civil wars and consequent fears for the stability of the newly independent country provided the setting and opportunity for the state military, the *Tatmadaw*, to assert greater influence during the post-independence period from 1948 culminating in the eventual military take-over in 1962. Upon taking control, Gen. Ne Win, author of the coup, reportedly declared "Federalism is impossible. It will destroy the Union" (TNI 2013, 3). The concern that federalism would result in a weakened national state was countered by promoting a discourse of national unity, which denied cultural and religious plurality and allowed the enactment of increasingly restrictive and oppressive policies by the ruling junta. These policies consolidated political and economic power for the military at the expense of civil liberties across the population, and prompted an increase in both political and ethnic resistance (Holliday 2011, 59). The ethnic conflicts are therefore intrinsically linked to the pro-democracy struggles, despite the tendency to approach these conflicts independently.

Pro-democracy Struggles

Successive military juntas from 1962 to 2011 reinforced an environment of authoritarianism and oppression during which democratic opposition and social activism were highly constrained and fraught with risk. While opposition was present throughout the military dictatorships, the late 1980s saw civil dissatisfaction with the ruling junta galvanised in response to currency devaluations in which many lost their savings (Holliday 2011, 54). The resultant widespread demonstrations of 1988, which reached a head in August (giving name to the 8888 movement), propelled many democracy activists into the spotlight, including the founders of the National League for Democracy (NLD) the late Win Tin and Daw Aung San Suu Kyi, daughter of Gen. Aung San. Students were at the forefront of these demonstrations, in part led by the same unions that had previously supported independence movements. The resultant popular uprising provoked a violent response from the ruling military in which hundreds of protestors were killed. The uprising however did trigger elections in 1990, overwhelmingly won by the NLD, but which provoked a greater backlash from the military junta who refused to relinquish power and instead reorganised as the State Law and Order Restoration Council (SLORC). NLD party members, student union leaders and other democracy activists were arrested and imprisoned, including Daw Aung San Suu Kyi who spent a total of 19 years under house arrest. Subsequently, many activists and members of the All Burma Federation of Student Unions (ABFSU) fled into hiding in Myanmar's densely forested east, forming armed resistance groups from where they continued their campaigns for democratic change. Others fled into exile across the Thai border, engaging transnational networks of political and social activism (Maber 2016b). The legacy of these struggles is tangible, particularly in tertiary education systems associated with dissent (Lall 2008; Maber 2014) and has been echoed by contemporary student protests where members of the contentious student unions newly found themselves subject to arrest and detention.

September 2007 again saw tens of thousands of protestors take to the streets of Yangon, Mandalay and other cities. The mass demonstrations originally started as a result of fuel price hikes due to the removal of subsidies. Protestors were then joined by large numbers of monks and nuns who were motivated to demonstrate against violence on the part of security forces directed towards protesting monks in Pakokka, giving rise to the popular terming of the movement, the Saffron Revolution (Walton and Hayward 2014, 11). The military response was brutal and in several cases fatal. 1,072 protestors, including many monks, were arrested for political activities in the aftermath of the demonstrations with prison sentences being conferred of up to 65 years (Watchlist on Children and Armed Conflict 2009, 10).

Resource Driven Conflict Dimensions

Myanmar's richness in natural resources and the vast disparity in wealth distribution have long been in tension and recent state-led resource extraction activities are currently generating new, more class-based conflicts overlaying ethnic grievances. Gem, jade, gold and copper mines, oil and gas extraction sites and pipelines, hydropower dams, as well as logging sites and opium fields punctuate the landscape of the ethnic territories and are all sites of contention. While the military junta dominated these, benefitting particularly from agreements with China over hydroelectric power and Thailand over the oil and gas production, the ethnic military and political groups maintain they should have greater economic control of the resources in their areas as well as determination over the use of land (Myanmar Peace Monitor 2014). Many of the project sites for resource extraction are targets for violence and the increased militarization that they attract from government forces exacerbates tensions with non-state armed groups and local communities alike (BNI 2013, 1; WLB 2014, 22). Similarly, the extreme poverty that is experienced by many across all of the ethnic territories is seen as a direct result of government policies, such as the *4-cuts* (*pya ley pya*), to undermine the ethnic groups struggle for self-determination through limiting access to food, funds, information networks and recruitment (Laungaramsri 2011, 102; Myanmar Peace Monitor 2014; WLB 2014). Vast disparities in income distribution also fuelled urban unrest as wealth is concentrated in the hands of a small number of business tycoons with close ties to the military (BNI 2013, 17).

Migration, Displacement and Exile

Both within Myanmar and beyond its borders, displacement has affected those fleeing the ethnic civil wars, exiles from political tyranny, those whose homes have been lost to communal violence, forced relocations to make way for hydro-electric dams or economic development sites, as well as those affected by environmental disasters, such as Cyclone Nargis which struck in 2008. Internally, up to 300,000 have been displaced in IDP camps for much of the last 10 years (Myanmar Peace Monitor 2014), with Kachin State and Rakhine State seeing the highest levels of displacement. This figure rises to 650,000 when accounting for those displaced outside the formal camp settings (TNI 2013, 10). Across Myanmar's borders, refugees have fled overland and by boat to Bangladesh, India, China, Thailand, Indonesia and Malaysia. Thailand has historically been the most established site of refuge and exile with nine official refugee camps established along the Thai border continuing to house up to 130,000 refugees (TBC 2013, 16). A further two million migrants are thought to reside in Thailand both legally and undocumented (TBC 2013, 19). The communities along this border region have in many cases been resident for up to 30 years, and have been associated with pro-democracy campaigning and human rights monitoring as well as providing a base for ethnic minority resistance from the Eastern states (Maber 2016b).

While displacements are continuing, particularly with a recent surge of civilians to the West fleeing attacks in Rakhine State as discussed further below, communities on the Eastern borders are increasingly facing the possibility of repatriation back to Myanmar (UNHCR 2014; Maber 2016b). Adequately addressing the situation and needs of returning refugees and migrants remains a key concern before repatriation attempts accelerate. Particularly in relation to education, the issues of accreditation for prior learning and recognition of skills for students and professionals alike are a priority for consideration.

Processes of Political Transition and Reform (2010–2015)

The approval of the 2008 constitution, adopted at a time of immense distress within the country in the aftermath of Cyclone Nargis, paved the way for the military to manage a controlled transition to civilian rule. Elections were held in late 2010, the first since the NLD's annulled victory of 1990, and marked an official end to the military junta's leadership which had endured in its various guises since 1962. Although this led to the inauguration of a nominally civilian government, the process orchestrated through the new constitution ensured that the military retained a designated 25% of parliamentary seats and veto powers, entrenching military influence in all aspects of politics (GEN 2012). At the time, the elections were criticised by many international actors for not being free and fair (UN 2010). A major objection was the refusal to allow democratic opposition leader Daw Aung San Suu Kyi to stand in the elections, leading to their boycott by her party, the largest of the opposition, the NLD. Unsurprisingly, the military-backed Union Solidarity and Development Party (USDP) secured victory, with President Thein Sein (himself a former military general) taking office in early 2011 (UN 2010; Hlaing 2012) and many of the same military political figures reappearing in the newly reformed parliamentary bodies.

However, despite the contentious transferal of power, President Thein Sein began a process of widespread reforms, particularly seeking to expand economic opportunities with international partners (Hlaing 2012; Chalk 2013). While this economic expansion served the agenda of political and military elites who benefitted substantially from the process (Turnell 2015), the political and social reforms also created opportunities for civil society movements to expand, particularly aided by the relaxing of censorship laws, and exiled activists began to re-engage with government authorities in the hope of influencing reforms (Bächtold 2015). From 2011 onwards, the majority of detained political prisoners were released encouraging the lifting of economic sanctions on the part of Western governments (although restrictions remained in place for many individuals associated with the former military regime), and international and regional trade agreements flourished. Typifying the emergence of Myanmar as a potential economic partner, the country held the yearly chair of ASEAN for the first time in 2014 under the theme "Moving Forward in Unity to a Peaceful and Prosperous Community" (Government of Myanmar 2014), reflecting the dual designs of the government on brokering a large-scale peace deal and ensuring economic security.

During this period, reform processes were instigated across multiple sectors: sectoral reviews and legislation packages were initiated in education, land use, manufacturing and rule of law, amongst others. Censorship was relaxed and telecommunications expanded, bringing affordable mobile phones to the country for the first time in 2014 (Dolan and Gray 2014). Each process brought new frictions and doubts over the sincerity, and durability, of the reforms (Bhatia 2013; Huang 2013). Likewise, academic as well as popular opinion remained divided as to the motivations behind these reforms and the commitment to democratic change, with some viewing the political transition as a calculated opportunity for the military to consolidate legitimised authority (Jones 2014; Global Witness 2015; Bhatia 2013), while others saw greater progress in the expansion of civil political space (Singh 2013; OECD 2013).

However, the increased possibilities for co-operation nonetheless changed the landscape of political manoeuvring. Having boycotted the 2010 elections, the NLD did contest the 2012 by-elections, winning the majority of contested seats and ensuring a position for Daw Aung San Suu Kyi within the parliament. Subsequent elections were held in late 2015, this time under greater scrutiny, resulting in an overwhelming victory for Daw Aung San Suu Kyi's NLD. However, as Daw Aung San Suu Kyi herself is barred from occupying the position of President in the Constitution, the NLD took office at the start April 2016 under the official leadership of President Htin Kyaw. Nonetheless maintaining her leadership of the party, Daw Aung San Suu Kyi was instead appointed to the newly established role of State Counsellor. As yet there has been insufficient opportunity to gauge the full impact of this transition from military dictatorship to democratic transition, however constraints have evidently remained and new challenges emerged. Despite obvious progress, power has still largely resided in the hands of a minority of elite who have an inconsistent record of accepting change. In addition to the continuation of the unresolved ethnic conflicts, there has been a rise in intercommunal violence (highlighted below) inflamed by a rhetoric of ultra-conservative Buddhist nationalism, primarily targeting Muslim minority communities in the western region of Rakhine (Walton and Hayward 2014). This ongoing climate of conflict and increasing religious violence suggests that although transition is underway, sustainable transformation may remain elusive.

Contemporary Conflict Dynamics

Amongst the many changes that have taken place over the last few years of Myanmar's transitions, conflict has continued to intensify in several regions of the country. While the research for this book was undertaken in areas that have experienced greater stability in recent years, other areas of the country have been experiencing an increase in military offensives. In Kachin and Northern Shan States fighting renewed in 2011 after the breakdown of ceasefire agreements and has continued through both election cycles. In particular, clashes between the Kachin Independence Army (KIA), the armed wing of the Kachin Independence Organisation (KIO), and the Tatmadaw have escalated, resulting in the displacement of over 100,000 civilians currently living in temporary shelters in continuing insecurity (Pistor 2017). Since the NLD took office, military assaults have intensified in 2016 and 2017, significantly undermining the legitimacy of renewed peace processes and further accentuating mistrust in government-led peacebuilding efforts (Naw and Barter 2017).

In Rakhine State reports continue to emerge of the widespread humanitarian emergency as hundreds of thousands of Muslim Rohingya are fleeing violence and persecution in the state for neighbouring Bangladesh (UN 2017). The extent of the atrocities reported during military "clearance operations"[1] against communities perceived to be illegitimate or hostile are deeply worrying and worsening as accounts of the violence are still being revealed (OHCHR 2017a, b). However, while military assaults against ethnic minorities elsewhere in the country have often been met with indifference amongst the general populace, the so-called clearance operations in Rakhine State have found significant popular support, fuelled by a rise in prominence of religious conservatism, debates over national identity and a proliferation of misinformation on social media. Navigating the voracity and diversity of emotions surrounding the issues of identity, legitimacy and threat presents a challenge, including for international researchers, as Rosalie Metro has eloquently discussed in her opinion piece "We Can Oppose Ethnic Cleansing Without Accepting Simple Answers" (Metro 2017). The complexity underlying tensions and triggers belie simple summaries, and it is beyond the scope of this work to do justice to a detailed analysis of these conflicts. The discussion below therefore is intended to provide background to the context of religious tensions which have increased in recent years and subsequently erupted into the current crisis.

Rising Religious Tensions

Recent years have seen a rise in religious conservatism allied with Burmese nationalism which has resulted in violent inter-communal conflicts between Buddhist majority and Muslim minority communities. Sporadic outbreaks of violence between 2012 and 2014 included rioting, assault and arson in Rakhine State, Meikhtila, Lashio and Mandalay resulting in over 200 fatalities (Walton and Hayward 2014, 8). Violence centred between Buddhist and Muslim communities, with the Muslim ethnic minority group, the Rohingya, in Rakhine State coming particularly under attack as perceived non-legitimate residents. During this period, instability in Rakhine State resulted in the displacement of between 130,000 and

[1] This neutralising phrase is rapidly becoming the government and military's preferred framing of the atrocities, as illustrated by statements from the President's Office (OHCHR 2017b).

140,000 civilians, many of whom continue to be sheltered in IDP camps (UN OCHA 2013; Myanmar Peace Monitor 2014). Muslim schools were in some cases a target for this violence, with 4 teachers and 32 students at one school in Meikhtila being among those targeted and killed in 2012 (GCPEA 2013).

The influence of religion has been prominent throughout Myanmar's political and cultural history and continues to shape the landscape of transition, with religious affiliation infused with constructions of national and ethnic identity. 88% of the 56 million population are estimated to be Buddhist (Department of Population 2016), leading to a frequent association between national identity and Buddhism, reinforced through media and public discourse as well as education practices (Salem-Gervais and Metro 2012; Walton 2013). Christian communities account for an estimated 6.2% of the population of Myanmar, while Muslim communities constitute a further 4.3% of the population, with the remaining 1.6% of the population identifying as Hindu (0.5%), Animist (0.8%), with another religion (0.2%) or with no religion (0.1%) (Department of Population 2016).

Also underlying current hostilities are conflicting notions of recognition, legitimacy and national identity. Changes to citizenship laws in 1982 resulted in citizenship being denied to many who had previously been recognised as citizens including ethnic groups which were no longer legitimised, to those whose parents did not both hold citizenship and to those not born within Myanmar. As part of the military junta's attempts to push a unifying rhetoric, the new citizenship laws reverted to precolonial, highly subjective definitions of ethnic groups which predated 1823, and offered full citizenship only to those who could prove ethnic and territorial connections to these groups, setting up arbitrary notions of the 'indigenous' and 'authentic' inhabitants of geographical territories (TNI 2014, 5). The Muslim communities in Rakhine identifying as Rohingya were reframed as "Bengali illegal immigrants" (Fortify Rights 2014, 11; TNI 2014, 11), setting up hostilities with ethnically recognised Rakhine Buddhist communities. Without full citizenship status, those whose citizens' rights were revoked by the 1982 act are denied access to university enrolment, land ownership and inheritance.

While religious violence has historical precedence, tensions have been inflamed by the recent emergence of controversial ultra-nationalist movements, known as the 969 and the MaBaTha, led by a small number of extremist Buddhist monks who claim to seek to defend the Buddhist majority from perceived threat. Originally a fringe movement, the alarming support that the MaBaTha and 969 have received in recent years has resulted in their amassing startling political influence. The impact and influence of increased religious conservatism is particularly evident at a policy level in the rapid approval in 2015 of a package of legislation, known as the 'Protection of Race and Religion' bills which reinforce an association of national identity with Buddhism (GEN 2015). The legislation includes provisions to restrict interfaith marriage and women's choices for religious conversion, and allow for limitations to birth numbers or mandated birth spacing in communities that are (perceived to be) rapidly expanding (Walton et al. 2015). The bills, and the political support they received, further validate constructions of Buddhist national identity and also reinforce gender inequalities limiting women's rights to choice and self-determination.

Ethnic Grievances and the Role of Education

Having discussed the historical and contemporary contexts to Myanmar's varied conflicts and political transitions, the focus now turns to outlining the ethnic grievances that inform positions within peace negotiations and the role that education has played within these. Acknowledging the plurality of priorities and stances adopted by the different Ethnic Armed Groups (EAGs), their varying historical roots and contexts, as further discussed in the subsequent section, there are nonetheless certain grievances that are shared by many groups in relation to treatment by the state and military forces. The summary table below lists these grievances, drawn from peace documentation and secondary sources. Two fundamental grievances which are common across the range of actors relate to political autonomy in a federal state and cultural recognition, as one peacebuilding staff member of an international donor summarised: "*This is about recognition. This is about having their rights*" (int. 76). For analytical reasons we have categorised these grievances according to their economic, socio-cultural, political and environmental nature, however many of these grievances evidently overlap between those categories (Table 3.1).

Table 3.1 Shared grievances for ethnic armed groups

Shared grievances for ethnic armed groups[a]	
Economic	Control over natural resources and unequal distribution of revenues
	Land rights and ownership
	High levels of poverty in ethnic states
	Lack of infrastructure (electricity, transport, roads)
	Forced labour (incl. in economic development projects and military porters)
	Arbitrary taxation
Social/cultural	Low levels of literacy in ethnic states
	Lack of protection for cultural practices and heritage sites incl. banned celebrations of festivals
	Lack of recognition of ethnic languages incl. learning in mother-tongue
	High incidence of drugs in ethnic areas (selling or addiction)
	Threats to religious freedoms
Political	Claims for a federal union and political authority
	Failure to respect Panglong Agreement
	Restrictions on forming political parties
	Rejection of 2008 Constitution
	Human rights abuses incl. military violence against women, arbitrary detention
Environmental	Land confiscation and relocations
	Impact of development projects and extraction sites incl. hydro-electricity dams, industrial zones, mines
	Impact of drug cultivation in some territories

[a]Sources: Ethnic Armed Organisations Conference (2013), Myanmar Peace Monitor (2013), BNI (2014), TNI (2013)

Within these grievances as listed above, it already becomes apparent that education has substantial relevance. The politicisation of education under the military regime, as well as the lack of appropriate resource allocation to the education sector as a whole, have had significant impacts on matters of access, quality and relevance in contemporary Myanmar (as explored further in Chaps. 4 and 5).[2] Such issues have consequently exacerbated educational grievances, adding fuel to conflict drivers. The desire to preserve ethnic cultural heritage and the sense of threat posed to this identity by the Bamar majority state is reflected in the significance of the role of education in building an ethno-national state. As expressed by the same donor staff member as cited above:

> [That] is what this conflict is about. It's about recognition of the culture or rights or their identity or their ethnicity and in education it's key, they want to see formal school with teachers that are allowed to train or to teach in their ethnic languages. So this is what they said conflict is about. (int. 76)

One of the key issues to bear in mind is that the positioning of social service delivery as a point of negotiation is not only an abstract desire to preserve cultural identity and autonomy, but relates to very tangible consequences for current services that are already being administered by ethnic organisations in the absence of the state. Unresolved issues of decentralisation and education autonomy are therefore central to addressing ethnic concerns, where there is a desire to protect services from the perceived dominating authority of the central government. While under-resourcing is a driver of the conflicts, an expansion of state services, including MoE basic education schools, is not always the desired solution. Suspicion persists that the centralised education system serves the interests of the majority rather than ethnic minority populations, which problematises the issue of redistribution and a 'simple' expansion of state provision of resources to education and its delivery. Although this is not the case universally in all the conflict-affected states, in Mon State where much of our research was conducted, the establishment of parallel systems of education by the Mon National Education Committee (MNEC) occurred as a direct result of the New Mon State Party (NMSP) extending its authority beyond military action to social service provision tailored to a Mon-identity construction. Education in MNEC schools therefore prioritises Mon history and culture with Mon language as the medium of instruction for primary levels (WPRC and HURFOM 2015), an issue which is further discussed in Chaps. 7 and 8. The impact of state-provided education being perceived as a tool of the government to dominate and manipulate populations has significant implications for pathways forward to address both conflict drivers and educational grievances.

---

[2] In 2000, the Ministry of Education received only 7.5% of the national budget, while the Ministry of Defense was allocated 40% (CRPP, 2000 cited in Lwin 2000). Although since reforms began in 2011 education budgets have increased they remain low (MoE 2013; UNESCO 2014), and have been a point of contention for student protestors and opposition groups (int. 110)

Outlining the Peace Processes

While ceasefires were sought by the successive military regimes throughout the 1990s, they were not accompanied by meaningful peace dialogues nor the withdrawal of troops by either party, resulting in the multiple disintegration of the agreements and cyclical recurrence of fighting (Watchlist on Children and Armed Conflict 2009, 9). In 2011, President Thein Sein renewed peace talks leading to new ceasefire agreements being signed with four non-state armed groups (NSAGs) and a further nine the following year, meaning that of the 17 major NSAGs engaged in combat 14 were now engaged in ceasefire arrangements and some peacebuilding dialogue (BNI 2014, 4). Three remained officially combatant, with the Kachin Independence Army (KIA) resuming fighting in the same year, 2011. As highlighted above, sites of conflict remain at their most severe in Rakhine, Kachin and Shan States (including extensive fighting in Northern Shan State despite the ceasefire with SSA-N). In the previous years there have also been on-going occurrences of military violence in Kayin State particularly around the Myawaddy-Mae Sot border (Myanmar Peace Monitor 2015).

As the research in the subsequent chapters of this collection was undertaken in the build up to the elections of 2015 and before the NLD took office, this section explores in more detail the peace negotiations that were being undertaken at that time. Acknowledging that there are multiple dimensions to Myanmar's conflicts, including political and religious tensions, this section examines formal policy arrangements directing attention particularly to the processes of formulating and articulating this policy more so than its enactment. It therefore takes as its focus the conflict and peace negotiations between the government and the ethnic armed groups.[3]

Renewing the Peace Processes (2011–2015)

After taking office in 2011, President Thein Sein sought to renew peace negotiations, consolidating bilateral ceasefire agreements with 14 EAGs during the course of 2012 (EBO 2013). These agreements formalised or replaced many previous ceasefire arrangements that had frequently not articulated concessions by either party, nor resulted in a reduction in fighting. As such, they demonstrated a new commitment by the USDP government to engage in peace dialogues, as was acknowledged by several of our respondents, including an international staff member involved in the peacebuilding sector we interviewed:

[3]As illustrative of the overlapping conflict dimensions, the All Burma Student Democratic Front, although a non-state armed group (NSAG) and not an ethnic armed group (EAG), is included in the ethnic ceasefire negotiations as a UNFC alliance member.

> There's not a great track record of written agreements being signed between the parties to the process. So the fact that the government was able to do that and was eager to do that is positive. (int. 94)

Commitment was also made to secure a nationwide ceasefire agreement (NCA), initially anticipated to be signed in mid-2013 (Crisis Group 2015). However, in the lead up to the general elections of November 2015, there was still a lack of agreement over the signing of this NCA, resulting in a rushed and unfinished process of dialogue that came under significant scrutiny during the subsequent election. With multiple interests and agendas evident across the large numbers of actors and parties involved, the process was lengthy and delicate, but arguably some progress was made, as expressed at the time by the same respondent as above: "*The trajectory is broadly upwards and the achievements of the last couple of years are substantial. Not irreversible, but substantial*" (int. 94).

The figure below aims to provide an overview of the various governmental and non-government actors involved in the process of peace negotiations, as well as the status (and absence) of the different national and bilateral ceasefire agreements (Fig. 3.1).

As of November 2015, 8 EAGs had agreed to sign the NCA, falling short of 15 that the government had hoped would sign, out of a total of over 20. A major point of contention (explored further below) had become the issue of which groups were included under the agreement; the ethnic coalition, also named the Union Nationalities Federal Council (UNFC), contended that a further six of its members that were excluded from the NCA should also be added (Keenan 2015). Additionally,

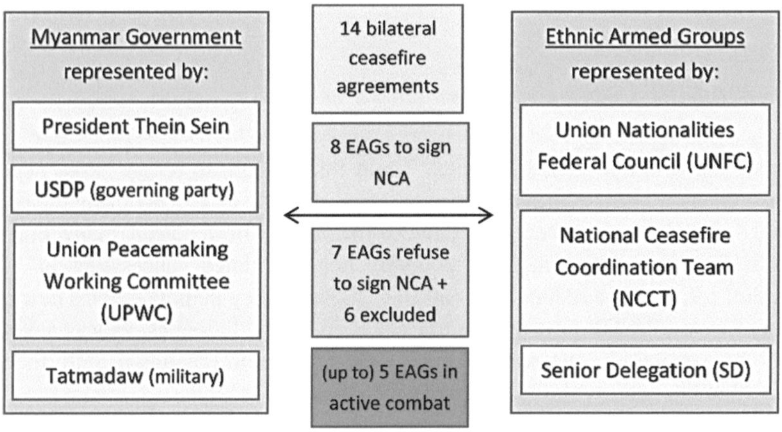

Fig. 3.1 Status of peace negotiations prior to elections, October 2015

combat is still active, most intensely in Kachin and northern Shan states with multiple EAGs, raising doubts as to how representative the NCA could be.[4]

Some international commentators have noted the perceived lack of agreement or coordination amongst the multiple EAGs (Kuppuswamy 2013, 3). However, such a perspective risks ignoring the question of why it should be expected that the various ethnic groups, whose motivations for armed struggle and whose experiences and arrangements with the state have been quite different, should have a unified response. One of the key challenges for peacebuilding initiatives in Myanmar is the very different states of conflict that affect the different regions. So while populations in Kachin and Northern Shan States are experiencing active fighting, continued casualties and ongoing displacement, Mon State has seen relative stability since the 1994 ceasefire agreement. This has evident implications for the expectations and aims of the different ethnic parties. While there are similarities and overlaps in the grievances expressed by ethnic actors, as indicated in the section above, there are also variations in the details, contextualisation and desired responses. Additionally, this also impacts the priorities of different regions in terms of service delivery and the extent to which issues of social service delivery, including access and control, may feature on the peacebuilding agenda for different groups. Consequently, states such as Kayin, Kayah and Mon that have established parallel systems of education closely linked to the EAGs may prioritise education issues within peace agreements more so than Chin State, which does not have such equivalent non-state education structures.

Ethnic alliances and frictions within them have been a feature of the conflicts since the 1950s (Keenan 2015), reflecting the different historical positions and ideologies behind the movements. Conversely, however, the desire for federalism has been a common motivation for the multiple groups and the UNFC has presented this as a united goal. Additionally, the UNFC has sought greater inclusion of periphery EAGs within the national-level dialogues. These overlapping issues and interests, therefore, reinforce the need for a contextual, and sub-national or local understanding of both the interconnected as well as the different conflict drivers.

The Roles of Varied Actors in the Peace Process

As highlighted in the diagram below, the process of peace negotiations in Myanmar between 2011 and 2015 reflects the nature of the conflicts, which had not seen significant international involvement. While previous ceasefire agreements under the military junta were directly between the Tatmadaw and the individual ethnic armed

[4]The 8 EAGs signing the NCA are the Karen National Union (KNU), the Democratic Karen Benevolent Army (DKBA), the Karen Peace Council (KNU/KNLA-PC), the Chin National Front (CNF), the Pa-Oh National Liberation Organisation (PNLO), the Arakan Liberation Party (ALP), the Restoration Council Shan State (RCSS/SSA-S) and the All Burma Students' Democratic Front (ABSDF) (Keenan 2015).

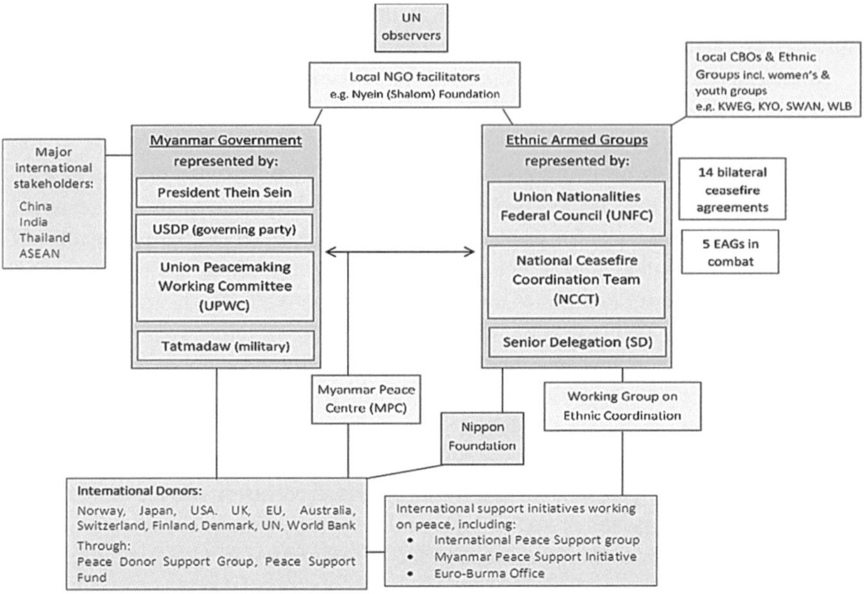

Fig. 3.2 Actors in the peace process, 2011–2015

groups on an *ad hoc* basis, the peace processes initiated in 2011 were largely led by the new USDP government. The Tatmadaw, however, continue to play a significant role in the process, both in terms of military representation in negotiations and also with regard to political influence within parliament and the ruling Union Solidarity and Development Party (USDP) (Fig. 3.2).

Peace negotiations took place between government and EAG representatives, with a small number of international observers from the UN being present at some meetings.[5] Additionally, local facilitators, such as from Nyein (Shalom) foundation, participated as mediators in some dialogues. The major peace supporting organisation through the negotiations was the Myanmar Peace Centre (MPC), subsequently replaced in 2016. Established in 2012 by the government and led by USDP Minister Aung Min, the MPC was seen as more closely aligned with government interests, despite being ostensibly designed to be a neutral organisation (int. 22). International support for the process was largely limited to funding through specific multi-donor peace funds, with financial support for the MPC largely coming from the Norwegian-led coalition of donors, the Peace Support Donor Group. Other internationally funded support initiatives included the Myanmar Peace Support Initiative, which concluded activities in 2015, and the Euro-Burma Office which continues to report on progress from Chiang Mai and also supports the Working Group on Ethnic Coordination to facilitate inter-ethnic collaboration. These initiatives largely worked

[5] Some additional international observers have in the past attended isolated meetings including delegates from China and the UK.

to increase discussion and contact to raise periphery support for peacebuilding in communities beyond the peace negotiations. The Japanese Nippon Foundation played a slightly different role to other international donor organisations and has worked in more direct contact with the EAG representatives to the UNFC to formulate their peace plans during negotiations. While there was little civil society consultation on the government side of the process, EAGs were and continue to be more closely associated with youth and women's organisations. Consequently, civil society groups such as the Karen Women's Empowerment Group (KWEG), the Karen Youth Organisation (KYO), the Shan Women's Action Network (SWAN), or the Chiang Mai-based Women's League of Burma (WLB) – among others – have promoted awareness of the peace processes in their communities, however their direct involvement remains limited.

International actors have been very much on the periphery of these negotiations, with occasional UN observers permitted to attend. As the International Crisis Group noted: "the peace process is home-grown, without any international mediators, and it should remain so – this has been one of its great strengths" (2015, 2). Those in the international community supporting in the process similarly articulated the position that "*we want to respect the national nature of the peace process*" (int. 51). However, as highlighted by those involved in negotiations, the absence of international agendas does not necessarily reduce complications:

> Being a locally owned process is what you want, and you want international stakeholders, donors to ideally support local solutions. But there is a balance, because where there's local ownership there's also entrenched biases and mistrust, and that runs very deep. (int. 94)

The UNFC at times requested more international observers to be part of the process (Myanmar Peace Monitor 2014), reflecting an underlying anxiety over power structures within negotiations. However, occupying this position with neutrality is a challenge. Amongst both local and international policy makers there was a sense that Myanmar's recent history of isolation and lack of international, or at least Western, engagement amplifies the challenges for new international connections: "*it makes it incredibly difficult for international partners to influence the process*" (int. 94). Equally, even when invited, the role and communication pathways for international actors is not always clear, as one international staff member revealed:

> Unlike other post-conflict or conflict settings where they have maybe as their counterpart a ministry of peace and reconciliation, we don't have that yet in Myanmar. (int. 51)

Further, international involvement which has largely involved funding being directed through local partners, has also been contentious. Between the elections, international donors fomented closer ties with the USDP government through bilateral trade agreements and development partnerships, and were consequently increasingly seen as allied with state authorities over ethnic concerns. This has been visible for example in hostile community responses at a local level to the Norwegian-led multi-donor funded Myanmar Peace Support Initiative (MPSI) (KCSN 2014). This also has continuing implications for education policy, where the same international partners (including the EU, JICA, and the World Bank) continue to participate in the formulation and implementation of education reforms as well as funding peace initiatives. The nature of these relationships as well as the peace agreements more broadly remain precarious: "*A small thing can undermine it and we should be very careful that we are not overly enthusiastic*" (int. 51).

Women in Conflict, Peace and Reform Processes

In recent years women's rights activism in Myanmar has garnered greater space for advocacy and brought increased attention to the ongoing gender inequalities they experience. Ethnically aligned women's organisations,[6] many originating in the 1990s, have frequently been associated with the ethnic armed struggles for auto-determination (Hedström 2016), navigating a precarious path between rejecting the frequently violent subjugation of women by the military state and simultaneously renegotiating gender roles within their ethnic traditions (Laungaramsri 2011). Combined with cross-border networks with exile groups in Thailand,[7] these women's organisations balanced seemingly non-political endeavours (providing education and healthcare to women and children in conflict) with more overtly politicised campaigns such as reporting on the systematic rape and abuse of ethnic women by the military (WLB 2014). Sexual and gender violence, experienced by many women across social, political and geographical divides (see for example GEN 2015), has also been pervasive across Myanmar's conflicts and has been well documented by ethnic women's associations and humanitarian organisations (see for example KWO 2010; SWAN 2002). Widespread incidents of rape and sexual assault by military personnel have been reported, leading to an understanding of such violence as deliberate attempts to undermine community cohesion (Laungaramsri 2011; WLB 2014). However despite women's distinct experiences of conflict and their contributions to ethno-nationalist struggles, they have been largely absent from previous attempts to negotiate peace.

Prior to the 2011 renewal of the peace process, the former ceasefire arrangements were arrived at solely by closed and often unwritten agreements between the military commanders of the Tatmadaw and the EAG in question (Lahtaw and Raw 2012: 7). Consequently, women played no part in these negotiations as they were, and largely continue to be, excluded from active participation and leadership roles in the military and EAGs, reflecting women's marginalisation from positions of leadership more broadly. As the current process of peace negotiations is more open (to media, observers and small numbers of participants beyond the armed groups), there has been hope for greater inclusion (Lahtaw and Raw 2012, 7). Small numbers of women have also participated in the formal meetings as representatives from the

[6] Examples of such organisations include the Shan Women's Action Network and the Karen Women's Organisation. See also Maber (2016a).

[7] Although the majority of its 13 member organisations are based within Myanmar, the Women's League of Burma (WLB) itself is based in Chiang Mai, Thailand.

EAGs, including most prominently Naw Zipporah Sein of the KNU, herself a former teacher, who led the UNFC Senior Delegation. However, overall the space available for women to participate in the peace process has been disappointing, with government representation and government associated organisations such as the Myanmar Peace Centre being notably male dominated (Swedish Burma Committee 2013; AGIPP 2015).

This reflects women's (lack of) inclusion in the political and reform environment broadly, where even in those spheres, such as education, where women have traditionally played a greater role, they continue to be marginalised and excluded from positions of influence (Maber 2014). Additionally, despite superficial commitments to the UN Security Council Resolution 1325 on *Women, Peace and Security*, references to women are overwhelmingly absent from the ceasefire texts, including the national ceasefire agreement. The absence of women from peace negotiations and documentation is particularly concerning given the impact of conflict on women's lives (WLB 2014), and reflects the reluctance of national and international policy makers to demonstrate genuine commitments to addressing women's concerns. There are indications that this is beginning to change, thanks in part to the efforts of civil society activists and organisations such as the Alliance for Gender Inclusion in the Peace Process, launched in 2014, which have brought increased attention to the need to ensure women's participation and distinct contributions to peacebuilding do not remain neglected. However, there continues to be a need to genuinely listen to and actively address women's priorities, including, fundamentally, by ensuring greater representation in political and decision-making arenas (GEN 2015; AGIPP 2015, 2017).

The Political Nature of Peacebuilding

While, as noted above, the commitment to securing nationwide peace agreements drew praise, particularly from the international community, the motivations behind these peace efforts have also been questioned. In line with a dominant international agenda that promotes a liberal peacebuilding model (as discussed in Chap. 2), the peacebuilding discourses have typically incorporated a strong economic rationale. President Thein Sein himself summarised the USDP government's motivations as:

> A failure to end the conflict with ethnic groups would be an obstacle to economic development and that is why efforts are being made to end the conflicts is the key foundation to peacebuilding in the country. (Kuppuswamy 2013, 5)

In addition, there have been questions around the sincere drive or prioritisation for the USDP government to foster processes of national (ethnic, political and economic) *reconciliation*, as the status quo might actually serve better the aims of the government and army (Kuppuswamy 2013, 8). However, many saw the NCA as a legacy for President Thein Sein, suggesting that the failed attempts to secure a complete NCA before the November 2015 elections reflected a failure of the USDP to win confidence in its leadership.[8]

Equally, some ethnic and civil society organisations remain suspicious of the process which they perceive to be designed to appease international donors and trade partners in order to secure greater financial benefits (Lintner 2015). Others also suggest that the quest for the NCA diverted attention away from meaningful political dialogue at a state level, trapping the process in a "*holding pattern*" (int. 101, conflict advisor) which undermined confidence in the peace processes more broadly, as another international conflict advisor working in the peace processes expressed:

> As far as explicitly implementing word for word the [bilateral ceasefire] agreements, it hasn't happened. And there's a few reasons for that, I guess the main one has been this diversion of attention to a nationwide ceasefire agreement. (int. 94)

Consequently, the extension of the ceasefire negotiation process to the detriment of implementing agreements already in place undermined peacebuilding momentum and failed to address the causes of conflict. As the same advisor highlighted: "*implementation arrangements is one main criticism of those bilateral agreements. KNU signed, you know, three years ago – where's the peace dividend?*" (int. 94). It is arguably this notion of reconciliation, as it has been expressed under Union rubric without emphasis on subsequent peace dividends, which is problematic for many ethnic constituencies. Attempting to delay political dialogue therefore undermines the deeply political nature of the ethnic conflicts. Pointing to the counter-productive implications for the peacebuilding process of the pursuit of a national ceasefire agreement disconnected from dialogue on political and socio-cultural grievances, the respondent continued: "*you're not going to get military successes without thinking about the interim arrangements for the provision of social services, so it's a big obstacle*" (int. 94). Likewise, the fundamentally political claim by the EAGs to federalism remains an unresolved point of contention. As this central driver of conflict is left undiscussed, it is difficult to build trust in ceasefire arrangements, a point acknowledged by donors and policy makers: "*I think the suspicion on the part of the ethnic organisations will always be that you are trying to get them subsumed into a unitary public system*" (int. 3).

The hope, with both the bilateral agreements and the continued push for the NCA, seems to be that if the documents of peace are in place, they can be added to later on – either to include more parties, or to flesh out specificities. However, this liberal model of peacebuilding, which sees the quest for negative peace prioritised, does not support building trust that these agreements will be any more meaningful than the previous broken ceasefires of the 1990s. Equally, the lack of a peace dividend, or tangible benefits at a local level, does little to dispel the suspicion of shallow motivations on the part of the government, whether it be the USDP government

[8] This view was expressed by several interviewed in the context of the research, including in ints. 9 and 110 with community leaders engaged in peace and education advocacy.

of the time or the newly incumbent NLD. A clear logic emerges from interviews with international organisations that highlight a chronological approach to peace processes which prioritise a negative peace, taking the NCA as the starting point that will later be followed by political dialogue across the EAGs (ints. 3, 13 and 101). This chronology also reflects the government's own projected pathways for peace negotiations, that saw union level political dialogue and the implementation of "regional development tasks in terms of education, health and communication" (Myanmar Peace Monitor 2014) as occurring only *after* the NCA had been achieved. However, as has been highlighted above, attempting to separate out military, political and social issues within the peacebuilding framework may not serve the ends of advancing confidence in the peace process as key conflict drivers are neglected.

As was consistently expressed by international and national actors involved in the peace process, the nature of negotiations is "*very fluid, complex and very political*" (int. 83). These political elements are reflected in multiple ways, including in: the motivations of ethnic armed groups; the manoeuvring of the USDP ahead of the 2015 elections; the continued political influence of the Tatmadaw; and the renewal of peace processes after the NLD's election victory. The attempt to segment the peace process, so that political dialogue is withheld until after agreement has been reached on a nationwide ceasefire, risks failing to acknowledge these influences.

Peace Processes and Challenges for Reforms Post-2015

Upon taking office in 2016 the NLD government relaunched the peace processes under a rhetoric of reconciliation. The MPC was replaced with the National Reconciliation and Peace Centre (NRPC) by the President's Office and, as discussed at the outset of this chapter, negotiations were restyled as large-scale "21st Century Panglong Union Peace Conferences". As yet, however, these events have centred on establishing stakeholders' positions and have afforded little tangible progress in advancing the substance of agreements or commitments to the NCA (TNI 2017). Apparent movements towards democracy and achieving durable peace also risk being overwhelmed by the current crises, as conflicts intensify and trust in a genuine commitment to reconciliation is undermined.

There are indications however that the space for incorporating discussions of social service provision into peace negotiations may be expanding towards a more inclusive style of deliberation (Walton 2017). Likewise, efforts to incorporate youth movements into peacebuilding discussions have also been apparent, with youth representatives invited to take part in discussions held before the launching of the official peace dialogues (Phyo 2016; PSF 2017). In the current policy environment, reforms are progressing across multiple sectors simultaneously and just like the wider peacebuilding process described above, the education reforms continue to be no less politically charged. The reforms in the education sector, and specifically the passing of the National Education Law in 2014, were some of the most overtly political and contentious policy changes introduced by the USDP government and continue to pose considerable challenges. Beyond this, the reforms coincide in their agendas, as one peacebuilding policy maker commented of the education reforms:

> They are doing and preparing things which are supposed to be discussed in the peace process. Most of the provisions are the foundation of peace building from [an] education perspective. (int. 13)

Treating these reforms independently without establishing links between them can therefore reinforce territorialism and potentially lead to further mistrust. An expansion of these intersections follows in the sections below.

Locating Education Within the Peacebuilding Architecture

At an overt level, education has not featured prominently in the text of peace agreements for the bilateral ceasefires or the NCA. Indeed, the peace process and the education reform processes have been kept separate, with many key stakeholders interviewed on the government side not seeing a connection. Although in broad terms references to the need to consider responsibilities for social service provision feature in the documents reviewed in the context of the research (NCA draft 2015), largely the assumption appears that education, and social services broadly, will feature more prominently in subsequent discussions:

> There's an awareness, there's an appreciation of the significance, but it's just not at the forefront of these negotiations…There's a lot of expectation that these sort of issues need to be dealt with in a more consolidated way through the political dialogue process. (int. 94)

Following the pathway laid out for negotiations, political dialogue after the signing of the NCA is therefore anticipated to address social issues including education. As one observer highlighted:

> Particularly post [bi-lateral] ceasefire agreements, that's when it becomes important. That's when the ethnic armed groups often begin to look around at what their role is and what they're doing [with regards to social services]. (int. 3)

However, while social service delivery may not prominently feature in the phrasing of the ceasefire agreements, participants in peace talks commented on the frequency with which issues of service provision, and in particular education, are mentioned within current discussions (int. 101). This suggests a potential disconnect in the extent to which agreements are fully addressing the grievances articulated by the ethnic groups as well as the variations in priorities for different actors. The demand for a federalist union reflects the desire of ethnic groups to exercise autonomy over their resources, human as well as natural, and to protect their cultural identity. Education is therefore central to the ethnic desire for self-determination, and connects closely to their demands for redistribution, representation and recognition.

The location of education, like other social services, within peace negotiations reflects the interests of those who physically take part in the discussion. The

Tatmadaw have neither experience nor interest in social service provision and consequently are unlikely to prioritise its role. Likewise, the Union Peacemaking Working Committee (UPWC) was dominated by political representatives for the USDP, themselves largely former military officials, who were more commonly drawn from the Ministries of Defence and Border Affairs rather than Education, Health or Social Welfare. This fuelled the perception that education would not be a primary concern within the ceasefire negotiations, as exemplified by the words of one respondent involved in peacebuilding policy-making:

> From my perspective, the main stakeholders in the peace building, they won't see education as a tool to solve the conflict for this stage. They won't see education as a tool for long-term sustainable peace building process. (int. 13)

This may equally be the case for those representing the EAGs in negotiations, who are largely senior male combatants. However, the EAGs vary greatly in size, in number and in role, meaning that they have different motivations and grievances and consequently each interact differently with concerns over education. In states such as Mon, Kayin and Kayah, where the EAGs are closely associated with the parallel systems of schooling that operate under their own curricula, education is a more prominent concern and more closely aligned with ethno-auto-determination. Likewise, the All Burma Student Democratic Front, while not an EAG, is also an alliance member of the UNFC, and is likely to prioritise current education reforms more explicitly in negotiations. Additionally, the protracted nature of the conflicts has led EAGs and associated community based groups to take responsibility for the provision and delivery of social services in the ethnic conflict areas where the state has limited access or may not be welcome. Consequently, for many of these armed groups, the question of responsibility over service delivery is very much embedded within current processes of peace negotiations, as well as central to claims made for a federal union.

The potential role of education reform in addressing these issues is therefore acknowledged, though still subject to much contestation, as is illustrated by the two quotes below. One international stakeholder involved in observing the peace processes stressed:

> I know that this issue of education would be addressed. You know the education law in this country is very controversial, particularly because [of the] diversity of all these ethnicities and how this education would address those issues. (int. 76)

However, a national counterpart revealed a different perspective, seeing more separation between political processes of education reform and the peace negotiations:

> In the peace process, people are not much into this education. They don't talk much about this peace [and] education issue. [But] in the political dialogue [it's] education policy, education law, at the moment, education. (int. 22)

The importance of inclusion of social sectors, including education, is one of the main arguments put forward by the theoretical framing of the Research Consortium, as outlined in Chap. 2. This claim is supported for the case of Myanmar by a recent (DFID funded) report by Kim Jolliffe for The Asia Foundation. In this report,

Jolliffe (2014) argues that interventions in social sectors have a significant opportunity to contribute to peacebuilding, in a moment when Myanmar's peace negotiations with contested areas show potential, but are still fragile. This report draws our attention to three important issues to consider here. Firstly, because resistance to the dominance of a Burman-led state by ethnic groups lies at the basis of many of the (ongoing or past) root causes of conflict, efforts to boost the government's legitimacy through social service provision – including (formal) education – carry a danger of deepening rather than mitigating conflict. The right to provide social services is closely tied to issues of authority, power and legitimacy, and hence are closely related to the ethnic nationalist struggles (2014, 7). This connects to our own analysis that education is deeply political, and for that matter its potential positive as well as negative 'faces' (Bush and Saltarelli 2000) are crucial to consider in any holistic peacebuilding approach. Secondly, Jolliffe points us to observe that in the absence of government provision in contested territories, various civil society networks (sometimes but not always connected to ethnic armed organisations) have firmly institutionalized their roles as local social service providers, in some cases supported directly by international aid. And thirdly, we need to recognise how the recent substantial inflow of aid has both positively and negatively impacted on Myanmar's ethnic conflict, either through strengthening or weakening confidence in the peace process and related (non-)state governance institutions (Jolliffe 2014, 2–3 and 25).

Addressing Educational Grievances

The table below summarises the educational grievances that were emphasised by respondents during the research. Drawing on the theoretical framework of the research these grievances are presented in relation to the three dimensions of social justice – issues of redistribution, of recognition and of representation. Opportunities for supporting peacebuilding though education therefore exist in addressing these grievances in ways that are accepted by all parties. Potential routes towards reconciliation are therefore also outlined in the table below. These are seen as suggested opportunities that have begun to emerge through both the peace and reform process and therefore should not be taken as prescriptive recommendations (Table 3.2).

The following chapters of this collection reveal further insights into the nature of these educational grievances and the challenges and opportunities which present themselves in seeking to address them.

Table 3.2 Educational grievances and pathways for reconciliation

Educational grievances for ethnic actors (Based on interview data)		Pathways for *reconciliation*
Redistribution	• Poor educational outcomes and lack of post-education job opportunities; • Unequal distribution of education resources incl. financing and material resources (e.g. textbooks); • Deployment of teachers, particularly based on language ability; • Disparity in teacher salaries between geographical locations and ethnic and state systems	• Reform that benefits all parties; • Increased support for teachers within all educational sectors through (conflict-sensitive/ peacebuilding) training, and fair compensation for well-being; • Recognition of the contribution of education and social service grievances to conflict; • Consequent acknowledgement among international, state and non-state actors of key position of education in peace process; • Building trust in commitment to both peace agreements and education; • Participation of actors from across educational sectors (state, ethnic, monastic and community) and all (school, community, state, national and international) levels in dialogue processes; • Curricula reform to ensure more inclusive content; • Demands from youth/students call for education that supports critical awareness of the historical/present socio-political and economic situation, and to enhance agency in terms of employment, political empowerment and inclusive forms of socio-cultural identity-formation
Recognition	• Language of instruction; • Prominence of rote learning in Myanmar language; • Suppression of critical thinking skills as mechanisms of manipulation to maintain a pliable population; • Exclusive association of Buddhism with national identity (e.g. through prayer in schools and curriculum content); • Lack of pathways to accreditation for non-state teachers and students; • Lack of acknowledgement of cultures and histories	
Representation	• Marginalisation of non-state actors in setting education agenda; • Curriculum content incl. lack of positive representation of ethnic groups; • History curriculum as glorifying *Bamar* military campaigns and heroes; • Discrimination against women from positions of leadership within and beyond education[a]	

[a]Although gender inequalities are not limited to ethnic grievances and are felt by all women in Myanmar, ethnic women's organisations, such as the Mon Women's Organisations (MWO) have been strong advocates for women's greater participation in leadership roles

Conclusion

Historical underpinnings to Myanmar's conflicts indicate the origins of grievances and the deep rooted mistrust that persists in peace processes. Prior to 2011, while the political environment did not allow space for ethnic parties to participate at a national level, the fundamental issues of rights to self-determination failed to be inclusively addressed. While there have been significant steps forward in engaging multiple groups in structured dialogue and negotiation processes, the prioritisation of achieving a Nationwide Ceasefire Agreement has continued to promote a liberal peacebuilding model that delays discussion of key grievances. However, without addressing these core grievances there are risks that patterns of conflict recur.

It is recognised that education has and continues to be a key grievance for many of the armed ethnic groups, other elements of civil society, and minority groups. Education reform is therefore deemed vital to securing peace dividends through improved service delivery and a renewed focus on inclusion and equality of provision. Considering the security and economic focus of the USDP government's peacebuilding agenda, and the convenience of the status quo for those in power, actual transformations towards a more sustainable peace are volatile. At present, this pattern appears to be enduring, as intensifying military offensives undermine the apparent commitment to inclusive peacebuilding. A challenge for Myanmar now is to incorporate a more sustainable peacebuilding approach that matches the rhetoric of reconciliation.

References

Alliance for Gender Inclusion in the Peace Process (AGIPP). (2015). *Women, peace and security policymaking in Myanmar*. Yangon: AGIPP.

Alliance for Gender Inclusion in the Peace Process (AGIPP). (2017). *Analysis of Myanmar's second union peace conference 21st century Panglong from a gender perspective*. Yangon: AGIPP.

Bächtold, S. (2015). The rise of an anti-politics machinery: Peace, civil society and the focus on results in Myanmar. *Third World Quarterly, 36*(10), 1968–1983.

Bhatia, R. (2013). Contours of change in Myanmar—and future prospects. *Strategic Analysis, 37*(1), 110–112.

British Academy and École française d'Extrême-Orient. (2015). *Language choice in higher education: Challenges and opportunities*. Manchester: Oakleigh Consulting Limited.

Burma News International (BNI). (2013). *Economics of peace and conflict*. Chiang Mai: BNI. http://www.mmpeacemonitor.org/images/pdf/economics_peace_and_conflict_eng.pdf

Burma News International (BNI). (2014). *Deciphering Myanmar's peace process: Reference guide 2014*. Chiang Mai: BNI. http://www.mmpeacemonitor.org/images/pdf/deciphering_myanmar_peace_process_2014.pdf

Bush, K. D., & Saltarelli, D. (2000). *The two faces of education in ethnic conflict: Towards a peacebuilding education for children*. Florence: UNICEF Innocenti Research Centre.

Chalk, P. (2013). *On the path of change: Political, economic and social challenges for Myanmar*. Special Report. ASPI.

Crisis Group. (2015) *Myanmar's peace process: A nationwide ceasefire remains elusive*. Yangon: Crisis Group. http://www.crisisgroup.org/~/media/Files/asia/south-east-asia/burma-myanmar/b146-myanmar-s-peace-process-a-nationwide-ceasefire-remains-elusive.pdf

Department of Population. (2016). *The 2014 Myanmar population and housing census – The union report: Religion*. Myanmar: Ministry of Labour, Immigration and Population.

Dolan, T. & Gray, S. (2014). *Media and conflict in Myanmar: Opportunities for media to advance peace*. United States Institute of Peace. Washington, D.C.

EBO. (2013). *EBO briefing paper: Myanmar peace process*. EBO. https://euroburmaoffice.s3.amazonaws.com/filer_public/c3/34/c334ad07-573a-40b9-bedf-90bcedcfeccf/ebo_brief_no_1_2013_peace_process.pdf

Fortify Rights. (2014). *Policies of persecution – Ending abusive state policies against Rohingya Muslims in Myanmar*. Fortify Rights. http://www.fortifyrights.org/downloads/Policies_of_Persecution_Feb_25_Fortify_Rights.pdf

GCPEA. (2013). *Country profiles: Myanmar*. GCPEA. http://www.protectingeducation.org/country-profile/myanmar

Gender Equality Network (GEN). (2012). *Myanmar women in parliament 2012*. Yangon: GEN.

Gender Equality Network (GEN). (2015). *Raising the curtain: Cultural norms, social practices and gender equality in Myanmar*. Yangon: GEN.

Global Witness. (2015). *Guns, cronies and crops*. London: Global Witness.

Government of Myanmar. (2014). *Moving forward in unity to a peaceful and prosperous community*. http://www.asean.org

Hedström, J. (2016). We did not realize about the gender issues. So, we thought it was a good idea. *International Feminist Journal of Politics., 18*(1), 61–79.

Hlaing, K. Y. (2012). Understanding recent political changes in Myanmar. *Contemporary Southeast Asia, 34*(2), 197.

Holliday, I. (2011). *Burma redux global justice and the quest for political reform in Myanmar*. New York: Columbia University Press.

Huang, R. L. (2013). Re-thinking Myanmar's political regime: Military rule in Myanmar and implications for current reforms. *Contemporary Politics, 19*(3), 247–261.

Jolliffe, K. (2014). *Ethnic conflict and social services in Myanmar's contested regions*. Yangon: The Asia Foundation.

Jones, L. (2014). The political economy of Myanmar's transition. *Journal of Contemporary Asia, 44*(1), 144–170.

Karen Women's Organisation (KWO). (2010). *Walking amongst sharp knives: The unsung courage of Karen women village chiefs in conflict areas of Eastern Burma*. Thailand: KWO.

Karenni Civil Society Network (KCSN). (2014). *Where is genuine peace? A critique of the peace process in Karenni State*. Myanmar: KCSN.

Keenan, P. (2015). *All-inclusiveness in an ethnic context*. EBO Background Paper. https://euroburmaoffice.s3.amazonaws.com/filer_public/01/95/019513d3-e0e5-4ca1-8f7f-fc208f6cbc7c/ebo_background_paper_4.pdf

Kuppuswamy, C.S. (2013). Challenging the reconciliation process: Myanmar's ethnic divide and conflicts. Institute of Peace and Conflict Studies. India. http://www.ipcs.org/issue_select.php?recNo=511

Lahtaw, J. N., & Raw, N. (2012). *Myanmar's current peace processes: A new role for women?* Centre for Humanitarian Dialogue.

Lall, M. (2008). Evolving education in Myanmar: The interplay of state, business and the community. In M. Skidmore & T. Wilson (Eds.), *Dictatorship, disorder and decline in Myanmar* (pp. 127–149). Acton: ANU Press.

Lall, M., & South, A. (2013, August). Comparing models of non-state ethnic education in Myanmar: The Mon and Karen national education regimes. *Journal of Contemporary Asia, 22*, 1–24.

Laungaramsri, P. (2011). Imagining nation: Women's rights and the transnational movement of Shan women in Thailand and Burma. In T. Salman & M. De Theije (Eds.), *Local battles, global stakes: The globalisation of local conflicts and the localization of global interests* (pp. 99–117). Amsterdam: VU University Press.

Lintner, B. (2015). How the west was won. *The Irrawaddy*. http://www.irrawaddy.org/magazine/how-the-west-was-won.html

Lwin, T. (2000). *Education in Burma (1945–2000)*. Thinking Classroom Foundation. http://www.thinkingclassroom.org/uploads/4/3/9/0/43900311/lwin_t._2000._education_in_burma_1945-2000.pdf

Lynn, N. H., & Slow, O. (2017, May 30). Mixed results at latest Panglong peace conference. *Frontier Myanmar*. https://frontiermyanmar.net/en/mixed-results-at-latest-panglong-peace-conference
Maber, E. (2014). (In)equality & action: The role of women's training initiatives in promoting women's leadership opportunities in Myanmar. *Gender and Development, 22*(1), 141–156.
Maber, E. (2016a). Finding feminism, finding voice? Mobilising community education to build women's participation in Myanmar's political transition. *Gender and Education, 28*(3), 416–430.
Maber, E. J. T. (2016b). Cross-border transitions: Navigating conflict and political change through community education practices in Myanmar and the Thai border. *Globalisation, Societies and Education, 14*(3), 374–389.
Metro, R. (2013). *Histories of Burma*. Yangon: Mote Oo.
Metro, R. (2017, December 15). We can oppose ethnic cleansing without accepting simple answers. *Tea Circle*. https://teacircleoxford.com/2017/12/15/burma-and-the-rohingya-crisis-we-can-oppose-ethnic-cleansing-without-accepting-simple-answers/.
Ministry of Education (MoE). (2013). *CESR rapid review of Myanmar basic education policy and proposed way forward. Phase 1*. Yangon: MoE.
Myanmar Peace Monitor. (2013). Ethnic Peace Plan. Myanmar peace monitor. http://www.mmpeacemonitor.org/peace-process/ethnic-peace-plan
Myanmar Peace Monitor. (2014). Government peace plan. Myanmar peace monitor. http://www.mmpeacemonitor.org/peace-process/government-peace-plan
Myanmar Peace Monitor. (2015). Monitoring archive. Myanmar peace monitor http://www.mmpeacemonitor.org/research/monitoring-archive
Naw, H. & Barter, D. (2017, March 3). As Kachin conflict escalates, fears rise and trust collapses. *Frontier Myanmar*. https://frontiermyanmar.net/en/as-kachin-conflict-escalates-fears-rise-and-trust-collapses.
NCA draft text. (2015). Nationwide ceasefire agreement (NCA). Unpublished document.
Nyein, N. (2016, August 31). 21st century Panglong Conference Kicks Off in Naypyidaw. *Irrawaddy*. https://www.irrawaddy.com/news/burma/21st-century-panglong-conference-kicks-off-in-naypyidaw.html
OECD. (2013). *Multi-dimensional review of Myanmar: Volume 1. Initial assessment. OECD development pathways*. Paris: OECD Publishing.
OHCHR. (2017a). Interviews with Rohingyas fleeing from Myanmar since 9 October 2016. OHCHR.
OHCHR. (2017b). *Mission report of OHCHR rapid response mission to Cox's Bazar*. Bangladesh: OHCHR.
Paung Sie Facility (PSF). (2017). Youth and everyday peace in Myanmar: Fostering the untapped potential of Myanmar's youth. PSF. http://www.paungsiefacility.org/uploads/3/0/1/8/30181835/youth_paper_english.pdf.
Phyo, P.T. (2016, June 13). Youth policy draft slated for October. *The Myanmar Times*. https://www.mmtimes.com/national-news/20819-youth-policy-draft-slated-for-october.html. Accessed 15 Dec 2017.
Pistor, N. (2017). *Life on hold: Experiences of women displaced by conflict in Kachin State*. Myanmar: Trocaire https://www.trocaire.org/sites/default/files/resources/policy/life-on-hold-trocaire-oxfam-2017.pdf.
Raw, L.S. (2016, October 19). Myanmar: The Dilemma of Ceasefires but No Peace. *TNI*. https://www.tni.org/en/article/myanmar-the-dilemma-of-ceasefires-but-no-peace.
Salem-Gervais, N., & Metro, R. (2012). A textbook case of nation-building: The evolution of history curricula in Myanmar. *Journal of Burma Studies, 16*(1), 27–78.
Shan Women's Action Network (SWAN). (2002). License to rape. SWAN.
Singh, U. B. (2013). Do the changes in Myanmar signify a real transition? *Strategic Analysis, 37*(1), 101–104.
South, A. (2008). *Ethnic politics in Burma: States of conflict*. London: Routledge.

Swedish Burma Committee. (2013). *Where are the women? Negotiations for peace in Burma*. Stockholm: Swedish Burma Committee.
The Border Consortium (TBC). (2013). *Poverty, displacement and local governance in South East Burma/Myanmar*. Thailand: TBC.
Transnational Institute (TNI). (2013). *Burma's ethnic challenge: From aspirations to solutions*. TNI. https://www.tni.org/en/briefing/burmas-ethnic-challenge-aspirations-solutions
Transnational Institutes (TNI). (2014). *Ethnicity without meaning, data without context: The 2014 census, identity and citizenship in Burma/Myanmar*. TNI. https://www.tni.org/en/briefing/ethnicity-without-meaning-data-without-context
Transnational Institute (TNI). (2017). *Beyond Panglong: Myanmar's national peace and reform dilemma*. TNI. https://www.tni.org/en/publication/beyond-panglong-myanmars-national-peace-and-reform-dilemma
Turnell, S. (2015). Burma's economic transition: Hopes and hurdles. *Social Research: An International Quarterly, 82*(2), 481–506.
UN. (2010). Statement attributable to the Spokesperson of the Secretary-General on Myanmar elections. UN. http://www.un.org/sg/statements/?nid=4911
UN. (2017). Violence drives more Rohingyas to Bangladesh; in Myanmar, Pope appeals for tolerance – UN. http://www.un.org/apps/news/story.asp?NewsID=58172#.WjrXnjfLi00
UN OCHA. (2013). *Myanmar: Children affected by Rakhine conflict miss a year of school*. UN OCHA. www.unocha.org/top-stories/all-stories/myanmar-children-affected-rakhine-conflict-miss-year-school
UNESCO. (2014). *Education for All 2015 National Review Report: Myanmar*. UNESCO. http://unesdoc.unesco.org/images/0022/002297/229723E.pdf
UNHCR. (2014). *Stories from Myanmar refugees*. UNHCR. http://data.unhcr.org/thailand/storyline.php
Walton, M. (2013). The "Wages of Burman-ness:" Ethnicity and Burman privilege in contemporary Myanmar. *Journal of Contemporary Asia, 43*(1), 1–27.
Walton, M. (2017, September 7). Political communication and transformative citizenship in Myanmar (Part II). *Tea Circle*. https://teacircleoxford.com/2017/09/07/political-communication-and-transformative-citizenship-in-myanmar-part-ii/
Walton, M., & Hayward, S. (2014). *Contesting Buddhist narratives: Democratization, nationalism, and communal violence in Myanmar*. Washington, DC: East-West Center.
Walton, M. J., McKay, M., & Mar Mar Kyi, D. K. (2015). Women and Myanmar's "Religious Protection Laws.". *The Review of Faith & International Affairs, 13*(4), 36–49.
Watchlist on Children and Armed Conflict. (2009). *No more denial: Children affected by armed conflict in Myanmar (Burma)*. New York: Watchlist on Children and Armed Conflict http://watchlist.org/reports/pdf/myanmar/myanmar_english_full.pdf.
WCRP & HURFOM. (2015). *Inaccessible and under-resourced: Concerns over education in rural Mon communities*. WCRP & HURFOM. www.rehmonnya.org/reports/Final-Edition.pdf
Women's League of Burma (WLB). (2014). *If they had hope they would speak*. Chiang Mai: WLB.

Chapter 4
Myanmar's Education System: Historical Roots, the Current Context, and New Opportunities

Ritesh Shah and Mieke T. A. Lopes Cardozo

Introduction

According to Lorch (2007), Myanmar's contemporary education system is symptomatic of a weak state where institutions are unable to provide for the welfare of its citizens. Paradoxically, this has led to a flourishing number of quasi and non-state actors filling the void. This includes the strengthening/re-establishment of a range of parallel systems, including: monastic and faith-based schools that have been partially co-opted into the state system; separate ethnic minority schools/systems that have been given space for manoeuvre due to cease-fire pacts signed since 1989; a flourishing private education system; and numerous INGO and NGO actors who have established small-scale, non-formal education projects around the fringes of state provision (particularly in the Early Childhood Care and Education (ECCE) and tertiary spaces). The consequences of this multitude of actors and providers are further considered in this section—in relation to access, quality and equity—to understand the current issues and concerns plaguing the system at present.

R. Shah (✉)
Faculty of Education and Social Work, University of Auckland, Auckland, New Zealand
e-mail: r.shah@auckland.ac.nz

M. T. A. Lopes Cardozo
University of Amsterdam, Amsterdam, The Netherlands

M. T. A. Lopes Cardozo, E. J. T. Maber (eds.), *Sustainable Peacebuilding and Social Justice in Times of Transition*,
https://doi.org/10.1007/978-3-319-93812-7_4

Historical Development and Evolution of a National Education System

Pre-colonial Monastic/Sangha-Led Education

Prior to colonisation, education was largely the responsibility of the monasteries. Monastic education is recorded to have started as early as the eleventh century amongst the lowland Theravada Buddhist population, and specifically amongst the (majority) Bamar ethnic group. Such education was typically rural and community-based, decentralised, and open to all boys irrespective of their class or background. While the education provided in these schools was generally free, the *Sangha* itself typically relied on the community for all its needs.[1] Important about monastic education, was the strong ideological foundation on which it was founded. A key aim of such education according to Cheesman (2010, 48–49) was to "'civilise' non-Buddhist groups into extending into the peripheral territories as a means to assimilate people into the lowland polities." For this reason, monastic education played a key function in pre-colonial Myanmar as, "…an explicit link between the people and their religion, and by extension, their state. It transmitted standardized cultural and intellectual matters across all sectors of society. It instilled a valuable sense of discipline that allowed rulers to maintain control over their subjects and reinforced a respect for tradition and hierarchy" (Cheesman 2010, 49). Amongst the majority Buddhist population, monastic schools were highly effective in supporting the development of basic literacy skills in Burmese and Pali languages, and important elements of Buddhist doctrine.

British Colonial 'Western' Education

The British colonial administration established an alternative to monasteries as the primary place of learning. Mass 'Western' style education, predicated on the teaching of English language, was promoted and supported by the colonial administration. Graduates of these schools soon made their way into government service, to the exclusion of traditional leaders. Monastic schools quickly lost their prestige to the English language, church/government run schools and became seen as the poor man's bastion (Cheesman 2010, 51), and the colonial education system formed part of the British 'divide and rule' tactics (Lwin 2000). This contributed to a decline in demand for education in general, as most Burmese lacked access to the few English schools that had been set up. Firstly, this was due to the high fees and related costs involved, and secondly, some also questioned if they wanted to participate in this colonial education system (Lwin 2000). Literacy rates across the British

[1] The Sangha is the centuries-old Buddhist monastic order that historically played a key role in governing the monastic school system (Cheesman 2010: 45).

administered areas dropped markedly. Some attempts were made by the British to co-opt monastic schools into the education system, through the provision of grants-in-aid, and roving teachers to provide instruction in additional subjects to those typically taught. Monastic schools viewed such involvement with suspicion and maintained an arm's length from the colonial administration. In response, the administration set about constructing a greater number of vernacular language schools that aimed to undermine the power and reach of monastic schools (Lwin 2000).

1930s Multi-tier System

What resulted by the 1930s was a multi-tiered system of schooling distinguished primarily by language of instruction and locus of control: (1) vernacular schools (either Burmese or a recognised local language) that were run by local authorities; (2) monastic schools which remained completely outside the state system; (3) vernacular/English schools run by the colonial administration; and (4) English only, private schools run by the church. Vernacular and monastic schools remained the only schooling opportunity open for the masses. Teachers in these schools, however, were often less well qualified academically and poorly remunerated for their services. The end of colonial rule in 1948 stratified education along several lines. Firstly, by loyalties or opposition to the colonial government, with monastic schools increasingly seen as the bastions of Burmese nationalism. Secondly, stratification happened by language of instruction, and thirdly, by educational opportunities and outcomes. As Lwin (2000, 5) notes, "[colonial education] did not guarantee equality of opportunity in education for all children," and instead education during this time was marked by high levels of polarization and alienation.

Post-WW II

Following WWII, a process of educational rehabilitation commenced and was financed out of the British military budget. In 1947, a report commissioned by the educational rehabilitation committee was released and proposed a significant overhaul of the entire Burmese education system. Underpinning the reform was an idea that education should be more accessible, adaptable and available to a greater proportion of the population through the introduction of free, compulsory, universal primary education.[2] Key recommendations included: (1) the abolishment of the three-tiered systems of education and consolidation of all schools and teachers into a state-controlled, provisioned and managed system; (2) free education for all citizens at the primary and post-primary levels (up to end of Standard IX or children

[2] Lwin notes in the post-WWII period the compulsory component of this ambition was deferred in recognition that teachers needed to be trained, schools provided and resources afforded.

15 years of age) and state subsidization of higher education; (3) an overhaul of the curriculum to introduce subjects that reflect the agrarian and rural lifestyle of most of the population, as well as religious education (i.e. Buddhism); (4) the promotion of Burmese and English as equal languages of instruction, but with a recommendation that indigenous vernacular languages be the language of instruction in situations where neither of the above languages was the predominant one in the communities served; and (5) a proposition to shift assessment regimes away from an examination-focus towards a portfolio of student progress through a report card system (Lwin 2000).

Post 1948 Independence

After Burma achieved independence in 1948, the recommendations from this report were considered in the creation of the new nation's national education system. Elements adopted included an insistence on Burmese as the language of instruction, with English adopted as a second language of instruction from the fifth standards, and establishment of primary (infant to fourth standard), middle (infant to seventh standard) and complete teaching units (infant to ninth standard). A system of free education for all students in the state system was also instituted, and the notion of compulsory education was piloted in the capital Rangoon. In 1953, education was included as a key priority sector within the government's Welfare state plans with the ambition that education support all citizens to gain literacy skills, support national reconstruction, imbue a sense of citizenship/allegiance towards the nation, and perpetuate practices of democracy. Additionally, a new curriculum was instituted which reorganized the education system into three levels: primary, middle and high school stages.[3] Non-state education providers, specifically private schools, Christian schools and Buddhist monastic schools were accepted and integrated into the post-independence system and given permission to maintain their autonomy under the 1951 Private Schools Act. These providers maintained approaches, including the teaching of English from an earlier age, the inclusion of religious education within the curriculum, and a focus on academic (or religious) education versus vocational education, which maintained the semblance of the stratified system that existed prior to independence. Thus, while access to education improved in this period, inequities within the system were maintained and as Lwin (2000) contends, were potentially exacerbated along new fault lines—between academic (private)

[3] Curriculum content was reoriented towards "practical and prevocational subjects" and a focus on fostering co-operative living promoted. At middle and high school levels, pre-vocational and vocational subjects were developed but differentiated along gender and local needs. The new policy also specified that only one vernacular language—Burmese—would be the medium of instruction, with English introduced as a compulsory second language from post-primary onwards (Lwin 2000).

and vocational (public) schools, medium of instruction, urban-rural (on access, opportunity and requirements for compulsion), and gender.

Military Regime's Impact on Education After 1962

Following the country's military coup and installation of military rule in 1962, the direction and focus of education changed radically. Underpinning the new government's vision for education was the idea that it would promote livelihood opportunities, be founded in socialist moral values, and give precedence to science. Implicit in the government's plans for education was a clear push for the modernization imperative. Priority was given to subjects that were perceived to advance economic growth and development, such as medicine, engineering and other math and science based disciplines, particularly at the university level. Barring Buddhist monastic schools in rural areas, all other types of non-state schools were nationalized (Lwin 2000). Over time, however, monastic schools were also more tightly regulated and controlled by the state. All *Sangha* were required to register with the government and accept ongoing state oversight, and later were centralized under the control of one common council. These policies served to reduce the power of individual monks and more tightly ascribe the educational programs within monastic schools to only teaching its own novices (Cheesman 2010). By 1980, according to Martin (2013 186), "the education activities of monks was monitored and censored, as was the curriculum." In 1993, the government recognized that it could not effectively provide mass education to all, and opened the door to monastic schools teaching to a wider section of the community. New monastic schools were required to open under the provision that they register themselves with the government.

This has led to monastic schools today falling into one of two categories: (1) those that confine themselves to Buddhist teachings and/or include the teaching of some basic literacy skills but remain outside of state control; and (2) those that have adopted the government curriculum, are registered with the MoE and Ministry of Religious Affairs, and have in essence, become part of the formal education systems (Lorch 2008). The impacts of this second category of schools in terms of educational quality, access, and equity are discussed in the next section.

After 1962, Burmese was affirmed as the language of instruction and, with occasional variances, little space was given to the inclusion of other indigenous vernacular languages. A narrative was developed in the curriculum during the military regime that focused on stressing the "Burmanness" of the nation, stressing Burmese culture as the norm of national identity, and important for the sake of national unity (Walton 2013; Salem-Gervais and Metro 2012). This sense of identity also extended to religious identity. While post-independence regimes had sought for the secularization of schooling, the government's platform of socialism included in it the blending of material and religious elements of society. In schools, this extended to students paying homage on a daily basis to 'Five Gratitudes' that included Buddha, Dhamma, and Sanga as well as teachers and parents.

According to Callahan (2003 cited in Lall and South 2013), the precedent set during this time worked to assimilate and disempower ethnic minorities. From an early age, education quickly became a politicized mechanism for the military state to "prevent children from learning how to think" by "invok[ing] ideas of loyalty and the image of obedient citizens" (Lwin 2000, 15–16). This, according to Walton (2013) has been "one of the main grievances underlying more than half a century of armed ethnic conflict", and has precipitated the growth of schools that have been set up by various armed ethnic resistance groups. This is again discussed in the next section.

Schooling Structure Dating Back to the Military Regime Period

It was during this time that the structure of schooling that remains in existence until today took shape. The schooling sector was split into three distinct components:

- Primary education (the first 5 years of schooling from Standard 0 (KG) to Standard IV);
- Middle schooling (the subsequent 4 years from Standard V to VIII);
- And high school (final 2 years of schooling from Standard IX to X).

With passage of the 1974 Constitution, primary education was compulsory, middle school semi-compulsory, and high school dependent on the will of the student (Martin 2013, 180; Lwin 2000). In primary school, subjects included as part of the curriculum were Burmese, English, mathematics, history and geography. Science was introduced as part of middle school with the same subjects continuing through high school. In general, this schooling curriculum and structure was deemed to give primacy to particular types of academic knowledge, rather than the development of life, vocational, moral or citizenship skills (Lwin 2000).

Students were required to sit exams at the end of each standard and given a "pass-fail" mark. In Standard VIII, at the end of middle schooling, a high stakes assessment was introduced which determined the future academic trajectories student could take—those that did well (A-list students) could go onto studying science subjects in high school, while those who didn't were relegated to arts subjects.[4] Similarly at Standard X, another high stakes exam was introduced and results determined if one could go onto university or were relegated to vocational streams. This examination regime stratified the education system, and acted to slot students into particular life trajectories from an early age (Lwin 2000). It also informed the nature of teaching practices in the classroom, and focused attention on the rote learning of facts through memorization and a culture of competition rather than collaboration. Examinations also became an instrument of the military, with students who were

[4]According to Lwin (2000) this was later changed so that irrespective of marks, students could continue to take classes in both the arts and sciences stream in to high school.

members of the Union Solidarity and Development Association (USDA), a group with loyalties to the regime, awarded 16 extra marks (Lwin 2000, 16).

Banned/Restricted Higher Education Post 1988

The tertiary sector in particular, has evolved in a politicized fashion. Against the backdrop of the country's 1988 'Democratization' movement, tertiary students, especially those studying in urban institutions, engaged in mass protests. This led to universities frequently being shut – sometimes as long as a decade – by the government, and students becoming subject to persecution (Maber 2014; Lall 2008).[5] It also led to staff and students in higher education being closely monitored (Martin 2013).

As a way to reduce the perceived threat coming from this group of educated youth, under the guise of promoting "equitable educational development" the government over time acted to increase the number of tertiary institutes, yet at the same time fragment them by discipline and location, with the belief that it would reduce civil unrest this way (Tin 2000; Martin 2013). The government has also promoted distance education programs, moved undergraduate study programs away from urban areas, and relocated universities to new sites in a ploy to disperse a 'critical mass' of dissent (Lall 2008, 132). Rangoon University, one of the country's first tertiary institutes, was split in half so that it no longer offered programs in medicine, teaching and engineering. Various Ministries as well as the Civil Service Selection and Training Board were given the authority to establish single discipline universities. The military, for example, has established institutes for engineering and science for students in the military circle, which were generally better resourced and of enhanced quality in comparison to others. The government has also acted to limit participation of ethnic minority groups in higher education. For example, those who are unable to prove their citizenship according to the country's 1982 Citizenship law, are effectively barred from gaining entry into universities.[6] For the ethnic Chinese and Indian populations of the country, this has effectively limited their options for tertiary study, and even when successful in gaining entry, these groups are often precluded from studying professional subjects like technology and medicine (Lwin 2000, 10).

---

[5] For example, following the 1988 student protests, all universities were shut for a period of 2 years, and further strikes during the 1990s led to a series of closure that in total amounted to 3 years. In Yangon, universities were shut for 10 out of 12 years between 1988 and 2000 (Lall 2008).

[6] This law specifies that citizenship is only available to those who can prove ancestry resident in Burma prior to the first British annexation in 1824. It makes it nearly impossible for ethnic Chinese and Indian inhabitants of the country to gain full citizenship and instead remain in the country on Foreign Registration Cards.

Current Parallel Systems of State, Non-state and Non-formal Forms of Education

Currently, schooling in Myanmar operates within multiple sectors, the largest being the government administered state sector through which the Ministry of Education is responsible for providing basic education. Over 47,000 schools provide education to students at primary, lower-secondary/middle, and upper-secondary levels, with approximate enrolment given below (Table 4.1).

Outside of the state system, monastic, ethnic and community-based schools (the latter two not represented in the data table above) play an important role in offering access to non-state education for children who may otherwise have none. These are outlined briefly below.

Monastic Schools

Monastic schools operate in all states and regions across the country, with over 1500 schools registered with the Ministry of Religious Affairs (MoRA), serving around 300,000 children (Government of Myanmar 2016). Most monastic schools offer primary education but some cover the middle and high school grades. Those that are registered use the official state primary and middle school curricula, but also teach about Buddhist culture and way of life. Because no fees are charged and food is provided, these schools are able to reach some of the poorest children. They cater primarily to poor children in the communities in which monasteries are located, including orphans, children of migrant workers and those sent away from remote areas (UNICEF 2012). Some schools are also able to teach children to read and write in their own ethnic languages, which makes them an attractive alternative for ethnic minority groups (Cheesman 2003). Most monastic schools teach novices and put children together and provide their educational services regardless of race and religion. Monastic schools are often more affordable, making use of donations for food, clothing and classroom resources and can provide a more accessible learning environment to those less able to access the state sector due to cost, accessibility and social exclusion. They do not require parents to purchase uniforms or books, but do

Table 4.1 Number of schools and students across the education sector (Government of Myanmar 2016)

	No. of schools	No. of students
Upper secondary	3513	0.9 million
Lower secondary	6224	2.8 million
Basic education	35,650	5.1 million
Monastic schools	1538	0.3 million
Private schools	438	0.1 million

sometimes require parents to pool their funds to pay for teachers or build facilities (Lall 2011).

While monastic schools are important in improving access to education, the same issues around educational quality in terms of class sizes, teacher qualifications/capacity and curriculum materials that exists in the state system, also manifest themselves in this sector (Cheesman 2003; Lorch 2008; Lall 2011). There is also a question of whether monastic schools also have an indoctrinating agenda behind them. Some monastic schools have been set up as a direct response to the establishment of schools run by Christian churches or mosques, and are established specifically to counter or even prevent the growth of these minority religions. Some monastic orphanages require every child who wants to live in their compound to wear a Buddhist novice's robe. Even in orphanages where this is not the case, Christian or Muslim children are sometimes encouraged to convert to Buddhism (Lorch 2008, 157). In light of our analytical lenses on the 4Rs, and processes of transformation towards peacebuilding, a deeper understanding of the role of faith-based education in Monastic schools and beyond is essential in order to further understand how issues of identity-formation (recognition), tolerance and intergroup understanding and living together with 'others' (reconciliation) are playing out.

Ethnic Minority-Run Schools

In ethnic minority and remote areas of the country a number of community, quasi-state or (I)NGO established educational schools have also been set up, which are not officially registered or accounted for by the state (and in official data as reflected in Table 4.2). This is largely because of a lack of comprehensive data on this sector, signalling the very loose associations these schools have historically had with the state as a product of ethnic-based conflicts (Government of Myanmar 2016, 100). In some instances, communities have established these schools in response to a lack of proximate access to government educational facilities. Communities will often self-fund and/or nominate a teacher from within to operate the school. Depending on the degree to which these schools are co-opted by the state to supplement education provision, communities are afforded some autonomy within these settings to deviate from the official curriculum and provide work and life skills to their students that are locally relevant. These community-based schools are increasingly of interest to

Table 4.2 Enrolment rates in ethnic schools (Jolliffe 2014)

State	No. of schools	No. of students
Kachin	279	23,000
Kayah	505	50,351
Kayin	1294	141,623
Mon	142	13,000
Shan	200+	*unknown*

donors, particularly UNESCO, who have pushed for the strengthening and/or establishment of these institutions as a mechanism of promoting non-formal education at the local level (Lorch 2008). Additionally, in many ethnic minority areas, resistance groups have managed to set up and administer their own schooling systems. Some examples of this are schools being run by the Kachin Independence Organization (KIO), the New Mon State Party (NMSP), and the Karen National Union (KNU). In these areas, the schools were set up as a direct response to the perceived marginalization that these ethnic groups encountered within the state system. There are at least 2420 ethnic schools across primary, middle and high school levels serving upwards of 228,000 students (Jolliffe 2014):

These parallel ethnic school systems vary significantly across the states in terms of size and the number of constituents they serve, their access to resources and sources of funding, and their approaches to curriculum design.

For many in this alternative schooling system, the teaching of identity, language and history (and in some cases religion) of the ethnic group are particularly stressed within the curriculum. Such curriculum also aims to valorize the ethno-nationalist struggle against the state (Salem-Gervais and Metro 2012). Teachers who could teach these subjects were locally recruited and employed, relevant curriculum resources and texts developed, and separate education departments established. Additional ethnic education programs are also run through churches or monastic schools in these areas (Lall and South 2013). However, not all ethnic states in conflict have parallel education systems; communities in states such as Chin and Rakhine rely primarily on government schools for education provision.

At present, one of the significant questions is how this sector of non-state provision can be effectively integrated into the government's ambitions for education reform. The NESP identifies a key challenge being,

> …the extent to which they are mainstreamed in other organizations involved in basic education provision, such as monastic schools, private sector schools, community-based schools, schools funded by non-governmental organizations and schools managed under ethnic education systems. Therefore, the MOE needs an effective partnership mechanism in place that brings these organizations together to share information and explore opportunities for collaboration. Effective co-ordination between the MOE and these organizations has the potential to make a significant positive contribution to the achievement of the NESP goal[s]. (Government of Myanmar 2016, 92)

The issue for the ethnic education authorities, however, is a fear that this drive for coordination might lead to the wholescale co-opting of their systems by the state, which effectively reduces the autonomy and independence for which they have long fought. This tension is explored in greater depth in the next chapter.

Alternative Non-formal Education

A sector that has been severely neglected by the state is non-formal education (NFE). In a society where almost 50% of children do not complete basic education, and where the vulnerable youth population may lack important livelihood and literacy skills, the fact that access to alternative education pathways is limited is a concern. According to UNICEF (2012), there has been no NFE budget or dedicated directorate within the Ministry set up to support this. Instead, provision has largely fallen on civil society, in particular NGOs and the international community. Lorch (2008) notes how a number of NGOs are involved in vocational or life skills training for youth, an observation which is supported by our own data collection and analysis when looking at education initiatives for youth (Chaps. 8, 9, and 10). Many target poorly educated school leavers or dropouts, and aim to support these individuals' entry into the labour market. These programs often lack recognition within government and are vulnerable to funding ebbs and flows from international donors. The piecemeal and small-scale nature of these initiatives often makes scale-up difficult, and as a result a large population of youth remain underserved by such initiatives (UNICEF 2012).

Passage of the new National Education Law in 2014, however, has begun to change this situation, by recognizing the role of NFE in Myanmar's education system, and also identifying its relevance and importance for the millions of children currently out of school. Chap. 5 of the law specifies the need for the Ministry to: (1) encourage implementation of out of school programs with non-state providers; (2) implement basic literacy programs; (3) provide equivalency programs for out of school children so they can re-integrate into the formal education system or access technical vocational education and (4) provide continuous learning opportunities, including self-learning education to improve citizens' knowledge and skills. Following on this, the NESP (2016, 160) sets a target of ensuring that, "learners will be able to access and graduate from quality assured, certified and nationally credentialed alternative education programs," signaling a stronger role for the state in recognizing, regulating and expanding opportunities in this area. How this unfolds in practice is still to be seen, but the fact that projections in the NESP signal a budget allocation for non-formal education provision that is 400% higher in 2017–2018 than it has been in previous years is an encouraging sign (Government of Myanmar 2016, 238).

Private Education and Tutoring

Myanmar at present also has a burgeoning private education taking shape. While private schooling was not officially sanctioned by the state, the number of supplementary or shadow education providers in the primary and secondary sector nonetheless grew tremendously in recent decades. Since the passing of the new Private Schools Law in late 2011, the path has opened for new private schools to officially register, expanding and legitimising the private education sector. They are responding to the highly competitive and assessment driven culture of the compulsory schooling sector, and the desire of middle and upper-class families to provide their children with a competitive advantage, including preparation for overseas study. It is also a response to what Lall (2008, 128) puts forward as, "a state that no longer provides the minimum education needed by its citizens."

Likewise, attending private tutoring outside school, has become commonplace amongst the middle class, particularly in urban centres. Often children will attend primary school in the morning, and then attend these extra tuition classes in the afternoon/evening. Anecdotally, the woeful underpayment for teachers' wages through the state payroll, has led many teachers to offering up their services to teach these classes, often at the expense of their regular waged employment in state schools. Recognizing the importance of these extra education classes to children's academic success, a number of NGOs and university students have established and operated low or no-cost schools for children from poor backgrounds. The problem with many of these operations, however, is that they are staffed by under/unqualified people and run with large class sizes—defeating the purposes for which they were set up (Lorch 2008).

Current Issues in Myanmar's Education System: Access, Quality and Equity

It is important to note that the statistics presented in the below section are often seen as contentious and problematic, as they often do not capture the full story of the situation in the country. This is largely due to the inability of census processes to enter into conflict-affected and border regions of the country without it being seen as a tool of political manipulation (TNI 2014).

Early Childhood Care and Education

Across the education spectrum, access indicators in Myanmar remain poor. While participation rates in formal ECCE have improved dramatically in the span of 10 years, the majority of children aged 3–5 do not have access to such opportunities. UNICEF (2012) illustrate in its *Situational Analysis on Children* that access to ECCE is strongly related to wealth and region. Allowing for regional variations, typically children living in poverty and more remote/ethnic minority dominated or conflict-affected regions were those least likely to be accessing ECC services (Government of Myanmar 2016). Historically, the government has not invested significant sums in ECCE, particularly outside the central lowlands. Interesting about ECCE is that the Ministry of Social Welfare, rather than the Ministry of Education, has held responsibility for the development of the sector. This has allowed community-based organizations, NGOs and INGOs to establish informal programs throughout the country and served to make the state a smaller actor in service provision in this sector (UNICEF 2012). In the past couple years, however, the government has signalled its intent to invest much more of its resources in ECCD, with a clear commitment to increase children's access to quality early childhood education services for those most disadvantaged. Passage of a ECCD Policy in 2014, and the clear prioritisation of equitable provision with the NESP are signals that there is (at least discursive) commitment to filling this gap, particularly for non-urban and remote areas of the countries.

EFA Progress

Myanmar, as a signatory to the MDGs and EFA, has made some progress towards the education focused MDGs on Universal Primary Education (UPE) and gender equality. In recent years, the national government under a series of national plans has focused on increasing enrolment rates, and improving rates of primary school completion (UNESCO 2007, 2014). Quantitatively, improvements have been demonstrated in that greater numbers (84%) of primary aged children were attending school in 2010 (UNICEF 2012), compared to a UNICEF report from a decade earlier noting that more than 40% of children in the country had never set foot in school (cited in Lwin 2000). At that time, a significant issue noted was a lack of schools, where one school was noted to be serving between 5 and 25 villages, depending on the region of the country, with border areas having minimal access to schools (Khin Maung Kyi et al. 2000, cited in: Lall 2008). The past decade has seen a significant amount of school construction and the implementation of multi-grade classrooms in areas where teacher shortages and/or classroom space shortages have been acute. That stated, there remain considerable disparities in terms of net primary attendance rates across the country.[7] The 2014 EFA additionally indicates gender parity for students at primary and secondary levels, with some regional variations where girls' enrolment is slightly lower in Rakhine state. However, given the difficulty of obtaining reliable data for many areas, these figures may not reflect experiences at a more localized level, further discussed below.

Access

Many access related issues are most acute amongst populations who are marginalized in contemporary society—those from minority ethnic groups, those who live in remote or border areas of the country, are from a lower socio-economic background, are refugees/IDPs, or are living under the threat or consequence of conflict and/or natural disaster. For example, in conflict-affected or ceasefire areas of Kayin

[7] According to the 2014 census, 35.72% of children aged 5–17 do not attend school, amounting to 4.5 million children. While recognizing the data might be incomplete and not portray a full picture, the census data illustrates how, possibly, there remain considerable disparities across the country with Shan showing the lowest school attendance rate at 57.4% and Chin (78.5%), Kachin (75.2%) and Kaya (72.58%) the highest (2014 Census).

(Karen), Kayah (Karenni), Shan, and Rakhine (Arakan) States, only one out of ten children were able to attend primary school in 2005 (Watchlist 2009). In these regions, forms of direct and indirect violence, including the destruction or occupation of schools by military forces, the planting of landmines on access routes to schools, and the intimidation and/or harassment by military forces of teachers and students all preclude ongoing participation of children in schooling (GCPEA 2014).

Girls' Access to Schooling

Nationally, gender equity targets in primary education have been met in terms of enrolment, but it is unclear to what extent inequities exist at a local level. A general trend in Myanmar is for more girls than boys to be enrolled in schools, particularly in the east, with this disparity growing even further into secondary education. However, a disaggregated analysis by township has not occurred and is necessary for a full picture of gender related issues in schooling (UNICEF 2012). For example, there is some suggestion that for poor households in particular, families will make economic-based decisions on which of their children to send to school, a process that often disadvantages girls (Watchlist 2009). Additionally, as Maber (2014) suggests, the qualitative experiences of children in schools, due to approaches to discipline and instruction, may also create particular forms of disengagement from schooling. Some women have reported that monastic schools in their area (Shan State) would only accept boys, so while their brothers received an education there was no accessible school for them to attend. The high incidence of sexual assault by the *Tatmadaw* and the risks associated with travel in zones of active fighting also contribute to preventing many girls from accessing schooling (WLB 2014). Likewise, while girls may be officially enrolled in a school, their household, caring and farming responsibilities often result in sporadic attendance. At tertiary level, higher numbers of women are typically enrolled than men, however, access to courses is highly gendered, as also highlighted below. Rather than being an indication of women's opportunities in society such statistics belie the devaluing of tertiary education as not providing a route to employment that attracts status and financial reward (Maber 2014).

Secondary School Attendance

Considering that almost half of the students entering primary school do not make it until the end, it is no surprise that participation rates in secondary schooling remain low. While 95.3% of those children who do successfully complete the last year of primary transition to lower secondary, gross enrolment rates for secondary school stand at approximately 53% (UNICEF 2012). This is largely due to the high rates of attrition in basic education, with the majority of children failing to reach the last year of their primary schooling. Regional and socio-economic differences are more pronounced at secondary level than they are at primary. For example, only 28.2% of children from the poorest households were in secondary school, compared with 85.5% from the richest households; secondary school attendance rate was 74.7% in Yangon but only 30.9% in Rakhine (UNICEF 2012). Reasons for dropout are varied, and include: economic factors (i.e. direct and opportunity costs), a perceived lack of educational quality/relevance, the ongoing impacts of conflict/natural disasters, and access-related issues such as distance to the nearest school (Lall 2008; Lwin 2000; UNICEF 2012; MoE 2013).

Higher Education's 'Exclusive' Expansion

In recent years, tertiary education has undergone mass expansion. The number of higher education institutions has gone from 32 in 1988 to 156 in 2008. Today every state and division has a minimum of three tertiary institutions to cater to its needs (Lall 2008). Given the issues around access at lower levels of schooling, however, pathways into tertiary education remain limited to those who 'survive' through to the Standard X examination, and successfully pass it. Corruption and nepotism into popular courses and universities remain an issue, and stand as a barrier to candidates who score well on the examination, but lack appropriate connections (Lwin 2007).[8] Additionally, tertiary learning is significantly gendered, despite high numbers of female students. For a number of university courses, including medicine, women are required to have a higher grade than men to qualify for admission, and in some institutions courses such as geology admit only male students (Maber 2014). Furthermore, the politicization of higher education, and in particular the scrutiny given to students and staff within it, offers them very little space for dissent and manoeuvre. The government frequently targets leadership of student unions and academic staff, and arrests and/or dismissals are a common occurrence (GCPEA 2014).

Within higher education, quality of instruction remains varied, but is generally deemed to be of poor quality (Lwin 2007). A key issue at present within the sector is that due to a multitude of government ministries who manage and oversee higher education institutions, patterns of funding and quality assurance vary greatly. Additionally, subject courses at present are poorly aligned with current and future employment opportunities in the country, and many graduates lack appropriate skills for entry into the labour market (MoE 2013).

Declining quality in higher education has also led to a burgeoning demand for students seeking alternatives for tertiary studies outside the country. To meet this

[8] Additionally, access to scholarships for local or international study, through newly introduced government scholarships, though academic institutions or through International and regional NGOs require students to have a certain level of academic preparation that is still beyond the reach of many.

demand, institutions have been set up to prepare students for the entry requirements of foreign universities (particularly in English), assist with Visa applications, and support their move over to the foreign university. There has been little regulation of these providers, and it has catered primarily to the urban elite of Yangon who have the resources and ability to send their children to such places. Lwin (2000, 15) notes, that the growth of this private shadow education system, "brings about unnecessary inequality of opportunity for pupils, resulting from differences in family means and geographical background."

Outside of issues of quality and access to higher education, are also issues over control of the sector. A significant source of contention in the reform process of recent years has been over the degree of control that the state should have over university governance and decision-making. As Chap. 5 specifies in more detail, through a process of negotiation, and amendments to the initially passed National Education Law, there is now some scope for universities to govern their own affairs. The challenge, however, as the NESP signals, is finding that balance between autonomy and state oversight. Using an equity-based argument, the government contends that, "If too much autonomy is given to HEIs [Higher Education Institutions] then it may be difficult for the government to insist that HEI's take special measures to provide access…to students from disadvantaged backgrounds…[and] ensure policy directives are implemented…too much central oversight…can be just as damaging in terms of impeding change." (Government of Myanmar 2016, 192).

Funding and (Under)Investments

In relation to issues of **redistribution**, a key issue alluded to at the outset of this section is the lack of appropriate resourcing to education in the country. In 2012, the government spent approximately 0.7% of its GDP on education (World Bank 2015, as cited in Government of Myanmar 2016), well below the average for countries in the region. As a percentage of the overall budget, Myanmar also spends very little on education—ranging between 4% and 7.5% depending on the year and estimates used (MoE 2013). Since 2012, as a result of reforms, public spending on education has been increasing, however, this remains the lowest level of investment in the ASEAN region, where ASEAN and developing Asian countries invest around 12% of public expenditure in education or on average 4% of GDP (World Bank 2015, as cited in Government of Myanmar 2016). The longstanding lack of sufficient funding provides little opportunity for the Ministry of Education to make significant headway in reforming an education system that is seen by many to be fundamentally broken.

The underfunding of education has led to a lack of sufficient educational facilities in many locales, with ramifications for the teaching and learning process. Overcrowding in classrooms is common. While nationally student to teacher ratios are suggested as being 34:1 (MoE 2013), this masks the disparities in class sizes that exist in rural/remote settings where up to 100 students in a single classroom may be a normal occurrence. Conversely, in remote areas class sizes may be very small, resulting in multiple grades being taught together with one teacher. Additionally, while the government has managed to get more students into school using existing infrastructure through such multi-grade classrooms, teachers remain poorly equipped to manage instruction in such settings. Teacher shortages in remote or conflict-affected areas as well as adequate preparation for low-resource settings remain under-addressed.

Since the start of the reform process in 2011, however, there have been substantial increases of almost 250% in the government's budget for education. This has led to a reduction in the household spending on education, as the government bears more of the cost (from 60% household/30% government in 2019–2010, to the opposite by 2013–2014). Despite these increases there is recognition that if the government would like to achieve the transformations it specifies in terms of improving access, quality and equity in the education system, it will need to substantially increase its financing to education on an annual basis somewhere between 10% and 20%, to result in the education budget by 2021 equating to about 2.3–3% of total GDP (Government of Myanmar 2016, 240).

Cost of Education

Since 2007, the government has made a commitment to providing free primary education to all children, yet reports suggest that due to the chronic under-resourcing of the education sector, many families are still required to pay fees or purchase texts/uniforms as a precondition for sending their children to school (Watchlist 2009). According to a UNICEF report (2012, 86), these costs preclude up to 30% of children from attending school. Ethnic parallel education systems receive very little or no funding external and consequently the costs of these schools, including teacher stipends, are largely born by the communities they serve (WPRC and HURFOM 2015). Inequalities in teacher salaries across the different education sectors have also been a point of grievance, with ethnic education providers questioning why government sector teachers are paid higher salaries in their regions compared to local teachers (Saw Law Eh Moo in Michaels 2014).

Curriculum

Although now in the process of reform, current national state curriculum remains rigid, subject/content driven, inflexible to adaptation to different contexts and backgrounds, and devoid of a developmental approach (UNICEF 2012; MoE 2013; Gray 2014). Content has pushed a singular national identity through the dominance of Bamar cultural and military history (explored further in Chap. 3) as well as the association of national with religious identity. Under the banner of developing moral character amongst the student population, Buddhist cultural courses and rituals have increased in schools since the late 1990s along with content in textbooks. By contrast, references to other religions have been entirely omitted from schoolbooks (Cheesman 2003, 57). The current curricula, teachers' guides and resource books have not been assessed in terms of quality of content, gender sensitivities, age and developmental appropriateness (UNICEF 2012; Sugiyama 2013). A specific concern has been the utilization of textbooks (specifically history texts) as a mechanism of legitimating the military regime through an anti-colonial, nationalistic discourse (Salem-Gervais and Metro 2012). Such narratives work to establish a process of 'othering' which establishes a clear set of protagonist and antagonists actors in contemporary national narrative.

The In-/Exclusion of Languages in Education

A key tension in past and present reform efforts has centred around language of instruction, to which we now pay more focused attention. Traditionally, the state has seen the promotion of the Burmese language as central to the promotion of national unity. This holds truth despite the incoherence and contradictions in language policy, linked to attitudes to the use of English amongst elites, which are underpinned by a legacy of colonialism. For instance, Burmese is supposed to be the official language, but there is still a lot of government paperwork that is only in English, including passports. Moreover, the insistence on conducting certain areas of life in English (medicine, technology, law), in addition to much teaching at the tertiary level, also suggests that there is a historically rooted attachment to English, co-existing with the aspiration to make Burmese the dominant national language.

However, despite such inconsistence, there was a backlash from ethnic actors who felt that the promotion of Burmese was done at the expense of recognition of other languages and cultures. It is important to note that until the 1962 coup, some scope was afforded for the teaching and/or utilisation of ethnic language in state education. Typically, this involved the teaching of ethnic language and/or literature until the 2nd standard as a separate subject. After the junta, however, ethnic languages and ethnic literature was banished from state education (Nyein (Shalom) Foundation 2012). Since 2011 there has been a reawakening of discussion around the role of languages other than Burmese in classrooms.

One of the key areas of focus for the government's current reform process, for example, has been around language(s) of instruction. The rapid assessment of the basic education sector, done at the start of Phase One, clearly identified that the language policy needed to be changed due to a number of concerns. One is that the Child Law of 1993 specifies that, "*every child shall have the right to maintain his or her own cherished language*." In effect, this right has been violated, given that since 1988 use of languages other than Burmese was not permitted in state education. Additionally, the report notes that the language barrier is perceived as a significant cause for drop out from non-Burmese contexts. The report concludes that while the policy environment until the time of the CESR has "*constrained development of expertise in bilingual language and learning issues, as well as in educationally sound strategies for addressing the range of bi- and multilingual contexts that exist in Myanmar*" (MoE 34). At the same time, there existed opportunities within the reform process to develop a clear language policy that was more inclusive and equitable and better acknowledged the range of bi- and multilingual contexts that exists in Myanmar.

UNICEF, as part of its PBEA activities in Myanmar has supported a process of facilitated dialogues around the topic. The aim according to a report was to "*canvas policy alternatives for issues already being debated and which are the cause of conflict, tension or policy paralysis*", specifically "*alternatives to the mandated use of Myanmar as exclusive medium of instruction in state schools*" (UNICEF 2016, 6–7). Those involved in these dialogues noted the power of bringing different stakeholders with starkly different interests into the same space to talk about a deeply political and difficult issue. Over time, the idea was to clear up misconceptions about what was 'allowed' or 'appropriate' in terms of language teaching, based on bringing together representatives from the state along with the ethnic actors. This opening up of a space for conversation between individuals and groups who for decades had not sat in the same room was also seen to create opportunities for policy change in regards to the teaching of ethnic languages in Mon State.

Other actors have embarked in advocacy efforts aimed at changing perceptions that learning in a language other than Burmese is to the detriment of a child's schooling success. For example, the Nyein (Shalom) Foundation (2012) produced a report based on interviews and reading assessment data of over 600 ethnic minority children and their families from Kachin, Karen, Mon, Chin, Rakhine, and Shan states. The study found that many learners understand little in school because of the language of instruction being Burmese. This then effects their performance on measures such as average reading time for a passage, word recognition and retell, where ethnic minority children perform significantly worse than native Burmese speakers. The study concludes that the current paradigm of Burmese as the sole language of instruction puts non-native speakers at a significant disadvantage in terms of success in schooling, and puts them on the path to dropping out of school. It recommends a policy for ethnic languages to be used as much as possible in primary schools, reflecting the conclusions of educational research more broadly.

The 2014 Education Law recognises the role of languages other than Burmese in the classroom, but does so in a limited way. It states, "*If necessary, things can be explained orally in children's mother tongue*" (MoE 2014, 5). It also states how ethnic languages can be taught as a subject. This directive is a direct rebuff to attempts by many in civil society to see the dominant ethnic language of a particular school/classroom be the primary language of instruction. This stands in contrast to the governments' main conviction that Burmese is still an important unifying factor for the country, and potentially even more so in a move towards federalism. Such forms of implicit resistance to practical change are evident in very partial or even insufficient approaches to the implementation of substantive textbook and curricula reform. Despite the aspiration to include 20% "local content" and provide textbooks and teacher manuals as mentioned above, there are real dangers that their potential to address ethnic grievances and frustrations will be thwarted given inaction due to major systemic implementation challenges.

Thus, despite the advocacy efforts to date, the promise of a state education system that acknowledges and embraces diversity, and affords opportunities for multilingualism remains unmet. This has consequences not only for social cohesion, but also the degree to which this education system can be inclusive and equitable to all. As a report by Lo Bianco suggests:

> Significant challenges remain for minority languages and new methods and practices of language planning are urgently required to foster national unity – methods which go far beyond 'consultation' as a modality of seeking endorsement or compliance of populations. There has been serious disparity between the perceptions of minority groups and officials as to the aims and experience of language education. (Lo Bianco 2015, 35)

Student protests that followed passage of the Education Law in September 2014 were in part the product of a sentiment that demands by NNER, ethnic education authorities, and other elements of civil society for acknowledgement of children's rights to learn in their mother tongue being unmet under the legislation drafted. In February 2015, the government agreed to reconsider the law through several amendments. One proposed amendment would have granted "*the right to use concerned ethnic languages as a medium of instruction beginning with early childhood*", but was voted down by lawmakers 394 to 98. A more progressive proposal by the NNER for "*mother tongue-based multilingual education*" never made it into either house's amendment bill (Snaing 2015).

In summary on the challenges of inclusive language approaches in education, the lack of acknowledgement and support for mother-tongue instruction remains a key grievance. Lo Bianco (2013, 27) notes the importance of language in the region as a "marker of ethnic identity and a mediator of cultural, symbolic and material resources." In the case of Myanmar, Bianco points out that "language and ethnicity have been central to violent conflicts, which have arisen in response to the attempted creation of a singular Myanmar identity by a centralised military government" (Lo Bianco 2015, 12). This has underpinned the promotion of Burmese language to the exclusion of other languages. Little policy space has previously been given thus far to addressing the multilingual educational context of Myanmar and the "language-barrier" because of this, and the language of instruction continues to be a significant reason for drop out and demand for education from non-state educational providers (UNICEF 2012, 86–87). The lack of educational resources and opportunities in the local language is perceived as a frustration and unfair treatment of those who speak minority languages, while conversely the reinforcement of local languages through various forms of education can support lessening such frustrations.

Conclusion

As this chapter has shown, Myanmar's education system at present is plagued by a number of challenges that are the product of its historical evolution, decades of armed conflict, chronic underfunding, and a system that is highly fragmented and de-facto decentralized. This has led to a situation today where there remain significant concerns about unequal access, poor educational quality, and the rising rates of inequality that are the result of these conditions. This, it is argued, has been a key source of discontent and grievance for many in Myanmar and either perpetuated or fuelled conflict over time.

At the same time, the past few years have seen a political commitment to redress some of these issues through a significant reform of the education system. This reform process, described in more detail in Chap. 5, has led to passage of a new National Education Law and a new strategic plan which sets an ambitious vision for the coming few years. The chapter has highlighted some of the possibilities *and* challenges that need to be addressed when moving from policy rhetoric into transformations of education practices and outcomes. Hence, while this chapter presents a picture of careful optimism about the *possibilities* for recent changes to redress long-standing inequities and grievances—particularly in regards to concerns around inequitable **distribution** of educational opportunities and outcomes, a lack of **recognition** for the particular concerns and issues facing minority-group learners, insufficient **representation** or recognized autonomy to local actors to provision for and manage education—there remain serious questions about how well this can contribute to a broader process of **reconciliation** against the context of conflicting demands on education, a complex system of parallel forms of education provision and hence varying mandates for education.

References

Cheesman, N. (2003). School, state and sangha in Burma. *Comparative Education, 39*(1), 45–63.

Cheesman, N. (2010). The incongruous return of habeas corpus to Myanmar. In N. Cheesman, M. Skidmore, & T. Wilson (Eds.), *Ruling Myanmar from cyclone nargis to national elections* (pp. 90–111). Singapore: Institute of Southeast Asian Studies (ISEAS).

GCPEA. (2014). *Education under attack 2014*. New York: GCPEA.

Gray, S. (2014). *Peace and development conflict sensitivity analysis: Child and youth framework*.

Jolliffe, K. (2014). *Ethnic conflict and social services in Myanmar's contested regions*. Yangon: The Asia Foundation.

Kyi, K. M., Findlay, R., Sundrum, R. M., Maung, M., Nyunt, M., Oo, Z., et al. (2000). *Economic development of Burma: A vision and a strategy*. Stockholm: Olof Palme International Center.

Lall, M. (2008). Evolving education in Myanmar: the interplay of state, business and the community. In M. Skidmore & T. Wilson (Eds.), *Dictatorship, disorder and decline in Myanmar* (pp. 127–149). Acton: ANU Press.

Lall, M. (2011). Pushing the child centered approach in Myanmar: The role of cross national policy networks and the effects in the classroom. *Critical Studies in Education, 52*(3), 219–233.

Lall, M., & South, A. (2013). Comparing models of non-state ethnic education in Myanmar: The Mon and Karen national education regimes. *Journal of Contemporary Asia., 44*, 298–321.

Lo Bianco, J. (2013). *Language and social cohesion: Malaysia, Myanmar, Thailand*. Desk Review.

Lo Bianco, J. (2015). *Myanmar country report. Language, Education and Social Cohesion (LESC) Initiative*. Unpublished report.

Lorch, J. (2007). Myanmar's civil society–a patch for the national education system? The emergence of civil society in areas of state weakness. *Journal of Current Southeast Asian Affairs, 26*(3), 55–88.
Lorch, J. (2008). 9The (re)-emergence of civil society in areas of state weakness: The case of education in Burma/Myanmar. In M. Skidmore & T. Wilson (Eds.), *Dictatorship, disorder and decline in Myanmar* (pp. 151–176). Acton: ANU Press.
Lwin, T. (2000). *Education in Burma (1945–2000).* Thinking classroom foundation. http://www.thinkingclassroom.org/uploads/4/3/9/0/43900311/lwin_t._2000._education_in_burma_1945-2000.pdf
Lwin, T. (2007). *Education and democracy in Burma: Decentralization and classroom-level educational reform.* Washington, DC: International forum for democratic studies.
Maber, E. (2014). (In)Equality and action: The role of women's training initiatives in promoting women's leadership opportunities in Myanmar. *Gender and Development, 22*(1), 141–156.
Martin, R. (2013). Myanmar: Governance, civil society and the developments in education. *Education in South-East Asia, 20*, 173.
Michaels, S. (2014). *They know nothing about ethnic education.* The Irrawaddy. Available online at: http://www.irrawaddy.org/?p=68985.
Ministry of Education (MoE). (2013). *CESR rapid review of Myanmar basic education policy and proposed way forward. Phase 1.* Yangon: MoE.
Ministry of Education (MoE) (2014). *Comprehensive education sector review.* Yangon: MoE. http://www.cesrmm.org/index.php/en/
NESP – Government of Myanmar (2016). *National education strategic plan 2016–21.* Government of the Republic of the Union of Myanmar Ministry of Education, Available online at: planipolis.iiep.unesco.org/sites/planipolis/files/ressources/myanmar_nesp-english.pdf
Nyein (Shalom) Foundation. (2012). *Policy paper on language in primary education in the republic of the union in Myanmar.* Yangon: The Shalom Foundation.
Salem-Gervais, N., & Metro, R. (2012). A textbook case of nation-building: The evolution of history curricula in Myanmar. *Journal of Burma Studies, 16*(1), 27–78.
Snaing, Y. (2015). *Most student demands unmet as MPs pass amendment education law.* The Irrawaddy. Available at: http://www.irrawaddy.org/burma/most-student-demands-unmet-as-mps-pass-amended-education-law.html
Sugiyama, R. (2013). *National curriculum review in Myanmar: Technical input for CESR working group.* Tokyo: PADECO CO., Ltd.
Tin, H. (2000). Myanmar education: Status, issues and challenges. *Journal of Southeast Asian Education, 1*(1), 134–162.
TNI (2014). *Transnational institute 2014 annual report.* Amsterdam: TNI. Available online at: http://annual2014.tni.org/
UNESCO. (2007). *World data on education: Myanmar.* Geneva UNESCO-IBE. Available online at: www.ibe.unesco.org
UNESCO. (2014). *Education for All 2015 national review report: Myanmar.* Geneva UNESCO, Available online at http://unesdoc.unesco.org/images/0022/002297/229723E.pdf
UNICEF. (2012). Baseline study: Child-centred approaches and teaching and learning practices in selected primary schools in child-friendly school focused townships in Myanmar.
UNICEF. (2016). *The state of the world's children 2016.* New York UNICEF. Available online at: https://www.unicef.org/sowc2016/
Walton, M. J. (2013). The "wages of Burman-ness:" Ethnicity and Burman privilege in contemporary Myanmar. *Journal of Contemporary Asia, 43*(1), 1–27. https://doi.org/10.1080/00472336.2012.730892.
Watchlist on Children and Armed Conflict. (2009). *No more denial: Children affected by armed conflict in Myanmar (Burma).* Available online at http://watchlist.org/reports/pdf/myanmar/myanmar_english_full.pdf
WLB (Women's League of Burma). (2014). *If they had hope they would speak.* Chiang Mai: WLB.
World Bank. (2015). *Myanmar public expenditure review 2015.* Yangon: World Bank.

Chapter 5
Education and Policy Challenges of a Situation in Flux

Ritesh Shah, Khin Mar Aung, and Mieke T. A. Lopes Cardozo

Introduction

Concerns about the country's education system, set against the backdrop of Myanmar's current process of economic and political change, have spurred what many argue is the most significant reform package in education to date. Initiated in 2011, and followed by a comprehensive review of the entire education sector in the following 3 years, a new national Education Law was passed initially in 2014, and subsequently amended in 2015. This was followed in 2016 by the passage of a new 5-year education strategic plan which presents a costed approach for achieving the significant ambitions of the reform package in cooperation with the country's development partners. In the latter parts of this process, the NLD assumed control of the civil government, but maintained and supported the momentum which had occurred under their predecessor government. Some small changes, particularly in terms of implementation were made. This was particularly true on matters of language of instruction. Some of the key shifts are discussed in subsequent sections.

Important about this strategy is that it takes a long-term, developmental view to reforming Myanmar's education sector. It does not mention or acknowledge the ongoing conflict occurring in parts of the country. It also fails to recognise ongoing tension in Rakhine State which at the time this chapter was drafted, had led to a large-scale humanitarian crisis as hundreds of thousands of Rohingya Muslims fled

R. Shah (✉)
Faculty of Education and Social Work, University of Auckland, Auckland, New Zealand
e-mail: r.shah@auckland.ac.nz

K. M. Aung
World Education, Yangon, Myanmar

M. T. A. Lopes Cardozo
University of Amsterdam, Amsterdam, The Netherlands

M. T. A. Lopes Cardozo, E. J. T. Maber (eds.), *Sustainable Peacebuilding and Social Justice in Times of Transition*,
https://doi.org/10.1007/978-3-319-93812-7_5

into Bangladesh to escape state-sponsored violence against them. The reason for the absence of such discussions in the reform texts is discussed in more detail later on in the chapter.

The major part of the chapter traces the evolution of the reform process in terms of its justificatory narrative, and the ways in which the reforms acknowledge and redress grievances of the past. A key argument made throughout this chapter is that on the surface (and using different yet connected terminology) claims are made to notions of redistribution, representation and recognition—particularly towards recognised ethnic minority groups—yet the substance of the reforms is largely one which some might argue is devoid of actual recognition of the country's history and conflict-affected context. Reasons why this might be the case and the competing actors involved are explored, and we identify the various interests involved in shaping these reforms.

It is important to note that the bulk of data collection and analysis that occurred in the writing of this chapter occurred in 2015, prior to the National Education Strategic Plan (NESP) being finalised and adopted by the new government. Several references are made to the draft NESP which was completed in early 2015. Interestingly, what was observed when comparing the draft to the final version of the NESP from 2016 was an even further elimination of references to conflict, peacebuilding and social cohesion. For that reason, in parts reference is made to the draft, rather than final version—because these quoted texts no longer exist in the final version. The deletion of this material says something in itself about the idea of "peacebuilding being everywhere and nowhere"; a concept that is explored more explicitly later on in the chapter. Drawing on a combination of the draft and final NESP also provides a foundation for discussing the policy making process in more depth.

Impetus and Drivers of Current Education Reform in Myanmar

In his inaugural speech on 30 March 2011, former President U Thein Sein committed the government to a wholescale reform of the education sector as part of a broader package of reforms that aimed to herald the country's transition to a liberal democratic state. The Framework for Economic and Social Reform (November 2012) subsequently set out a policy framework for reforms to the education system that would consider issues of access, quality and management within all levels of the sector. In February 2012, the Ministry of Education (MoE) agreed to undertake a Comprehensive Education Sector Review (CESR) as a response to this agenda.[1] It was argued in the Terms of Reference for the review that it was,

[1] With impetus for the review coming from the President's office rather than the Ministry itself, overlaps in perceived responsibilities and tensions in agendas and motivations have been a feature of the reform process since its instigation.

> …required in order to ensure that there is a full and comprehensive understanding of the current status of education in Myanmar, regarding access and quality across the sub-sectors; as well as current strengths and gaps in policy, capacity, management systems, financing and partnership. This will support the implementation of priority reforms and the assessment of realistic policy options to form the basis of a costed, strategic education sector plan. These, in turn, have the potential to address the challenges and greatly accelerate progress towards realisation of Myanmar's education and socio-economic goals. (MoE 2012, 2)

The primary rationale for this reform has been and continues to be driven by an imperative to 'modernise' an education system that is perceived to be antiquated and irrelevant to Myanmar's current position in the regional and international global political economy. Specifically, Myanmar's 'democratisation' as well as accession into ASEAN have led to a desire to construct citizens and a state that are perceived to be able to participate in this new political economy. Education is perceived as a key vehicle for doing so. According to one international interviewee:

> The generals realised they were going to join the outside world, and that they were part of an education system that wasn't preparing anybody for it…and therefore they saw [reform] as key for becoming like their ASEAN partners. (int. 10)

The language of modernisation is inherent in the Ministry of Education's vision and motto which are to ensure that the country's education system, "promotes a learning society capable of facing the challenges of the Knowledge Age" and that it helps to build "a modern developed nation through education", respectively (MoE 2012, 1). This is also reflected in the rationale for the Comprehensive Education Sector Review (CESR) and ensuing development of the National Education Strategic Plan (NESP). The CESR, for example specifies that through this review and the development of a new education sector plan, opportunity will be afforded to "greatly accelerate progress towards realisation of Myanmar's education and socio-economic goals" (MoE 2012, 1). According to a separate ADB report:

> The education reform strategy and development plan sits within a national development process that is focused on poverty alleviation, rural development and decentralization. (2013, 6)

Related to this, the draft National Education Strategic Plan's chapter on access, quality and inclusion stresses the importance of improving inclusive access to quality education provision from a human capital and economic development paradigm. Specifically, the chapter, citing research from the World Bank, argues that improving access will: "…have a high impact on poverty reduction although its impact will not be realized in the short-term" (3).

In sum, the key driver for reforms at present is focussed on improving educational service delivery to ensure that the education system promotes, rather than hinders, broader macro-economic reform processes. As described by one individual involved in the CESR process, the consolidation and focus on improving service delivery, rather than considering the function of education in promoting peacebuilding or even a peace dividend was because it was a politically 'neutral' focus that all sides could agree on. This person believed that, "*improving teaching and learning in schools/getting textbooks to students and better management of schools… they are exactly the same [in terms of competing interests from different stakeholders around reform]... they are not going to deviate too much...in terms of a setting of the policy agenda*" (int. 8). Another international consultant believed that while inherent in the drive to improve access and quality of the education system is the ability to broker a peace dividend between citizens and the state, the lack of visible manifestation of such language meant that peacebuilding was, "*everywhere and then it's like nowhere*," in the current process unfolding (int. 79). The consequences of this *implicit peacebuilding rationale* are further explored in both this chapter as well as those on teachers and youth.

Contestations and Challenges in the Lead Up to the New Education Strategic Plan

Competing or Aligned Agendas?

One of the key principles stressed when the CESR first began was a desire to ensure a level of coherence and coordination within and between CESR activities and other policy reforms and initiatives in the sector. The Terms of Reference specified that, "Over the time period of the CESR, it is anticipated that there will be many other inter-related processes taking place...the CESR will synergise with and tap into these wider processes as far as possible" (MoE 2012). In addition, given the multiple actors and sub-sector studies that would be carried out as parts of each phase of the CESR, there was a promise that strong coordination would ensure that a clear and consistent purpose was shared across these activities.

Yet, with 72 consultants (national and international) and 19 different sub-sector studies carried out in Phase 1 alone, coordination has proven to be a particularly difficult challenge despite the intentions highlighted above. It was noted by one international donor staff that the significant number of individuals and agencies involved required, "*a [full-time] coordinator...drawing up an Excel spreadsheet of consultants that were coming in and were going out...[it was] an absolutely huge logistical challenge*" (int. 79). A consultant working within the early stages of the reform process also felt that the entire process has been,

> ...very haphazard and poorly organized... with no clear conceptual framework...well they had a rapid assessment which set the stage but I didn't get the sense from that that there was a lot of strategy and thinking around … [it] should have led to a clear road map and agenda but they went into phase 2 which involved a much larger number of studies that were even more disparate in nature. (int. 8)

This lack of coherence and a clear conceptual framework also meant that when it came to prioritising activities within and between the various sub-sectors, vested interests came in the way of coherence. The same respondent noted that:

> we have got some subsectors [which are] heavily influenced by lots of donors involved and its quite messy because they have contrasting opinions and things and pull government colleagues in different directions. (int. 8)

A similar tension has also existed between the CESR process and other policy initiatives in the education sector. Driving much of this tension has been a desire amongst those in government to make some quick visible changes to the education sector—referred to as the "quick wins", and the CESR's desire to support a process of systemic, sustainable reform. One interviewee felt that,

> there was this tension between the long-term sustainable sector planning and the strategic process, based on evidence and [the desire of politicians for] we want something now. (int. 79)

The CESR process aimed to develop a strong evidence-base and use such evidence to drive policy decision-making. The use of data, and particularly the employment of evidence-based decision-making was driven by a belief, particularly amongst the international community, that doing so would result in greater transparency, and force issues to be decided on the basis of data, rather than political agendas. While theoretically, this rationalist and technical approach may have allowed decisions about the (re)distribution of resources to be more equitable, those involved in the process believed that this approach may have been "politically naïve", particularly, "*...to think that in this currently highly charged environment politicians can wait two years...there was a need to show some concrete results intermediate along the way*" (int. 79).

There was a sense that the multiple actors, actions and interests involved in the reform led to situation by 2015–2016, where the desire for rapid, visible change precluded the initial aim of CESR—which was to provide a comprehensive, coherent view. As one individual working on the sidelines of the reform processes at that time noted,

> ...It feels a little overwhelming in terms of the amount of change which is underway and the depth of that change that is being undertaken...so although the broad Education Law has been passed now all of the bylaws, rules, regulations, subsections...they're all called different things... they're being written like mad....with all this frenzy...I think the speed and pressure for reform is compromising the ability to get really good work done. (int. 4)

This sentiment was reiterated by another respondent who felt that the intense drive to produce new policies was frustrating efforts to ensure coherence between the different pieces of action occurring:

> This is something we keep telling [the Ministry]...make sure that your subsector laws match with the Education Law ...but also match between themselves... make sure that they match with your [long term goals]...and make sure the NESP is aligned to them... that's why the NESP is also a bit late compared to what was foreseen ...and now the Education Law will be reviewed...which means that the bylaws will be delayed. (int. 6)

Thus, the expectation of producing some visible change, balanced against the desire to ensure coherence, "*...was an uneasy compromise*" where "*this interface between technical and political processes, this interdependence and how the one influences the other*" has manifested itself in clear tensions (int. 79). UNICEF and other international actors whom are supporting CESR maintain a belief that the reform process has the potential to lead to an educational system that is more equitable for all. The challenge, however, has been to maintain a coherence and commitment to this vision through the multiple actors and individuals involved in the process, and across the various stages and activities which are occurring within this set of macro reforms.

Both the influx of international consultants as well as policy priorities—such as the provision of school grants, school based management, the introduction of competency based frameworks for teachers and other educational professionals, and investment in child-centred pedagogies—all testify to the formative role of international policy borrowing in shaping Myanmar's educational reform process. However, the comments discussed above highlight the lack of coherence that resulted from the involvement of so many actors, leading to representatives from the Ministry of Education feeling overwhelmed by the proliferation of global educational agendas and technical advice. From a sustainable peacebuilding perspective, these are warning signs for a potential lack of context responsiveness, which might exacerbate rather than address grievance and inequality. These findings in Myanmar mirror the critiques presented by other scholars on international policy borrowing in the broader field of education (see also Verger et al. 2012).

Participation and Voice in the Reform Process

The CESR Terms of Reference also stressed that a guiding principle of the reform process should be that it would be "an inclusive, participatory process". This would involve various departments/Ministries of government as well as a wide range of educational stakeholders, including representatives of different ethnic groups and the monastic sector. It was envisaged that this process would engage with key constituencies including parents, students, communities, teachers, head teachers, and education officers at the State/Regional and township levels. Moreover, CBOs, academics and development partners in shaping and refining the reform agenda. The CESR Phase One report (MoE 2013, 19) argues that the findings and recommendations present "diverse opinions" based on comments received from a range of educational stakeholders. Yet it became evident in speaking to those observing and witnessing processes of consultation and participation that such efforts were both insufficiently participatory or representative.

One significant reason given for this was a lack of understanding, willingness or ability to participate. One international respondent believed that there was an unwillingness to participate from the opposition groups themselves:

> …it is important to recognize that [the government] did invite all these different people to come and talk to them […] but politically they just… I got a sense that they just didn't want to engage. (int. 8)

This respondent went onto an example to illustrate this point: "…*The ministers have invited the students to a number of meetings...recently…and they haven't been willing to attend*" (int. 8). Yet, from the perspective of those in the opposition there was a willingness to participate, it was rather government officials who were unwilling or unable to enter into a meaningful dialogue with them. The National Network for Education Reform (NNER) is the major civil society group for education, set up in 2012 specifically to bring together actors and activists across education sectors. The NNER, has close associations with political opposition and ethnic groups through the multiple positions of the networks' leadership and members.[2] There was therefore perceived to be political conflicts of interest for the government to engage with NNER too closely (ints. 79 and 22). Likewise, the cumbersome bureaucracy involved in facilitating such politically charged meetings was identified as obstructing discussions and potentially provoking recriminations (int. 4). The highly oppositional and political dynamics that existed between NNER and the government was therefore perceived to preclude effective dialogue. One observer further described how, "*Distrust was so embedded for so many years, there wasn't a sort of safe space to have a dialogue…*" (int. 79). This then led to a sense of a one-sided type of communication, where while NNER was expected to participate in the government reform process, reciprocity in terms of engaging with NNER's separate reform platform was not equally considered by the government. An individual working within the reform processes expressed this as follows:

> I think neither side is able to trust each other too much so we had … we facilitated sessions where the CESR shared their review findings and then we had another one where the NNER shared their findings of their country-wide consultation, but you couldn't get the two in the same room. The NNER came to the government one but the government for all sorts of different reasons weren't able to come to the NNER one. (int. 4)

In another instance, around the drafting of the new Education Law, questions of whether or how NNER should be invited ultimately led to them being excluded from the consultation process, which in turn fuelled a stronger grievance on the part of NNER.

> They organized a high-level consultation on the outputs [of the law reform process] in March last year. The president was going to be there, the Minister of Education, States, regions...and then there was a lot of unclarity about the NNER about if they were or were not invited. And our understanding is that they were invited, but [with a limited number of representatives allowed]. I don't think the limits on [the] number of attendees was ever specified, so when they arrived for the meeting with a large contingent, [the government] stopped them. In the end NNER wasn't at the meeting, that was the result. So they called a press conference the day of the meeting. Saying [NNER] reached out to them but [the government] didn't reach out to us. Because meanwhile the NNER was doing their own national consultation around policy documents they produced. (int. 4)

Moreover, when consultation did occur, there was a strong sense that it was limited in both breadth and depth. Often consultation was described as more a case of 'telling' various stakeholders what the findings were, and not opening conclusions reached in the various stages to contestation or debate. As one consultant described:

---

[2]The blurred boundaries of the roles of leading NNER figures came to a fore in early 2015 during the student protests as the NLD sought to distance themselves from the political position of the NNER, removing a key leader from the party executive committee (Mratt Kyaw Thu 2015).

> The government did go to the states and regions, and it put forward the parts of [CESR findings]…but the way they did it, they basically went in and said 'this is what's going to happen, does anybody object?' No, good, right we consulted. (int. 10)

The same individual recalled another meeting where civil society was invited to attend and provide input to the government on the draft Education Law:

> A member of [civil society] was talking about something, and this was a consultation meeting… and the minister said well that's already been decided so there was no point of going over that. So consultation is very much giving information. It's a powerpoint up on the wall and saying this is what we're going to do. The word consultation is used very easy…because you say we are going to involve everybody…but they're not actually doing anything. (int. 10)

Another respondent similarly described how there was a strong perception that the Ministry was:

> …go[ing] too far ahead [so consultation] will be seen as confirmation rather than input…. people feel that its already cooked, and are not really wanting…input…they just want us to tick the box. (int. 79)

The reach of such consultations was also limited. The same consultant involved in the planning of these meetings described how:

> …originally they wanted to have consultations in every state, but in terms of capacity and trying to get dates...they ended up doing it regionally. I think it was doing the right thing, but not enough of it…[often in these meetings] it was not so clear who was [invited] and who was not, [and so] it was probably more government people than civil society people represented. (int. 79)

Finally, the government legitimated the passage of the Education Law in 2014 as a reflection of a diverse range of viewpoints and interests—in essence a product of the consultation process itself. They argued that protests led by groups such as the All Burma Federation of Student Unions (ABFSU) following the law's initial passage were misinformed and based on false pretensions. As Metro (2014) identifies, "advocates of the law counter that it already includes much of what the students' desire". Yet, the claims of the protesters "suggests that ministry officials have not yet succeeded in informing stakeholders about their larger efforts at reform, in building consensus around them or in creating trust regarding their aims" (Ibid.).

While UNICEF and QBEP partners, for their part, pushed for the consultation process to seek the view of all stakeholders irrespective of gender, ethnicity, religion, political affiliation, and to include, rather than exclude important non-state actors, it would appear that in actual practice, a fairly limited consultative approach was employed. One observer noted that UNICEF's expectations may have been unrealistic, particularly in a context where "*it is not something this country has been exposed to for the past 50 years*" (int. 51). His perspective was that expecting an inclusive and participatory consultation process to do just that, because it was part of a "*two or five year project cycle*", would inevitably disappoint. The danger was that in a setting with conflicts still ongoing and peace agreements with different groups still very tentative, any promises that were perceived to be unmet could, "*undermine [the peace process]*" (int. 51). Additionally, during the times of the run up to the elections of 8 November 2015, there was both, tension and uncertainty in the political environment more broadly which affected trust and confidence in reform processes specifically. Likewise, the protests that have occurred around the Education Law are concerning and revealing of such grievances, as they are the direct expressions of a felt lack of *representation*.

Continuity or Change? The National Education Law

The National Education Law passed in 2014 was supposed to provide a foundation upon which key legal framework issues identified in Phases One and Two of the CESR could be rectified, as a prelude to the implementation of the new NESP. As it turned out, however, the Education Law turned into a political issue and grievance in itself, largely because of a perception from large segments of society that the law does not go far enough to challenge or change the status quo. Stakeholders such as students, teachers' unions and civil society organisations, who had campaigned to be included in decision making, have felt ultimately side-lined, as those with direct involvement in policy formation remained confined to a small circle of officials. After the passing of the National Education Law in September 2014, students and members of the NNER publicised their dissatisfaction through seminars, public events and protests. In March 2015, student demonstrations reached a height as protesting students seeking amendments to the law met a brutal police response that resulted in dozens of arrests. It was a graphic reminder of the consequences of this fundamental mistrust that pervades across generations, political affiliations and ethnic identities (amongst others). Table 5.1 provides a summary of some of the languages embedded in the emerging legislation and policy documentation of both the government and NNER—using the 4Rs framework—and compares them.

On one hand, what is evident are some clear similarities in key principles of what the government is proposing and what NNER was asking for, particularly in terms of broadening educational access, offering up greater autonomy to schools and universities, and creating greater mechanisms for the recognition of ethnic groups other than the Bamar. Both NNER and the government agree on the need to ensure that school-aged children have free, unfettered access to an education that is non-prejudicial and exclusionary. Where they differ is on how far this access should extend, with NNER arguing that it should extend to youth and individuals of any age. Similarly, NNER and the government agree on the need to better preserve and support languages and cultures other than the Bamar majority. For the government, however, this is focussed on the preservation, maintenance and strengthening of the languages and cultures of 'national races' while for NNER the focus is on ethnic group language and cultural preservation and maintenance—an important distinction in the context of Myanmar. Thus, in several areas, while the government has made some moves towards NNER's policy agenda, there is a sense it hasn't gone far enough. One individual, working on the inside of the reform process for the government, reflected on this challenge identifying that:

Table 5.1 A comparison between the National Education Law and NNER's Education Policy using the 4Rs framework

Topic	National Education Law (2014)	NNER Educational Policy submitted to parliament
Redistribution	Every school-aged child has the right to education that enables them to develop their full potential while respecting the environment and the rights and values of others	School-aged children and youth (of any age) must have equal opportunities to pursue education
		The compulsory years of education will be mandated and enforced by law and will be free for all students
	Once free, compulsory education has been successfully implemented at the primary level it must be extended step by step (to higher grades)	There must be no discrimination against students on the basis of their birthplace, the region where they live, their ethnicity, culture, religion, social background, poverty, wealth, gender, or physical disability
		All citizens have the right to lifelong education
		All high schools operated with funds from the federal budget must be free
		Both university education and vocational education will be valued equally
		Regional departments of education will take responsibility for sending mobile teachers to students who live in regions far from schools
Recognition	Education must value, maintain, and improve the languages, literature, culture, and traditions of the national races	Education must be free from the influence of religious groups or political parties. It will value human dignity and freedom of religion
	Monastery schools and schools operated by religious organizations must use only the Ministry of Education's basic education curriculum, syllabus and textbooks in accordance with the standard national education curriculum	Educational policy must give priority to the preservation of the environment and the maintenance of the ethnic languages and cultures which will contribute to long-term, sustainable development
	The national language, Myanmar, will be the language of instruction for basic education. If necessary, things can be explained orally in children's mother tongue	Emphasis will be given [in Early Childhood Education] to the development of the children's mother tongue. The basic education curriculum will be written by experts based on the national education policy. Each region has the right to freely develop this curriculum further based on the curriculum guidelines approved by parliament
		In each region, at the primary levels, the ethnic language agreed on by majority decision will be used as the school language. In multi-language areas, the school language will be decided by the school administrative body of each school
		In middle schools in ethnic areas, where Burmese is not the mother tongue, Burmese and the ethnic language will be used in a bilingual way. English will be taught as a subject

Representation	Every level of education must be up-to-date and include diverse perspectives and views while promoting good character and producing human resources which will benefit the building of the nation	[Primary and secondary] school will be administered by a School Administration Body made up of the principal, teacher representatives, parent representatives, and respected community leaders. The School Administration Body will be responsible for enrolling students, hiring teachers, writing curriculum [see point 9 below on "developing" curriculum], testing of the school's teaching, learning and student achievement, and financial management of the school
	Coordinating Committee for Higher Education will check and approve all budget requests for each of the universities related to it prior to submitting them to the central government	Each university has the right to set its own admission requirements
		The universities and colleges will be free from the direct control of any government ministry. They will receive permission to operate from the University Administrative Council, but will be autonomous
		The University or College Administrative Council will be made up of professors from various subjects, management and financial officers, representatives of the university or college teachers, representatives of the student's union, as well as nationally recognized experts and academics
		Each department in the university or college will write their own curriculum
		Universities and colleges have the right to freely pursue research and to freely publish their research findings
		Each university and college has the right to freely communicate with and pursue educational activities with other recognized universities inside or outside the country
		Students have the right to freely form groups such as a Students' Union, sports teams, and arts and culture clubs
		Teachers have the right to freely form a Teachers' Union
		Teachers and students who have reached the legal age have the right to join a political party of their choice. They must show mutual respect for other views and opinions
		The University Administrative Council must take into consideration students' evaluations of their teachers

(continued)

Table 5.1 (continued)

Topic	National Education Law (2014)	NNER Educational Policy submitted to parliament
Violence	Every school-aged child has the right to education that enables them to develop their full potential while respecting the environment and the rights and values of others	There must not be any failing of exams by students in the basic education schools
	Human dignity and freedom of religion will be respected in places of formal education	Students have the right to freely express their ideas and views. Rather than designating views as right or wrong, priority will be given to the reasonableness and logic of the idea
	Good learning environments will be created and maintained for the long-term	Universities and colleges must be places that promote learning and provide a secure learning environment
	There must be mutual respect between teachers and students, and teachers must teach without physically or mentally harming students	
Gender	No mention	No mention

> The government is saying well, we've put [provision for teacher and student association] in the law and people are going, yes, but there isn't a proper meaningful representation… [NNER is] say[ing] that alright, we see that you are making some moves but … your comprehension of representation isn't what we're looking for. (int. 4)

What has to be noted is that in 2015, after months of protests, the Education Law was amended. Several of the issues under discussion were taken up in the National Education Amendment Law of 2015.[3] With regard to the preservation and support to ethnic languages and cultures, the 2015 Amendment mentions the state and regional government now has the responsibility to develop the local curriculum. In addition, the Amendment states that at primary level it is now allowed to use the respective ethnic language and medium of instruction in some schools.

Who Should Control Education?

On matters of autonomy—at both the primary, secondary and tertiary levels—the government and NNER take starkly different positions on how much independence should be granted from the centre. For example, curriculum control is implied under the government's draft law to remain in the hands of the state, while NNER advocates for greater curriculum autonomy to local schools and communities. It can be argued there is some degree of decentralisation included in the 2015 Amendment, with the State and local government now having a say in the development of the 20% of the curriculum designated as 'local', which includes subject areas such as ICT, Income Generating Programmes (IGP), life skills or ethnic languages.

University administration under the 2014 government's law, particularly around important issues like budgeting, remains tightly under their control, while NNER advocates for universities to become self-regulating/governing entities. No provision is afforded in the 2014 National Education Law for the existence of student or teacher unions at the university level which is left to individual institutions to define in their own charters. This again is a significant historical and current grievance for NNER and ABFSU. Many of these issues are raised in a statement issued by NNER in August 2014 in response to the National Education Law being passed by the Parliament. Consequently, there is some attention paid in the Amendment of 2015 to these issues of university autonomy, as it states that universities should be free to find their own funding, and that the management of respective universities should be the responsibility of the university council.

Nevertheless, for those involved in NNER, there is a sense of grave disappointment that despite promises of significant change, there has been very little movement on the government's side. One group of academics claimed outright that, "*the people's voice' [was] ignored*" in the reform efforts (int. 100). A leader of the group attributed this to the fact that the reforms were driven by a small group of individu-

---

[3]This new law is made available for instance by the ILO (in Burmese only): http://www.ilo.org/dyn/natlex/natlex4.detail?p_lang=en&p_isn=100492&p_country=MMR&p_count=100.

als who were in essence, vestiges of the military government of times past (int. 96). The group of reformers working with government were seen by many to be a "*narrow representation*" of the broader interest groups in education on the outside, namely, "*…Bamar, and people from the education community, so we're not necessarily having a group that is so aware of all of the issues of everyone else in the country*" (int. 79). Added to this is the recognition that, "*[the] Ministry of Education has always been very politically sensitive… it's always been one of the most conservative ministries to work with and very set in its ways*" (int. 4). A strong sentiment, particularly from key segments of civil society, is that despite the rhetoric of change, little has actually changed substantively in how the government has carried out the reform process. An article from University World News quotes U Thein Lwin from the NNER: "there were changes to some of the wording but not the substance of the National Education Law" (Phaw Waa 2015).

Peacebuilding Logic "Being Everywhere and Nowhere" in Reform Texts

A key area of UNICEF's work in supporting the reform process has been to ensure that a peacebuilding rationale is considered in the work that was to be undertaken. This commenced in the early stages of CESR, where a consultant employed by UNICEF ran a series of workshops in 2014 for the CESR team. The key messages shared by UNICEF at these workshops were that:

1. Education needs to be delivered effectively, equitably and conflict sensitively in order to ensure that it is a driver of durable peace rather than a cause of division and conflict in society;
2. Getting educational reform right in Myanmar by ensuring that it is conflict sensitive and inclusive in its design and delivery will advance the nation's prospects for peace and prosperity. Getting it wrong will risk undermining a potential pillar for peace and the country's ability to realise its full potential;
3. Educational policies and practices have the potential to cause harm as well as good, particularly if they are conflict insensitive (Harris 2014).

Additionally, one of the key recommendations from Phase One of the CESR is to "use education as a tool to strengthen peaceful coexistence among ethnicities and exchange strategies," (MoE 2013, 41) and to:

> encourage more cooperation between the MoE and international/local NGOs in border areas and areas that have no peace. In doing so, the Ministry should first develop trust from the people and then collaborate according to the Nay Pyi Taw Accord. (MoE 2013, 41)

It is identified that in Phase Two of the CESR detailed studies of educational provision in conflict-affected regions of the country would be undertaken, yet this work was never completed.

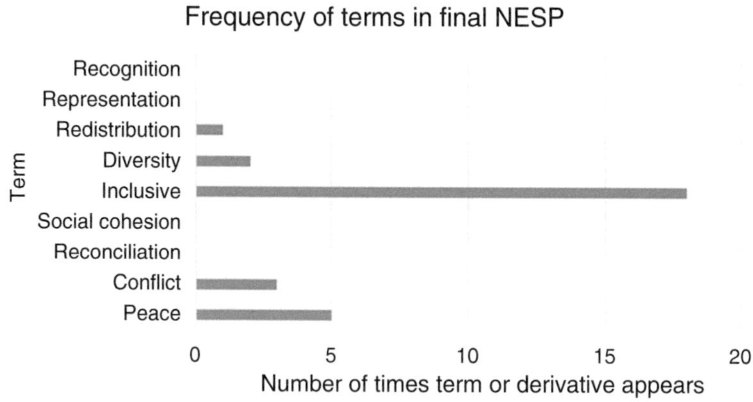

Fig. 5.1 Frequency of peacebuilding terms appearing in NESP (2016)

Content analysis of the final 2016 NESP suggests that concepts of peacebuilding and conflict were mentioned infrequently, and understood rather narrowly (see Fig. 5.1).

Firstly, in the NESP the government specifies clearly that "education will play a key role in securing the lasting peace and security of the nation" (7) and that "education…is a key driver to support the democratic and peace-building process" (32). The NLD's education minister has also been quoted as acknowledging the past grievances held by minority actors about the education system, and specified that, "educational development in ethnic minority areas is directly linked to the success or failure of Myanmar's peace process" (Htut 2016). On the other side, however, there is no specification in the 2016 NESP of how it might concretely do so. This signals that the current political climate prefers to move beyond the past, and in a way leave aside a commitment to reconciliation, rather than to recognise the enduring legacies which sectarian and ethnic-based conflicts in the country have and continue to have on the country's current development trajectory.

Secondly, what also becomes clear is how education is situated very firmly within the liberal peacebuilding lens (Paris 2004, 2010), with the 2016 NESP arguing that

> Myanmar has embarked on a period of profound political, economic and social change involving three major transitions to: a democratic governance system, a market-oriented economy and peace within its border area. (32)

Education's role is to service this market-oriented economy, to "achieve the national goal of Myanmar becoming an upper Middle Country by 2030" (Ibid, 32). In other words, peace is not an outcome in and of itself, but rather the security it might afford is intended to drive the country's growth and prosperity.

Thirdly, we analysed how conflict in the same document is viewed as a reason for inequalities in educational access and outcomes, but inequality itself is not specified as a driver of conflict. For example, the 2016 NESP acknowledges that living in conflict-affected areas can act as a demand-side barrier to accessing quality education, and that there is a need to disaggregate access-related indicators by several dimensions, including whether children live in a "post-conflict" setting in the country (72). The NESP, however, is silent on how education itself may and might continue to be a driver of conflict. The result is that the NESP largely portrays the country's conflict-affected situation as a past condition, rather than an ongoing concern, and very little specification is given to how education structures, systems and processes might be part of the transformative remedy. In particular, issues of reconciliation are notably absent.

Fourthly, the need to recognise diversity is mentioned largely within the parameters of the Education Law and its subsequent amendment, which offers opportunities for the learning of ethnic languages and culture, and the use of ethnic languages as a classroom language. In the NESP, priority is given to the development of the 20% local curriculum, namely the development of textbooks for teaching national races, languages and booklets that reflect culture and tradition of national races groups. In relation to new textbooks, the 2016 NESP specifies that, "All new textbooks and teachers' guides will be trialed with a selected sample of schools across the country in order to ensure their relevance and suitability for Myanmar's diversity" (117). Yet, links of these efforts to peacebuilding are only mentioned once, in the chapter on early childhood, where the 2016 NESP specifies that "Research in other countries has shown that culturally and linguistically appropriate ECCD services can also help achieve peaceful relations among ethnic groups" (73). Importantly, while the NESP places recognition of language and culture more centrally, this is only for those ethnic groups who are national races. It implies that groups such as the Rohingya, who are not 'counted' as national races, will not be included in the reformed system.[4] Additionally, the Education Law repeatedly mentions education being offered to citizens, who are defined as: "…someone who, according to Myanmar law, is a citizen, visiting citizen, or person who has been granted citizenship as well as foreigner who have been given legal permission to study" (draft NESP 2015 Chaps. 1 and 2). Given Myanmar's exclusionary citizenship laws,[5] there are several minority groups who under this definition will not be guaranteed the same rights of access, quality and relevance of education as granted to others.

Fifthly, the 2016 NESP also only briefly alludes to the importance of redistributing access to education from a peacebuilding perspective, arguing that:

[4] 135 ethnic groups are officially acknowledged. Changes to citizenship laws in 1982 resulted in citizenship being denied to many who had previously been recognised as citizens including ethnic groups which were no longer legitimised, which included the Muslim Rohingya (TNI 2014, 5).

[5] In the 1982 Citizenship Law, full citizenship was offered to only those who could prove ethnic and territorial connections to groups who arrived in the country prior to 1834, setting up arbitrary notions of the 'indigenous' and 'authentic' inhabitants of geographical territories (TNI 2014, 5). The Rohingya communities were reframed as "Bengali illegal immigrants" (Fortify Rights 2014, 11; TNI 2014, 11), setting up hostilities with ethnically recognised Rakhine Buddhist communities. Others such as those from Chinese and Indian heritage had their citizenship rights similarly revoked by the 1982 act.

> Increased funding needs to be spent more equitably and more efficiently, with some redistribution directed to geographical areas of educational disadvantage and lower socio- economic groups, combined with gender-responsive budgeting. (56)

Access to quality and relevant education is even of more concern for displaced school-going children, for instance in Kachin and Shan States, who due to continuous violent conflicts in the ethnic areas are forcedly displaced. Even though in some cases these students might be able to still learn in their own languages, there are often scarce resources like teachers, text books and other teaching and learning materials to support forced migrant students in their learning.

Analysis of both the draft and final NESP and Education Law would suggest that overall, a peacebuilding logic or language is notably absent from key reforms that will set the scene for the country's educational landscape moving forward. As was stated by one participant, with the logic of peacebuilding being "*everywhere and then…nowhere*," (int. 79) in current policy texts, the danger is that important components of education contributing to positive peace are being squandered for the sake of political expediency. According to several individuals involved in the reform process, the reason to not push the peacebuilding agenda more strongly in such reforms was over concern that it could politicise the process even more. One individual, involved heavily in the NESP process noted that, "*people have intentionally avoided [discussing conflict/peacebuilding] because it is too difficult…too sensitive…too much of an unknown*" (int. 8). When asked about the visible absence of a discourse of peacebuilding in the NESP, this person went onto discuss how, "*It's too obvious to talk about it in a conflict-post-conflict language so [we use] a stealth approach to addressing issues of concern*" (int. 8). Using the language of strengthening and improving service delivery was perceived by reformers and development partners as a way of, "*…helping the government to deliver results...[that will] then …achieve all of these things automatically*" (int. 8).

Peacebuilding is presumed to automatically occur from efforts to improve service delivery of education, which may not be the case, particularly when concerns around recognition and representation, let alone reconciliation, are not adequately considered in the policy texts itself and in the policy development process. Another development partner supporting the efforts acknowledged that, "*I'm not sure the 4Rs are well represented or taken care of in the sector plan…..and its surely a weakness of it*" (int. 6), and another respondent described conflict-sensitive and peacebuilding perspectives in these texts as "*a periphery issue*" (int. 4). When thinking about why this might be, another individual observing the development of the NESP from the outside noted:

> We have a lot of technical experts in education helping the team to develop their chapters, but they are education experts and not necessarily Myanmar experts…[they're] doing a sector planning as it was any other country. And…people are uncomfortable to acknowledge that there is no peace and there is no social cohesion…it's easier to pretend that it's already there. (int. 79)

Summing this up, we find the description of peacebuilding "*being everywhere, and nowhere*" to accurately reflect the current state of affairs when reviewing the absence or presence of a peacebuilding logic in current reform processes. It is everywhere in the sense that there seems to be a recognition of the need to place education reform process in the actual context of inequalities and frustrations, while it is mostly absent due to the often strategic neglect of the direct connotations to peacebuilding or related terms, or perhaps a lack of awareness and capacity to effectively address the reform process in a conflict-sensitive manner. In doing so, there runs the danger, as Harris (2014) reflected on, that the reform and policy direction as they seem to take shape potentially might do more harm in the future, rather than address the root causes that drove many aspects of the conflict in the first place: a lack of fair *redistribution* of resources and opportunities; a reflection of *recognition* of the various linguistic and cultural needs and aspirations of all those living in the country (and not only those granted citizenship); a sincere *representation* and a participatory process that not only informs, but rather engages with oppositional and minority perspectives—including the perspectives of teachers and students/youth alike; to in the long run, enable some first steps to addressing the grievances expressed through and inflicted by education through *reconciliation*.

Addressing Inequalities: The Quick Wins Platform

Against the backdrop of the sector redevelopment process described in the preceding section are a series of significant policy initiatives that have been started by the former government since 2011. These actions are predicated on the pressure, identified in the prior section, for quick visible actions which address some of the ongoing grievances held regarding the state of the education system at present. As has been discussed in Smith and Elison's (2015, 11) literature review, an important aspect of education acting as a peace dividend may be a focus on "highly visible improvements in service delivery rather than long term systemic reform." Doing so may help the state to (re)gain legitimacy by improving citizens' subjective perceptions of the quality and effort which it is putting into redressing public concerns about education. This point was acknowledged on more than one occasion by those interviewed. For example, a representative from an international organisation felt that: "*the enormous build-up of frustration, about the underfunding, about the declining quality, about the centralized control, about the exclusion, so many elements that civil society is angry about in education*," (int.79) meant there was a strong imperative for the government to show progress quickly.

Since 2011, there is evidence of clear efforts on the part of the government to reduce access and quality related barriers in the education system, particularly in the basic education sector. This is particularly true in regards to redistribution efforts by both increasing overall expenditure to education, and to reallocate resources already available.

Specific changes include:

- **Increased salaries for all teachers:** From April 2012, all civil servants, including primary and secondary school teachers on permanent contracts were given an allowance of 30,000 Kyats per month on top of their salary (approximately $38 USD). Government staff serving in remote and conflict-affected townships and sub-townships saw their salaries doubled, in addition to the monthly stipend of 30,000 Kyats. Daily wage teachers also say their salaries nearly doubled (from 1100 to 2100 Kyat/day). An additional salary increment of 20,000 Kyats for each civil servant was put in place in April 2013. The aim of improving salaries, particularly for those serving in remote and conflict-affected areas, is to improve retention of staff deployed to such areas, and redress traditional distributional imbalances in regards to student-teacher ratios (NESP 2016, 38).
- **Construction of new school facilities:** In 2015–2016 the government made a commitment to constructing 3000 new ECCD classrooms onto existing primary schools, and building 2000 new classrooms for secondary schools based on a mapping exercise. Additionally, 2795 libraries are to be constructed in secondary schools throughout the country. Priority is to be given to remote and border areas.
- **Ensuring the establishment of kindergarten level in all schools:** By the end of 2016, the government committed to ensuring that all 44,401 primary schools have instituted kindergarten level as part of the basic education programme.
- **Increasing the teaching workforce:** 72,000 primary teachers have been appointed as 'daily wage' teachers to support effective teaching and learning process as well as to increase the number of teachers in primary schools.
- **Scholarships for deserving students:** A scholarship programme, managed at the township level has been instituted since 2012 to high achieving students who are unable to complete or transition to middle or high school due to financial constraints. According to data presented in the draft NESP, the scholarships for those in middle schools have increased to 20,000 Kyat/month with 1002 scholarships awarded in 2013–2014; and scholarships for high school aged students are valued at 30,000 Kyat/month with 414 students receiving this award in 2013–2014.
- **Increased government financing to education:** The education budget had been increased from 0.6% of GDP in 2009–2010 to 2.1% of GDP by 2013–2014. The government views this as critical to their financing of free and compulsory education at primary level, with the possible later extension to middle and secondary.
- **Provision of school grants:** Through support of the World Bank, and the Government of Australia the government has provided school grants to all state schools for basic maintenance needs in an attempt to, reduce the burden of school maintenance costs on the community.
- **Addressing hidden costs of education:** Acknowledging the 'hidden costs' of attending school, the government has since 2012, provided all primary students with free textbooks and exercise books, and granted them 1000 Kyats to purchase stationery costs.

These initiatives were generally lauded by the international community as a signal of genuine concern and political will to address past educational grievances. One individual acknowledged the importance of what the (former) government had done arguing that:

> Education is very high profile… every child every family is affected by education and if [the government] can be seen to be doing well or getting results then obviously it's helpful… So for instance the textbook exercise where all of the children got a new textbook was really something which was very visible and reached all children. (int. 4)

In line with this, and making explicit reference to some of the 4Rs, the same individual went on to recognise how such efforts could be linked to concepts of redistribution, recognition and reconciliation:

> …The government is making enormous effort to enlist equity in all schools, so everyone is getting school grants now with World Bank support…[this includes] school grants to monastic schools… so that's extremely progressive. They're looking at textbooks this year… this year's budget is one set of textbooks for every child which is very progressive and uniforms for every child so yes, from a recognition point of view [the government is acknowledging that] all children are equal…And reconciliation...[it is about] getting those visible outputs there to every school in the country. (int. 4)

However, in seeking to universalise current reform efforts as benefiting "every child" such comments risk overlooking the continuing implications of an inherently discriminatory state educational system in which non-state schools are under and inequitably resourced.

From the government's perspective, there is a sense that these quick wins efforts are 'apolitical' and non-objectionable to any side. It is for these reasons that it is believed that action can be taken in the absence of consultation or further discussion:

> Improving teaching and learning in school, getting textbooks to students and better management of schools… they are exactly the same [interests across the political spectrum]… they are not going to deviate too much...in terms of a policy agenda. (int. 4)

The only danger, according to this interviewee, was the government setting up a precedent of high expectations that it would need to deliver on into the future:

> School grants are there… the ball has started rolling [and] it is very hard to bring those back… one set of textbooks per child has been promised…those things are out there, those promises are made... the government can't just stop. (int. 4)

The promises made have meant that wittingly or not, the international community has been asked to support aspects of this quick wins agenda. The World Bank and Government of Australia, for example, have been the organisations that have funded the provision of school grants to all state schools. Other development partners, have supported other components of the programme, such as the funding and/or training of teachers in the monastic sector, the training of head teachers on school based management, and the provision of educational facilities and materials in border, remote and conflict-affected areas where the state still finds it difficult to penetrate. The need for the development partners to support the government's ambitious new agenda was universally recognised by those interviewed. According to a representative of one agency:

> We see the need to substitute the state in some areas especially for school construction and especially for teacher training…There's a lot which is said about the content of the national education sector plan but in a sense nothing has started…so teacher training is still the same…so the quality of education is still as poor as it was before. (int. 6)

Often, such support was explicitly targeted at sectors and regions where it was deemed that grievances, inequities and a lack of government support were strongest. The international community, in essence, often played an important role in trying to rebalance the locus of resources and support in efforts to strengthen or gain traction behind the peace process. The same interviewee mentioned how:

> For example [our support] in Rakhine is about establishing a balance by addressing the needs of those who are in a difficult situation … in a more equal manner…it is about continuing to provide education to the kids but also using that as a kind of peace dividend. (int. 6)

This higher level of engagement with state actions to redress past grievances did not come, however, without levels of mistrust or suspicion by those traditionally aggrieved by inequities. As the next section discusses in greater detail, there was concern about the (former) government's 'true intentions' behind this new focus. With the international community increasingly involved as a partner in such actions, knowingly or not, they too were being viewed with the same concern. One international advisor felt that:

> There is this sort of nation building/state strengthening agenda in a context where the state has been perceived as illegitimate by many citizens, but certainly in conflict-affected areas. The government over some many years has been adopting militarized assimilation policy through education and the expansion of state services (education, health etcetera) into the ethnic areas. I think there is a perception of the different ethnic groups that the international community is facilitating [the] expansion [of] problematic state education into these autonomous areas. A classic example would be the World Bank allocating millions of dollars to support school grants and that's all in government schools, but in conflict-affected areas. (int. 87)

There were also some concerns raised, however, about how these actions sat alongside the CESR/NESP process. For instance, with the deployment under the quick wins programme of over 72,000 day-wage teachers into schools, new questions surface about how these new teachers may or may not be eventually incorporated into the professional (and qualified) workforce which the reforms hoped to build over time. Even the more 'simple' actions as part of the quick wins strategy were perceived, by some development partners, to not have sufficient long-term insight:

> Quick wins are trying to address gaps…..by building middle school classrooms so that there's less of an [inequality]… so that children are able to stay on at school beyond primary… I think that's a really good intent…[but] one of the challenges is I think looking at those plans really strategically… so for example when we saw the government's education budget, details was to the level of a paintpot and one set of easels per classroom… but there wasn't an overall rationale for what was the purpose for that whole package…and that's needed so that addressing inequalities in a coherent way [is done]. (int. 4)

With a matter like the deployment of 'unqualified' day wage teachers into hard to staff areas, namely conflict-affected and border regions, there could be a long-term consequence in terms of establishing a system where qualified teachers remain in the majority heartland with less qualified teachers operating in the fringes—creating potential differentials in terms of actual or perceived educational quality. As experience has shown from other countries in the region, such as Timor-Leste, this could lead to new forms of grievance or concern in the long-term (Shah 2012). A 2015 report by the Myanmar Education Consortium highlights many negative impacts of the hiring of these daily wage teachers, and questions whether this component of the quick wins package has addressed or worsened educational inequalities. Specifically, the report notes that, "teachers often are unmotivated and keen to return to their home areas which results in long periods of absenteeism", and that the program has also, "attracted the teachers of some ethnic education systems, contributing to a loss of teachers in those systems" (MEC 2015, 27).

Educational Governance: A Push and Pull Between Centralisation and Decentralisation

A significant concern raised about the Quick Wins programme is the sense, that purposefully or not, it aims to increase the control and reach of the state into sectors that have traditionally sat as distinct to the state system, namely the Monastic schools and the schools run by ethnic actors. The increasing role of the state, in terms of funding teacher salaries, providing learning resources, and allowing development partners to engage more deeply with non-state actors, is part of a broader agenda of bringing together a fragmented education system under one umbrella—what some have referred to as a convergence agenda.

A key component of the peace dialogue process is to identify ways in which the activities of state and non-state actors can be (re-)integrated into a single system. For a number of years, non-state actors have been extensively involved in substituting for a lack of state attention and/or meeting the demands for the promotion of an alternative ethnic narrative within the schooling experiences of local communities in conflict-affected and border regions. The fragmentation of social service provision is seen by the state as a threat to national unity, and thus convergence of educational provision under the auspices of the state is seen as critical to the notion of a unitary, federalist system of power sharing. As one peace advisor identified:

> The connector part of that is the peace processes and education service delivery…the convergence of education…reassimilation of refugee and IDP children…the alternative or complementary education systems in the state and border areas…makes education very important in the broader agenda as well. (int. 4)

That stated, there remains deep suspicion amongst those who for decades have now actively fought for their autonomy to cede control back to the state, even if ultimately the aim is to devolve control back to the regions and ethnic groups. Another peace advisor acknowledged that, "*…the suspicion on the part of the ethnic organisations will always be that you are trying to get them subsumed into a unitary public system*" (int. 3). At the same time this interviewee felt that education was an important "*entry point*" for commencing a process of convergence: "*where you can do stuff that's practical and actually useful in terms of service delivery…and helps to continue to build trust*" (int. 3).

As some cease-fire agreements have been signed in recent years, there is hope for greater integration and dialogue between the parallel system and the state apparatus. The draft NESP, for example acknowledged the important role of ethnic schools in substituting for the absence of state presence in the past, and argued that:

> The contribution of these schools needs to be recognised. Ideally there should be space within government systems to allow coexistence and coordination between the two systems, including for children's ability to transition between these schools and take government exams. (draft NESP 2015, Chap. 3, 42)[6]

Such integration is already happening. In Mon State, for example, the longer standing cease fire has meant that Mon education authorities have expanded their presence into government controlled areas of the state through 'mixed' schools. Here, the government curriculum is followed, but indigenous language is maintained in instruction at primary school level. In Karen state, however, the more recent nature of the cease-fire has meant a lack of integration until now. Outside of full alternative schooling provision, education authorities in these areas have also set up summer learning and after-school programs to supplement state education provision, and ensure that students' ethnic identities and languages are maintained (Lall and South 2013; Lorch 2008).

That stated, the draft NESP is also cognisant of the concerns raised by such convergence in terms of an encroachment of state control into affairs that have traditionally been maintained by separatist, ethnic actors. It acknowledges that:

> Relationships between some ethnic education providers and the government is more tentative and these education providers may not wish to share information about their schools; they also see government attempts at increasing provision in areas that they cover as a threat if it is not properly managed. (draft NESP 2015, 42)

Indeed, concerns about such convergence were raised quite clearly in interviews with representatives from both, the monastic and non-state (ethnic) education sectors. From the monastic sector, one representative felt that the government's payment of teacher salaries was ultimately about it exerting greater control over the quality and nature of the education being provided within its schools:

> Now in the monastic schools, the government provides the teacher salaries. [The government's feeling] is …schools are not qualified in the teaching or management. I agree [with] that. We need to provide and strengthen the monastic schools systematically. If the principals even set up the schools, if they can't do the quality in education system, this school should be closed, I agree. But don't control our schools through [increased] contribution. (int. 15)

[6] It is notable that this same acknowledgement, however, was not made in the final NESP produced in 2016 where this statement has been removed.

The same individual argued that what was needed was not more resources, but greater autonomy for the sector to reform itself. According to this respondent, the state's increased support of the sector was "*only about being under [their] control*" and did not acknowledge that many monastic schools, "*have the ability, they have infrastructure…enough resources*" (int. 15).

For non-state actors and conflict-affected minority communities who have traditionally borne the costs of educating children in their jurisdictions, increased resourcing to their schools from the state was welcomed. At the same time, concerns were raised that it should not occur at the expense of reduced autonomy, as expressed by a local staff member of a donor organisation:

> [Ethnic actors are saying] education should be taken responsibility by the government. The government says… OK but only if you use the same curriculum [as government schools]… but we want to have our own curriculum…we want our ethnic language as medium of instruction…we want to include our history…it is only the cost and the responsibilities [that] should be [with] government. (int. 74)

What is occurring, is an interesting pull towards *recentralising* control over a system that has become fragmented along identity-lines (by religion and ethnicity), while at the same time a discourse, at least in current reform efforts, to then *decentralise* control of education back to regions, states, townships and schools. The push to decentralise control, within the framework of the CESR, is driven by a logic of improving the distributional and representational inequalities that have been part of educational service delivery for some time. It is believed that districts, townships and schools, with the right information, can better serve the needs of their communities and identify pockets of disadvantage.

Constitutional reforms and the present government's Framework for Economic and Social Reform have instituted an architecture for decentralisation (or deconcentration) to occur. Specifically, each of the seven states and seven regions has a state or region education office. Under each state or region education office are several newly-created (since 2012) *khayaing*, or District Education Offices, below which are Township Education Offices, one for each of the 325 townships of the country. However, a key issue remains the extent to which the state-level administrative infrastructure is equipped with decision-making authority, rather than simply bearing the burden of increased bureaucracy.

On the part of the government and some actors within the international community, however, there is a sense that the decentralisation process needs to be managed carefully. There is limited internal capacity at present to manage education both in a community's and the nation's best interest. As one individual working for the government in the reform process noted, "*You're not going to say let the communities run the schools and the government is not going to have anything to do with education,*" rebuffing the claims of groups such as NNER whom are asking for immediate, greater autonomy over educational decision-making (int. 8). Rather, decentralisation is perceived within current policy circles as a process that needs to be handled carefully and led through careful capacity building and strict controls and how devolution is carried out. According to the same individual:

> [The] government is quite keen on decentralization … [but] put in place a very strong mechanism for financial control and things… I think that would be something that the government would have to do. (int. 8)

Capacity development activities at the sub-national level, particularly for actors like UNICEF through its Mon Whole State Reform project, are driven by a logic that a federalist state model will be the inevitable outcome of the broader peace process. Current efforts aim to prepare state, district and township education authorities for anticipated key administrative, fiscal and policy decisions:

> What we are doing is sort of capacity building... One of the gaps is that people... at the education officers at sub-national level have never been trained…so when decentralisation does come in whatever form it will be, we need to prepare them so that they understand what their role is, so that they can say... here is my plan. (int. 5)

The aim is to avoid problems that have plagued decentralisation reforms in other post-conflict settings (see Dupuy 2008), and ultimately to embed a culture of evidence-based decision-making into the ethos of these actors. The belief is that by focusing on evidence and logic rather than emotion or instinct, decisions will be made by these actors in transparent and equitable ways (QBEP Joint Improvement Plan, UNICEF 2014). What is important to note about this current capacity-building activity is that it is anticipatory and speculative, rather than reflective of the actual roles and responsibilities such actors have at present. As UNICEF's own concept note from the Mon Whole State Approach describes:

> Eventually the education system will inevitably have to pursue some form of decentralization with local level planning, management and supervision of education programmes in order to adequately respond to the changing context, as well as to respectably fulfill the demands of the clients. It is critically important for the country to establish an effective means of decentralizing management of education to State/Region, township and school levels.

It is important to note that promises of decentralisation remain exactly that: promises of things to come, rather than a reflection of what exists at present. Recent research carried out in Mon State and Yangon found that:

> There has been limited, unclear 'deconcentration,' resulting in a certain amount of responsibility shifting to lower levels of administration, but people at these lower levels do not have decision-making authority commensurate with, or related to, their responsibilities. Government policies concerning education and decentralization have not been clearly defined. Instead, the institutional and organizational culture in the Ministry of Education continues to be top-down. (Zobrist and McCormick 2013, 4)

From a peacebuilding standpoint, this raised concerns for these authors who note that:

> …a lack of autonomy at lower levels of administration may prevent the Ministry of Education from being able to address and implement politicized aspects of education provision, including the provision of services in ceasefire areas, in languages other than Myanmar, and more widely, in being responsive and accountable to local populations. (Ibid)

Hence, what exists is an uneasy tension between on the one hand a state which has expressed an intent to address issues of redistribution, representation and recognition through the decentralisation of a strongly centralised system, while on the other hand the connected process of convergence raises questions about whether this limits opportunities (at least in the short term) for trust building and reconciliatory developments, and particularly for minority ethnic groups, to continue to vocalise and represent their interests for schooling.

Conclusion

This chapter has sought to indicate how peacebuilding is implicitly part of broader discourses of social inclusion, equity and improved access for those traditionally neglected by the national state, rather than being explicitly mentioned in key policy texts. Additionally, while a draft version of the NESP had included greater mention of some of these issues, the final 2016 NESP had eliminated most mention about the country's past and current conflict. Education reform was firmly positioned within Myanmar's process of economic liberalisation, and a key aspect of its engagement with the global marketplace. This is not to say, however, that the importance of a socially cohesive and harmonious population was not recognised. Rather, the belief was that by improving service delivery—with a key focus on redistributing resourcing and addressing access-related constraints—traditional grievances against the state would be resolved. Yet, what the chapter has also shown is how questions about representation and recognition of perspectives and voices from civil society, non-state actors, and ethnic education authorities remain unanswered, and in fact, the process of reform has made visible these social ruptures.

Specifically, despite a rhetoric of broad participation in the reform process, consultation about the NESP and Education Law has been fairly limited and unrepresentative with many key national stakeholders feeling sidelined. While a number of actors and sectors have been involved in the NESP, these are largely representing the interests of outside actors (i.e. the international community). This is most apparent when it comes to questions such as language of instruction and control of the education system as whole. This has resulted in the reforms being perceived by many to be endogenously rather than indigenously driven.

Importantly, the prioritisation of visible and rapid change (e.i. the Quick Wins) has taken precedent over the need to better consider ways in which education has and continues to be a key and structural grievance of those marginalised by the national state. Thus, despite the belief that the reform package has an implicit peace-dividend built into it, with its promise for more accessible, relevant and quality education, it is big on platitudes but short on concrete promises. As described by one interviewee, the logic of peacebuilding is at once "everywhere and nowhere." As argued at the outset of this book, for education to truly contribute to peacebuilding, root grievances that are the product of education service delivery and governance must be addressed. This, we argue, has not been a key reform focus as of yet.

References

ADB. (2013). *Republic of the Union of Myanmar: Support for education sector planning*. Asian Development Bank.

Dupuy, K. (2008). Education for peace: Building peace and transforming armed conflict through education systems. Oslo: International Peace Research Institute, for Save the Children Norway. Available online at http://toolkit.ineesite.org/toolkit/INEEcms/uploads/1050/Education_for_Peace_Building_Peace.pdf

Harris, S. (2014). *CESR workshop: Handout 1 – Education and conflict sensitivity*.

Htut, S.Y. (2016). Minister ties improved education for ethnic minorities to peace. *Myanmar Times*. Available online at https://www.mmtimes.com/national-news/22474-minister-ties-improved-education-for-ethnic-minorities-to-peace.html

Lall, M., & South, A. (2013). Comparing models of non-state ethnic education in Myanmar: The Mon and Karen national education regimes. *Journal of Contemporary Asia, 1*, 118–140.

Lorch, J. (2008). The (re)-emergence of civil society in areas of state weakness: The case of education in Burma/Myanmar. In M. Skidmore & T. Wilson (Eds.), *Dictatorship, disorder, and decline in Myanmar* (pp. 151–176). Canberra: ANU E-Press.

MEC. (2015). Analysis of education services in contested regions of Myanmar final report. *Myanmar Education Consortium*. Online: https://mecmigration.files.wordpress.com/2016/05/mec-contested-areas-report-july-20151.pdf

Ministry of Education (MoE). (2012). *Terms of reference for Myanmar, comprehensive education sector review*. Yangon: MoE.

Ministry of Education (MoE). (2013). *CESR rapid review of Myanmar basic education policy and proposed way forward. Phase 1*. Yangon: MoE.

Mratt Kyaw Thu. (2015). Students continue to march as NLD expels education expert. *Myanmar Times*. Available online http://www.mmtimes.com/index.php/national-news/13018-students-to-step-up-strike-as-four-party-talks-fall-through.html

NESP. (2015). National Education Strategic Plan 2016–21 comprehensive education sector review phase 3. MOE Department.

NESP – Government of Myanmar. (2016). *National Education Strategic Plan 2016–21 Government of the Republic of the Union of Myanmar Ministry of Education*. Available online at: planipolis.iiep.unesco.org/sites/planipolis/files/ressources/myanmar_nesp-english.pdf

Paris, R. (2004). *At war's end: Building peace after civil conflict*. Cambridge: Cambridge University Press.

Paris, R. (2010). Saving liberal peacebuilding. *Review of International Studies, 36*(2), 337–365.

Phaw Waa, N. S. (2015). Amended law excludes autonomy, union recognition. *University World News*, 26 June 2015, 373. Available online http://www.universityworldnews.com/article.php?story=20150625173908808&query=Myanmar

Shah, R. (2012). Goodbye conflict, hello development? Curriculum reform in Timor-Leste. *International Journal of Educational Development, 32*(1), 31–38.

Smith, A., & Ellison, C. (2015). *The integration of education and peacebuilding: A review of the literature*. Research Consortium on Education and Peacebuilding/University of Ulster. Available at https://educationanddevelopment.wordpress.com/outputs-research-consortium/

TNI. (2014). *Transnational Institute 2014 annual report*. TNI. Available online at: http://annual2014.tni.org/.

UNICEF. (2014). QBEP Joint Improvement plan.

Verger, A., Novelli, M., & Altinyelken, H. K. (2012). *Global education policy and international development: new agendas, issues and policies*. Huntingdon: Bloomsbury.

Zobrist, B., & McCormick, P. (2013). *A preliminary assessment of decentralisation in education*. Experiences in Mon State and Yangon Region.

Part II
Teachers and Peacebuilding

Chapter 6
Understanding the Changing Roles of Teachers in Transitional Myanmar

Elizabeth J. T. Maber, Hla Win May Oo, and Sean Higgins

Introduction

Within the context of Myanmar, teachers' space for manoeuvre as peacebuilders has been constrained and conditioned by a variety of issues. These include factors that may restrict teachers' opportunities to contribute towards peacebuilding in the classroom and create inclusive learning environments such as the timetables, assessment models and curricula they work with. However, beyond teachers' own practice, they also find themselves perceived and framed differently by a range of actors within education policy discourses, and frequently instrumentalised within the structure of the highly centralised state education system, which equally contribute to limiting contributions to building peace rather than exacerbating tensions. However, despite the many shared influences which constrain teachers' positions, individual teachers themselves express a wide variety of motivations, aspirations, experiences and practices that belie a unified conceptualisation of their agency. In this chapter we examine these varying roles, perspectives and positions for teachers across Myanmar's education systems, with a particular focus on the experiences of government school and MNEC school teachers as they adapt to the changing educational and post-conflict landscape of Mon State. We go on to relate these experiences to opportunities for promoting peace and social justice, looking in detail at the

E. J. T. Maber (✉)
University of Cambridge, Cambridge, UK
e-mail: ejtm2@cam.ac.uk

H. W. M. Oo
B.S.I. Learning Academy, Yangon, Myanmar

S. Higgins
University of Amsterdam, Amsterdam, The Netherlands

M. T. A. Lopes Cardozo, E. J. T. Maber (eds.), *Sustainable Peacebuilding and Social Justice in Times of Transition*,
https://doi.org/10.1007/978-3-319-93812-7_6

history curriculum and processes of curriculum reform as offering opportunities to address historical tensions and inequalities.

Our research data was gathered between January and April 2015, with the school year ending in March, resulting in a limited timeframe to engage with ongoing school practices. As a result, data was largely not gathered through observations within classrooms, but occurred through interviews and small group discussions conducted both within and beyond the bounds of learning institutions. These interviews included: members of the Ministry of Education; government school teachers, head teachers and Township Education Officers from two townships in Mon state; MNEC school teachers and head teachers from three townships in Mon state; teacher educators and university lecturers in the Yangon region; group discussions with community education teachers from seven states; the head of a monastic school; representatives of teacher unions and the NNER; and national and international staff of (I)NGOs and international agencies conducting teacher training and education support as well as engaged in education reform and drafting the NESP. The research presented in this chapter therefore draws from interviews and group discussions with 115 respondents.

Beginning with an overview of the position of teachers in contemporary Myanmar society, the subsequent section draws attention to the interlinked dimensions of the gendered nature of the teaching profession, the influence of low salaries in contributing to teachers' motivations and attitudes towards their roles, and the widespread practice by many school teachers of after-school tuition.

Positioning Teachers in Contemporary Myanmar

Traditionally in Myanmar, teachers have been held in high esteem within communities, and students are expected to hold a similar level of respect for their teachers as they do for the *Sangha* and their parents. Concurrently, teaching has long been viewed as a profession of goodwill, interest and self-sacrifice (Lwin 2000; Tin 2000). The status of the profession, however, has been undermined by the chronic underinvestment in the education sector as a whole. Nonetheless, the traditionally high status afforded to teachers within the country's rigid social structures creates strong hierarchies between teachers and students, with the latter expected to be subservient to their teachers. Teaching practices have generally followed teacher-centred and authoritarian pedagogies, with a prominence of rote learning, instruction and replication rather than learner-centred or participatory approaches. As it is generally seen as inappropriate for students to engage in dialogue or shared decision-making with their teachers, this creates significant challenges to shift classroom pedagogy towards more child-friendly practices. Tin (2000) notes that teachers as a group have been, "highly conservative and traditionalist" (115), and resisted attempts to shift pedagogy away from rote learning. Lall (2011) however, in exploring the more recent push of child-centred pedagogies by international agencies within monastic schools, revealed a more nuanced picture, suggesting that this conservatism is of a principled nature. Namely, the belief of teachers, parents, and head monks, is that a 'western approach' serves to undermine the traditional hierarchical structures of respect for teachers and elders, and potentially could create a culture clash in homes and classrooms if implemented. Such beliefs have also led to a resistance on the part of teachers to changing practices of corporal punishment, which are still widespread, inside classrooms (UNICEF 2012). With diverging presentations of teachers' roles and positions, the sections below examine some of the influencing factors affecting teachers before exploring the varied perceptions encountered in the research.

Gender and Teaching

Teaching in Myanmar is a highly gendered profession, with over 80% of teachers in the state sector being women (MoE 2013), with the result that there may be "*in many schools, [only] one or two or three male teachers*" (int. 19). Issues of gender and expected roles for men and women are therefore closely related to teaching practices and have implications for the perceptions of teachers and their duties as well as for understanding policy impact such as in deployment. Gender hierarchies are also reproduced in the sector, with the result that although there is a high proportion of female teachers at primary, middle and high school levels, amongst head teachers the proportion drops (MoE 2013), and more senior positions are commonly held by men. This pattern was also evident in the research process, with the majority of teachers interviewed being female, head teachers interviewed reflecting a more even balance and township education officers being predominantly male.

Many attributed the high numbers of women in teaching to the low salaries of the profession which has contributed to a lowering of the status traditionally afforded teachers. One teacher educator explained:

> In Myanmar, mostly teachers are women. I think because of salary. Men are the leaders of their families. So they should get high salaries, but in Myanmar teacher salaries are very low. So mostly men don't want to take teachers' duty. (int. 19)

This was also perceived to have been exacerbated over the last decade, as one retired male teacher reflected on the feminization of the teaching profession he had witnessed:

> Most of the teachers are women and there are few men...it is very rare to find [male teachers], you see. [At] the time we are working, because when I joined the education department, I worked as a senior assistant teacher, [at] that time, there are a lot of men joining education, now you see the situation quite different. And [now] only women are joining, most of the people who are joining teacher professions are women. Men are not joining, because men are joining other professions or other area which is more like, financially more resourceful or something like that. So they are seeking such kind of jobs, you see. (int. 16)

Inequalities in status between male and female teachers were identified by several teachers interviewed, with some female state teachers identifying the process of deployment (discussed further in Chap. 7) as particularly disadvantageous. With teachers being deployed arbitrarily around the country once they have completed training, some female teachers reported feeling insecure in unfamiliar and remote areas (int. 122). Undertaking a teaching post in a remote or conflict-affected area was identified as a route to promotion, and consequently women felt disadvantaged in their career development where male teachers were more likely to be willing to take up or remain in such postings (ints. 122 and 123). The vulnerability of (particularly female) teachers to violence is also further explored below.

Beyond the state sector, high numbers of female teachers are also evident in ethnic and community education sectors, as one Mon teacher working in the MNEC sector highlighted:

> [For] MNEC about more than 90%, maybe 95% or 98% of the teachers are women. So they only have some point percent of [male] teachers at Mon national schools, among 800 teachers, maybe about 10 or 20 male teachers. (int. 52)

Again, low salaries were identified as a source of the feminization of the profession and an obstacle for women's equality both within society and within the family as female teachers were dependent on financial support. The same Mon teacher continued: "*We want … supporting salaries. That's not enough. If women have not enough income, then how can they support their family?*" (int. 52). Additionally, as many ethnic education systems are associated closely with ethnic armed groups and the struggle for auto-determination, ethnic schools have been identified as an accepted sphere for the female contribution to ethnic nation-building, which has reinforced the perception of teaching as a female role (Laungaramsri 2011; Maber 2016).

In the monastic sector, however, although many teachers come from the surrounding community and may be male or female, the masculine environment of the monastery and greater numbers of monks teaching leads this sector to be seen as more male dominated than other teaching contexts. In urban areas where there may be greater variety of available schooling options the effect of this masculinization may be limited (int. 15), as is apparent in the case study in Mawlamyine discussed in Chap. 8. However, in rural and remote areas girls and their parents can be less likely to consider monastic schools as welcoming learning environments limiting their educational pathways (ints. 4 and 23). Reflecting religious hierarchies, nuns do not occupy the same position of status within the community as monks, leaving the few nunnery schools that exist severely underfunded and lacking donations, with nuns teaching often without any access to training (int. 23).

The Influence of Low Salaries

Teacher salaries, as discussed in Chap. 5, while raised in recent years continue to be inadequate for many teachers to sustain an independent living. Prior to 2009, a primary school teacher's salary averaged around only 30,000 kyat ($22) per month, increasing to 40,000 kyat ($30) per month for senior middle school teachers (World

Bank 2015, 50). Annual increases in salaries since 2011 have seen these figures rise to an average of approximately 90,000 kyat ($67) per month for primary teachers and 145,000 kyat ($107) per month for senior middle school teachers by 2015 (World Bank 2015, 50). While the increase is significant, the monthly salaries nonetheless remain low and this pattern of low pay has compelled many teachers to take second jobs or to offer private after-school tutorials for a fee (UNICEF 2012) (further discussed below). Many rural families provide supplementary support to teachers in order to retain them, including additional salary, food, living quarters, water and firewood. However, this additional support for teachers located in remote regions has generally remained insufficient, and such communities suffer high rates of teacher attrition (UNICEF 2012). In some cases, teachers have sought bribes or favours from students to pass examinations, an issue that Tin (2000) suggests serves to undermine the traditional value and status placed on the profession.

A strong sense of duty and of performing a service was expressed by several teachers and teacher educators participating in the research. This was articulated both in relation to a Buddhist philosophical approach to teaching as moral guidance (ints. 19 and 106) and as a service to the community irrespective of religion (int. 124). For some Buddhist teacher educators, teaching this understanding of duty to trainee teachers was also seen as a service to the nation aligned with a sense of patriotism, as one female teacher educator expressed: "*I shall train them how to behave in the classroom, how to nurture the pupils, how to love our spirit, how to love Myanmar culture*" (int. 19). The same teacher educator continued:

> We all have low salary in education but we are used to this. So it is not important for us. So it is a factor for life but we've taken into account for salary. As well as my students, I always see that salary is very low, maybe low but we contribute our knowledge and practice as [best] we can. (int. 19)

This view of the role of teachers also led some more senior members of the teaching profession to express a certain suspicion of the current education reforms, associating them with a loss of dedication to service amongst teachers that was strongly linked to Buddhist notions of the teacher. As one senior teacher educator, now leading a resource centre, lamented: "*Teachers are motivated now by salary. It's a job where you can get an easy salary, now that salaries have increased. They are not motivated by duty [anymore]*" (int. 106). Such opinions reflect the impact of policy reform in changing the nature of the teaching profession and again point to the wide variety of conceptualisations that teachers bring to their own roles.

Further reform implications were hinted at in relation to the gendered nature of the teaching profession, where the majority of teachers and teacher educators are female. Anecdotally, it appeared that more male trainee teachers were applying to the education colleges in 2015 compared to previous years, with teacher educators speculating that they may have been attracted by the salary increase for teachers (int. 102). Follow up research will be required in the coming years to verify if this pattern is confirmed and to further explore the gender implications of such a shift for the profession.

The Practice of Tuition

The practice of offering private after-school classes is widespread in Myanmar, with many teachers offering tutoring to students in their homes or in informal private schools from primary through to high school grades. The practice has also very recently spread to higher education institutions, with students seeking private classes as an alternative to attending university lectures. One student recounted arriving for a university lecture to find that he was the only student in attendance and, not wanting to disturb his teacher who was working on the computer, he quietly left (int. 113). Such an alteration of the expected roles of teacher and student therefore has significant implications for the relationship of trust between teacher and learner.

In two separate discussions, a small group of teachers and a group of recent high school graduates in Yangon were asked about their experiences teaching and attending private tuition classes after school hours. Amongst teachers, tutoring was viewed as integral to the academic system to support unrealistic assessment targets: "*almost all of the students in our country depend on these tuition classes in order to achieve success in their academic years*" (int. 112). One teacher also highlighted the pedagogical freedom offered by private classes in comparison to what she perceived to be the constraining environment of the state school. However, the potential for private classes to undermine the role of teachers in the state system was also clear: "*on the other hand, teachers may rather pay greater attention on their private ones than teaching at school*" (int. 112). Anecdotes are numerous of teachers withholding teaching from their formal classes in order to encourage students to attend tuition, or not passing students who failed to attend paid classes (ints. 4, 16 and 125). The most commonly identified motivation is the need to supplement meagre teacher salaries, supported by those interviewed who encouraged reform as a way to alleviate the pressures:

> In fact, I hate such tuition. But academic staff are broke with the government salary only. So it should be all inclusive and integrated approach to reform the best custom. (int. 112)

Teacher trainers were also critical of the practice, seeing it as eroding their authority as skilled professionals, and identifying students and parents as driving the expansion of tutoring by desiring 'answers' for the rigid assessment system:

> It's also from the students' side, because they only want a short cut that they want to memorize. So [the] easy way, I mean. [...] And then, in order to pass the exam, they [...] prefer the private tuitions. (int. 19)

Conversely, although overall it is hoped they could manage without it, students themselves had mixed views of attending tuitions. Sharing the view of some teachers on the positive learning environment, some students appreciated the close attention they got from teachers in private classes arguing that "*more attention can be gained by teachers in private tuition due to the smaller size of it compared to school and university*" (int. 113). However, they also identified the practice as undermining teachers' roles as well as the relationship between teacher and student:

> If a student [relies too much] on private tuition, there will be lack of respect between students and teachers at school since students won't pay much attention on what they have

> been taught at school, and teachers also might not teach well by assuming that they will be taught at private tuition, which is also somehow related to the unethical behaviour of both students and teacher. (int. 113)

Some students additionally responded with sensitivity to their teachers' positions, showing they were aware of the financial motivations behind the extra classes and were sympathetic to their teachers' situations: "*since the paid salary is a bit lower than it should be, it is necessary for them to make money by means of private classes*" (int. 113). Equally, students identified the potential for reform in the education system to reduce the need for tutoring. The hope then, for both students and teachers alike, is that education reforms can promote more egalitarian teaching practices.

Varying Perceptions of Teachers' Roles

In addition to the influences which impact on teachers' positions within society as highlighted above, teachers are also perceived differently by different actors, particularly in the context of the education reforms instigated by the USDP government of 2011–2016. These framings have a tendency to amalgamate teachers into a homogenous group, which can have dual implications in both obscuring the varying practices and experiences of diversely motivated teachers, and also projecting a unified presentation of teachers' identities which excludes those who fall outside this vision. The sections below explore these contrasting presentations of teachers, first as they emerge from policy discourses around the education sector reforms and subsequently as teachers and teacher educators themselves expressed their roles.

Framing Teachers in Policy Discourse

Within the current education reforms we see multiple framings of teacher roles, but frequently without acknowledgement of their varied identities, capacity and agency. So in the context of the 'Quick Wins' platform, discussed in Chap. 5, 30,000 primary teachers have been deployed around the country as daily-wage teachers with very limited training as preparation. Such responses to the acute shortage of teachers, especially in remote and conflict-affected areas, are generally welcomed. However, the implication that pressures on schools will be eased merely with more individuals in classrooms, without acknowledging the skills those teachers require, may be problematic. Likewise, questions have emerged as to who is categorized as a teacher. The National Education Law, originally passed in September 2014, defines a teacher as "someone sufficiently qualified and who teaches a particular level or standard of education" (Union of Myanmar 2014, *translated*). The fact that the many teachers beyond the government schooling system, in monastic, community and parallel ethnic education sectors are largely without formal training (further discussed in Chaps. 7 and 8), renders this categorization of teachers contentious and exclusive. Likewise, there is a failure to acknowledge or address discriminatory structures that allow access to teacher training programmes, as highlighted by one national trainer working within an international organisation:

> Something that comes up outstanding in Rakhine is the issue of teachers' bias in conflict[-affected] populations. This is really difficult because there is a lot of [discrimination]. Some are teaches as well and in Rakhine in most places, the Muslims can't be teachers, either having been trained as teachers or more important those policies, legal blockages to Muslim people entering civil service. (int. 77)

The exclusive nature of civil service and teacher education has implications for multiple marginalised groups, who fail to see themselves represented within education structures. Disabled students and young adults similarly drew attention to the fact that people with disabilities are not permitted to enrol in teacher training, leading to an absence of any teachers with disabilities within state schools (int. 126). This lack of representation is further compounded by a lack of attention to the needs of students with disabilities within teacher education programmes, reinforcing the perpetuation of learning environments that frequently fail to be inclusive of marginalised groups.

In general, perceptions of teachers as individuals are vastly lacking in discourses, with the result that teachers continue to be instrumentalised within the education system. This tendency neglects the vast differences between teachers' practices, which most directly affect students' experiences in schools. One cause identified by a former teacher and teacher educator was the lack of monitoring:

> When the technical monitoring team came to those school, their focus is not on what is really happening in the classroom, teaching – learning process. And their focus is on what kind of material the school has and so on, you see. (int. 16)

Consequently, the reality for students in school with regard to the quality of teaching they receive can be underappreciated. For teacher policy planning therefore, a major challenge lies in addressing these vast variations in practice where there is often little information available. The highly different contexts for schools in terms of geographical situation, security, resources, personnel and student composition, are also not readily understood by international actors, often on short term assignments and in the absence of significant qualitative data (int. 79). This has led to some frustration at the large numbers of international consultants connected to the CESR and the drafting of the NESP, which, while drawing heavily on a global understanding of teacher policy and sector planning, has not always been perceived as sufficiently contextualized (ints. 79 and 110).

Teachers' Own Perceptions of Their Roles

In comparison to the homogenising view of teachers that can appear in both policy and popular discourse, teachers themselves highlighted the varied nature of teachers as individuals, often citing observed 'good' and 'bad' behaviour amongst colleagues (ints. 16, 19 and 20). It is also apparent that teaching is not a static profession as teachers often held multiple roles and individuals, particularly in ethnic schools and community settings, had often worked in different spheres before becoming teachers (ints. 17, 23 and 124). Likewise, particularly in the government sector, many teachers left the profession after a few years, or changed position to work more broadly on education or development issues beyond the classroom (ints. 103, 110, 122 and 123).

While teachers expressed differing motivations for their work, a frequent recurrence within discussions amongst teachers in both Yangon and Mon State were tensions between what they hoped for their role and the practicalities of the tasks they faced. Reflecting the traditional position of teachers within Myanmar society, teachers across the range of school systems viewed themselves as leaders in their communities, as this teacher trainer in Yangon expressed:

> We are community leaders, I think. So not only teaching in the schools is important but also leadership role in community is a bit important. (int. 19)

This was articulated as a source of opportunity, but was hindered by the additional tasks teachers felt they were burdened with. Teachers from primary level to university lecturers were exasperated by the demands placed on their time beyond the roles they saw for themselves as teachers. Teachers felt exhausted by the dense curriculum that allows little space for creativity (ints. 20 and 21), and by non-teaching tasks that include overseeing car parking and patrolling school grounds (ints. 100 and 110). This was also particularly a problem for university lecturers who were unable to undertake research as their teaching and administrative tasks were so heavy, leading one lecturer to comment "*teachers are security guards now!*" (int. 110). Older teachers expressed sympathy for their younger colleagues as demands were seen to have increased: "*they don't have time to prepare for their lessons, so they are just entering the classroom without any preparation*" (int. 16). Internationally supported training, techniques and additional subjects such as life-skills were also sometimes seen as merely adding to this workload (ints. 93 and 110). As one government school teacher in rural Mon State confessed:

> Sometimes the new techniques we are learning now are complicated and we don't know what to do. Only when the monitor comes do we prepare records – for their sake, we are not really doing it. Teachers are too tired so they cannot row the boat. (int. 93)

Additionally, as further discussed below, the perception of the respected status of the teaching practice, despite low salaries, may accentuate the frustration that some government school teachers expressed when feeling their position was not welcome in a community (int. 16) or their authority not respected by students (ints. 19 and 20).

Perspectives on Teacher Preparation

While teacher education will be discussed more thoroughly in Chap. 7, the perspectives of teacher educators and teachers from varying sectors on the preparation and support for their roles also resonate with the ways in which teacher practice is understood. Consequently, a brief discussion of teachers' experiences of training is included here before examining accounts of observed teacher practice in the classroom.

Generally, teachers at primary schools are trained at Education Colleges and have completed the 2-year Diploma in Education. To qualify to teach at the upper secondary level, government teachers are required to attend the 5 year bachelor degree in education (B.Ed.) course (recently increased from 4 years) provided by one of the two Universities of Education in Yangon and Sagaing, in comparison to lower grade teachers who can train at one of the 22 Teacher Education Colleges around the country. Once qualified, teachers may be deployed to teach at any location across the country, with limited influence over where they might be placed.[1] Likewise, those teachers who have completed their bachelor degree in B.Ed. are appointed at middle or high schools regardless of their preferred specialism, as highlighted in the text box below.

A Former Teacher's Account of Her Training

Researcher with the Research Consortium and co-author, Hla Win May Oo, here writes of her experiences training as a school teacher in 2001–2005.

Upon the successful completion of my matriculation exam, I joined the Yangon Institute of Education (IoE), which is now renamed as the Yangon University of Education, in 2001, at the age of 17. There are two Universities of Education in Myanmar, one in Yangon and one in Sagaing. I transferred to Yangon IoE from Sagaing IoE as the latter is very far away from Sagaing Town due to transportation problems and other shortages (as it was newly established at that time).

There were only 48 of us who met the criteria to join the IoE directly right after the matriculation (called direct intake). There were only a few direct intake candidates at that time. Before then, the candidates at the Institutes of Education had been those who had finished their Diploma in Education at an education college and had some years of experience in the primary schools (called College of Education, or COE, intake). So there were still a great deal of COE intake trainees. In 2002, it went on like this, but later on, they started allowing more direct intake trainees.

The B.Ed course in our days was a 4-year program. Now it takes 5 years to complete it. During the first 2 years, we studied all the subjects like Myanmar, English, Mathematics, and any two of those science or arts subjects; from Chemistry, Physics and Biology if you specialized in Science, whereas for those who were Arts majors, they were to choose any two from History, Economics and Geography. There was no one taking any arts subjects in my batch.

(continued)

[1] This has led to reports of teachers offering financial incentives to those within the administration so that they might be allocated a post in their preferred location (int. 122).

During the 3rd and 4th years, we went on studying our chosen two science/arts subjects and we were to major in only one from the other subjects (Myanmar, English or Mathematics). Those above mentioned subjects are called academic subjects, and we also studied educational subjects such as Educational Psychology, Educational Theory, Educational Administration, Educational Statistics and Educational Methodology, etc. There are also PGDMA (Post-graduate Diploma in Multi-media Aided Teaching) and PGDT (Post-graduate Diploma in Teaching) offered at Yangon Institute of Education. Any graduates can take the entrance exam and upon passing this, they can join these courses. If they are assigned at schools where there are no multi-media aids like computers, they become teachers who teach the subjects for which there are no teachers assigned.

Despite your specialization at the institute, you are required to teach any subjects that you are assigned by the principal when you become a teacher at a basic education school. I have some science specialized friends having to teach arts subjects and English majored ones teaching Myanmar and so on. Those who were not happy with it ended up resigning from their teaching posts. Upon completion of the B.Ed, the trained teachers are appointed nationwide. There are some drop-out teachers, meaning they don't work at government basic education schools, due to transportation problems and lack of safety at the remote areas. I am one of those drop-out teachers. Some of my juniors dropped out after working for some months or a year due to the practices of the principals and education officers which they found unbearable or unacceptable.

The logistics, upheaval and expense of undertaking such training can make it difficult for aspiring teachers from ethnic minority and rural areas to access these institutions. As a result, the correct or incorrect association of government school teachers as belonging to the majority (Bamar, Buddhist) population is further reinforced, often leading to such teachers being perceived as outsiders in the areas they are deployed. One teacher educator had observed a stark contrast between the ways in which community teachers and government teachers were welcomed within the same township, highlighting tensions between teachers resulting from deployment practices:

> The community love [the local community teachers] and they also provide them residential quarters and also something to eat and whatever they have. And when such kind of things are happening, government appointed teachers said they should also... the community should also support them in that way. But they are not, you see, treating children in the way that community appointed teachers are doing. So ... there are some kind of conflicts in some areas. (int. 16)

Differences between teachers working in the various education sectors were further highlighted by education practitioners' own contrasting views of teachers' practices. Within the ethnic education sector there was a pride expressed by teachers and head teachers that their pedagogical approaches to teaching were more progressive and sensitive to student needs than in the government schools, as one MNEC head teacher explained:

> For the assessment, in our project township, we include more about children participation and their feelings. Now, in the exam, when we ask them to write about the plants that grow in the water, the students can write what they know not exactly from the textbooks ... even the township officer give the guideline to focus on the children feelings and opinions and participation and we give marks on that. The students here can express their own opinion and we don't have limitation for their answers. (int. 60)

This also reflects the conclusions of research conducted on contrasting student experiences in formal state and non-formal community learning environments, where students characterized their interactions with state school teachers as dominated by fear (Maber 2016). In contrast, learning experiences in community education environments, in this case provided by ethnic-affiliated women's organisations, were appreciated because of the more egalitarian relationship with teachers, where students felt more confident to ask questions and to share 'teaching' roles within the classroom with their peers (Maber 2016).

Discussions of the perceptions of teacher roles and practices amongst teacher educators also revealed perspectives and examples of observed practice amongst teachers that are rarely reflected within either policy or literature, and which demonstrated a widely differing spectrum of behaviour. One example had been witnessed of a teacher displaying the results of the class examination months before students had taken the test:

> So I asked the headmistress 'the examination is only going to take place in February and the result is already there [in September]. Why do [it] like that?' She said 'because when we announce that list, pass list, it is the same whether it is now or whether it is in February'. (int. 16)

In this scenario, teachers demonstrated a casual disregard for the potential of their students to learn and develop. However, as illustrated in the text box below, other observations were cited of government teachers who had developed strategies for mutual language learning with students in ethnic minority areas, learning selected phrases from students' mother-tongue language to aid communication in class, or voluntarily teaching language classes or agricultural skills before or after the school days according to the needs of their students (int. 16). Likewise, Township Education Officers were encountered in Mon State who encouraged mutual language learning in their schools (int. 39). Such examples of cooperation in schools across ethnic divides were present, but had often gone unnoticed amid a climate of limited shared information (int. 89).

A Teacher Trainer's Account of Observing Plural Language Use

With over 100 different languages spoken in Myanmar and many in ethnic territories not speaking the official national language of Burmese, the issue of language of instruction in classrooms has been a central tension in education policy (South and Lall 2016). However, the practices of individual teachers within formal classrooms may facilitate moments of smoothing through introducing opportunities for multi-directional language learning.

Interviewed in Yangon, a senior teacher trainer who had spent two decades training in the state education sector, reflected on an instance he had observed while travelling to monitor teacher progress in state schools, which highlighted strategies employed by individual teachers in working with multiple languages in the classroom. The experienced trainer recounted observing a newly qualified state school teacher who was deployed to Shan State repeating the two phrases she had learned in Pa-Oh language:

> How do you call it in Pa-Oh? [and] This is called – in Myanmar. So she learned only that …two phrases and she started communicating with the children. (int. 16)

In so doing, the teacher not only encouraged Burmese language learning amongst her students but also placed herself within the frame of learning as a student of Pa-Oh language, creating a momentary disruption in the hierarchy of the class. The teacher trainer continued, explaining the strategies of the observed teacher in seeking to support horizontal learning between students:

> Another thing is she also asked the parents, saying 'I would like to teach your children how to speak in Myanmar language. Can you send your children one hour ahead in the morning and also one hour ahead in the evening?' So people are very pleased. So they are sent one hour ahead and she organized such kind of meeting. (int. 16)

In these extra classes before and after the school day the teacher encouraged students of varied ages to practice their Myanmar language together and learn practical phrases from each other. The anecdote illustrates the continued possibilities to undo fixed roles, albeit briefly, which persist even within highly constrained environments. However, the structure of school days is unyielding in this case, and consequently the teacher resorts to creating these moments for alternative peer learning beyond the framework of the school day. Likewise, although the teacher is herself attempting to build connections through reciprocal learning of Pa-Oh language, the educational policies prioritising the promotion of Burmese (and in some cases English) as the language of instruction, curriculum and assessment remain unchanged. Such practices therefore remain dependent on the nature and inclination of individual teachers, rather than affecting institutional change, as the teacher trainer recounting the observation reflected: "*she got this kind of idea [herself], she didn't get it from the training*" (int. 16). Nonetheless, these alternative relationships will be carried through in the course of the day, potentially enacting small changes in the learning experiences of the individual students.

The varied practices of individual teachers, as well as the differences in position and motivation between teachers working in the different education systems, have significant impact in contributing to inclusive or exclusionary environments for learners within the classroom. In situations of conflict, these practices can have substantial implications for contributing to tensions or to promoting reconciliation. Consequently, the following sections examine in more detail the roles and specific situations between conflict and peace of teachers participating in the research.

Between Conflict and Peace

As expectations of the roles and practices of teachers vary, so likewise the opportunities for teachers to contribute positively to peacebuilding are also varied and frequently constrained. Reflecting the dual potential for education in conflict-affected contexts to exacerbate tensions or to contribute to peacebuilding (Davies 2010; Bush and Saltarelli 2000), the multiple dimensions of teachers' identities, skills and practices within the different education systems can likewise support or hinder peacebuilding. Additionally, teachers may themselves be targets of violence and the precarity of their situation leads to increased insecurity in their position. The subsequent sections explore these dimensions of teachers' positions between conflict and peace, concluding with an exploration of the subject of history teaching as expressed by government and MNEC school teachers in Mon State.

Navigating Experiences of Violence

Given the nature of teacher deployment across the country, the vulnerability of teachers to direct violence in conflict where they may be isolated from familial and social support networks was raised by several teachers and trainers (int. 15), and also intersects with the gendered nature of the profession, as discussed above. As many teachers are women, they expressed a vulnerability when being placed in remote or conflict-affected areas that they were unfamiliar with (int. 122). While some teachers reported a great sense of connection to their community environments when teaching, and saw these as a source of support (ints. 16, 20 and 21), others felt they had not made, or were not given the opportunity to make, these embedded relationships that might contribute to a reduced feeling of vulnerability. For many women across Myanmar, from diverse religious, ethnic and political backgrounds, the presence of soldiers in the highly militarised areas is a source of threat (WLB 2014). Therefore, even despite positive relationships within the school environment and with parents, female teachers may feel no more secure in their position. Teachers working across the different education sectors experience these insecurities differently. The much-publicised case of rape and murder of two Kachin community teachers in Northern Shan State[2] in 2015 was referenced on several occasions by teachers and trainers interviewed, and held a particular resonance for community teachers and those trainers that frequently travelled to visit schools across the country. The attack may ultimately not have been a deliberate attack on teachers, but rather an opportune assault on women, however it underscores the particular risk that female teachers experience. With very low salaries, or in this case as volunteers, the teachers are often not able to access secure housing. Risks are also prevalent in travelling for teachers, trainers and students alike, particularly where the laying of landmines has been a common practice by multiple parties to the conflicts.

While teachers may experience violence, they can also be both complicit in and responsible for its reproduction. Although not addressed in policy texts, corporal punishment is still widely practiced, as reported by teachers and teacher educators:

> There are many cases I have witnessed with my own eyes … you have to kneel; put your knees on floor and stand with your knees on the floor [for] thirty minutes. And also he put some kind of seeds [under the knees]. (int. 16)

Such practices were seen as reflecting and reinforcing a wider culture of violence, which frequently characterised hierarchical relationships. As one international education staff member highlighted, the challenge for training was reflected in "*how to maintain this [training] in the classroom without the use of intimidation, fear or violence in their students, who are coming from homes where that's still the way to control the children.*" (int. 78). As is further explored in Chap. 10, teachers were also viewed by others as complicit, intentionally or otherwise, in the reproduction of dominant hierarchies that reinforce marginalisation through their failure to promote critical thinking skills and to deviate from curriculum texts (int. 110). Pedagogy, educational structures and exam systems can therefore support reproductions of violence through rewarding obedience, repetition and replication rather than negotiation, lateral thinking or mediation skills. Likewise, the teaching of history was particularly identified as problematic in reproducing discourses of dominance over minority groups, as is further explored below.

Teachers' Views of the History Curriculum and Its Relation to Peacebuilding

As also discussed in Chap. 8, the teaching of history in schools has been contentious and a particular grievance amongst ethnic minorities, which has exacerbated conflict and social divisions. While the case study in Chap. 8 focuses on the experiences and inequalities identified by ethnic Mon teachers within the MNEC schools, here

[2] The rape and murder was alleged to have been carried out by soldiers stationed in the area, however the subsequent investigation failed to confirm this.

we explore the perspectives of both MNEC and government school teachers on using current history curricula and their hopes for the revised curricula which are forthcoming.

Teachers in both government and ethnic school systems were aware of their obligation to work within prescribed history curricula whose content was partisan and could generate inter-ethnic animosity. One teacher in a Mon-ethnic MNEC school highlighted the division between a Mon and a Burmese centred history curriculum, pointing out that *"our heroes are their enemies and our enemies are their heroes"* (int. 61). Another recognised the exclusive concerns of the history curriculum taught in ethnic schools: *"right now the MNEC curriculum is talking only about Mon"* (int. 61). Such views reflect Metro's findings that history textbooks used in government schools have been perceived to be *"Burman centric"* by ethnic minorities, while *"ethnonationalist organisations that run schools aspire to teach children the history of their own ethnic group as opposed to the history of Burma as a whole"* (Metro 2013, 150). Teachers in both systems also expressed their awareness of their limited pedagogic practices recognizing that they were generally teacher led: *"the students have to follow what the teachers say and if they make any mistakes they lose marks"* (int. 60). Such views indicate teachers' awareness of their location as agents within a prescriptive curricula that reinforced division as well as functioned to deter students from critical questioning of a received body of information.

However, while mindful of working within such constraints, teachers also demonstrated faith in the possibilities of the subject to impact positively on the growth and behaviour of young people. History was perceived, both within MNEC schools and government schools, to be a subject that offered young people a body of role models of ethical behaviours as well as situations from which they could learn and *"imitate"* (ints. 60, 61 and 93). From the subject young people could *"take the good things as examples and avoid the bad things"* (int. 93). For one government school teacher the subject offered *"lessons from the past… in order not to become like this again in the future"* (int. 60). Moreover, its potential for developing in young people *"a love of the nation"* (int. 60) was also underlined. The subject's relevance also extended to its role in contributing to peacebuilding. Current curriculum reforms being overseen by the Mon National Ethnic Committee were noted as motivated by an awareness of the importance of the subject to improve opportunities for peacebuilding (ints. 58 and 61). A particular concern was the glorification of violence within the current history curriculum for ethnic schools. As Metro has noted, one of the goals of the MNEC reforms of their history curriculum is to *"encourage a spirit of unity with other ethnic groups and avoid perpetuating conflict"* (Metro 2015, 5).

Recognising the subject's potential to contribute to peacebuilding, some government school teachers critiqued the biases of curriculum content as undermining the subject's potential to encourage views and attitudes that would ameliorate ethnic discrimination. Such critiques resulted in some teachers acknowledging their mediating role in rendering the content of the subject more acceptable to ethnic minority students. For example, a teacher in a government school expressed awareness of the potential of its Bamar dominated content to generate alienation amongst ethnic minority students. She drew attention to her commitment to presenting the subject in such a way as to de-emphasise its contribution to inter-ethnic animosity:

> We always discuss in the meeting about how can [we] teach it to be peaceful… and we tell them that all ethnic groups live in Myanmar country so that they must say we are all Myanmar citizens. (int. 60)

Moreover, other teachers explained how they glossed subjects that appeared to legitimate ethnic conflict such that *"we consider to teach them as if it is not the ethnic war and it is just the war of the king to get the land"* (int. 60). The ethnocentricity of the curricula taught within the ethnic system was also critiqued such that one informant noted that *"if the history is biased people from different ethnic groups cannot have peace"* (int. 58). Such examples illustrate how some teachers in Myanmar, even within a prescriptive curriculum, aim to "swim against the current", as Metro has pointed out (Metro 2015, 12). These rather courageous teachers provide their students with an experience that runs counter to the ideological biases of prevailing curriculum orthodoxies.

A similar desire to offer students a different learning experience from that commonly used in history teaching was evident in teacher's discussions of using creative pedagogical methods to stimulate interest and motivation. Aware that teacher led exposition might bore students, some teachers from both ethnic and government schools reflected on creative ways of communicating the subject including role plays, or making connections between the past and the present (ints. 59, 60 and 61). As one teacher from a rural township noted:

> For the history teaching we teach the lessons from the textbooks and we tell them what is happening now, so they can relate things. The teacher has to prepare more to do this. (int. 60)

When asked about their views on reforming the content of the curriculum, some teachers in both government and ethnic schools mentioned the inclusion of history post-Myanmar's independence to enable the subject to be more relevant to students (ints. 60 and 93).

However, even while pointing to the role of the subject in breaking down ethnocentric prejudices, teachers also appeared to convey an attachment to exclusive and sectarian understandings of the subject. When invited to specify what the content of the history curriculum should be for their schools, some teachers within the ethnic system emphasised that its sole focus should be on the history and traditions of their Kings and their people (int. 59) within a narrative that stressed their unique suffering and sacrifice (ints. 42 and 59). Such views were underpinned by a perception of the subject as a vehicle of preservation of a distinctive ethnic cultural identity and its inter-generational transmission. As one teacher put it, *"the purpose is not to lose their Mon identity and carry it on to the new generation"* (int. 61). Here, teachers' views resonate with attitudes current within the larger Mon ethnic community and local historians (McCormick 2014b). Their understanding of the purpose of the subject reflects that mission to "write a singular past" (McCormick 2014a, 300) which McCormick has explained is a result of a sense of "impending danger" that their "language, culture and history" is under threat (McCormick 2014a, 309).

Aligning with such viewpoints on the function of history, teachers implicitly present themselves as guardians of their culture, responding to grassroots community expectations.

Opportunities for Promoting Peace and Social Justice

Listening to teachers' perceptions and experiences underlines on the one hand the capacity of the curricula to frame their practices in such a way as to undermine their roles as agents of social cohesion. On the other hand, we heard evidence of teachers working against the 'curricular grain' and seeking to counter its potential to breed inter-ethnic animosity in the spaces of their classrooms and relationships with students. This confirms evidence cited by Metro (2015, 7) that even within a highly authoritarian and repressive educational system, in which students and teachers have been punished for using their creative thinking skills, in schools some are "using the system in a different way" (Metro 2015). However, such examples of the exercise of peacebuilding agency outside of curricula expectations also co-exist with teachers articulating highly exclusive and ethnocentric conceptions of the subject and its truths. Teacher agency, particularly in relation to history teaching as outlined above, is conditioned by community expectations of the role of certain subjects in the preservation of distinctive ethnic identities, compromising the prospect of using the classroom to promote inter-ethnic understanding. In seeking to mobilise history teaching for ethnocentric as well as more tolerant and pluralistic purposes linked explicitly to peacebuilding, these Myanmar teachers present what has been referred to as the "double-sided nature of their role" (Horner et al. 2015, 40). Yet perhaps the most important message to emerge from our research is the relevance of engaging the teacher voice in order to build understanding of the complex impacts of curricula in driving, defining and compromising their agency as peacebuilders.

However, the possibilities for teachers to contribute to peacebuilding within and beyond their classrooms were not limited to those teaching history. As highlighted above, some teachers identified a role for themselves as builders of peace within their communities. Perhaps unsurprisingly, this characterisation was more commonly identified by those working in communities more directly affected by conflict, including by Mon teachers working in the MNEC schools. One teacher for example indicated:

> The teachers and head teachers see themselves as peace builders in the classroom and also in the community, because they are not only teaching but also help students with their behaviours. In the community teachers have to work with the parents on both children's learning and behaviour. (int. 63)

As the quote above suggestions, notions of building peace however were largely attributed to teaching interpersonal behaviour to students to avoid fighting in the classroom, while also acknowledging the need to address students' wellbeing. Likewise, another MNEC teacher also reflected:

> We can develop […] the spirit of working together, teach them to help them have a good standard of living and this will help them not to fight. (int. 59)

Equally, MNEC teachers were more likely to express this position than government or Yangon based teachers, pointing to differing priorities in the school systems. Emphasis amongst these teachers was placed on positive experiences in the classroom as building a peaceful environment: "*in socializing and in their work and also in teaching if the teacher can teach the lesson with fun then that brings to peace*" (int. 93).

Beyond the formal texts of the national policy reform, which make little reference to the opportunities within education to contribute to peacebuilding, some local and international organisations recognised this opportunity. The potential for teachers to play a greater role in mediating conflict was acknowledged by these (national) staff in training initiatives, stemming from their position within the community:

> Because teachers are respected in community. When the teacher comes in and plays the role of sort of handling the conflict, playing the role of the connector or reconnector, it's acceptable. (int. 50)

Likewise, within organisations associated with the peace processes, there was also a recognition amongst staff members which was not reflected in political practice:

> For the country to go ahead with the sustainable peacebuilding process, the teachers are very critical. They are the medium connecting, like improving the youths, for students to understand the country, to understand each other and the foundation of the country in every sector. So the teacher is very important, the teacher needs to understand contemporary issues and conflict issues and needs [to be] more proficient in their language, their subjects. (int. 13)

However the tension between this potential contribution of teachers to peacebuilding and the role that is expected of them by the state "*to get through the curriculum and for the children to pass the exams*" (int. 4), was clearly acknowledged by education staff:

> Teachers have no time. They are busy with chapter end test which they are assigned and need to finish the chapters. They need to prepare their students for these tests. (int. 46)

In this, the current process of curriculum reforms potentially offers an opportunity to reformulate texts and timetables alike in such a way as to allow greater openings for peacebuilding practices to take place within the classrooms. These revisions are being rolled out across the school years sequentially, beginning with the primary curricula and later moving on to middle and high school level. Consequently, as a final focus of this chapter, the curriculum reforms being supported by JICA at primary level are examined below, drawing on interviews with JICA and MoE representatives.

Curriculum Reforms

Under JICA support, Myanmar's primary level basic education curriculum is being reformed in a process which started in March 2014 and is due to complete in October 2019 (int. 84). The revised curriculum framework has only recently received approval from the minister. This project involves the development of a national curriculum framework, which integrates skills development into the coverage of all subjects. These include communication, problem solving, critical thinking, logical thinking, scientific processes, and innovation. The project also involves a major review of the content of subject textbooks to orient them away from their presentation of information for pupil memorization towards a more skills-based approach to subject learning, which is seen to encourage critical thinking and problem solving. Given the fact that textbooks in Myanmar have not been substantively revised for 30 years (int. 84), this is a particularly ambitious and potentially transformational – yet not unproblematic – undertaking.

Managers of the project are aware of its far-reaching implications for the potential transformation of teacher practices in Myanmar given the current dominance of rote learning and knowledge transmission in preparation for tests. As one informant working on the new content pointed out, "*current textbooks are based on the teacher-centred approach. So, we are using a totally different approach*" (int. 84) which encourages student enquiry and active learning. Thus, curricula and textbook reform are perceived as interconnected with reforms to teacher education as well as assessment systems. A key aim of the project is therefore to foster teachers who can deal with the new curriculum framework through reform of the curricula of teacher education colleges. To this end, in conjunction with textbook production, the project is also generating teacher guides. Moreover, another strand is to re-orient the current assessment system away from factual testing towards evaluating pupils' acquisition of skills and understanding. Textbooks are foreseen to offer suggestions as to how this may be implemented.

The project is thus important in bringing teacher practices into relation with curricula and assessment systems. Within the context of Myanmar's fractured education system, this is a particularly ambitious project. Institutional divisions within the ministry that have separated curricula development from teacher training have not facilitated such connectivity. However, this perception of the inter-relation between curricula reform and teacher education is embedding at ministerial level. In relation to the JICA reforms, an informant from the Department of Education Planning and Training (DEPT) pointed out that teacher education cannot be understood in isolation from curriculum reform (int. 75). This project has the potential to remove some of the systemic obstacles, which have undermined teachers' ability to diversify their teaching practices. However, this would need to go hand in hand with changing teachers' obligation to an assessment system that encourages rote learning for tests and to overcome a shortage of resources to support the implementation of new approaches to learning (Metro 2015).

The project's managers are aware of the scale of the challenges of teacher implementation, given its radical departure from the patterns of teaching and learning that teachers in Myanmar are deploying. Indeed, one noted that: "*if we totally shift dramati-*

cally, maybe the teacher cannot catch up" (int. 84). Such perceptions are particularly relevant and evince an awareness of what Metro has termed the "danger of over-ambitiousness" when aiming to implement innovative solutions (Metro 2015, 13). Indeed, project managers place a high priority on the importance of developing appropriate approaches to teacher professional development. Thus, one commented that:

> Once the curriculum is developed and the textbooks are changed, if the teacher doesn't change, the new curriculum will not be realized. That's why teacher training is very important. (int. 84)

Thus, project managers saw the goal of training to be equipping teachers to be able to develop a range of skills in pupils – communication, critical thinking, problem solving – through active and participatory learning, but nevertheless to balance this approach with attention to more familiar subject content. Project managers suggested that a blend in training of more traditional whole class approaches linked to the communication of subject content, together with supporting teachers to diversify their learning strategies, would be the most plausible way of securing teacher ownership of the curriculum reforms (int. 84). Such attempts to build on existing practice rather than aim for radical transformation echo the strategies being deployed in other teacher education reforms (discussed further in Chap. 7).

While not explicitly referring to peacebuilding – which informants pointed out was linked to their awareness of sensitivities within the Ministry at the time (int. 84) – various components of the content of the new curriculum relate to the inculcation of relevant values and behaviours. This was the case for subjects such as social studies and its inclusion of moral and civic education. Moral education addresses several themes including relation to self, to other people, to group and society and to nature and the universe, as well as particular values including appreciation and respect, rights and responsibility, integrity, good manners and culture and social cohesion. While not referring explicitly to drivers of conflict in Myanmar, their generic focus on pupil development of behaviours, knowledges and skills linked to inter-personal and societal communication and understanding overlaps with the broadly relational dimensions of peacebuilding processes at the local scale.

Specific components of envisaged content, including the reduction of references to the military in social studies, indicate a commitment to the opportunity to use the curricula to delegitimise violence. Given the legacy of control over the history curriculum and textbooks in Myanmar by the military state for the purposes of nation-building (Salem-Gervais and Metro 2012) if followed through, this is a radical departure. Violence is also addressed through the treatment of such topics as bullying in school. Moreover, the selection of ten famous people in Myanmar to be studied within social studies aims at inclusivity by ensuring representation from different ethnic groups (int. 84). Including such peacebuilding related content, curriculum developers were aware both of the need to respect Ministry sensitivities while doing justice to their sense that curriculum reform should reflect national renewal and aspiration. In the words of one curriculum manager: *"this is the new textbook and Myanmar will be a democratic country"* (int. 84). Nonetheless, current plans for textbooks to be written only in Burmese – as well as uncertainty about how the curriculum will use the freedom to include 20% local content – suggests the curriculum's limitations in relation to addressing pressing issues of social justice linked to a lack of recognition of the diversity of cultures and representation of ethnic groups.

Conclusion

There has been a tendency to instrumentalise teachers as quick solutions to educational challenges, rather than to consider their particular identities, capacity and agency. Understanding the varying positions and framings of teachers within contemporary Myanmar, as well as learning from the practices and perspectives of teachers themselves, supports greater uncovering of their roles in conflict and in peacebuilding.

Traditionally teachers have been held in high esteem within Myanmar, which offers an opportunity for teachers to take on positive mediating and leadership roles within their communities. However, the status of the profession has been undermined by chronic underinvestment in the education sector, leading to teachers suffering material hardship, insecurity and often seeking work beyond their school environment. The low salaries that teachers receive have contributed to the feminization of the profession, however, despite the high numbers of women in the teaching workforce avenues for promotion and decision-making roles in the sector preference men. Several female teachers spoke of their feelings of insecurity in being deployed to remote and conflict-affected areas, which contributed to teachers dropping out of the profession or not being eligible for promotion. Gender considerations are therefore a significant dimension to any changes in the education structures.

While teachers saw a role for themselves in relation to building positive and peaceful inter-personal relationships with pupils and in the wider community, they frequently reported being exasperated by unrealistic expectations linked to an over-dense curriculum and additional responsibilities within and beyond the school. This contributed to a tension between the recognition of the potential peacebuilding agency of teachers and the instrumental, exam-oriented expectations of the state that require teachers to act as obedient civil servants. Through the examples encountered within the research, the strategies that some teachers employ to help advance notions of peacebuilding within their classrooms and their communities offer indications of the opportunities that may be expanded upon.

However multiple constraints continue to limit such opportunities, as evidenced in the accounts of history teaching in Mon State. Although teachers within government and ethnic systems were aware of the potential of history to contribute to peacebuilding, they were constrained by existing curricula frameworks. Additionally, for certain teachers, their own (community-driven) attachment to sectarian approaches to history, undermined their commitment to exploiting the subject's potential to contribute to social cohesion. Current processes of curriculum revision should go some way to contributing to improved teacher practices in such areas, however the imperative remains for training to be carefully linked to its innovative focus.

References

Bush, K. D., & Saltarelli, D. (2000). *The two faces of education in ethnic conflict: Towards a peacebuilding education for children*. Florence: UNICEF, Innocenti Research Centre.

Davies, L. (2010). The different faces of education in conflict. *Development, 53*(4), 491–497.

Horner, L., Kadiwal, L., Sayed, Y., Barrett, A., Durrani, N., & Novelli, M. (2015). *Literature review: The role of teachers in peacebuilding*. University of Sussex: Research Consortium Education and Peacebuilding. Brighton, UK. Available online at https://educationanddevelopment.files.wordpress.com/2014/11/the-role-of-teachers-in-peacebuilding-literature-review.pdf

Lall, M. (2011). Pushing the child centered approach in Myanmar: The role of cross national policy networks and the effects in the classroom. *Critical Studies in Education, 52*(3), 219–233.

Laungaramsri, P. (2011). Imagining nation: Women's rights and the transnational movement of Shan Women in Thailand and Burma. In T. Salman & M. De Theije (Eds.), *Local battles, global stakes: The globalisation of local conflicts and the localization of global interests* (pp. 99–117). Amsterdam: VU University Press.

Lwin, T. (2000). *Education in Burma (1945–2000)*. Thinking Classroom Foundation. Chiang Mai, Thailand. Available online at http://www.thinkingclassroom.org/uploads/4/3/9/0/43900311/lwin_t._2000._education_in_burma_1945-2000.pdf

Maber, E. J. T. (2016). Cross-border transitions: Navigating conflict and political change through community education practices in Myanmar and the Thai border. *Globalisation, Societies and Education, 14*(3), 374–389.

McCormick, P. (2014a). Writing a singular past: Mon history and 'modern' historiography in Burma. *SOJOURN: Journal of Social Issues in Southeast Asia, 29*(2), 300–331.

McCormick, P. (2014b). Ethnic histories: Reflections from the field. *Journal of Burma Studies, 18*(1), 123–135.

Metro, R. (2013). Postconflict history curriculum revision as an "intergroup encounter" promoting interethnic reconciliation among Burmese migrants and refugees in Thailand. *Comparative Education Review, 57*(1), 145–168.

Metro, R. (2015). Students and teachers as agents of democratization and national reconciliation in Burma. In R. Egreteau & F. Robinne (Eds.), *Contemporary Burma/Myanmar* (pp. 209–223). Singapore: NUS Press.

Ministry of Education (MoE). (2013). *CESR rapid review of Myanmar basic education policy and proposed way forward. Phase 1*. Yangon: MoE.

Salem-Gervais, N., & Metro, R. (2012). A textbook case of nation-building: The evolution of history curricula in Myanmar. *Journal of Burma Studies, 16*(1), 27–78.

South, A., & Lall, M. (2016). Language, education and the peace process in Myanmar. *Contemporary Southeast Asia: A Journal of International and Strategic Affairs, 38*(1), 128–153.

Tin, H. (2000). Myanmar education: Status, issues and challenges. *Journal of Southeast Asian Education, 1*(1), 134–162.

UNICEF. (2012). *Baseline study: Child-centred approaches and teaching and learning practices in selected primary schools in child-friendly school focused townships in Myanmar*. Yangon: UNICEF.

Union of Myanmar. (2014). *National education law*. Nay Pyi Taw: Union of Myanmar.

Women's League of Burma (WLB) (2014). *If They had Hope They Would Speak*. Chiang Mai: WLB.

World Bank. (2015). *Myanmar public expenditure review 2015*. Yangon: World Bank.

Chapter 7
Navigating Teacher Education Reform: Priorities, Possibilities and Pitfalls

Sean Higgins and Naw Tha Ku Paul

Introduction

While focusing primarily on teacher education and reform initiatives affecting teachers, this chapter firstly locates these within the context of wider issues related to teacher governance and accountability. It highlights the legacy of centralised and authoritarian control over teachers' work and discusses recent initiatives towards decentralising teacher governance to townships. It also spotlights continuing inequalities in the distribution of resources to schools in remote and marginalised areas, as well as between schools in the formal and parallel education systems – including the monastic sector and ethnic education systems; and the resulting challenges experienced by teachers deployed to these contexts. Secondly, it reflects on recent initiatives to enhance teacher accountability again highlighting context-specific challenges and possibilities.

The third section starts out by looking at macro level systemic issues related to teacher education. It clarifies the current avenues for training and professional development available to diverse constituencies of teachers in a complex and fractured landscape of provision. It then reviews current teacher education curricula, pinpoints areas requiring reform, while also highlighting the challenging cultural political economy context that shapes and constrains the possibilities for change. Indeed, since the writing of this paper, elections in November 2015 have given the National League for Democracy a majority of seats in Parliament. The findings reported in this chapter, like those of other contributions to this book, are based on data gathered prior to this change during the rule of the USDP government which is referenced throughout the text.

S. Higgins (✉) · N. T. K. Paul
University of Amsterdam, Amsterdam, The Netherlands
e-mail: s.higgins@uva.nl

M. T. A. Lopes Cardozo, E. J. T. Maber (eds.), *Sustainable Peacebuilding and Social Justice in Times of Transition*,
https://doi.org/10.1007/978-3-319-93812-7_7

Attention to the curricula of teacher education is followed by more micro level analysis drawing from four case studies of teacher education initiatives developed by international and local actors. These highlight a diversity of entry points and approaches and provide insights for further reflections on how such interventions address the peacebuilding agency of teachers, as well as their strengths and weaknesses in relation to achieving coherence, sustainability and context-responsiveness.

The chapter draws on the voices and viewpoints of a range of actors - including teachers, teacher trainers, head teachers, international actors, education officials and community based stakeholders – in the Mon and Yangon areas of Myanmar. It also spotlights various dimensions of teacher education and its wider context including issues of governance and accountability, curricula content, as well as the cultural political economy factors (as introduced as an analytical framing in Chap. 2) conditioning and constraining reform. Bringing these various lenses and perspectives together, along with concrete references to current and ongoing interventions that illuminate key issues, it reveals the complexity, challenges and possibilities of teacher education reform in contemporary Myanmar.

A Note on Methodology: Talking to Teachers in Myanmar

The research consortium spoke to 115 teacher related respondents including head teachers, teachers and teacher trainers between January and April 2015. Local researchers conducted all interviews in Burmese and, where necessary, in Mon language. They were aware of the reticence of teachers to discuss their work and feelings and the consequent challenge of engaging teachers in a dialogue. This may be understood as a product of teachers' experience of a centralised and authoritarian management structure, discussed below, which does not encourage teachers to express individual viewpoints.

Teacher Governance and the Legacy of Centralisation

In Myanmar, the historical legacy of a strongly centralised and authoritarian system of governance and control has and to a great extent still impacts on the way teachers and teacher educators are managed. This is especially true of the country's formal education system of teacher recruitment, deployment, and training (detailed below), while in contrast the parallel education systems - including the Monastic sector and the ethnic education systems - seem to be more responsive to locally defined demands of communities. Some of the teacher educator interviewees expressed how the centrally controlled system by the national government undermines the ability to effectively meet the needs of a wide diversity of local communities, while at the same time paying little attention to the needs and priorities of its teacher educator force. One informant pointed out that teacher educators were moved around the country in militaristic fashion "*like an army*" (int. 102).

With current (still minimal) shifts to more decentralised forms of governance, data from Mon State suggests that township education officers felt somewhat more ownership over the monitoring aspects of teacher's work, feeding in to slowly changing forms of accountability. UNICEF's Township Education Improvement Plan is directly intending to support this shift, through building the capacity of township education officials in Mon State. As mentioned by one township education official, *"now we are supporting the facilities for the children to have equality in education for all the children including the ethnic people and the Mon national schools"* (int. 39). Nevertheless, some officers mentioned feeling rather constrained within existing centrally controlled forms of decision-making on other aspects of teacher governance (recruitment, deployment and remuneration), as it is yet unclear what authorities they can exercise with regards to teacher accountability. Furthermore, our data suggests there may be a possibility of the misuse of newly gained decision-making power by township education officers to be driven by personal whim, rather than strategic decision-making that supports inclusive collective needs.

The Deployment of Resources and Teachers: Challenges and Inequities

A related issue with regard to teacher governance is the perceived imbalance in the distribution of educational resources between teachers working in the state and ethnic and/or monastic systems. As further illustrated in the case studies in Chap. 8, our data shows how those educators in remote areas or otherwise marginalised positions (being part of a non-government school system) felt undermined by a lack of resources (textbooks, classroom furniture), as well as human resource matters (training, enough teacher staff etc.) (ints. 15 and 110). One informant from the monastic sector highlighted the inability of principals to meet the needs of large numbers of rural children who wish to pursue their education beyond primary level. Because of the lack of investment in middle level schools these students tend to drop out (int.15). A recent report (WCRP and HURFOM 2015) on education provision in Mon rural communities confirms the low resource constraints, teacher shortages, and poor school infrastructure in village schools.

Reinforcing the findings outlined in Chap. 6, our data also confirmed a gendered impact in terms of deployment. As many teachers are single women those interviewed attributed this position to their not wanting to take up teaching posts in conflict-affected or remote areas where they felt isolated, far removed from their families and without structures of social support (ints. 122 and 123). Others also identified this as a cause of the lack of promotion for female teachers to positions of administrative authority as they were disadvantaged compared to male colleagues who received benefits from having spent time in 'difficult' schools, in conflict-affected and remote areas (int. 123).

In relation to the deployment mechanisms, teachers and teacher educators interviewed largely felt unprepared and unsupported to meet the challenges of being deployed by central level government in any place around the country. Firstly, it was expressed how in remote areas teachers may be expected to teach various subjects and at different levels; something for which they often are not trained. A teacher trainer pointed out that:

> There are some challenges for some new teachers. In some cases, if it is remote areas or faraway places, there aren't enough teachers, so they have to teach 3–4 subjects. So, if you are specializing here in biology, maybe you might have to teach history or geography if there is lack of teachers. So that is challenge. And also, you are preparing as a senior assistant teacher but there [are] no teachers at the junior secondary school classes, so you have to teach the subjects that you are not familiar with. That is another challenge. Sometimes as a new teacher, you have to listen and follow [what] the principal said or the dean said. (int. 21)

This situation of clashing expectations between the head teacher and incoming teachers was perceived to lead to frustration and tensions at the school level. Also identified as problematic in this regard was the lack of support available to teachers once they were deployed:

> Another thing is teachers are, once they are trained, they are sent to school and there is no follow up support system. So, in the remote area, teachers cannot get technical support, any kind of support, you see. And they need [it] in their work. So, there is no follow up technical support. (int. 16)

Secondly, in addition to a lack of professional preparedness, the material hardships faced by teachers deployed in remote areas, and the insufficient salaries, undermined their wellbeing and job motivation. These include a lack of appropriate and affordable housing for teachers, difficult or unavailable transport, and a lack of safety (especially for female teachers).

In the absence of incentives, these precarious conditions lead teachers in remote areas to experience decreasing levels of job motivation and eventually to leave their job. Reflecting on her reasons for deciding against continuing to work in a remote area, one informant reported "*transportation problems and lack of safety*" as well as "*the practices of the principals and education officers which they found unbearable or unacceptable*" (int.122). Moreover, a recent report on the policy of hiring daily wage teachers points out that it "will not resolve the disparity in educational conditions…. A strong system of incentives to remote schools should be introduced and a periodic transfer system among all teachers should be considered" (Muta 2015, 2). The demoralising combination of harsh material conditions, challenging relationships with school leaders, lack of affordable accommodation, unrealistic expectations in relation to teaching roles and subjects and inadequate training all undermine the well-being and effectiveness of teachers deployed to rural areas. Finally, at the moment teacher educators felt that there was no adequate training for teachers to be sent to conflict-affected areas, which will be further discussed below.

Teacher Accountability: New Developments and Ongoing Challenges

Against a shifting landscape of centralization and some preliminary decentralization shifts, the government, supported by UNICEF and other international donors, has been driving first steps towards a new system of teacher accountability. This new system referred to as the "competency framework" is not necessarily unique to Myanmar, and according to CESR documentation draws on teacher management reforms implemented in "Western" contexts, albeit not uncontested. The competency framework aims to enhance accountability through identifying competencies for various educators – including teachers at different levels, teacher educators as well as management staff – through a participatory process of consultation. They are also seen to provide codes of conduct for these various educators at different scales. These jointly agreed compilations of competencies then are foreseen to be used to hold those different educational stakeholders accountable for their work. Reflecting further on the potential pitfalls below, the national government and international actors see the benefits of this framework in that it can provide a shared language of expectations, potentially to encourage dialogue and understanding between the various educational professionals (e.g. teachers, head teachers, teacher educators and township education officers). The peacebuilding potential is then perceived to result from the enhancement of clarity over tasks and responsibilities between those professionals, which can increase collaboration and mutual understanding, a finding which is also supported in the literature (Horner et al. 2015). Referring to this process, one education specialist pointed out that:

> If we could take those competencies and post them on a wall, and as the community could better understand what could be expected of the head teacher and the education officer, they would be able to help each other and critique each other and encourage each other towards a more shared language and goal. (int. 89)

Our data on this topic speaks specifically to the way initial steps have been taken in Mon State, and recognising the unique nature of Mon with regards to other parts of the country. Reflecting on the data, and supported by literature on the topic of teacher accountability (Robertson 2012), there is a danger that the generic nature of competency frameworks and a looming lack of context- and conflict-specificity is largely unresponsive to the needs of Myanmar's diverse regions. Firstly, drawing unproblematically on international best practices might not be the ideal solution in a conflict-affected situation, where numerous educators are operating in non-state and other parallel systems. There are other systems of teacher accountability operating in the country, such as community-based systems of teacher support and control, which are largely ignored and marginalised. Here, accountability is more framed at local levels around the appropriateness of the background of the teacher (e.g. ethnicity, language, gender, age, commitment to the locality, and the importance of local knowledges). Secondly, given the fractured nature of the education system, a generic competency framework developed at the central (majority-dominated) level potentially exacerbates tensions and feelings of being ignored and excluded. Thirdly, then, the internationally driven, neoliberal-inspired efficiency agenda that drives such a framework to shift responsibility to local levels and individual teachers (Robertson 2012), has the potentially negative effect of continuing or reviving authoritarian/coercive systems of control over teachers, rather than providing much needed support in difficult working conditions. Finally, these competencies are often developed with an image that is much more favourable than the actual under-resourced school reality most Myanmar teachers face.

Teacher Training and Education

Having highlighted key issues relating to the governance, accountability and deployment of teachers, the following section now addresses their training and education. It first offers an overview of the diverse pathways available. This is followed by an analysis of curricula content, the politics of teacher education reform and a review of a selection of interventions, community based and international, which aim to enhance current provision.

Teacher Training and Professional Development Routes in Myanmar

The process of teacher recruitment, training and promotion in the state sector remains severely flawed at present. As highlighted above, this recruitment and promotion process has led to a concentration of inexperienced and unqualified teachers in primary education, and exacerbated concerns about the quality and relevance of education—a matter that then continues to fuel drop outs from the system (UNICEF 2012). Additionally, teacher training institutions struggle with challenges including: inadequate skills in pedagogical teaching; poor facilities, equipment, and information resources; overcrowded curricula; and lack of supervision. Moreover, school leaders are not equipped to be instructional leaders, and are instead promoted based on years of service and qualification. Little training is offered to these leaders once they enter into the job (UNICEF 2012).

However, across the different sectors, the opportunities for teacher professional development vary considerably. Figure 7.1 below provides an overview of pre-service and in-service training for state, monastic, ethnic and community schools.

As depicted in the figure below, formal pre-service teacher training prepares teachers to enter the government system through two Institutes/Universities of Education, located in Yangon and Sagaing. These deliver a 4 year B.Ed course, recently increased to 5 years, that qualifies teachers to teach at secondary and upper secondary levels. The 22 Education Colleges located throughout the country offer

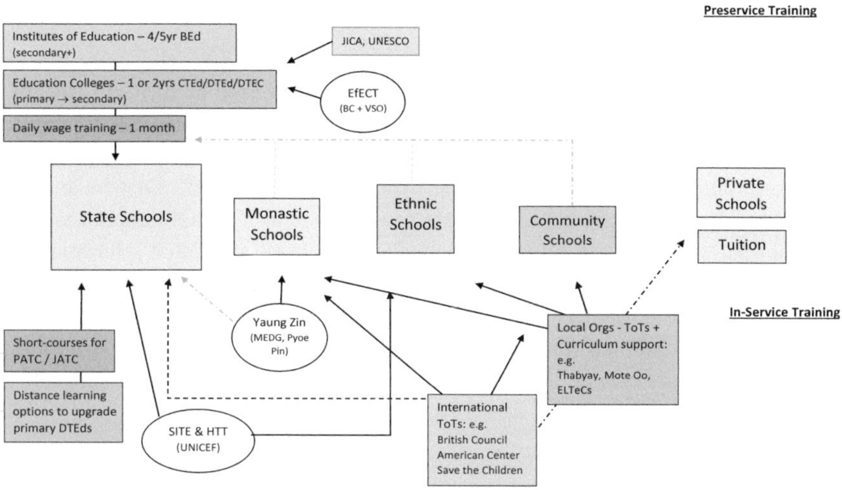

Fig. 7.1 Education sectors and teacher training. (Design by Elizabeth Maber)

2-year courses, which prepare teachers to teach at primary and lower-secondary levels respectively. Once in service, there is some (although limited) opportunity for state teachers to up-grade their skills. Additionally, the recent introduction of daily-wage teachers through the ‘Quick Win’ platform enables junior teachers to be deployed in schools as assistants after 1 month of training. In contrast, the non-state education sectors have no formalised pre-service training. Here, teachers are recruited directly from the community, often beginning on a voluntary basis. Once in service however, monastic, ethnic and community sector teachers may have greater access to professional development through teacher training initiatives supported by international and local NGOs. International actors (with the exception of UNICEF and one JICA supported initiative) were not allowed to implement training programmes in the government education system prior to 2011, and consequently organisations such as Save the Children and the British Council worked exclusively with the non-state sectors. The result is that although non-state teachers may have few or no formally recognised pre-service qualifications, where trainings were available and accessible, some have been trained in more learner-centred pedagogies. Since 2011, the education reform process has enabled international actors to work with the state, resulting in partnerships, which include UNICEF SITE and head teacher training and the British Council and VSO supported EfECT (discussed below). Finally, opportunities for contact and shared learning across the sectors are also beginning to open up. The Yaung Zin teacher training programme, developed and implemented within the monastic sector is an example, again outlined below, which may be adopted more widely across the state sector in future.

Current Teacher Education Provision and Potential for Reform

As noted by Hardman, there has been a "growing recognition by the Government of Myanmar and its donor partners that a focus on pedagogy and its training implications need to be at the heart of the commitment to improve student retention, progression, and learning in Myanmar" (Hardman 2012, 3). Driven by such considerations, teacher education reform has emerged as a particular national priority (Hardman 2012, vi). Reports on the analysis of current provision (Hardman et al. 2013; MoE 2014) contain recommendations on the reform of curricula and pedagogical practices in training institutions, as well as offering suggestions to systematise teacher professional development linking pre-service and in-service training. They also pinpoint a range of areas of teacher education that require urgent reform, including:

- The commitment of teacher educators to a transmission model of teaching;
- An overcrowded curriculum with little opportunity for private study and reflection, but rather focused on an end-of-unit assessment system;
- Challenging physical environments in which teachers work, especially in remote areas;
- Weak partnerships between teacher training institutions and the schools in which students do their teaching practicum;
- Lack of professional development opportunities for teacher educators to enhance their "knowledge, understanding and practice of effective pedagogy" (Hardman 2012, vi) as well as to develop mentoring and coaching skills;
- Limited attention to practical challenges faced by teachers including multi-grade teaching, the teaching of languages other than Burmese and inclusive education (Hardman et al. 2013, 31).

Lall's study of the promotion of child-centred approaches in teacher training offered by international aid organisations has drawn attention to the considerable cultural and logistical challenges that undermine its effective implementation by teachers: "NGOs and INGOs who are importing western educational practices to other countries… should adapt models to local contexts before implementation" (Lall 2011, 231; see also Lall et al. 2013). Other reports similarly caution against "the simplistic polarisation of pedagogy into teacher-centred and child-centred" so that "there is a better balance and blending of local cultural practices in the different regions of Myanmar with internationally informed teacher education reforms" (Hardman et al. 2016, 116). Such insights underline the need for training interventions to be carefully tailored to the lived experiences of teachers and the cultural and contextual factors conditioning their work in Myanmar.

Navigating Teacher Education Reform in a Highly Politicised Context

Our informants drew attention to institutional as well as a range of cultural political economy factors, which rendered such interventions to reform and enhance teacher education difficult to navigate. One was the current division within the ministry of education, which split teacher training from school curriculum development, with the former being overseen by the Department for Teacher Education and Training (DTET) and the latter by the Department of Basic Education (5). As one informant from DEPT put it,

> you cannot look at teacher education alone, you have to look at curriculum reforms as well… so I think the Ministry has to co-ordinate among these different agencies who are involved in teacher education. (int. 75)

Current restructuring within the Ministry with the possibility of establishing a "*teacher education department*" (int. 75) may facilitate such co-ordination. Moreover, constraints of access to teacher education colleges and schools as well as obligations of international aid agencies to work closely within the parameters set by the Ministry have narrowed their field of manoeuvre (int. 4). One informant suggested that this had entailed challenges in reaching out to non-state educational actors including teachers in ethnic and monastic systems, but nevertheless progress had been made on ensuring trainings were as inclusive as possible (ints. 48 and 131). Another issue was the sometimes-controversial nature of aspirations to reform the content of teacher education, in particular in relation to building conflict sensitivity into the curriculum. The view was expressed that a cautious approach, which stressed the continuity of such subject content with traditional curriculum priorities, had been an essential prerequisite for ensuring its acceptance within the Ministry of Education (ints. 48 and 74). One informant noted that *"it was too sensitive politically to work with teachers for peace elements… so we had to go step by step"* (int. 48).

Pointing to the challenges of navigating teacher education initiatives within the current policymaking environment in Myanmar, another informant from an international aid agency observed that *"it's not going to be an easy thing to do in a very complex environment and when there's a lot of rhetoric which can be destructive"* (int. 4). Together, then, these viewpoints are a reminder that teacher education initiatives are interacting with a highly politicised and challenging context that influences what is realistic and feasible.

Case Studies of Teacher Education Initiatives

Nevertheless, operating within such constraints, there has been a recent proliferation of teacher education interventions within the country. The data for the following analysis of a selected number of teacher education interventions is drawn from a range of stakeholders, enabling a combination of insights from programme managers in aid agencies, teachers who have experienced trainings as well as the perspectives of government officials. This selection combines in-service and pre-service trainings as well as long-term projects. It includes trainings addressed nationwide to non-state teachers in the monastic system, as well as initiatives targeting head teachers and teachers in government and ethnic community schools in Mon State. The research team did not find evidence of evaluations of the impact of these initiatives. However, the following comments are not intended to be evaluative but rather to offer reflections on their strategies to develop the capacity of teachers and where relevant to clarify their contribution and potential to supporting their peacebuilding agency. Together they illustrate the creativity and diversity of approaches to the challenge of enhancing teacher education provision in contemporary Myanmar.

Site Training UNICEF

UNICEF's SITE programme (School based in service Teacher Education) training is offered to in–service primary teachers in Mon State including those working in government, monastic, and ethnic managed schools. It was piloted in 2011 and started in 2012.

The SITE training offered by UNICEF to in-service primary teachers in Mon State uses self-study distance learning modules in which teachers draw on their classroom experiences and collaborate with other teachers and their head teachers within inter-school clusters (UNICEF, SITE Programme Guidelines 2014). Its primary focus is on the development of teacher pedagogical skills through ten study units. These include materials on child friendly schools, reflective teaching practices, lesson planning, learning through interaction and collaboration, developing students' basic skills, and assessment of learning. The programme is intended to ground professional development strategies in the daily realities of classroom life experienced by teachers as well as through structured self-assessment of their practice. Experienced teachers are encouraged to work with less experienced colleagues to develop practical teaching skills with an important mentoring and support role envisaged for the head teacher (ints. 5, 7 and 46). This approach resonates with recent international thinking on effective ways of building and changing teacher's practices which emphasise both the formative impact of developing "learning communities at the school and cluster level" (Hardman 2012, 7; see Horner et al. 2015, 50). It also responds to a perceived need for teachers to develop their practice through joint, ongoing reflection about the pedagogical processes they choose to use.

This site-specific, teacher-driven, and collaborative model of professional learning was underlined as a key rationale of SITE's approach. Moreover, it was recognised as a departure from previous training modalities within Myanmar. As one education officer put it: "*this is an attempt to move teacher education from workshop methodology to self-learning on the job training... coaching, mentoring, group discussions, journal writing…*" (int. 5). One informant drew attention to the innovative nature of SITE's grassroots rather than "top down" approach to teacher development, given the authoritarian structures of control during previous regimes. It was pointed out that the model of teacher learning envisaged was "*nothing unusual in many countries around the world but for Myanmar, this is quite revolutionary*" (int. 5). Such comments are a reminder of the challenging cultural contexts within which more participatory approaches to teacher education are aiming to take root.

The British Council English for Education College Trainers (EfECT) Programme for Teacher Educators

The British Council's EfECT (English for Education College Trainers) started in 2013 and was initiated as a result of discussions between then President Thien Sein and then UK Prime Minister, David Cameron.

This intervention is notable for offering context-specific and culturally responsive support to enhance the agency of a professional group, teacher educators, whose capacity development and needs are often overlooked within conflict affected contexts (Hardman 2012, 20). This inattention serves to "minimise the effectiveness of their contribution to the education of teachers at the PRESET and INSET stages" (Hardman 2012, 20). Addressing this challenge, The British Council EfECT programme provides English and pedagogical training for teacher educators over a period of 2 years. It works in 20 education colleges, 2 Institutes of Education, the National Centre for English Language, and the University for the Development of National Races. The programme has supported around 1575 teacher educator beneficiaries. The first year of the project aimed to help improve English proficiency in the context of the expectation that academic subjects are taught to trainees through the medium of English. Its attention to developing educators' pedagogical practices addresses concerns about the dominance of whole-class non-interactive teaching methods within training colleges as noted above. However, the programme's aim of avoiding imposing western pedagogic frameworks of best practice is well aligned with the emphasis in recent international research on the need for context-responsive and culturally sensitive teacher education (Lewin & Stuart 2003). The programme takes an emphatically practical rather than theoretical approach to the development of educator's pedagogical skills.

Internal qualitative evaluations of the EfECT programme, which elicited the most 'significant change' as a result of participation, have underlined the increased self-esteem and professional confidence enjoyed by teacher educators. Moreover, informants highlighted the appeal of learning an international language, which had symbolic as well as practical relevance because it represented the possibility of extending their communicative possibilities as well as their intellectual horizons. This is an important acknowledgement, given the widely recognised low morale of this professional group and their difficulty accessing international developments in education (Hardman 2012, 21). While EfECT is an intervention targeted at in-service professionals, it is also intended to benefit pre-service students who will benefit from the enhanced professional skills of their teachers. In its careful tailoring to cultural context and particular professional needs, the programme illustrates a distinctive approach to enhancing the agency of a key but neglected professional group.

UNICEF's Head Teacher Training

Another group whose needs are frequently neglected are school leaders, whom UNICEF's Head Teacher Training engages with. This training is currently offered in 34 townships to 5000 head teachers. Through providing training in management and instructional leadership, the programme affirms their pivotal role as agents of change and key figures not only in their schools but also in the wider community. Course content contains management tools including school self-assessment and planning, staff development as well as how to build community links (ints. 6, 7 and 48). This is delivered to heads through a cascade model of training with master trainers from the DEPT. In relation to the recognised need within CESR evidence gathering (Hardman 2012), to establish systemic professional networks or "clusters," the training's focus on the pedagogical agency of the head teacher as an "instructional leader" is particularly important (ints. 5 and 48). In these clusters, teacher educators, school leaders, as well as township education officers are brought together to support classroom teachers in developing their pedagogical practice. Empowering school leaders in this particular aspect of their role is an important aspect of the intervention, understood to address a neglected feature of their leadership responsibilities at present (ints. 5, 36 and 48). Explaining the project's rationale, one informant pointed out that:

> We've noticed very much that they needed to be empowered with the sense that they are a leader of teaching and learning, that they can create an environment, that they can rally teachers to talk about teaching and learning, to coach and mentor each other. (int. 36)

Head teachers recognised the impact of the training on their skills:

> By attending head teacher training… compared with before I improved my management skills and developed better relationships with teachers and [learned] how to teach systematically. (int. 60)

They also mentioned their acquisition of administration skills to enable them to monitor and record school attendance and write development/improvement plans (ints. 63 and 74). Acknowledging the scarcity or absence of resources to support their day-to-day professional practice, head teachers placed particular value on the course materials. These were perceived as useful sources of practical advice to refer to on a daily basis: "*I always put the book on the table – how to manage and monitor the school and teachers – all the questions are in that book*" (int. 60).

Envisaging teacher professional development as a collaborative endeavour that mobilises the support of other teachers, head teachers as well as township education officials and educational administrators, SITE trainings respond to Metro's call for a systemic approach that goes beyond individual teachers working on their own (Metro 2015). Such approaches are more likely to yield that critical mass necessary to supporting individual teachers to develop their practices (Metro 2015).

Yaung Zin Teacher Training Programme

The Monastic Education Development Group's Yaung Zin competency based trainings are offered to unqualified primary teachers in 256 schools nationwide within the monastic and other community based systems.

The Yaung Zin Teacher Training programme developed by local and international agencies uses a competency-based approach to teacher professional development. The course consists of eight modules which focus on: leaning needs and learning styles; teaching and learning strategies; lesson planning; classroom management; assessment; professional development; being a reflective practitioner; and working with parents and community (Yaung Zin n.d.-a, 3). These are covered in 31 days of full time training. Its competency based approach resonates with an agenda emerging from the CESR to re-frame teacher professional development around a national teacher competency framework (Hardman 2012, vii; MoE 2014, 30). The value of this strategy as a vehicle for changing teacher behaviours and practice is explained in the programme literature which notes the usefulness of competencies in "identifying clearly what a professional teacher needs to know and be able to do in the classroom, recognising the importance of context, and taking account of the human resources available" (Yaung Zin n.d.-a, 7).

However, in specifying the importance of context and resource constraints as conditioning the exercise of competencies, the Yaung Zin programme avoids the potentially generic and decontextualized processes of teacher accountability that competency frameworks can sometimes lead to. Indeed, a significant feature is its affirmation of the community role of the teacher (Yaung Zin n.d.-a). The programme's inclusion of a module on Working with Parents and the Community which is "based on a real case study of a community and its monastic school" (Yaung Zin n.d.-a, 6) illustrates this links with the community specific context in which teachers work.

Like other interventions and responding to national concerns as outlined above, the priority of the Yaung Zin programme is "teaching and facilitating learning" (Yaung Zin n.d.-a, 4). A key feature of its approach is the use of school based mentoring to follow up the initial training (int. 15). This enables "*discussion on their difficulties in their practical teaching*" (int. 15) reflecting a concern to link teacher development with the classroom realities they face on a daily basis. The training also adopts a systemic approach in which enhancing the agency of the teacher is one component of a broader strategy to build the capacity of other stakeholders including head teachers, parents, and wider community (int. 15). This is significant in understanding teachers' development of their practice as a process, which is crucially influenced and potentially supported by a range of actors, in particular their head teachers. Similar to UNICEF's head teacher training, Yaung Zin's attention to this professional group is based on the view that they are key agents of change in schools. As one informant put it *"to change the education system in the monastic school, the principal is the very important leader... their visions and mindsets are very important"* (int. 15). Moreover, their role in the wider community is also recognised such that *"the majority of the monastic school principals are the leaders in their community"* (int. 15).

Situating teacher education within its community context and approaching teacher development through competency acquisition supported by on site, classroom based mentoring, the Yaung Zin programme resonates with many of the recommendations for teacher education reform which have featured in CESR discussions.

Teacher Education and Peacebuilding: Some Reflections

A notable feature of all the teacher education interventions reviewed is their frequently implicit and indirect approaches to enhancing the peacebuilding roles of teachers. These possibilities were uncovered by researchers when engaging with teachers who were reflecting on the impact of training on their daily professional realities. Thus, while not explicitly referred to as peacebuilding, the development of pedagogical and managerial skills through the trainings was understood by teachers and head teachers to be relevant to the micro-realities of their roles and responsibilities to establish peaceful relationships in their schools and with their local communities. So, for instance, the focus on school development planning within head teacher training was perceived by trainees as potentially a strategic vehicle through which they could make decisions on infrastructure or resourcing priorities, linked to the reduction of conflict and tensions (int. 63).

For example, head teachers pointed out how planning to improve school infrastructure through the erection of wall partitions would help to reduce tensions between teachers and students, arising from high noise levels and the likeliness of quarrels between groups of students being taught in one large open space (ints. 59 and 63). The opportunity to build school-community relationships through school improvement planning procedures was perceived to be conducive to peacebuilding processes:

> If we get teaching resources from the school improvement plan we will be able to work together with the parent teacher association – together we can build up peace. (int. 63)

In a similar way, teachers on the SITE training identified aspects of course content – in particular, the emphasis on child-friendly approaches, avoiding discrimination, creating a safe environment, avoiding corporal punishment, using problem-solving techniques such as discussion, giving students a chance to talk freely, referring pupils misbehaviour to the school council – as all supportive of their roles as peacebuilders, especially as this was construed in terms of building positive relationships with children and communities (ints. 59, 63 and 64). The relevance of trainings to the interpersonal and relational dimensions of their peacebuilding roles – with other teachers, students, and parents – were particularly underlined by teachers (ints. 60 and 63). The centrality of interpersonal relationship building within a community context to these teachers' perceptions of their peace-related role aligns with the findings of Horner et al.'s review on teacher agency (2015). This found that:

> [T]he way teachers teach is as important as what they teach in facilitating the knowledge, skills and attitudes that facilitate or obscure peaceful futures. Teachers are part of both the school community and the wider community where the school is situated. (Horner et al. 2015, 9)

Teachers recognised that the knowledges and skills acquired from trainings, while not explicitly tied to a peacebuilding agenda within the course content, could nevertheless support their participation in such social processes. Such reflections on the relevance of their training highlights the importance of the creative, perhaps unexpected ways in which teachers mediate and apply its content to extend their agency as peacebuilders within their particular school contexts.

Key stakeholders acknowledged the implicit and latent integration of peacebuilding dimensions of teachers' practices within trainings, with particular emphasis on the peacebuilding potential of child-centred pedagogical approaches. A government official pointed out with regard to the SITE trainings that "*it is not explicitly stated as such, but there are some ideas and principles already provided through different modules*" (int. 75). Indeed, all the trainings reviewed included implicit or more direct content bearing upon the peacebuilding roles of the teacher. Thus, within the Classroom Management module of the Yaung Zing programme, one of the identified competencies is that the teacher should "demonstrate mutual respect, applying equity principles and lack of bias in dealing with student diversity, gender, race, ethnicity and religion" (Yaung Zin n.d.-a, 2). As one of the indicators of such inclusive teacher practice, the module draws attention to the importance of recognising the cultural and ethnic diversity of Myanmar. In the specification of teacher competencies currently being developed within the MOE, teachers are expected to be "context sensitive, avoid discrimination and create an environment that promotes respect for diversity and social cohesion" (UNICEF n.d.). One education specialist thus pointed out that peacebuilding was infused throughout the competencies especially all those "*related to communication*" (int. 46).

This mode of infusing, rather than explicitly referring to, a peace or conflict-related dimension within teacher education may be understood as a strategic response to the potentially controversial and contested nature of the notion of peacebuilding within Myanmar's government as discussed above (int. 48). Moreover, within the mandates of aid agencies, the explicitly peacebuilding implications of education interventions may be subservient to the privileging of the restoration of service delivery provision. As pointed out by one informant from an aid agency, "*we are not so much trying to say that we do this for peacebuilding.... we're doing that for the children's education system... so that they can live peacefully*" (int. 74). Such perceptions from practitioners underscore the challenges of embedding an explicit peacebuilding logic into teacher education, given other context-specific pressures on policy and programming.

However, some interventions did explicitly engage with the peacebuilding agency of teachers. For instance, the addition of Conflict Sensitivity to UNICEF's head teacher training addresses issues of conflict resolution. This emerged out of a recognition within aid agencies and amongst recipients of initial training for head teachers that handling conflict and building peaceful relationships between students, staff and the wider community was a key aspect of the school leader's role (int. 48). As one education specialist put it, the aims of such trainings were "*how to create a peaceful working environment in his or her school*" (int. 48). Indeed, in identifying conflicts over practical community issues like digging a well for water or building a fence to keep a buffalo out – where the "*role of the head teacher is very important*" (int. 48) – these head teacher informants underscored their responsibilities as key community actors. Trainings were perceived to provide school leaders with basic concepts and strategies of conflict resolution which they would then adapt in relation to their contexts: "*we provide the basic concepts because each area has a different scenario – some suffer with fighting government and armed groups*" (int. 48).

Starting out, by contrast with a particular scenario of likely conflict for a teacher in the monastic system, the Yaung Zin programme includes a module to discuss "ways to manage conflicts relating to traditional beliefs and cultural norms concerning Monks" (Yaung Zin n.d.-b, 12). Here the teachers' ability to develop skills to navigate relationships within rural communities, in which monks are socially powerful actors, is stressed as an aspect of conflict resolution. Thus, the module states that, "it is important for teachers to know how to get the support of key decision makers to facilitate working effectively with parents and community" (Yaung Zin n.d.-b, 12). Both these initiatives illustrate the essentially relational understanding of teacher peacebuilding agency, in which training was perceived to empower them to solve inter-personal conflicts (ints. 48 and 75).

In relation to broader peacebuilding dynamics, the opportunities which trainings offer for bridge-building between government and non-state teachers across former professional divides was perceived as an important benefit by both groups (ints. 59, 60 and 63). For instance, teachers and head teachers from government and ethnic schools' systems participating in the SITE and head teacher trainings recognised that the trainings had given them opportunities to build trust, share resources and discover common ground in their professional challenges and concerns. They were perceived by many as a chance to overcome the legacy of earlier divisions (ints. 58 and 60). Reflecting on the benefits of the head teacher training, one head noted that "*we share and discuss on how to teach lessons and how to discipline students*" (int. 58). Another noted that "*we have to work with other head teachers so we see that it is effective. Each area is different from the other so we share our knowledge"* (int. 58). Some sense of the role of trainings as spaces for trust building is evoked in the comment of one MNEC teacher who observed:

> At first government teachers looked down on us as we were not fluent in Burmese, so [we] could not participate in the training sessions, but then after a time the government teachers also tried to understand [us] speaking in Mon language. (int. 59)

For one ethnic teacher, the trainings were an opportunity to challenge what was perceived as an unfair belittling by government teachers of students and teachers within the ethnic education system (int. 63).

However, teachers working within the ethnic education system also drew attention to the challenges of attending trainings, given their awareness of the disparity of resources between government and ethnic run schools (ints. 58 and 63) and the resulting differential capacity to implement what was learned. Thus, one head teacher working in the ethnic system pointed out that *"for the government school teachers they are permanent, but our teachers turn over every year – we need to work with new teachers so we have difficulty"* (int. 63). Ethnic teachers also drew attention to the linguistic challenges they encountered in trainings where the medium of instruction was Burmese: *"our teachers are not fluent in Burmese so they think we do not have capacity but Burmese is not our language"* (int. 41). Such comments are a reminder that while providing new spaces for professional and social collaboration - and thereby contributing to broader peacebuilding dynamics - the training of teachers take place within a political economy environment in which legacies of educational inequity and lack of cultural recognition persist. Paradoxically, these may be reproduced in trainings.

Implementing Teacher Education Reform: Challenges and Constraints

The programmes reviewed are all relatively recent in origin and implementation. However, it may be opportune at this point to reflect on various broader issues which they raise linked to the overall logic and sustainability of teacher education initiatives in Myanmar. In so doing, it is illuminating to apply the theoretical framings of the 4Rs used throughout this book to understand how teacher education in particular may or may not contribute to broader processes of social justice.

Firstly, their very diversity of approaches and priorities, while a strength at one level, may also reveal a lack of co-ordination between aid agencies to ensure coherence and complementarity within a long-term strategic vision. Taking an overview of current initiatives, one informant expressed the view that there was a lack of coherence in the response to key informative baselines studies such as that of Hardman (2012) (int. 8). Some informants from aid agencies did acknowledge their tendency to work without sufficient reference to each other and indeed sometimes in competition (int. 5). The result is that perhaps while each individual intervention has many strengths, the proliferation of initiatives directed to the improvement of teacher development lacks a collective rationale that might be gained from greater co-operation.

Secondly, and linked to the absence of coherence, are the difficulties of long-term planning for sustainable impact as a result of the short-term priorities of donor funding (int. 74). Given the needs for teachers to develop their practice over time, with proper support systems and follow up to trainings, this is a major structural weakness of initiatives which are mostly short term and therefore ineffectual in promoting sustainable changes. Our data revealed considerable frustrations amongst some programme managers about uncertain financing flows. Here teacher education intersects with the nationwide and systemic challenge of redistribution of resources given the inequities between the state and monastic/ ethnic systems. Short-term-ism and inadequate funding of interventions to secure long-term follow up may exacerbate existing inequalities.

Thirdly, the interventions reviewed mobilise a range of approaches to understanding teacher agency. Some are emphasising the teacher's key role in the community and others profile the teacher in relation to more generic skills and competencies. Knowledge pooling through current training initiatives may enrich strategies to take account of the plurality of contexts of teachers' work and the challenges they face. Here the content of teacher education initiatives benefit from taking into account the voices and vantage points of teachers and are thereby responsive to the micro-practices of their work. Ensuring all interventions provide opportunities to consult teachers in this way may ensure that teacher education contributes to achieving the social justice goal of representation.

Fourthly, while the implicitness of the peacebuilding dimension of teacher education may indeed be a necessity given the politically sensitive nature of the issue within the country, it was clear from our engagement with teachers that some of the knowledges and skills they were learning were perceived to be relevant to the micro realities of their self-defined roles as peacebuilders. There may be an opportunity here to root training – both pedagogical and managerial – more directly and explicitly in the situations and circumstances linked to peace-related processes that teachers are facing and attempting to navigate on a daily basis. Such a situated approach, attuned to the micro-contexts of teachers' conflict resolution practices, may greatly enhances teachers' capacity to effect reconciliation processes.

Fifthly, there is perhaps a danger that in the urge to draw on so called international "best practice" from OECD countries, local knowledges and expertise in relation to teacher roles, especially as it has developed within community education, may be side-lined. There lies a danger in losing the valuable, context-responsive indigenous practical wisdom of current teachers (Metro 2015). Metro concludes convincingly that "Burmese teachers are a valuable resource that have apparently been underutilised in the government's current attempts at education reform" (Metro 2015, 223). In relation to the filtering into Myanmar of expertise from abroad, a report on teacher education has observed that:

> International borrowing is inevitable and often useful for the development of teacher education. However, models and theories developed in one context should not be imported uncrit-

> ically to others. Teacher education curricula are needed that, while sometimes using cross-national insights as points of departure, also build on local teacher knowledge, experience and examples of good practice. (Lewin & Stuart 2003, xvii)

While some of the programmes reviewed above have made attempts to respond to the views of community teachers, the need to build on and start from local knowledges and experiences is particularly important in the Myanmar context, where an influx of international consultants may have distorted this need for a balance between the international and the local in defining content and priorities of teacher education. By acknowledging and valuing the situated knowledge of local teachers, teacher education has the potential to realise a key social justice goal of recognition. In the case of teachers this should privilege attention to the lived realities that condition and constrain their exercise of agency.

Sixthly, teachers communicated some level of frustration at the tension between the structural constraints they were working within and the expectations of trainings in terms of time required for study, meetings, and investment in implementing pedagogical strategies (ints. 59, 60, 64 and 93). Teachers also expressed how expectations within trainings are often unrealistic. Teachers are assumed to employ child-centred approaches, in a context of constraints on time, energy, resources, physical infrastructure, high pupil numbers, parental and community expectations of teacher-led learning, and their work within an assessment regime linked to regular testing. Failure to take account of the lived experience of teachers within trainings may therefore be counter-productive and further undermine low morale. Evoking an experience of being asked to do the impossible, one teacher pointed out that "*in Myanmar we say it is like trying to capture frogs with a basket that has a big hole in the bottom*" (int. 93). Such comments underscore the importance of tailoring professional development interventions and related ongoing systems of support to the contexts and realities of teachers' lives as well as being realistic about the pace and level of change that can be expected. Here again, recognition of Myanmar's teachers within the diverse micro-contexts of their work is at stake.

Finally, there is a danger that the understandable emphasis of teacher education on capacity building will raise expectations in relation to resource distribution and financial investment which are complex and difficult to realise, thereby causing disappointment and undermining motivation and belief in the relevance of such trainings. This conundrum is clearly a reflection of attempting to reform teacher education in an uncertain and volatile cultural political economy environment, where issues of redistribution, representation, recognition and reconciliation are directly felt and experienced by teachers involved.

Conclusion

This analysis of teacher education interventions in contemporary Myanmar has revealed several key challenges. These include: a tension between the recourse to international best practices and the particularities of teachers' local needs and knowledges; the difficulties of navigating reforms within a volatile cultural political economy landscape and the ongoing legacy of an authoritarian and highly centralised education system; the dangers of collusion by international actors with the reproduction of power asymmetries between different teacher constituencies; and the difficulty of making appropriate judgements about what is realistic and feasible in relation to the pace and scale of reforms.

However, within such a challenging context case studies have also revealed the creativity of international and local actors in developing carefully targeted approaches to enhance teacher education in times of transition. These include site-based collaborative clusters, community rooted content, tailored competency frameworks and a focus on the agency of teacher educators and head teachers. Further reflections have highlighted issues relating to their coherence and sustainability and a tendency to overlook indigenous community based teacher knowledges. Finally, the generally cautious and implicit nature of peacebuilding within training initiatives undertaken is a reminder of the intersection of teacher education reform with a volatile and sensitive political landscape.

References

Hardman, F. (2012). *Development of a teacher education strategy framework linked to pre and in-service teacher training in Myanmar*. Yangon: UNICEF.

Hardman, F., Aung, W., & Myint, A. A. (2013). *Development of a teacher education strategy framework linked to pre and in-service teacher training in Myanmar*. Yangon: UNICEF.

Hardman, F., Stoff, C., Aung, W., & Elliott, L. (2016). Developing pedagogical practices in Myanmar primary schools: Possibilities and constraints. *Asia Pacific Journal of Education, 36*(1), 98–118.

Horner, L., Kadiwal, L., Sayed, Y., Barrett, A., Durrani, N., & Novelli, M. (2015). *Literature review: The role of teachers in peacebuilding*. University of Sussex: Research Consortium Education and Peacebuilding. Available online at: https://educationanddevelopment.files.wordpress.com/2014/11/the-role-of-teachers-in-peacebuilding-literature-review.pdf

Lall, M. (2011). Pushing the child centred approach in Myanmar: The role of cross national policy networks and the effects in the classroom. *Critical Studies in Education, 52*(3), 219–233.

Lall, M., San, T. S., San, N. N., Myat, T. T., & Khaing, L. T. T. (2013). *Teachers voice–what education reforms does Myanmar need?* Yangon: Myanmar Egress.

Lewin, K. M., & Stuart, J. S. (2003). *Researching teacher education: New perspectives on practice, performance, and policy, multi-site teacher education research project (MUSTER)*. (Synthesis Report. No. 12882). London: Department for International Development (DFID).

Metro, R. (2015). Students and teachers as agents of democratization and national reconciliation in Burma. In R. Egreteau & F. Robinne (Eds.), *Contemporary Burma/Myanmar* (pp. 209–223). Singapore: NUS Press.

Ministry of Education (MoE). (2014). *Comprehensive education sector review*. Yangon: MoE. http://www.cesrmm.org/index.php/en/

Muta, H. (2015). *Evaluation study on "Having at least five teachers at one school" policy in 2014: Has the regional disparity in educational conditions diminished?* Unpublished research paper for the Government of Myanmar.

Robertson, S. L. (2012). Placing teachers in global governance agendas. *Comparative Education Review, 56*(4), 584–607.

UNICEF. (n.d.). *Concept note on support to decentralisation: A whole state approach (Mon State)*. Internal document. Accessed 2015.
UNICEF. (2012). *Baseline study: Child-centred approaches and teaching and learning practices in selected primary schools in child-friendly school focused townships in Myanmar*. Yangon: UNICEF.
UNICEF. (2014). *School based in-service teacher education. SITE Programme Guidelines*. Internal document. Accessed 2015.
WCRP & HURFOM. (2015). Inaccessible and under-resourced: Concerns over education in rural Mon communities. WCRP & HURFOM. www.rehmonnya.org/reports/Final-Edition.pdf
Yaung Zin. (n.d.-a). *Yaung Zin competency based training programme: Introduction to the Yaung Zin Teacher Training Programme*. Yangon: Yaung Zin.
Yaung Zin. (n.d.-b). *Yaung Zin competency based training programme: Working with parents and the community*. Yangon: Yaung Zin.

Chapter 8
Non-state Teachers in Mon State: Teacher Identity and a Struggle with Inequality

Taru Niskanen and Katharina Buske

Introduction

Monastic education and ethnic education are parallel education systems to the state education in Myanmar. While monastic education provides education for over 8.400 (MIMU 2016) of the most disadvantaged children in Mon State, the ethnic education sector in Mon State provides education for approximately 24.000 (Rehmonnya 2017) with many more ethnic students in other parts of the country. Largely, todays officially recognized monastic education system exists due to the failure of the state to provide education services for all of its citizens (Lorch 2008). The most important distinction between publicly organized education and monastic education is that the former is governed by the Ministry of Education (MoE) while the latter by the Ministry of Religious affairs (MoRA), which are two separate entities within the government system. However, the curriculum employed by both systems is the same, designed nationally by the MoE. Ethnic schools in turn employ mostly their own curriculum in their own language and are completely independent from any governmental institution. They are organized and run by ethnic educational organizations that have developed during the decades of conflict, some of them being more successful than others. In Mon State ethnic education is provided by the Mon National Education Committee (MNEC) and has a rather successful history.

The school system is operated by teachers who are the key determiners of the quality of education. Teachers' professional identity – the way they see themselves as teachers and their professional work – is reflected in their practice through occupational commitment, job satisfaction, self-efficacy and motivation, which in turn affect learning outcomes (Canrinus 2011). This chapter starts from building on the notion of teachers' professional identity within monastic schools. Teachers' professional identity has this far remained unexplored within the studies on monastic

T. Niskanen (✉) · K. Buske
University of Amsterdam, Amsterdam, The Netherlands

M. T. A. Lopes Cardozo, E. J. T. Maber (eds.), *Sustainable Peacebuilding and Social Justice in Times of Transition*,
https://doi.org/10.1007/978-3-319-93812-7_8

education sector in Myanmar (e.g. BIMM & MEDG 2014). Instead, the studies (e.g. BIMM & MEDG 2014; Zobrist 2010) focusing on monastic schools in Myanmar emphasize mostly their needs in terms of facilities, learning materials and teaching methods. The chapter then continues by discussing the notion of identity within MNEC schools, with a specific focus on peacebuilding. The ethnic education system is highly dependent on the willingness and determination of the ethnic teachers to contribute to the educational development of their people. Hence, this case study seeks to engage with the nexus between the role of ethnic history teachers and their contribution to peace. It tries to broaden the understanding on how to enhance the chances for peace through history education in the aftermath of ethnicity-based conflicts by focusing on the teachers' identity and work environment. Given that in many other countries the function of history teaching is to build a national identity create a feeling of "otherness" towards other nations (McCully 2012), this power of history teaching becomes extremely important in post conflict contexts, where ethnicity is a big source for constructing identity. Therefore this case study focused exclusively on the experiences of history teachers. The Mon education system that is the focus of this case study is a particularly interesting case, because it is often described as a prime example of cooperation between an ethnic education system and the government. As Weldon (2010) indicates, more research is needed on how the experiences, emotions and beliefs of teachers not only filter the curriculum they are teaching, but also alter their role as "peace agents". This case study seeks to contribute to exactly that knowledge gap in the literature. In the context of Myanmar, the different ethnic identities in the nation state pose simultaneously a very interesting hurdle and a potential tool for the peace process.

While firstly discussing the two case studies on their own, the chapter concludes by bringing together the topics of inequality and religious and ethnic identity much present in the two case studies outlined here.

Methods

Both case studies presented here draw primarily on research conducted with non-state teachers in Mon State relating to their experiences of teaching. The fieldworks were carried out between September 2015 and March 2016. Thus, the research data reflects a specific geographic area and time period and what is presented in this chapter does not claim to represent the entire country nor the most recent political shifts.

The case study by Niskanen draws from critical realism (Bhaskar 2013; Archer et al. 2013). The specific approaches employed to form the theoretical and analytical tools are the strategic relational approach (Hay 2002; Jessop 2005) and an ecological agency framework (Priestley et al. 2012). Out of the 59 officially recognized monastic schools in Mon State, 4 urban schools for undertaking the core interviews were chosen. The selection was made according to criteria of schools being different from one another in terms of size and the proportion of novice monks therein.

The qualitative research by Niskanen employed an exploratory research design (Brown 2006), drawing on the following inquiry techniques: in-depth semi-structured and open-ended interviews with teachers at four monastic schools (n = 27); informal interviews with principals and administrative personnel at four monastic schools, and civil society actors (n = 23); and non-participatory observations of the monastic schools. The total number of participants was 59. A timeline interview method was used to extrapolate the participants' life histories, professional backgrounds and motivations to teach. The primary unit of analysis were 11 individuals within 4 monastic schools currently engaged in teaching. A purposive sampling technique was used in seeking the predefined group of individuals. In the schools, the respondents were either pointed out by the principal monk or as a result of a discussion between the teachers themselves. The process of data analysis was done deductively. Towards the end of the fieldwork period, reflections emerging from the data were presented to and discussed with the principal monks, staff and teachers during a final visit to the monastic schools. The presentation of the preliminary findings enabled a refinement of the emerging findings and served as a form of data validation.

The research by Buske is based on a mixed-methods approach and includes mainly focus groups (n = 7) and questionnaires (n = 61) with MNEC history teachers. In addition to these, data was collected through observations, identity mapping exercises, MNEC documents and interviews with MNEC representatives. Most of these sessions took place in either the MNEC schools themselves or the New Mon State Party (NMSP) offices of different townships.

The purpose of the focus groups in this research was to grasp multiple perspectives on the issues surrounding history teaching and peace (Kambarelis and Dimitriadis 2013) in a group of MNEC history teachers and involved around 20 open-ended questions. In regard to this particular tool and the role of the local interpreter, open discussions arose and my influence as a researcher was mitigated (Cresswell and Plano Clark 2011). The focus groups were organized in cooperation with the MNEC office based in Mawlamyine and were located in different parts of Mon State. Because of the history of the conflict, the MNEC schools operate mainly in rural areas, which made access sometimes difficult and time consuming. The questions for the focus groups focused on four main domains, namely; school environment, history teaching, peaceful society and identity.

To complement the qualitative data on issues around history teaching and peace, the research used quantitative questionnaires including 30 variables. Their purpose was to gather more comparable data, which helps supply detailed information about individual differences of participants. The indicators were separated into three different groups relating to teacher training and environment; ethnic, identity and values, and demographics. The questionnaire included both closed and open-ended questions (Porst 2011).

Case Study on Monastic Teachers' Professional Identity in Mon State

This case study explores the worlds of 11 practicing teachers at 4 monastic schools in Mon State, Myanmar. The specific research question answered is: What are monastic teachers' professional motivations and aspirations? In answering this question, the theoretical approach this case study adopts is explained first. Then, the context of monastic education within Myanmar is provided, followed by the main findings.

Defining Teachers' Professional Identity

In providing the theoretical frame of the case study, this section discusses the meanings attached to the conception of professional identity. The conception of professional identity is used in various ways within the field of educational studies (Beijaard et al. 2004). It can be broadly "defined as one's professional self-concept based on attributes, beliefs, values, motives, and experiences" (Slay and Smith 2011, 86). Some studies (e.g., Knowles 1992; Nias 1989) relate it mainly to teachers' *self-image* while other studies (e.g., Goodson and Cole 1994; Volkmann and Anderson 1998) emphasize teachers' *roles*, often in relation to other concepts such as reflection or self-evaluation (Beijaard et al. 2004, 108).

Professional identity is multifaceted: "Historical, sociological, psychological, and cultural factors may all influence the teacher's sense of self as a teacher" (Beijaard et al. 2004, 113). The way teachers see themselves as teachers and their professional work is "based on their interpretations of their continuing interaction with their context" (Canrinus 2011, 7). Such context factors include professional development opportunities, level of autonomy (Canrinus 2011) and perceived professional expectations from others, such as students, colleagues, parents and the broader society (Beijaard et al. 2004). Personal factors include for instance main reason for becoming a teacher, educational beliefs and experience in education (Canrinus 2011). This means that teachers' professional identity is closely related to their career motivations and aspirations, which are the focus of this paper. More specifically, the indicators of professional identity manifest themselves in a teacher's occupational commitment, job satisfaction, self-efficacy and motivation (Canrinus 2011). Another vital factor in the process of identity formation are the biographies and backgrounds of teachers, including factors such as early teacher role models and previous teaching experiences (ibid.).

Background

To better communicate the findings of this case study, this section explains the position of monastic education sector within Myanmar. Monasteries have functioned as centres of religious, cultural and social life including informal education for communities in Myanmar for centuries. In fact, monastic education – dating back to the times before state education emerged – was once the pillar of education in Myanmar and catapulted the literacy rate to one of the highest within Asia in the late 1940s and 1950s. Even after the emergence of state education system in the early twentieth century, monasteries continued to provide educational opportunities for the learning of basic reading, writing, and arithmetic skills in particular to those children whose access to state education was restricted because of long distance or lack of financial resources (Tin 2000).

The range of schooling that took place in monasteries began formalizing over 20 years ago, when monasteries throughout the country were systematically transformed into officially recognized schools that followed the government set curriculum (Education in Myanmar n.d.). Currently there are over 1.500 of such schools, located in every state and region and providing education for over 250.000 of the most disadvantaged children (MoE 2014). This accounts for around 16 percent of the total number of the country's primary and high school pupils (Myanmar Times 2013). These numbers are on the increase (MoE 2014). The majority (70.5%) provide primary education and the rest also lower secondary education (MoE 2014).

In Mon State, the teaching staff within the monastic school sector predominantly consist of female teachers rather than monks and nuns. Additionally, while nearly half of all monastic schools of the country have some boarding students, the total number of novice monks and nuns is way below 15% of the monastic student population (BIMM & MEDG 2014). This means that most of the students come from the surrounding neighbourhoods simply to acquire education that compares favourably to that in state schools. Despite the similarities, such as using the same curriculum and being formally recognized by the state, monastic schools have received little, if any, government support in the past (BIMM & MEDG 2014). Moreover, they still largely rely on donations from individuals and the community (ibid.).

Teachers' Identity Formed by Experiences, Motivations and Aspirations

This section discusses the 'personal' and the 'contextual' of teachers' professional self-identity. More specifically, the case study identifies five components of teachers' professional self-identity: (1) personal biographies and backgrounds of teachers; (2) religious (Buddhist) faith; (3) perceived professional expectations from others; (4) teachers' professional wellbeing; and (5) teachers' professional development opportunities. This is necessarily a simplified presentation of the complex processes of teacher professional identity formation and in reality the components are largely overlapping and interlinked.

This section argues that the impact of these components on monastic teachers' professional identity ranges from positive to negative. The positive motivating factors and resources include teachers' dedication to their own disadvantaged communities and being able to relate to their students' situations. Additionally, religious (Buddhist) values of self-sacrifice and service are an important positive resource to the teachers, driving teachers in their work. Religious faith arises as a key to understanding teachers' professional identity in this specific monastic school context, faith framing their motivations and activities as teachers. Somewhat contradictorily, monastic teachers might have compassion for the poor and be professionally motivated but on the other hand, many of them see teaching at a monastery as an undesirable long-term job. Teachers are challenged because of their lack of professional qualifications, insufficient salary and poor working conditions. At monastic schools, teacher management and professional expectations of obeisance mean that teachers have limited power in decision-making. Additionally, the perceived expectations from the students' parents create challenges. The hardships teachers experience in teaching generate negative self-perceptions of being underprivileged and feelings of inferiority to the public-school teachers. Therefore, many of the interviewed teachers are thinking about getting out of teaching at the particular monastic school and getting a position at a public school.

The Positive and the Negative of Teachers' Backgrounds

Most of the interviewed teachers come from lower socio-economic backgrounds. Despite poverty, nearly all of the teachers managed to pursue education in public schools, half of them having graduated from a university or being currently enrolled as a distance student.[1] While most of them have a solid education background, not many have prior experience in teaching before the current position and none of the teachers has a teaching certificate. Most teachers are relatively new in their current teaching position, with less than 2 years of experience at the school. At the other end of the spectrum is a group of senior teachers (including the two monks) who have been already teaching at the school for well over 10 years. All the 11 teachers interviewed are Buddhist, mostly female and predominantly of Bamar (i.e. Burmese) ethnicity, which is the dominant ethnic group in Myanmar. The median age is 30, while the youngest teacher is 17 and the oldest 70.

[1] All of the nine female teachers participating in this study have their educational background from public primary and secondary schools. One male teacher (monk), attended a school up to grade five until the building was destroyed due to war, after which he went to a monastery. The other male teacher (monk) continued studying Buddha education at a monastery after grade 8 at a public school.

The fact that the monastic teachers themselves come from lower socio-economic backgrounds has both weaknesses and strengths in relation to their work. The weakness is they have limited educational opportunities due to a lack of financial capital, which leads to a lack of professional qualifications: the interviews found that many teachers' education has been interrupted or challenged by the financial hardship of their families. For the same reasons many have not been able to pursue a teaching certificate. This indicates a mismatch between teachers' qualifications and the demands of the job. At the same time, due to their own backgrounds, teachers show empathy for their students' life situation. For instance, one interviewed teacher responded:

> Teachers need to understand their students, their lives and feelings. This means that (…) sometimes a student is in a very difficult position because parents really need help at home or elsewhere. It is not up to the student and in such situations teacher should not scold the student but be understanding.

In addition to compassion and understanding, it is noteworthy that teachers are essentially serving their own poor communities: a majority[2] of the interviewed teachers come from the same area where their current working place is located. This contributes to the dedication of teachers to serve/help their own poor communities.

Teachers Serving Their Communities

Teachers at the four monastic schools strongly view themselves as community leaders, which becomes visible through both ideology (status and religious faith) and practice. First, the way teachers talk about themselves in connection to the status teachers have in their community reflects their professional identity. Providing moral guidance by teaching "*good behaviour*" to the students is seen as an essential task of a teacher. Especially the male teachers (monks) express such goals, as can be expected in line with the Buddhist ideology. Furthermore, when discussing their own childhood school years, the teachers point out reasons why they highly admired specific teachers for specific characteristics: "*telling what is good and what is bad*", "*teaching clearly without need for tuition*", "*having a good nature and kind heart*", "*being caring like a parent*", "*providing free tuition*" and "*teaching communication skills*". These are the early teacher role models integral to their biographies, influencing teachers' self-perception today.

The data also shows that teachers' professional identity is closely tied to the idea of service and self-sacrifice. Service is a key feature of Buddhist faith and the interviewed teachers work in a highly Buddhist milieu of monasteries. Therefore, this self-perception is particularly present amongst monastic teachers. However, paradoxically, the reason why many young female teachers aim to become public school teachers is because they believe only then can they serve the nation. For instance,

---

[2] Seven out of the 11 come from a city where the 4 schools integral to this study were based and the rest 4 teachers come from smaller villages either within the same state or Kayin state.

one teacher commented: "*I want to teach in state school in my village because I want to serve national duty*".

Monastic teachers' status in general seems to be subordinate to their state-school counterparts. One male teacher (monk), for instance, points out how some teachers are not eager to participate in teacher education courses provided by the government because they feel being looked down on by the public school teachers. Additionally, many monastic teachers express opinions that public school teachers are in many ways in a better position.

Secondly, the day-to-day practices of teachers show how they actively work as leaders of their communities. This study identified the relationship with community and students as the main challenge teachers face in their day-to-day working environment. A reason for this, substantially discussed by the interviewed teachers, is the student composition. Since students come from lower socio-economic backgrounds, it is not surprising that students' home situations bring challenges to teachers. One teacher explains: "*Students cannot study at home. They cannot do their homework because parents need their help with work*". Such statements are common amongst the teachers. It is generally understood that monastic school kids' help is needed at home, which also results in absences and dropouts. Teachers seem to have developed many tactics to deal with the challenges regarding the relationship with community. Most importantly, there is a strong recognition amongst the interviewed teachers that talking with communities and getting the families on their side is a key in negotiating their constraints.

Professional Expectations from Others

Teachers' surroundings affect their identity as a teacher (Canrinus 2011). Within the schools visited for this study, patriarchal structures of governance are vastly present. As highlighted in Chap. 6, the gendered nature of the teaching profession in Myanmar reproduces gender hierarchies within the sector. This is also evident in the four monastic schools: most teachers are women, operating within a feminized profession that is, at the same time, a strongly male dominated environment in that monks are holding much higher prestige and mostly the ones holding administrative positions. The above links to issues of management of teachers and professional expectations of obeisance. Myanmar is characterized by a top-down management culture, and teacher governance and management within monastic schools are not free from such structures. Professional expectations of obeisance much present in the entire country in particular exist within the monastic sector where religious hierarchies are strong.

A second key point in connection to expectations is related to the fact that monastic education forms an opportunity for the economically marginalized parents to get an education for their children. It is safe to say that they see education as a source of power and therefore set expectations on the education. In teachers' opinion, a common approach by the students' parents is to compare the monastic schools to public schools. Explained by one teacher:

> Most parents take children to this school because they cannot afford government school (...) they expect teachers and the education to have the same level than government schools.

"*This is the biggest pressure*", asserts one principal monk. Hence, the professional identity of many teachers is impacted by their own perceptions of these expectations.

Teachers' Wellbeing and Future Aspirations

Teachers' emotional or mental condition with respect to happiness and enthusiasm at work is tightly connected to professional identity. Reflecting the discussions in Chaps. 5 and 6, the monastic teachers highlight the lack of pay as a factor that majorly affects their personal wellbeing. Eight out of the nine teachers receiving salary point out that the salary is insufficient.[3] Another factor affecting teachers' wellbeing is the apparent mismatch between teacher qualifications and the demands of their job, as already referred to earlier. In addition to lack of pay and qualifications, teachers' wellbeing is challenged with poor working conditions of monastic schools. Infrastructural constraints including the physical building, resources, curriculum and time-constraints are all factors that bring challenges, highlighted by the teachers.

Likewise, teachers' self-identity is connected to the ways they see themselves in future. The way they see themselves as teachers and their professional work develops "based on their interpretations of their continuing interaction with their context" (Canrinus 2011, 7), which include factors such as professional development opportunities and level of autonomy (Canrinus 2011).

Indeed, a wish for professional development comes up a lot: a need for enhancing one's teaching skills and general knowledge dominates amongst the teachers. Many express hopes that government and NGOs would organize teacher education courses. Interestingly, the interviews also prove insights about the divisions between the different education sectors in a way that monastic teachers feel inferior to public school teachers. Sentiments are expressed that there are problems of mixing public schoolteachers and monastic schoolteachers within a single course, as one individual explains in connection to government-organized course on child-centred approaches to teaching:

> Government teachers think they are better (…) and that's why monastic teachers don't like to participate the course. (…) There are many ways to teach but the government teachers (…) believe that their way is the only good one, not the other way explained by the monastery teacher.

To some extent, this corroborates what is written in the second case study of this Chapter about the resentment of the ethnic school teachers of public school teachers (see section below). The interviews with the 11 monastic teachers show that there is

[3] The two male teachers (monks) are excluded from this count as the monastic rules prohibit them to handle money or gain salary.

a resentment that the monastic sector is different from the state sector with the result that many monastic teachers feel belittled and underprivileged. The development of monastic teachers' professional identity takes place in relation to the other, in this case to the public-school teachers.

In terms of more long-term professional development aspirations, the data reveals that most of the teachers interviewed (6 out of 11) aspire to become a public school teacher – this despite the seeming dedication to the monastic school sector discussed earlier. More specifically, those who have been working at the school for a relatively short time tend to desire to become a public school teacher. Many of them want to pursue a teacher education degree or finish their studies at university and then work at a public school. Gaining experience at a monastic school helps to get into teacher Education College, which in turn guarantees a position at a public school. Explained by one teacher: "*I want to become a good teacher and next year will attend Education College for four months and then teach at a government school*". Indeed, one recent study has found that:

> [S]taff recruitment and retention was reported to be difficult – monastic schools compete with government schools for teaching staff, and cannot match the salaries offered in government schools. (BIMM & MEDG 2014, 3)

The findings presented in this section support such sentiments.

The reasons to pursue a position at public school include better financial security (such as higher pay and retirement money), serving the nation, enhancing teaching skills, and higher status. The government of Myanmar has recently decided to employ and train more than 100.000 teachers to public schools (Myanmar Times 2016). Where do these teachers come from? Based on this study, it is reasonable to predict that if access to public schools is made easier by lowering requirements, many monastic teachers might opt for that. This may pose a real risk that monastic schools could be losing many of their teachers to the public school sector, unless the monastic school position is made an equally attractive option. If monastic teachers do not have a feeling that they can develop professionally, if they do not get sufficiently salary or if they feel less valued in their current position at the monastic schools, the future image of monastic schools within the country's educational landscape might be uncertain. This is alarming since education services provided by the monasteries have an important function as a social safety net for those segments of Myanmar's society that cannot afford the costs of public education.

Case Study on History Teachers in MNEC Schools and Their Vision on Peace

This section presents the results drawn from the case study based on ethnic teachers in Mon State. In order to set the scene and introduce the main participants it starts with giving a small overview of the background situation and contextualises therefore the following empirical sections. After a brief theoretical excursion, the section continues discussing experiences of inequality that became evident through this research. Lastly, issues of identity such as language, ethnicity and religion are broached with the aim of giving evidence on consequences for the teachers' ability to act as 'peace agents'.

Theoretical Background of the Case Study

The role of teachers in the ethnic education system is one of particular interest when considering the important role those actors are given in the theoretical debate around education and peacebuilding. Teachers' identities become deeply internalised and bolstered with group memories (Weldon 2010). As Leach and Humphreys (2007) indicate, teachers not only act positively for the peace process but are also capable of representing their own biases in the classroom and reproducing inequalities. The perception of a teacher's representation of the past influences both teaching practices and attitudes (Murphy and Gallagher 2009). But as teachers are the ones transmitting collective memory, which is highly linked to identity building to future generations (Panteli and Zembylas 2013), the linkage between teacher environment, own background and performance as 'agents for peace' is extremely important. In post-conflict contexts especially the role of teachers in history classes is influential (Freedman et al. 2008; McCully 2012; Metro 2013).

Aside from the important role of teachers in peacebuilding, the teaching on history holds a great potential to lead children to a peaceful future for their country and is a major feature of identity and nation building. As Freedman et al. (2008, 666) argue:

> In the aftermath of conflict, revising the content of history curricula presents states with an important means of conveying new narratives of the past, which influence the national identity of citizens, particularly those of the next generation.

While the function of history in most countries is to build a national identity and shared history to create a feeling of "otherness" towards other nations (McCully 2012), this power of history teaching becomes extremely important in post conflict contexts, where ethnicity is a big source for constructing identity. McCully (2012) suggests that the creation of a unified national identity is especially difficult in contexts where different ethnicities have experienced discrimination over decades. The strong connection between the history curricula one is taught and the way one's own identity is built emphasizes why research on history teaching in post-conflict countries is so crucial (Cupcea 2014).

Teachers' Environment: A Clear Vision of Inequality

This section seeks to explain how inequalities between the state and the Mon education system are impacting MNEC teachers negatively and therefore curbing their ability to promote a sustainable peace process. It is argued that through enhanced cooperation between the MNEC and the government, inequalities in school facilities, salary or teacher trainings become more visible, which instead of fostering peacebuilding, endangers any transition from negative to positive peace long-term. As one teacher expressed is the discussion around equality for her the prerequisite for peace: "*Equal rights and then we can say it is peaceful Burma*" (F5, female teacher). This desire for equality and equal rights can be explained by the many inequalities teachers face in their personal lives as Mon people, but also in their position as teachers in MNEC schools. Fighting inequalities and guaranteeing equal rights is perceived as full recognition of the ethnic identity and would contribute to a peaceful Myanmar.

Inequalities in the Teachers' Position, Environment and Training: The Struggle for Recognition and Redistribution

One of the first steps of the government in 2011 was to increase the salary of social servants, including the base teacher salary (Lall 2016). One of the interviewees reported that the state teachers now earn around 150,000 kyat per month (for middle school teachers), which equates to around $110. On the contrary, the MNEC teachers earn 20,000 kyat per month at maximum (around $15). This increase in state salaries resulted in greater pay inequalities between state and MNEC teachers and had the effect of increasing discrimination against MNEC teachers, who feel less worthy.

Therefore, one of the biggest conflict issues that arose during the focus group discussions was the payment gap between state and MNEC teachers. The quantitative data suggests that many MNEC teachers are not satisfied with their payment, because it is most of the time irregular and not enough to make a decent living. More than 70% of the participants vary between categories from 1 to 3, with 1 meaning 'not satisfied at all' and 5 meaning 'totally satisfied' with their salary.

As one of the officers at the MNEC explained, most teachers get paid every 3 months, sometimes even longer due to budget constraints. This payment is handed out by their head teachers, who get the money from the township officer, who himself gets it from the MNEC office. Salaries have to take a long journey through the system before they arrive at the individual teacher, and although there is no evidence of corruption, it is a fact that the teachers occasionally do not get paid at all.

The unequal distribution of salary between the state and the MNEC teachers has strained relationships between the two groups, largely due to feelings of discrimination stemming from the salary discrepancy. Additionally, the MNEC teachers, as the quote below highlights, hold the government responsible for the problem, which has a negative impact on their perception of the government in general. Not only are the individual relationships damaged, but a new negative characteristic of the 'other' is also created – they willingly do not support MNEC to harm the Mon people. As the teacher described in this example:

> For the salary, for the allowance of the salary [we] already asked the government to pay more and the government [did] not allow. (F2, female teacher)

As one participant expressed, many Mon teachers believe that the government does not want to support MNEC on issues of the teacher salaries. This mind set nurtures resentment against the government and the state teachers, who are mainly Bamar, and increases the division between "us" and "the other".

The quantitative data slightly suggests that teachers who are more satisfied with their salary are more likely to believe in a peaceful future as all of the teachers who are totally satisfied with their salary, totally believe in a peaceful future. It seems that if the burden of worrying about surviving from one's salary is taken away and teachers are better able to provide for a family, they are subsequently encouraged to envision a peaceful future.

In discussing teacher training sessions, many teachers expressed how it helped them to become better teachers by learning new teaching methods, materials and skills such as time planning and management. One teacher indicated that the training removed a burden for her: "*Before [I] didn't join [the teacher training], [I] was tired of teaching.*" (F7, young female teacher). Such training allows teachers to perform better and the children are happier with the lessons. Most of the teachers had attended short in-service teacher training provided by the MNEC, which are normally anywhere between 10 and 45 days and are done alongside teaching in class. The two most popular ones among the teachers that were interviewed were "Reading and Writing for Critical Thinking" and "Child Centre Approach". When the teachers were describing a 'good teacher' from their perspective, the words 'child centred' and 'critical thinking' were often repeated. It suggests that the training sessions had an effect on the teachers' idea about what constitutes good teaching. The question remains how it is transferred in the classroom.

Although many of the teachers had teacher training, the data shows that not all of them got a certificate for it or were aware that they got one. Either way, the consequence is the same; teachers felt that their training was not worth as much as the training of government teachers, even though it helped them improve their own teaching skills. As one teacher described:

> Most say that the teacher teaching under the government school, they have more skill and then kind of they already graduated, a little bit they look down, they discriminate the teacher from the MNEC. (F7, female teacher)

This feeling of not being worth as much as the "other" side results in a hierarchy among teachers and education systems, further fuelling conflicts and disagreements. Most of the teacher trainings are not recognised by the government and this makes it difficult for MNEC teachers to compete with state teachers.

Inequalities between recognised certifications and training further divide the teacher groups and school system as MNEC teachers are limited to the MNEC system, which is not the desired aim when trying to foster cooperation in order to promote a peaceful coexistence. Although through a recent change of policies and a shortage of state teachers the government has increasingly employed MNEC teachers, it is not perceived as progress towards more recognition of ethnic teachers. MNEC teachers rather expressed the feeling that the government is 'stealing'

MNEC teachers because there is no alternative solution. The result is that MNEC teachers feel the government is exploiting them and causing the recruitment problem MNEC is facing. Hence, the attitude towards the government worsens and a peaceful cooperation is less likely.

Nevertheless, I did experience in some regions and schools an increase in cooperation between state and MNEC teachers. In some so called “mixed schools”, where MNEC sends a teacher to teach Mon language and history in state schools, or in monthly meetings between the school teachers encouraged by MNEC and the government. The mixed schools approach seems to be a good way of combining the two education systems, but it also entails some risks. The government indeed allows Mon language and history in state schools, but does not support the teaching. The financial and organisational burden is shouldered by the MNEC, and more particularly by the teachers. This uneven distribution of responsibility and resources makes it difficult for the MNEC and their teachers to sustain such practices in the future and doesn’t support a shared process of alignment. This example shows that while an increase in encounters and cooperation are forms of desired progress between the two former conflict groups, they can have negative effects if the cooperation is unequally divided, especially when the ethnic minority has to put in more effort than they can afford. It suggests that in order to strengthen reconciliation efforts such as by increasing encounters, other dimensions of the peace process, like the redistribution of these encounters, need to be settled first.

Some teachers expressed, as demonstrated in the quote below, that the monthly meetings stress them rather than actually supporting the intergroup relationships, although they acknowledge that it also has positive effects in the contact with each other:

> During their holiday they want to relax, but they have to participate in government group, no more time with the family, more time with the state. (F2, older group of female teachers)

Increasing cooperation and the number of encounters with the aim of developing a peaceful relationship between state schools and MNEC schools, has turned out to have the opposite effect, and is perceived as a hardship within the group of MNEC teachers. During many focus groups discussions, inequalities between the state teachers and the Mon teachers on various levels were talked about intensively. Although the salary is one of the biggest issues, the training and facilities also play a role. It is obvious that these inequalities are a major problem for the MNEC teachers to truly engage in a process of reconciliation with the state. Next to the discussion about inequalities, increasing encounters and cooperation between the two education systems became evident as well, whether on the school level, with the monthly meetings of the ‘mixed school’ approach, or on the MNEC office level, with increasing development of shared programs and meetings. Unfortunately, the inequalities become more visible by the increasing encounters between teachers. While the education systems were separate, MNEC teachers were aware of the differences, but did not have to face them on a daily basis. This increasing awareness of inequalities results in MNEC teachers holding the government responsible, which is counterproductive for the wider peace process the MNEC is involved in. The major finding is that although the cooperation between the MNEC and the state schools aims to contribute to the peace process, it is often a financial and time burden for the MNEC teachers and has a negative impact on the relationships. It is argued that through increasing encounters between individuals from the former conflict parties, bonds can be developed, which would help the individuals reconcile with the past. This case study suggests that the reconciliation dimension has negative impacts if the context, in this case that of teachers, is not considered. They are not prepared for these encounters and therefore cannot profit from them.

Inequality in the Political Sphere: The Lack of Representation

Inequalities were not only visible on a financial or resource level of teachers. Many participants expressed that the democratic system works unevenly for different groups of society and they felt disadvantaged. Hence, the general attitude towards democracy was negative, which will be explored in the following section. It provides an interpretation of the teachers' perception of democracy and critically analyses the impact on the peace process.

The former president of Myanmar Thein Sein said: "There can never be peace without democracy nor democracy without peace" (cited in Lall 2016: 104) and thereby stressed the government's view on democracy and its importance for the future of the country. The extent to which the system under the rule of Thein Sein was in reality a democratic system has been debated, but nevertheless, it demonstrates that democratic processes are valued by the national government.

> You know, our Mon we don't know about democracy. We know about our federalism. (F5, male head teacher)

This quote, above, expresses the idea I was repeatedly hearing from teachers talking about democracy. It is interesting for two reasons. The first part entails an argument many teachers were using, saying that people are not educated enough to participate in the elections or understand the democratic system. Secondly, the last part of the quote is related to the wish of self-determination. The teachers do not believe that democracy will change anything for ethnic minorities, but prioritise federal decision making processes, which enables them to be independent and autonomous within the country.

Although it was an extremely interesting time politically while this research was conducted, with the second democratic elections having recently been held (with the majority of votes going to the NLD) and it was close to the announcement of the new president, teachers in Mon State did not share the excitement: "*The democracy meaning is very good, very powerful. But after a while democracy is bla bla bla*" (F4, group of young female teacher).

The general attitude towards democracy is best encapsulated in this quote. It is explained by disappointments from the past and the legacy of the military dictatorship, that people are not yet able to believe the situation has changed and will have a long-term effect. Scepticism and indifference describes best the position most teachers were taking. The government was mostly referred to as the "Burmese government" which demonstrates how the teachers distance themselves and their ethnicity from democracy and the political entity. The distinction between "us and them" in political terms hinders nation-building efforts and decreases the government's legitimacy, which ultimately prevents the Mon people from identifying themselves with the new democratic nation: "*The teacher said, she doesn't believe, they [the government] are not working with us*" (F2, female teacher).

Hand in hand with the desire for equal rights and political representation, explained above, came the fear of losing what and who the Mon are. It is a result of being afraid that the Mon people, the language, the culture and their traditions could disappear. For the teachers, the solution to the problem is to protect it by reaching for autonomy. One female teacher indicates that a loss of nationality is always caused by someone taking it: "*We worry for our nationality, if someone destroys it or taking it*" (F2, female teacher).

Teachers in every focus group exclusively identified with the Mon ethnicity. Being someone was strongly linked to being Mon, which always entailed an element of exclusion towards others. Having ethnicity as the unifying element of the group goes hand in hand with separation from others. Some teachers accordingly expressed feelings of superiority as demonstrated in this quote: "*Yes, we are Mon. We don't feel national, we have more superiority*" (F3, female teacher). This demarcation especially from Burmese people is legitimised through religion and history, but also through factors such as the visual nature and the behaviour. One teacher listed unique Mon characteristics that legitimised this superiority:

> We have fight about things, but we are the first to meet Buddha. We are the first with donations (…), we are the first one to apply religion, we have the hair of the Buddha, we are the first ones to build a pagoda. (F3, older female teacher)

The connection between religion and the Mon identity is remarkable, introduced through the teachers into the classroom and therefore has a great impact on how identity is built through Mon education.

The "other" is created by legitimising a superiority that cannot be reached unless you are Mon. Its source is ultimately ethnicity, which no one is able to choose freely. In this sense it endangers a peaceful coexistence with other groups in the country because there can never be a unifying element. Nation-building efforts have no effect on the Mon teachers, because they don't identify at all with the nation. The wish for self-determination is a result of an ethnic identity that is described as unique and superior.

The MNEC has often been described as a prime example of how ethnic education can work with the state education system for many legitimate reasons, such as the combined curriculum, mother-tongue education and the possibility for students to transfer into the state education system (Lall and South 2014). As Lall and South (2014) suggest:

> State support and the development and rooting of ethnic identity is, therefore, essential for the multi-ethnic population to possess a sense of inclusion, which in turn will spur and enhance loyalty for a national language. (Lall and South 2014, 4)

This research raises the question of what happens if the ethnic identity is defined by an ethnic superiority and does therefore not enhance loyalty to the nation.

The findings of this research give glimpses of how identity is created in MNEC schools. Feelings of pride and exclusivity were often the main markers for the Mon identity. It was exclusively connected to the ethnicity and there were almost no identifications with something else, such as a concept of the nation. It was revealed that identity in MNEC schools do not promote a process of building an ethnic as well as a national identity, but quite the opposite. The identity building process in MNEC schools is therefore an issue that negatively affects the peace process.

Conclusion

This chapter has presented two case studies both conducted in Mon State Myanmar focusing on non-state teaching. Although the case studies are very different, they both feature the topics of inequality and religious and ethnic identity.

Teachers in both monastic and ethnic education speak about similar dilemmas regarding their lack of professionalism, job chances and salary. They seem to be well aware of their unequal position in comparison to the state schools in terms of redistribution of government resources to education. Largely, teachers in both monastic and ethnic education exhibit negative self-perceptions of being underprivileged and feelings of inferiority to the public-school teachers. This increasing awareness of inequalities results in MNEC teachers holding the government responsible, which is counterproductive for the wider peace process the MNEC is involved in. In the case of monastic schools, the inequalities result that many of the interviewed teachers are thinking about getting out of teaching at the particular monastic school and getting a position at a public school. Within MNEC education, the motivation to protect their ethnic identity somehow outweigh these constraints coming with the profession of an ethnic teacher. Within monastic education, religious (Buddhist) values of self-sacrifice and service are an important positive resource to the teachers, framing their motivations and activities as teachers. Other positive resources are teachers' dedication to their own disadvantaged communities and being able to relate to their students' situations.

The ongoing education sector reform taking place in Myanmar provides an opportunity to guarantee that monastic and ethnic schools receive a better share from the country's education provisions. This requires that the position of non-state education within the National Education Law (NEL), currently under revision, is clarified and that its many bylaws, regulations and subsections are formulated with holding non-state education sector in a position of high importance. It is recommended to open up the reform process especially for non-state education systems and organisations as they play a pivotal role in the provision of basic education for the rural ethnic population and should also be able to contribute their vision of education to the reform. Separating state and ethnic and monastic education is a step in the wrong direction if the aim is combining the education systems and appreciating differences in the country.

References

Archer, M., Lawson, T., & Norrie, A. (2013). *Critical realism: Essential readings*. London: Routledge.

Beijaard, D., Meijer, P. C., & Verloop, N. (2004). Reconsidering research on teachers' professional identity. *Teaching and Teacher Education, 20*(2), 107–128.

Bhaskar, R. (2013). *A realist theory of science*. London: Routledge.

Brown, R. B. (2006). *Doing your dissertation in business and management: The reality of researching and writing*. London: Sage.

Burnet Institute Myanmar and Monastic Education Development Group (BIMM & MEDG). (2014). *Monastic schools in Myanmar – A baseline study*. Yangon: BIMM & MEDG.

Canrinus, E. T. (2011). *Teachers' sense of their professional identity*. Groningen: University Library Groningen.

Cresswell, J. W., & Plano Clark, V. L. (2011). *Designing and conducting mixed methods research*. Thousand Oaks: Sage Publications.

Cupcea, A. (2014). History teaching in Bosnia Herzegovina during the conflict and post-conflict era. *Romanian Review of Eurasian Studies, 10*(1–2), 133–146.

Education in Myanmar. (n.d.). http://factsanddetails.com/southeast-asia/Myanmar/sub5_5f/entry-3117.html

Freedman, S., Weinstein, H., Murphy, K., & Longman, T. (2008). Teaching history after identity-based conflicts: The Rwandan experience. *Comparative Education Review, 52*(4), 663–690.

Goodson, I. F., & Cole, A. L. (1994). Exploring the teacher's professional knowledge: Constructing identity and community. *Teacher Education Quarterly, 21*(1), 85–105.

Hay, C. (2002). *Political analysis: A critical introduction*. London: Palgrave Macmillan.

Jessop, B. (2005). Critical realism and the strategic-relational approach. *New Formations: A Journal of Culture, Theory and Politics, 56*, 40–53.

Kambarelis, G., & Dimitriadis, G. (2013). *Focus groups. From structured interviews to collective conversations*. New York: Routledge.

Knowles, G. J. (1992). Models for understanding pre-service and beginning teachers' biographies: Illustrations from case studies. In I. F. Goodson (Ed.), *Studying teachers' lives* (pp. 99–152). London: Routledge.

Lall, M. (2016). *Understanding reform in Myanmar – People and society in the wake of military rule*. London: Hurst & Company.

Lall, M., & South, A. (2014). Comparing models of non-state ethnic education in Myanmar: The Mon and Karen National Education Regimes. *Journal of Contemporary Asia, 44*(2), 298–321.

Leach, F., & Humphreys, S. (2007). Gender violence in school: Taking the 'Girls-as-Victims' discourse forward. *Gender and Development, 15*(1), 51–65.

Lorch, J. (2008). 9: The (re)-emergence of civil society in areas of state weakness: The case of education in Burma/Myanmar. In M. Skidmore & T. Wilson (Eds.), *Dictatorship, disorder, and decline in Myanmar* (pp. 151–176). Canberra: ANU E-Press.

McCully, A. (2012). History teaching, conflict and the legacy of the past. *Education, Citizenship and Social Justice, 7*(2), 145–159.

Metro, R. (2013). Postconflict history curriculum revision as an "Intergroup Encounter" promoting interethnic reconciliation among Burmese migrants and refugees in Thailand. *Comparative Education Review, 57*(1), 145–168.
MIMU, Myanmar Information Management Unit. (2016). http://themimu.info/sites/themimu.info/files/documents/Sector_Map_Monastic_Education_2015-2016_MIMU962v04_30Aug2016_A3.pdf
Ministry of Education of Myanmar (MoE). (2014). *Education for all 2015 national review report: Myanmar*. http://unesdoc.unesco.org/images/0022/002297/229723E.pdf
Murphy, K., & Gallagher, T. (2009). Reconstruction after violence. How teachers and schools can deal with the legacy of the past. *Perspectives in Education, 27*(2), 158–168.
Myanmar Times. (2013). *Monastic education: In decline or on the rise?*
Myanmar Times. (2016). *Teacher numbers to grow by a quarter under reform plan*.
Nias, J. (1989). Teaching and the self. In M. L. Holly & C. S. McLoughlin (Eds.), *Perspective on teacher professional development* (pp. 151–171). London: Falmer Press.
Panteli, Y., & Zembylas, M. (2013). Teachers' perception of national identity and its intersection with gender: A phenomenological study in a conflict society. *Gender and Education, 25*(4), 379–395.
Porst, R. (2011). *Fragebogen. Ein Arbeitsbuch* (3rd ed.). Wiesbaden: VS Verlag für Sozialwissenschaften.
Priestley, M., Biesta, G., & Robinson, S. (2012). *Teacher agency and curriculum change*. Working papers (ESRC reference: RES-000-22-4208).
Rehmonnya. (2017). MNEC drafts Mon National Education Policy. *Rehmonnya*. http://rehmonnya.org/archives/4106. Accessed 25 Nov 2017.
Slay, H. S., & Smith, D. A. (2011). Professional identity construction: Using narrative to understand the negotiation of professional and stigmatized cultural identities. *Human Relations, 64*(1), 85–107.
Tin, H. (2000). Myanmar education: Status, issues and challenges. *Journal of Southeast Asian Education, 1*(1), 134–162.
Volkmann, M. J., & Anderson, M. A. (1998). Creating professional identity: Dilemmas and metaphors of a first-year chemistry teacher. *Science Education, 82*(3), 293–310.
Weldon, G. (2010). Post-conflict teacher development: Facing the past in South-Africa. *Journal of Moral Education, 39*(3), 353–364.
Zobrist, B. (2010). *Mapping teaching-learning and operational experiences in fifty monastery schools*. Report for Pyoe Pin Programme, Myanmar Youth Forum and Phaung Daw Oo Basic Integrated Monastic High School.

Part III
Youth and Peacebuilding

Chapter 9
Youth Agency for Peacebuilding in and Beyond Education: Possibilities and Constraints

Sean Higgins and Mieke T. A. Lopes Cardozo

Introduction

This chapter aims to situate and understand the situation of youth within current processes of social, economic and political transition within Myanmar. In so doing, and in alignment with the book's concern to illuminate the cultural political economy context in relation to the agency of youth as peace builders, it underlines the constraints, opportunities and horizons of action available to youth. It should be noted that the insights offered below draw on the research team's engagement with youth constituencies in Mon State and Yangon and cannot therefore be considered representative of the highly diverse and context-specific situation of youth throughout the country. Moreover, the socio-political landscape in the country is in a state of transition (see Chap. 1), and with unresolved peace negotiations in process, the conclusions presented here should be understood as provisional and appropriate at this particular juncture.

At the outset, the lack of evidence about youth in Myanmar is striking. Indeed, a particular concern expressed by the many participants in this research – including the staff of international aid agencies as well as government ministries – was their current lack of precise knowledge, based on reliable evidence, about the situation and aspirations of Myanmar's youth. This absence of data was perceived by many to undermine effective policymaking tailored to the specific needs and concerns of youth across the country, especially in relation to their economic situation. As one informant pointed out, "*the problem is you don't really know what is happening to the youths out there…job opportunities, education, the employment market*" (int. 1). Exacerbating this perceived knowledge gap, the absence of information sharing between local and international agencies and in particular the neglect by the latter

S. Higgins · M. T. A. Lopes Cardozo (✉)
University of Amsterdam, Amsterdam, Netherlands
e-mail: mlopescardozo@fmg.uva.nl

M. T. A. Lopes Cardozo, E. J. T. Maber (eds.), *Sustainable Peacebuilding and Social Justice in Times of Transition*,
https://doi.org/10.1007/978-3-319-93812-7_9

of the "*grassroots*" insights and "*practical*" knowledge of youth needs developed by local actors was also underlined (int. 81).[1] For example, the Ministry of Labour's current project in conjunction with the International Labour Organisation (ILO) focuses on gathering data across the country, linking labour market opportunities to planning, for enhanced vocational provision to meet youth needs. This is evidently an attempt to remedy one dimension of this evidence gap (ILO 2015, 86). Such initiatives testify to a broader recognition by both national and international actors that there is an urgent need to generate accurate knowledge as a crucial precondition for understanding and effectively engaging with the country's youth (int. 13). Within recent academic research on Myanmar, there is also a striking inattention to youth needs and concerns. It is noticeable that within assessments of the country's political and economic transition, relatively little is said about the younger segment of the population as opposed to broader civil society. This relative dearth of material on the situation of youth in Myanmar suggests that it is an important example of a broader neglect of attention to youth voices and needs in conflict-affected contexts.

Responding to this gap in knowledge, this chapter starts by sketching out the heterogeneous nature of those considered as 'youth' and continues by situating youth within Myanmar's current political and socio-economic transition. In doing so, we highlight certain important issues affecting youth agency including migration, inter-generational relationships and drugs. The second part of this chapter then moves to analyse current framings of how youth are understood, both within the continuously fluctuating policy discourses as well as by other key stakeholders. Finally, the multiple scales of youth activity and interaction will be considered, from intra-personal reflections, and inter-personal relationships all the way to engagement at national and international levels. This then leads us to the concluding argument that for diverse youth groups in contemporary Myanmar, and across levels of educational attainment, relative prosperity, dimensions of marginalisation and geographical location, a picture emerges of a rather restricted space for manoeuvre available to the younger generation within Myanmar's transition.

Locating Youth Within the Country's Social, Political and Economic Transitions

Reflecting the priority of the *Literature Review: Youth Agency, Peacebuilding & Education* (Lopes Cardozo et al. 2015) to reject assumptions of the homogeneity of youth, the research presented in this book aimed to include youth perspectives from a range of constituencies.

---

[1] Numbers indicated after quotations refer to our coding system employed as a research team, and congruent with Chaps. 3, 4, 5, 6, 7, 9, and 10.

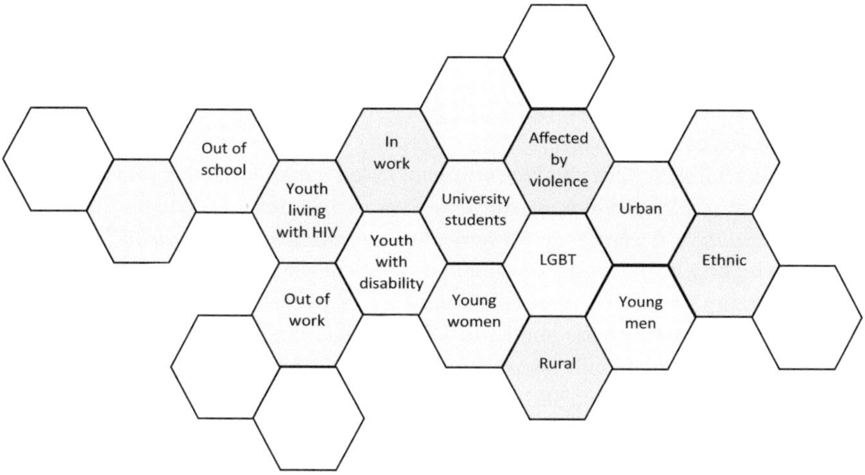

Fig. 9.1 Multiple youth constituencies included in the research. (Design by Elizabeth Maber)

Which Youth?

Youth engaged with in our data gathering were of different religious faiths, socio-economic backgrounds, and political affiliations and were between the ages of 16 and 30. Research took place in the Yangon area and in Mon State, although youth participants included ethnic identities beyond these two areas. An overview of the multiple constituencies primarily included in the research is provided in Fig. 9.1.

These categories of youth overlap and intersect so that individuals may identify with multiple or hybrid affiliations. Identity associations may take on greater significance in certain circumstances over others, and likewise may shift over time as alignments as well as spaces for agency, such as rural or urban, in or out of employment, are fluid and may change. Although not featuring prominently in our data gathering, it is acknowledged that youth may also be parents, carers, homeless, former or current combatants, they may be engaged in forced labour or sex work or subject to a variety of additional positions.

Experiences of Political/Democratic Transition

Youth informants from both urban and rural backgrounds recognised, albeit with a degree of caution, the potential positive impacts on their lives of the tentative opening up of political and social freedoms which have been associated with the country's political transition within the last few years. Many expressed their awareness of experiencing a new national liberalising trajectory stating that "*our country is on the path to democracy*" (int. 40), or involved in a "*democratic transition*" (int. 57).

Articulating a perception of the broad positive implications of recent developments for the presence and participation of youth within civil society, one rural youth informant participating in trainings and offering political and civic awareness noted that "*we have more right to speak freely, teach freely and show freely*" and that there are "*more rights on the cultural side*" (int. 57). Similarly articulating a sense of shifting societal dynamics another informant noted: "*in the past it is very difficult to lead in front of our community. But now [our] community is changing and [the] political situation is changing. So they start to practice democratising*" (int. 32). This also highlights the close association of political change with social transformation for young people. In particular, informants expressed appreciation for the expansion since 2011 of the number of civil society organisations and NGOs that were concerned with youth issues and how these started to provide meaningful spaces for their participation and support (ints. 40 and 57). As one youth CSO member put it:

> in the democratic transition we have more right to start up an organisation and there are more opportunities to attend the courses in NGOs or somewhere else, so the youth can get more chances…and there are many organisations which do the training, like capacity building courses or awareness training, but all are focus[ed] to get peace. (57)

Informants also associated liberalisation processes with new opportunities for offering support to youth to enhance their political awareness: "*now we can give the training freely with the politics in villages and towns*" (int. 57). This was also complemented by their enjoyment of easier access to printed newspapers and social media.

Constraints on Youth Political Engagement

However, optimism about new possibilities for youth held out by the prospect of ongoing 'democratisation' was tempered by a counter-veiling recognition of continuing constraints on youth participation and political engagement. Stakeholders expressed their awareness of the tokenistic appropriation of youth within decision-making spaces, where apparent inclusion masked exclusion from genuine influence and power (ints. 7, 94 and 13). Thus, even though youth might be invited to participate in more formal peacebuilding activities and meet "*high level people*", one informant concluded that "*Youth continue to be marginalised: you know we allow them to participate in the meeting but it's not structural influence*" (int. 7). Some informants, reflecting on experiences of participation in the youth wings of political parties, noted that they became dominated by elders so much that they no longer properly served their purpose as a channel to enable and promote participation. It was also recognised by youth participants themselves that "*in the democratic transition, youth are weak in political knowledge*" (int. 57), highlighting the legacy of inadequate education systems to prepare young people to participate in politics. This sense of frustration at the limits of exercising genuine influence, as well as the fear of repercussions from police and military that accompany political action have strong influences on participation. As one peer educator commented:

> Youth don't participate in the political because they fear the political. And in their mind, they always think that if they do politics, they will be in prison. For example, the students' protests that we have recently, when they hear the protest, they think about the 88 revolution because during that revolution many students died, so parents call and take back their children. (int. 57)

Further constraints on youth participation and their agency for transformation are discussed in the next Chap. 10. What is apparent from the foregoing discussion is the range of relationships to and experiences of the "political" within diverse youth constituencies in different contexts. These evidently cover a spectrum from activism and engagement – albeit frequently in circumstances of intimidation and violence – to passivity, fear and despair.

Youth Within the Economic Transition

Interestingly, for youth in Mon State and Yangon, who unlike youth in other states may not have directly experienced violent conflict, there was a frequent association of peacebuilding with opportunities for work and resulting possibilities of financial security. Here peace was explicitly understood as a sense of wellbeing, emphatically linked to rectifying perceived economic injustices. In a focus group discussion, a group of rural village youth similarly expressed their conviction of the relevance of well-paid work for theirs and their communities' wellbeing, pointing out that *"good business and income are the important things for peacebuilding"* (int. 44). The dignity and life-enhancing prospects that come from earning a living was perceived by many youth to provide the practical and emotional underpinning for their positive exercise of agency linked to peacebuilding and development within their communities. Thus one youth pointed out that *"in order to have the youth participating in the country's development process, we need job opportunities and methods"* (int. 57). When asked what he meant by "methods", this young man talked about the practical know-how to be able to produce good rubber products such that *"if they know how to, they can get more income and they can go to the schools and they will be educated and they can participate in the development process"* (int. 57). Here economic wellbeing was perceived to be the essential grounding for youth's capacity to learn relevant skills, and contribute to sustainable developmental processes. This was a view not only held by youth, but similarly by state-level stakeholders (int. 80), as is further illuminated below.

Youth informants recognised that Myanmar was undergoing an economic as well as political transition, associated in particular with renewed international investment in energy, mining, industry and agriculture. However, many perceived that such developments were benefiting an elite group of 'cronies' – high ranking business people who enjoyed patronage and economic benefits during time of military rule (Gravers and Ytzen 2014, 126) – at the expense of the majority of the population, especially rural youth. Thus one informant observed that *"in the democratic transition, there are more economic opportunities for the people who are rich but there are no opportunities at the ground level"* (int. 57). Such perceptions confirm the analysis of other commentators. A review of the country's recent economic trajectory concludes that "lack of public policy and investment support has limited the potential of a young and eager to learn population that could contribute to economic growth" (Findlay et al. 2016, 47). Youth perception of the state's disconnection from the economic plight of its citizens is captured in the comment of one informant on the treatment of farmers protesting at state land grabbing, who pointed out that: *"we can say that we have foreign investment and wide uses of cell phone and more cars"*, but he warns that *"they are not the improvements that we really want, like... you can see the farmers and workers because of their low pay, when they protest they go to the jail"* (int. 56).

Against this perception of their exclusion from the benefits of national economic growth spurred by foreign capital, youth expressed despair at the lack of employment opportunities. This seemed to be relevant both to the diverse constituencies of urban and rural youth, including school drop outs, as well as better educated youth (ints. 24, 44, 67 and 68). They also expressed frustration at the impoverishment caused to them and their families by narrow options of low paid casual labour (int. 38). Similarly, youth with high levels of education were also frustrated that it did not translate to adequate professional compensation or a better standard of living: "*the salary for youth is not related to professional [position] even though you are a doctor, you are not paid [a] professional salary*" (int. 114). Such concerns about high youth unemployment and under-employment were construed within a broader critique of inattention of the state to the social and economic needs of communities. Similarly, they also highlight deeply felt resentment that formal education is failing to provide a pathway to employment and improved living standards for young people.

A recent report on the need for improved vocational education provision confirmed this dismal picture, of the impoverishing consequences for youth of a lack of both work and work-related education opportunities, pointing out that "in 2013 approximately one million lower secondary school drop outs needed access to adequate and labour market relevant vocational education and training in order to break out of the cycle of poverty" (TVET, Sub-Sector Report 7,28). Paradoxically, while the nation's large youth constituency is perceived as an asset in relation to prospects for economic growth as shown below in analysis of state level policy on technical and vocational education – our youth informants emphasised their current experience of exclusion from labour market opportunities.

Migration as Impacting on Youth Agency

While this chapter's attention to youth agency assumes the presence of this demographic within Myanmar, it was, on the contrary, the scarcity or near absence of youth in the villages and communities of Mon State resulting from the impact of widespread economic migration which was a recurring concern amongst informants. As one informant bluntly put it, *"that groups is hard to find in the villages due to migration"* (int. 7).

Youth informants cited the frustrations of youth at the lack of employment opportunities and/or well-paid work opportunities in Mon State as a key economic driver of the exodus of their generation (int. 57). This frustration was particularly felt by well-educated youth who spoke of being ashamed *"for working on the same thing that illiterate people like, like rubber tapping and rice farming although they are graduates"* (int. 38). Some also pointed to a mismatch between what they had learned in their formal education and the employment prospects in Mon State: *"they can't use their education in reality, so most of the youth go to foreign countries to work"* (int. 56). Such frustrations were compounded by pressures to migrate to earn money in order to alleviate family poverty (int. 44) as well as the perceived economic success of friends who had gone abroad to earn and were sending remittances back home. Although our data reflects mostly on the situation in Mon State, similar observations are also relevant for instance in Shan State, Kayin State, Kayah State and Thanintharyi Region (ILO 2013).

Socio-cultural Impacts of the Political and Economic Transition on Youth Agency

This section highlights some of the social and cultural impacts bearing upon youth agency, and reviews them in relation to the above-sketched political and economic context of transition.

Changing Inter-generational Relationships

The scarcity of a youth demographic resulting from migration was perceived by many – including youth themselves – as a social tragedy for Myanmar, undermining the capacity of communities to benefit from the energies and skills of a key group in society. Thus, the negative impact of a youth absence on inter-generational leadership and knowledge exchange were noted. As one informant put it, *"it takes people of different generations to run a community right"* (int. 80). Moreover, young people themselves were aware that as result of being caught up within processes of economic migration their generation is unable – frequently unwilling – to contribute to the development of their communities. Many perceived the migration process as one that undermined a sense of commitment of youth to their communities.

Youth as well as national and international stakeholders agreed that a major influence on youth agency within Myanmar was their location within these changing inter-generational relationships. There was a widespread perception of a shift away from traditional social hierarchies in which youth were compliant and subservient to elders' dominance. One youth noted that *"in the past only the elders, rich people, authority people have to be leaders in the villages, but now things are changing"* (int. 32). Such shifts presented particular challenges as well as opportunities for youth. Many expressed an awareness and commitment to cultural norms obligating them to a passive role; as one put it, *"the culture makes us to be obedient to elder people"* (int. 57). On the other hand, there were new opportunities to forge more collaborative and co-operative relationships with elders through dialogue. Recognition of greater opportunities for youth leadership in village communities was perceived to be a by-product of such societal shifts (int. 32). Still, many youth continued to be committed to traditional social values, even as they welcomed the new social inclusion of youth. Thus, one youth pointed out that *"we need to bow our head when we walk in front of the older people, have respect [for] older people and have empathy to[wards] younger people"* (int. 38). However, such shifts posed challenges both for youth as well as elders, in particular related to the extent to which traditional cultural norms could be transgressed as youth took up new spaces to *"talk back"* to teachers and parents (int. 81).

Youth Resorting to Drugs

Youth and leaders of organisations working with youth expressed concern at what they perceived as mounting levels of drug abuse among youth. While field work was not conducted in the major drug producing states of Myanmar, nevertheless it was recognised that even within this context removed from the immediate major sources of supply, drugs were accessible and used by large numbers of youth (int. 7). The role of high unemployment, dropping out of school, and the impact of economic migration abroad on youth attitudes and behaviours were all cited as factors instigating youth to turn to drugs (int. 57). The availability of remittances from money earned abroad within rural villages was also cited as a factor encouraging drug use (int. 7).

Moreover, some youth questioned what they perceived as a strategy to arrest youth drug users rather than the suppliers (int. 57). Youth organisations working with youth on drug issues in rural villages in Mon State reported having to seek special security for fear of reprisals by drug traders (int. 56). This indicates the difficulty of addressing youth drug abuse given the range of vested interests committed to their continued production and consumption. Some youth felt strongly about what they perceived as the collusion of state authority in undermining youth agency by not taking action against drug dealers and instead criminalising youth consumers with heavy-handed law enforcement. For instance, one informant pointed out that:

> The police don't address the drug users and the government lets it happen, so it could mean that they are destroying the citizens intentionally.

Youth drug use is thus located in a complex mix of state collusion, the persistence of a prosperous drugs economy and the consequent challenges of interventions to address drug abuse, and is an area that calls for further research.

Youth-Related Policy and Framing

Having laid out the location of youth within Myanmar's current transition, and young people's experiences of current challenges in relating to this context, this section illuminates the way youth are framed and addressed at the policy level. It highlights the lack of a state level youth policy and policy coherence in this area. Policy coherence is weakened on the one hand by the number of ministerial departments attending to youth issues, including the Ministries of Labour, Education and Social Welfare, and on the other by a lack of co-ordination between them (int. 8). Some informants, youth as well as those working in government organisations, noted with regret the absence of a Ministry or a Minister devoted to youth issues (ints. 13, 14 and 18). Moreover, the lack of co-ordination of responses and programming in relation to youth by international agencies operating in the country was recognised as undermining the effectiveness of interventions (ints. 80 and 81). Being mindful of the attention to youth needs in the policies and programming of some non-governmental organisations, the overall picture remains of the absence of a coherent, systematic focus within national state and donor policy.

Youth as Framed Within National State Level Agendas

It was noted that the absence of a coherent institutional architecture at the state level for addressing youth issues was in part a reflection of a legacy of neglect of this constituency within national policy prior to the recent democratic transition. However, there was also a perception of a more recent *"huge cultural and structural breakthrough"* (int. 51) in the treatment of the country's youth within government, in which their needs, issues and voices were finally coming into view as an important component of national development. One informant noted that within the current transition there were genuine signs of a move away from previous paternalistic approaches to youth as *"babies that needed to be taken care of"* (int. 51) within earlier authoritarian top down modes of national governance. However, the limitations of this apparent cultural repositioning of youth within national policy priorities is underlined by others who point out that youth have been marginalised from both dialogue on current education reform processes and peace processes and that their concerns are not mainstreamed as a cross-cutting issue (int. 79).

The fact that attention to youth constituencies is frequently implicit or emerges indirectly as a component within broader governmental initiatives perhaps reflects this unresolved and uncertain re-evaluation of youth within national priorities. Some – including youth themselves – for instance have associated recent ministerial aspirations for more "*people centred*" governance with greater recognition and responsiveness to youth (int. 18). The willingness of government Ministries to organise workshops on youth related issues is also taken to reflect a new recognition of youth concerns.

Moreover, the potential role of youth in contributing to the country's economic growth and transformation is recognised within policy formation linked to a perceived urgent need to improve access to and provision of technical and vocational education (int. 8). Here the economic dimensions of youth agency are emphasised and their status as a key source of the nation's human capital. Youth are thus defined in relation to the exigencies of national economic growth within an expanding market economy (int. 86). What is striking is a recognition of absence of knowledge or understanding of youth needs linked to the labour market and employment. A national survey organised by the Department of Labour with the co-operation of the International Labour Organisation (2015) is the first one undertaken in the country in "a quarter of a century and will provide results that will shape the country's employment policy" (ILO 2015, 1). In relation to enabling a greater understanding of the needs of youth, the survey aims to produce labour statistics on the labour force and potential labour markets, child labour, and the school to work transition. Informants from the Ministry of Labour underlined the significance of this data gathering process in providing information about the regional diversity of labour market needs, which could inform the appropriate tailoring of vocational training for unemployed and out of school youth (int. 86).

Recognition of the inadequate quality and provision of technical and vocational education for the country as a whole also indicates a wider concern with youth well-being as influenced by employment and livelihood prospects (ints. 86 and 79). Thus, a report on Technical and Vocational Education forming part of the CESR research process (see Chap. 4) points out that the transformation shifts which the Ministry of Education commits to achieving is that "learners can access and graduate from quality assured certified and labour market responsive TVET which will enable them to find decent employment and secure their livelihood" (TVET Sub-sector report no 7, 1). While this can be seen as a promising response to youth demands for a dignified job, at the same time there lies a potential danger in instrumentalising youth as mere (potential) productive citizens, and leaving more political and socio-cultural aspects of youth agency and empowerment aside.

Youth Within the Policy and Programming Priorities of International Actors

There is wide acknowledgement amongst education staff of aid agencies that Myanmar's youth have been neglected within the priorities and programming of international actors overwhelmed by a multitude of other competing concerns within a challenging context (ints. 4 and76). Such inattention contradicted a general awareness that youth needed to be better targeted in programming and a conviction that *"more needs to be done on policy for youth"* (int. 4). Various challenges were identified, which had rendered youth-related programming problematic and difficult to operationalise.

Firstly, the dangers of offending political and cultural sensitivities by attending to a cohort sometimes *"perceived as trouble"* or being "*controversial*" was highlighted (int. 4). Secondly, the sheer heterogeneity of the country's youth constituencies – including disillusioned students, school drop outs, unemployed male and female youth, young parents and child soldiers, all with disparate needs and situations – made programming particularly complex. Thirdly, the inattention to developing programmes to support Myanmar's youth as agents of peacebuilding was attributed to a perceived lack of an evidence base to inform interventions (int. 3). Finally, it was recognised that the generic programming frameworks which aid agencies brought to conflict-affected contexts, such as TVET or equivalency programmes, undermined comprehensive and integrated analysis of the particularities of youth needs in Myanmar, undermining the possibility of context-responsive and meaningful interventions (int. 4).

Framing of Youth Within Myanmar Society

This section highlights the diverse array of approaches and perceptions of Myanmar's youth circulating amongst national and international stakeholders, civil society actors, the police and state security institutions, elders, and also as reported within the media. Bringing these together indicates the variegated understanding of youth agency, which ranges across a continuum, from highly negative to celebratory and indeed triumphalist (see Fig. 9.2). They also indicate the contradictory expectations held of the country's youth and their status as a constituency whose agentic significance is contested and uncertain.

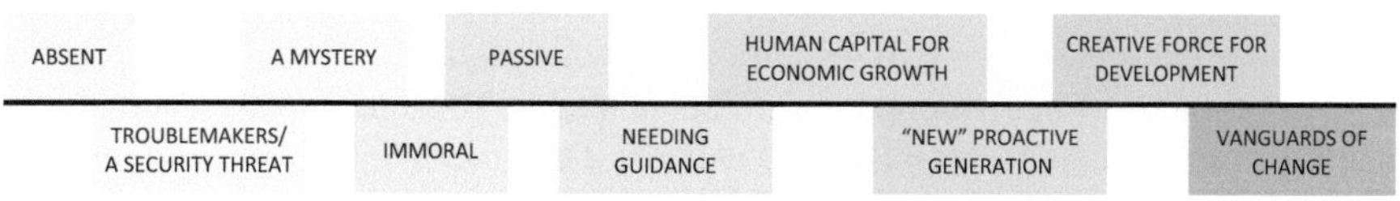

Fig. 9.2 Youth agency across a continuum. (Design by Elizabeth Maber)

Youth as Absent

As noted in the previous section on political economy factors impacting on youth agency, there was a widespread recognition of the absence of youth within Myanmar's rural communities caused by economic migration. Thus a manager of a youth initiative commenting on the challenging process of recruitment noted that "*we said we would like to have youth but the problem we found is that there are no youth in the villages of Karen and Mon state*" (int. 30). This exodus of youth in search of work opportunities was regarded as a social tragedy and a waste of the country's human resources.

Youth as a Mystery

One recurring theme is that youth in Myanmar are an unknown social group in the sense that there is an absence of reliable data and knowledge about their needs and concerns. Such views were expressed particularly in relation to understanding their economic situation. As one informant from an international aid agency put it: *"the problem is you don't really know what is happening to the youths out there... Job opportunities, education, the employment market..."* (int. 6). This view was corroborated by actors at the national ministerial level, who are involved in major national data-gathering exercises linked to youth employment needs. As one put it, there was a challenge to *"connect all the dots"* in relation to understanding the diverse situations of youth in different parts of the country (int. 86). The perception of youth as a mystery is also evident in anecdotal comments that elders within Myanmar culture are unable to understand a demographic whose attitudes and behaviours are currently changing rapidly. One informant evoked this incomprehension, pointing out that: *"I didn't do a study of this*" but observing that

> I came to feel that a lot of people don't know how to handle these transforming youth… I think that leads to comments saying that we don't understand 21st century youth. (int. 81)

Youth as Troublemakers/a Security Threat

There is a consensus among some informants that youth in Myanmar are not so demonised as drivers of conflict as in other conflict-affected contexts (ints. 3, 4 and 12). For example, one informant pointed out *that "youth are not stereotyped as a threat or problem per se, but in specific contexts are perceived as a threat, [as] those who are disaffected"* (int. 4). Yet, the view that certain sections of the youth population were unnecessarily troublesome, anti-social and unreasonable is present amongst a range of national and international actors. This charge was levelled frequently at student activists (ints. 6, 13 and 51). One informant expressed a level of frustration and impatience with *"those who keep protesting about the Education law... because they haven't been heard... that's fine... but do you know of any law that is meeting the needs of everyone?"* (int. 6). Thus interpreted, the behaviour of student activists was seen to have breached social and political protocols, such that they needed to be more mindful about: *"how your country works, and what is democracy and how far you can and how far you shouldn't go"* (int. 6).

Frequent press reports of the monitoring, arrest, detention, imprisonment and violence levelled at student activists – campaigning peacefully on educational as well as more recently on election related issues – demonstrate a more extreme version of the notion of youth as a threat to social order. In one report, the Home Affairs Minister is referenced as announcing that: "the students posed a threat to Burma's stability" (Irrawaddy, February 13, 2015b). Explanations of state interventions to control student protesters underscore the need to protect the "country's security, rule of law and to maintain regional peace" (Irrawaddy, February 13, 2015b). Reports of the monitoring of student protesters against educational reform by plain clothes police officers (Irrawaddy, March 2015a) underlines the perceptions of such groups as subversive, needing to be scrutinised and controlled. This framing is also linked to their projection as operating against national interests because of "being manipulated by groups seeking to destabilise the country" (February 6, 2015, The Associated Press) including "foreign organisations and ex-political hardliners" in the view of the Home Affairs Minister as quoted in Irrawaddy (February 9, 2015c). Such responses indicate the currency within the Myanmar's state and police authorities of a highly securitised projection of youth as subversive of social and national order, needing containment through monitoring, surveillance and regulation.

Youth as Immoral

Discussions of the country's youth constituency also focused on their lack of ethical behaviour and attitudes. Such views are not limited to elders' moralizing of young people, but were also at times articulated by young people themselves in reference to their peers:

> They are saying that the country's future is in the hands of the young people, but in the young people's hands we see alcohol, drugs and beer… so we can't think of our country's future. (int. 57)

What distinguishes these approaches is their adoption of a distinctively moralised framing, perhaps linked to religious values.

Youth as Needing Guidance

The view of youth needing guidance may result from the framing of youth as immoral, but it is also present particularly amongst educators with less moralising overtones. The view of youth as impatient, rather than overtly immoral, was also expressed by teachers who were frustrated at students' desires to get to the 'right answer' without spending time on learning processes (int. 19). Some pointed to the needs of youth for direction and values education in order to *"know right from wrong"* (int. 17) or *"to be patient and persevering"* (int. 17). This view of youth as 'in-formation' rather than as autonomous individuals connects to an infantilising of young people particularly from those in positions of state and/or community authority. References by Ministry of Education representatives to students wanting to engage the government in dialogue about education Law Reform as "children" who could not be given everything they ask for (Metro 2014) also illustrates this infantilising approach. Paradoxically this framing is also strongly connected to perceived failures in the education system to meet the needs of young people, particularly in developing critical thinking skills. Many of the young people interviewed also shared a related articulation of desiring more knowledge and access to information and in feeling under-prepared for the tasks they wanted to take on (ints. 14, 114 and 115). This frustration at feeling denied access to forms of knowledge they identify as needing is further elaborated in Chap. 10.

Youth as Passive

Many youth participants drew attention to the cultural expectations that they should always respect elders (int. 6). However it was also acknowledged that such expectations that youth should be deferential often meant that they were not listened to. So one informant pointed out that *"in Burmese culture they don't give space for youth to participate in decision making or whatever"* (int. 81). This, according to our respondents, results in a passivity and compliance with dominant cultural (and religious) norms.

Youth as Human Capital for Economic Growth

Several actors stressed the key role of the youth demographic as a human capital resource, which can potentially make a major contribution to the country's economic growth. Drawing attention to the country's rising yearly GDP but also to the challenge of managing the country's massive natural and environmental resources, one informant warned that *"if you don't work well with those stakeholder youths, it's a disaster"* (int. 76). This framing of youth is also present in the rationales and theory of change of TVET oriented interventions, as further discussed in Chap. 10.

Youth as a "New" Proactive Generation

Some informants emphasised the emergence of a "new" generation of youth characterised by their concern to be proactive in relation to community and national development. Such youth demonstrated an unprecedented concern to engage with the government, which distinguished them from previous generations of youth under the military regime who were obligated into compliance and passivity in relation to top down and authoritarian governance. So the approach of one youth leader was described as *"definitely the new generation of Mon youth in Myanmar*" (int. 81) because his vision of community development was based on his sense of a partnership between *"community and government... to make this happen"*. Such an approach was indicative of a newfound willingness of youth to exercise responsibility *"instead of just criticising"* (int. 81).

Youth as a Potential Creative Force for National Development and Peacebuilding

Linked to the perception of an emergent demographic whose attitudes and approaches differed from earlier generations of youth, was the view that their potential to contribute in innovative, out-of-the-box and dynamic ways to the nation's development, was currently being under-estimated and neglected. Within such framings their resourcefulness, energy and initiative was underlined as a resource to be harnessed. One informant noted that *"we are really excited about this... when you are 15 or 16 you are already quite ready to be active citizens"* (int. 18). The capacity of youth to be creative and innovative was perceived to be their particular strength. Thus a manager of a youth programme pointed out that *"I think the biggest potential of youth... they're so out of the box... they have a lot of ideas that are so unconventional... that shakes our fixed ideas and prejudices"* (int. 81). Such openness to new knowledges was evident in their ability to use *"technologies... and share these things in a much more dynamic way than us [elders]"* (int. 81).

This viewpoint is supported by media attention to youth mobilising social media to contribute to peacebuilding initiatives. One report headlined – *Myanmar youth strike a pose against hate in selfie campaign* (AFP 13 July 2015) – and explained how youth had used mobile phone technology and social media to promote cross-cultural friendships between Muslim and Buddhist youth within a context of increasing religious intolerance. Press reports that "Myanmar's political parties hope young voters will rejuvenate them" (Mizzima, 5 June 2015) also evoke the association of this demographic with the revitalisation of traditional institutions. While understood as constituting a threat to cultural norms (int. 81), this ability of the country's youth to bring distinctive qualities to development and peacebuilding was regarded by youth respondents as well as some of the national and international actors included in our study as one of the country's strengths (ints. 6, 33 and 80). Reiterating such views, a recent analysis of national prospects for economic growth entitled *Myanmar Unlocking the Potential* draws attention to its "youthful workforce" as a particular advantage along with "its strategic location, ample natural resources, and huge tourism potential" (ADB 2014, iv).

Youth as Principled Vanguards of Change

Located as agents within Myanmar's history, youth were also projected as principled and heroic vanguards of social change in Myanmar. Press reports linking current student protests with earlier traditions of radicalism capture this historicised understanding of youth agency. The Irrawaddy noted that:

> Students have been at the forefront of protest actions since pro-independence sentiment picked up steam against Burma's British Colonizers in the early 20th century. (Irrawaddy, February 13, 2015)

Others record the parallels between current activism and that of the '88 generation. These projections tend to emphasize the moral courage, bravery and conviction of stances taken up by students throughout Myanmar's history. A participant in the '88 uprising, commenting on recent police violence against student activists, noted that "they are just like me… they are in their 20s, I was about 20 then. They will be shocked and nervous now, after their first experience of violence" (Irrawaddy, March 16, 2015a).

In summary, this array of assumptions about the agency of youth forms a continuum from negative framings – as absent, mysterious and problematic – to celebrations of their potential contribution to change in their capacity as unique contributors to economic growth, and as creative and innovative, principled and courageous. It has also thrown light on their positioning within the distinct, sometimes contradictory agendas of various actors. These include concerns for security and social order, national growth and development, inter-generational changes, as well as the resonance of youth behaviour with the broader trajectory of Myanmar's history. In relation to the interest of this chapter in the spaces of manoeuvre available to youth, the emergent message is perhaps the complex and daunting challenge they currently face in negotiating such a variegated landscape of expectations.

Strategic Engagement at Multiple Scales

Youth participating in our research identified a range of supporting 'moments' of engagement that contribute to their felt sense of agency. By interacting in multiple ways across scales, ranging from peer relationships to exercising international influence, youth drew on a variety of connections – local national and international – to support their agency for transformation and where possible circumvent limitations. Figure 9.3 below highlights the levels at which these interactions occur, with further explanation detailed below.

Youth identified supporting and hindering factors across these levels, simultaneously drawing on multiple dimensions to exercise agency – or the capacity to take action – while also constrained by their contextual environment and positioning. Below, we start our discussion from the 'supra' level of international engaments, moving all the way over to the 'nano-level' inter- and intrapersonal levels. In doing

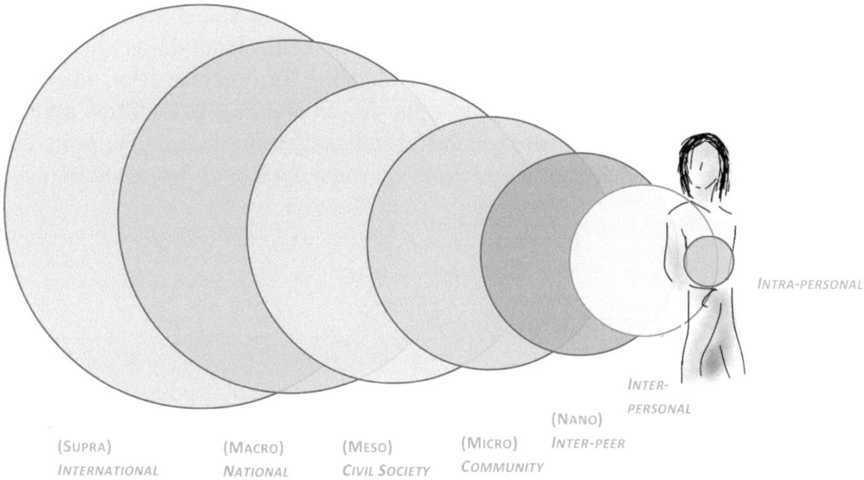

Fig. 9.3 Multi-scalar youth interactions. (Design by Elizabeth Maber)

so, we aim to broaden the often micro-oriented discussions around youth participation to acknowledge their involvement beyond the immediate level of peers and the community, and to provide a more nuanced analysis of spaces and connections that might be more restricting or enabling.

(Supra) International Level

International engagement included global youth movements, travel abroad for study and work, and participation in international events such as International Youth Day. Several youth leaders had participated in ASEAN youth programmes including forums, exchanges and cultural visits with the aim of both advocating for peace and promoting regional dialogue and shared learning (ints. 18 and 115). Similarly, community based or national level organisations working to facilitate these opportunities reflected the intention to contribute to local development amongst participants:

> They provide youth exchange programs, so many youths could apply for the youth exchange programs. Then after they come back, they can run their own organization and build network with the others, youth groups, so they can keep going. (int. 9)

Youth also identified the support of international organisations providing a space to bring young civil society members together such as British Council clubs (int. 114) and American Centre forums and debates (int. 104). This international contact was welcomed across the range of youth constituencies participating in our research, with underprivileged youth as likely to respond positively to international contact: "*satisfaction is earned while giving trainings to others and when working with foreigners*" (int. 24). For groups traditionally marginalised within Myanmar society, including young people with disability, LGBT youth and young women's rights activists, international and transnational networks were identified as supporting their advocacy work, both through access to funding for initiatives (int. 116) and through creating a feeling of solidarity (ints. 18, 23 and 88). In addition, several youth respondents also commented on the recently increasing access to information on internet and (inter-)national connections on social media, as discussed in other sections as well.

(Macro) National and State Level

Engagement at the national and state level was characterised as the most problematic arena for young people to influence. Beyond global initiatives that delineate a certain space for youth, participating in national level discussions or seeking to be heard by policy makers was a source of constraint. As has been highlighted elsewhere, the state is commonly associated with limiting the spaces for youth activities:

> Sometimes, it's hard to get due respect and impression from the government authorities just because they regard the youths as still young and not experienced enough. They don't see the capacity and capability of the youths in Myanmar yet. (int. 115)

Interactions with the state were often characterised by a strong impression of hierarchy. Frustration and fear was also expressed at the suppression of youth's freedom of movement and expression by continued surveillance of their activities by state and local government, as well as military and police authorities. Thus one informant pointed out that attempting to organise collective action amongst youth and peer training was difficult as "*the police and the village administrators call very often and disturb us indirectly if we do the training…so we can't say we have freedom for our country*" (int. 57). Other constraints on youth horizons of action included perceived state pressure on youth forums to avoid discussion of issues "*not encouraged by government*", which nevertheless pertained directly to youth's sense of wellbeing, including "*sensitive issues…unemployment, immigration, drug issues*" (int. 7).

However, while this space remains constrained and problematic, youth also acknowledged that government supervision was reducing in some areas (int. 115). One young civil society leader saw increased space available for youth movements as a result of working to build trust with state authorities: "*the views of some [in the government] have started to change and the condition is getting better compared to the past two years*" (int. 115). This expansion of spaces for collective youth networking was identified (int. 14) as an important result of liberalisation impacting on youth opportunities for advocacy and inter-regional reflection and collaboration on issues affecting them.

Youth Dissatisfaction with the Government

Concern was expressed that the liberalising momentum following 2011 had stalled such that "*in 2014 and 2015 the improvement is going a little backward*" (int. 56). Such viewpoints highlight the predicaments facing youth as they attempt to exercise agency within what they perceive as highly contradictory trends within state governance. Some rural and urban youth expressed a noticeable sense of alienation from the state and its apparatuses of authority, with some expressing strong views. One Mon youth noted that "*for the government, their strategy is to put the fear in the youth['s] mind about politics*" (int. 56). This general perception of a regulatory state concerned to exclude youth from political discussions was linked to a negative assessments of the conduct of militarised operation of state institutions. It was noticeable that rural youth in particular construed their dissatisfaction with the state as a result of a perceived inattention to the social and economic needs of their communities. One youth note that "*in the 2008 Constitution I don't see the paragraph for the public like building a preschool for the children and building a home for the aged...so I think we need more justice laws*" (int. 57). Moreover, he also noted that "*we are weak in protecting workers in the job... and we don't have a prescribed basic salary for the workers*" (int. 57). Such comments underline the diverse expectations of the democratic transition amongst different youth groups.

(Meso) Civil Society Level

The opportunities for youth to build networks, develop partnerships and gain skills and knowledge about human rights, advocacy and communication from civil society organisations, NGOs and CSOs was also welcomed. However, this recognition of the expansion of their political agency within spaces and networks available to them co-existed with their awareness of youth's inability to effect structural redistributions of power and resources to address underlying issues such as land rights and financial compensation for displaced landowners. This was due to a perception of the state's continuing desire to centralise control of land and resources. Working within the constraints of such broader political structures produced a paradoxical sense in youth that activism to effect significant social changes linked to redistribution and representation processes was being continually undermined and thwarted. It was also pointed out that many community based organisations addressing youth concerns were operating in an 'underground' fashion, without formal legal registration (int. 57), suggesting either limited approval of administrative authorities for their activities, or a reluctance for youth to formalise their operations, or a combination of these factors.

Engagement with civil society has enabled youth to form links between multiple levels of engagement, often supporting connections to international and transnational movements. For example, for the LGBT community, the recent growth of national and international civil society organisations concerned with human rights advocacy more broadly provides greater opportunities to raise public awareness of LGBT rights despite the ongoing prejudice they experience in society (int. 88). LGBT youth were involved in public awareness raising activities such as Human Rights Day, the International Day Against Homophobia and the Transgender Day of Remembrance, enabling them to gain visibility for advocacy work.

(Micro) Community Level

As highlighted in many of the case-study initiatives presented in Chap. 10, and in contrast to the earlier mentioned framing of youth as passive, youth often demonstrated a commitment to their communities, which motivated their desire to take action. This was at times motivated by a desire to address injustice or discrimination (int. 88), to protect and preserve a cultural identity (int. 68), or to help others overcome challenges they had experienced (int. 24). The perceived expansion of space for activism was also reflected in youth mobilisation at a community level, which has proliferated in recent years. Both youth-initiated as well as (I)NGO-led responses to emergency situations opened up spaces for community engagement of groups of youth, for instance after cyclone Nargis in 2008, and with the more recent flooding in 2015. Although deep-rooted divides persist, at the same time a shared sense of solidarity was articulated by many people in Myanmar in the aftermath of the cyclone and floods, supporting a rise in volunteerism as many young people rushed to offer support to affected communities. In contrast, and as mentioned elsewhere, migration patterns mean that many communities experience an absence of youth members.

(Nano) Inter-peer and Collectives of Youth

Considering the limited space for youth engagement with international and national levels, as detailed above, most of the youth programmatic interventions focus on the civil society, community and inter-peer levels. Collectives of youth are both youth-initiated and youth-led, as well as founded and supported by (I)NGOs, as was illustrated in the micro-case studies on non-formal education initiatives above. Peer learning was frequently identified as especially being supportive for youth agency (int. 24), while in one specific programme inter-faith and inter-ethnic encounters between youth with different backgrounds was seen to contribute to greater mutual understanding (ints. 7 and 32). As an example of youth collectivism, the textbox below highlights the benefits and challenges of Youth Forums in Myanmar.

Youth Forums: Benefits and Challenges of Collective Mobilisation for Change

Youth expressed their appreciation for the sense of solidarity they derived from establishing international networks of communication with youth in other countries, using social media and facebook, as well as learning from the operation of other youth forums in the ASEAN region (18). While the youth forums were celebrated as vehicles for new forms of collective action and social relationships, their leaders also highlighted the challenges faced by their inter- and intra-regional mobilisation of Myanmar's youth:

- Leaders of youth forums mentioned uncertain public spaces and experience of state repression, exemplified by reports of police harassment of a press conference, in which: *"young women were trying to explain to the media what happens to them and what kinds of [violence the] government commits to them"* (int. 18).
- Doing justice to the diverse and context-specific priorities of youth across the country was found problematic, as one leader pointed out: *"we try to make sure we do things in the nationwide level, that's concerned the whole region and the whole country* […] *we made sure the issues we discussed were representative, inclusive and grassroot: issues including youth and peace and youth and education"* (int. 18).
- Youth were *"passionate about their own region and sometimes [our] interests are different"* (int. 18), which rendered agreements on collective priorities and actions sometimes difficult to achieve.
- Youth leaders reported the existence of tensions between different generations of youth, such that those with more longstanding experience in such youth activism *"challenge and point out what is missing"* (int. 18).
- Youth struggled with practical difficulties when coming from conflict-affected contexts – not least because making the journey to attend a meeting was very challenging: *"They have to come like over 20 hours to drive from their place"* (int. 18).

The development of appropriate institutional, procedural and budgeting processes was challenging given that for instance one national network included 157 representatives from each of the states and divisions in the country. Hence, structural and personal constraints on youth, including financial and time pressures, as well as differing interests and priorities affect the ability of youth movements to be sustainable.

Intra-personal Levels

Finally, at the intra-personal level young people involved in (non-formal) education initiatives frequently cited the improved confidence that they attributed to this participation as a helping factor for their activities (ints. 24 and 117). Taking on responsibility and receiving recognition for their activities (ints. 14 and 24) contributed to this increase in confidence, in addition to building supportive friendships and relationships (ints. 18, 115 and 117). However, as was highlighted in the examples above, youth participants, activists, leaders and students are also subject to the stresses of financial, time and family pressure as well as over-work and exhaustion, which impacts their mental and physical well-being.

Conclusions

This chapter argued how despite the recent transition period since 2011, and consequent increased opportunities for (at least some groups of) young people's access to training, education, participation in civic life and access to information more broadly (newspapers, online (social) media), for most youth constituencies an overall picture emerges of a rather restricted space for manoeuvre. In a humble attempt to start to respond to a major gap in knowledge on young people's needs and challenges in Myanmar, this chapter drew on data collected from a range of youth constituencies in Yangon and Mon areas. This enabled the research team to listen to the views and voices of diverse groups of youth and do justice to our aim to represent the heterogeneous experiences of this demographic.

Listening carefully to the voices and experiences of diverse groups of youth in Mon and Yangon areas during the current period of transition since 2011 this chapter has revealed their hopes, fears, and frustrations and ultimately their restricted space for manoeuvre in relation to the socio-political, economic and cultural opportunities for change. Applying a strategic relational approach to analysing youth agency, this chapter has clarified various dimensions of their situation, notably the opportunities and challenges they face, the sources of support they draw on, and pervasive structural constraints that directly and indirectly impact on their potential and possibilities.

On the one hand the shifting socio-political landscape has opened up new opportunities to access social media, newspapers, political awareness training and new spaces to participate albeit cautiously – in civic life – articulating their viewpoints, in a context of a more general lack of acknowledgement of the political citizenship rights of youth. On the economic front, youth were aware of new possibilities opening up with international investment in Myanmar's and aspired to On the socio-cultural front, youth were mindful of shifting inter-generational dynamics which offered new prospects for youth initiative and indeed leadership in villages communities.

However, youth's space for manoeuvre within these new and unprecedented social political and economic trajectories are delimited by structural and societal factors. The continuation of exclusionary political processes offering youth only tokenistic participation as well as intimidating activities of police and the military constrain youth political engagement. Inattention to the employment needs and vocational training of youth in national state policies and programmes and education provision undermines possibilities that this constituency may benefit from new economic opportunities, which appear to be monopolised by elites. This leaves the majority of youth, especially in rural areas, faced with continuous levels of poverty, without sufficient income or work, undermining their ability to contribute to peace and development of their communities.

This chapter has also revealed various systemic factors at the national and international level that undermine prospects for supporting youth. The ability of the state to address the variegated needs of Myanmar's youth is limited by the lack of context and group specific data, of a coherent state level policy focusing on this constituency or a Ministry or Minister devoted to youth issues. Finally, youth are alienated from the formal education system which many feel is irrelevant, and particularly lament the inadequate provision of technical and vocational education linked to labour markets and the prospects of work. Moreover, the needs of youth have not been prioritised in the programming and policies of international aid organisations and donors, faced with many competing concerns.

Moreover, unhelpful, sometimes contradictory societal framings of youth, e.g. as security threats, forecloses recognition of this demographic as a positive national resource who may contribute to peacebuilding processes. Indeed, our data reveals a far more nuanced picture, inviting recognition of the social-cultural, political and economic commitment and collective as well as individual courage expressed by a range of young people. These show a spectrum of responses to the challenges they face – from activism and engagement, albeit in circumstances of intimidation and violence – to passivity, fear and despair.

In navigating their situations youth expressed appreciation for the support offered by the proliferation of local civil society organisations and NGOs in the transitional period. Many also saw an enhancement of their capacity to engage and enact with what they saw as peacebuilding efforts through the connections and solidarities that they forged at the international level with global youth movements, forums and related peer networking.

References

ADB (Asian Development Bank). (2014). *Myanmar: Unlocking the potential.* Mandaluyong City: Asian Development Bank.

Findlay, R., Park, C. Y., & Verbiest, J. P. A. (2016). Myanmar: Building economic foundations. *Asian-Pacific Economic Literature, 30*(1), 42–64.

Gravers, M., & Ytzen, F. (2014). *Burma/Myanmar-Where now?* Copenhagen: Nias Press.

ILO. (2013). *Assessing potential changes in the migration patterns of Myanmar migrants and their impacts on Thailand.* The International Organisation for Migration, Country Mission in Thailand & The Asian Research Centre for Migration: Chulalongkom University.

ILO. (2015). Myanmar: New labour force survey addresses data gap. International Labour Organisation. Available online at: http://www.ilo.org/global/about-theilo/newsroom/features/WCMS_378029/lang--en/index.htm

Irrawaddy. (2015a, March 16). *Burma's student protesters at odds with older activists as reforms stall*. Available online: http://www.irrawaddy.org/burma/burmas-student-protesters-at-odds-with-olderactivists-as-reforms-stall.html

Irrawaddy. (2015b, February 13). *Pass amendments and we'll go home, protesting students say*. Available online: http://www.irrawaddy.org/burma/pass-amendments-well-go-home-protesting-studentssay.html

Irrawaddy. (2015c, February 9). *Senior Minister says student protesters 'threaten stabilitiy*. Available online at: http://www.irrawaddy.org/burma/senior-minister-says-student-protestors-threaten-stability.html

Lopes Cardozo, M. T. A., Higgins, S., Maber, E., Brandt, C. O., Kusmallah, N., & Le Mat, M. L. J. (2015). *Literature review: Youth agency, peacebuilding and education*. University of Amsterdam, available online: https://educationanddevelopment.wordpress.com/outputs-research-consortium/

Metro, R. (2014) Decentralise education – Then what? *Myanmar times*. Available online at: http://www.mmtimes.com/index.php/opinion/12451-decentralise-education-then-what.html

Mizzima. (2015, July 13) *Myanmar youth strike a pose against hate in selfie campaign*. Available online: http://mizzima.com/news-domestic/myanmar-youth-strike-pose-against-hate-selfiecampaign#sthash.lrL3iVju.dpuf

Chapter 10
Prioritising Education: Youth Experiences within Formal and Non-formal Education Contexts

Elizabeth J. T. Maber, Naw Tha Ku Paul, Aye Aye Nyein, and Sean Higgins

Introduction

This chapter highlights the issues that diverse young people participating in the research raised as affecting their agency for transformation. Education emerged as a central factor for young people in shaping opportunities and in both constraining and advancing their possibilities for action, with formal and non-formal education practices being seen as offering differing opportunities to respond to youth concerns. A total of 80 youth perspectives (46 male and 34 female) informed these findings across the range of youth constituencies that make up our research. While the majority of the young people involved in the research were from Mon and Yangon regions, participants in the discussions referenced here also came from Ayewaddy, Bago, Kayah, Mandalay, Rakhine, Sagaing, and Shan and included Buddhist, Christian, Muslim and non-faith youth. Additionally, data is drawn from interviews with five youth leaders (four female and one male) which also focused on their ability to take action on the issues that concern them. To the extent that it was practicable, an effort was made to maintain gender-balance in our engagement with youth participants in all initiatives.

E. J. T. Maber (✉)
University of Cambridge, Cambridge, UK
e-mail: ejtm2@cam.ac.uk

N. T. K. Paul
Point B, Mawlamyine University, Mawlamyine, Myanmar

A. A. Nyein
Independent Researcher, Yangon, Myanmar

S. Higgins
University of Amsterdam, Amsterdam, The Netherlands

M. T. A. Lopes Cardozo, E. J. T. Maber (eds.), *Sustainable Peacebuilding and Social Justice in Times of Transition*,
https://doi.org/10.1007/978-3-319-93812-7_10

The chapter begins with an overview of the issues prioritised by youth during the focus group discussions and interviews. A brief discussion of these issues is provided, before exploring the perspectives expressed with regards to education in more detail. In particular, attention is drawn to gendered experiences within formal education and factors that were identified as constraining youth agency for transformation. Subsequently, three case studies of non-formal education initiatives for youth in Yangon and Mon State are presented outlining the ways in which these initiatives seek to enhance dimensions of youth agency, and the perspectives of those youth participating in them. Finally, the chapter draws together reflections on these varied learning experiences and youth agency for peacebuilding.

Positioning Education Within Priorities for Youth

In reporting youth perceptions of their priorities, we are mindful that they may not be in a position to identify all the factors which may enhance or undermine their agency, following Lukes' (1974) attention to covert and frequently unrecognised structural sources of disempowerment. It is acknowledged therefore that the issues raised here may only reflect a partial view of the concerns affecting young people and are also limited to the experiences of those 80 individuals taking part in the discussions. Nonetheless, within the breadth of concerns and priorities expressed by youth participating in the research, it is apparent that issues relating to experiences within education and the relevance of learning occupy a central position.

Building on the contextualisation of agency and diverse youth constituencies outlined in Chap. 9, the chart below illustrates a summary of the issues that were raised by youth participants in discussions as priorities for them, and the frequency with which this occurred. These issues were frequently identified as limiting young peoples' possibilities to take action in ways that would improve the lives of them-

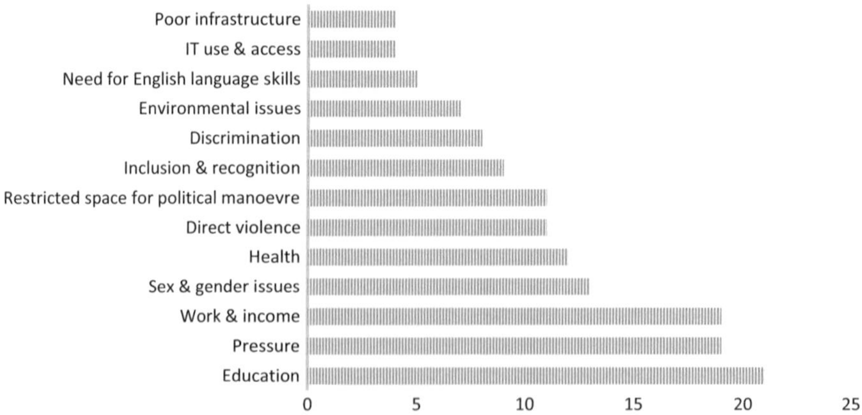

Fig. 10.1 Summary chart of issues raised by youth

selves and others. During individual interviews and small group discussions participants were asked to detail, either verbally or by listing them on paper, the issues that were primary preoccupations for them and that they saw as needing to be addressed in order to improve their daily lives. Figure 10.1 shows the themes of these issues and the number of times each was raised by different groups, with details of the themes being expanded under the subheadings below.

Education

As will be explored in greater depth below, experiences within education environments as well as the level and quality of knowledge that young people had access to was the most frequent concern that youth raised, stressing a feeling that their education had not prepared them to face the tasks that they wanted to achieve (ints. 24, 38, 44, 65, 68, 69, 114, 115 and 117). For five participants, the lack of opportunity to access formal schooling had contributed to their experiences of exclusion and marginalisation, with poverty being a particular barrier for those of lower socio-economic status (ints. 24 and 118). Likewise, negative experiences in education including discrimination by teachers or exclusion were also particularly highlighted by disabled and LGBT youth as frustrations that had limited opportunities available for these youth and had also contributed to the dis-incentivised remaining in school or continuing education (ints. 24, 88 and 116).

Pressures

Time commitments, particularly for those in employment, were strongly articulated as causing issues for young people (ints. 29, 114 and 117). Trying to balance family responsibilities with work and participating in further study or volunteering left young people exhausted and put stress on their relationships (ints. 29 and 114). One young man commented: "*After night shifts at work, I have to get up early to [study] in the early morning. I have to fight sleepiness with coffee*" (int. 117). Likewise, after-school tuition was also identified as contributing to pressures on students, both in terms of adding expectation that they obtain high grades in their school exams and in terms of reducing their time to relax after the end of the school day (int. 113). Despite health issues for some young people, the commitment to work, study, volunteering and activism demonstrated dedication on the part of these youth leaders both to improving their situation and that of their communities (ints. 14, 18, 114, 115 and 117). However, these stresses remain little researched, indicating a need for further attention to the psychological as well as physical impact of pressures experienced by young people.

Work and Income

The lack of job opportunities and the low salaries for those young people in employment was also frequently raised as causing difficulties, and was identified as a limitation for them to exercise agency and control over their choices (ints. 24, 38, 44, 57, 67, 68 and 88). However, poverty and a desire to maximise work opportunities were motivating factors for some to pursue education and to engage in community work to improve their situations (ints. 24, 57, 65 and 117). The low reward for these pursuits was a frustration, and the financial strain placed on individuals by volunteering was expressed as a tension that at times restricted their agency to participate (ints. 14 and 114).

Sex and Gender Issues

As also explored further below, the gendered nature of experiences within and beyond education environments was frequently articulated. The discrimination and inequality that were a feature of their experiences and witnessed in their communities were voiced particularly by the young women interviewed and by members of the LGBT community as concerns affecting their agency (ints. 24, 38, 67, 70 and 88). Violence against women, abortion, rape, early marriage and trafficking were identified as prevalent issues, interestingly more so amongst the marginalised urban youth interviewed than rural respondents, despite the widespread practice of these abuses in all areas. The importance of and need for sex education and knowledge of safe sexual practice were also stressed by these youth (ints. 24 and 88).

Health

General health problems, lack of access to health facilities and lack of specific awareness of HIV prevention, diagnosis and treatment were all raised as concerns (ints. 24, 69, 88 and 117), as well as a lack of reproductive health awareness (int. 24). In both rural and urban areas drug use was also highlighted as a prominent concern (ints. 24, 38 and 69). These were seen as limiting young people's well-being but also restricting their capacity to take action. Additionally, as also highlighted above, mental health, and specifically depression, was identified as an issue that was related both to the overburdening of young people due to financial, social and familial pressures (int. 117) and also an effect of cultural discrimination (int. 68).

Direct Violence

Many youth participants reported having experienced direct violence including in conflict areas, from authorities, within their communities, in schools and in the home. For some young people, experiences of direct violence in the community and in the home prompted their concerns for others in shared situations (ints. 24, 67, 88 and 116). For others, witnessing the effects of conflict supported their desire to advocate for peace (ints. 14, 18, 29, 65 and 68).

Restricted Space for Political Manoeuvre

Being required to get permission from authorities before undertaking any activities was often raised as imposing limits on youth actions (ints. 65, 59, 115, 116). As one youth leader highlighted: "*it's not culturally acceptable to do things or activities without the elder or authorities' permission*" (int. 115). The perspective highlights the cultural nature of this restriction, not limited to an effect of authoritarian rule. Likewise, restrictions on movement (int. 69), the lack of spaces for youth (ints. 29 and 65), lack of political provisions (ints. 14 and 18) and the oppressive character of the Constitution (ints. 14 and 69) were all identified as further limiting youth space for manoeuvre.

Inclusion and Recognition

Issues of inclusion and recognition of rights were highlighted by those who felt excluded, particularly with regard to ethnic or cultural identity (ints. 67, 68 and 69), and marginalised in education systems (int. 116). In addition, a number of youth leaders identified the need for a "*people centred*" model of development and reform as being important to address the concerns of young people (ints. 14, 18 and 65).

Discrimination

Similar to expressing a desire for inclusion, discrimination on the bases of ethnicity (ints. 65, 67 and 68), gender (ints. 18, 24 and 38), sexual orientation (int. 88) and disability (int. 116) were all identified as issues impacting young people which limited their agency. One disabled activist confessed "*it is too difficult for [the community] to change their negative attitudes towards disability*" (int. 116). However, in these cases education was frequently identified as a means to combat negative stereotypes and discrimination. In this case, the same activist continued, "*to overcome this challenge, these concepts are provided in training and advocacy in understandable versions*" (int. 116). Experiences of discrimination were therefore sometimes a motivation to prompt action and bring youth together.

Environmental Issues

For some youth, environmental issues were highlighted (ints. 14, 38, 67, 68 and 69). These were of particular concern for those who were directly affected by extraction sites for oil, gas and minerals (ints. 14 and 38). The need to protect natural resources was therefore associated more with the impact of industry on young people's present lives than in relation to a future hope for conservation. Land rights were also similarly raised by those who were directly affected by the arbitrary confiscation of land (int. 67). These issues were also closely connected by young people to the concepts of peace and justice (ints. 14 and 68) as highlighted below when connecting to young people's priorities for peace.

IT Use and Poor Infrastructure

Other issues prioritised by the youth interviewed were poor infrastructure, IT use and access, and the need for English language skills. Infrastructure, particularly in relation to the lack of transport (ints. 18, 68 and 69) and lack of electricity (int. 69) for remote and rural youth offered constraints. Making use of IT and English language classes (ints. 24, 38, 57, 67 and 117) were seen as opportunities for young people to connect beyond their immediate experiences.

Relating Priority Issues to Peacebuilding

Notably, in these discussions peacebuilding was not frequently raised explicitly by youth themselves, but emphasis was placed on the challenges that they experienced as the concerning issues for them. While it was recognised that a priority for peace was an end to war and fighting, the majority of youth we spoke to were not directly affected by fighting. Rather, these youth respondents tended to characterise experiences of structural violence as disrupting their goal of peaceful existence as well as experiences of inter-personal violence highlighted above, including police brutality or gender based violence. Nonetheless, when asked directly in subsequent discussions, priorities for peace for these young people reflected their experiences of constraint and included "*easing tension between families, societies and communities*" (int. 24), "*doing business peacefully*" (int. 117), or as one group discussion of rural youth identified: "*Only if we get true peace, the mountain will remain, we can do farming freely, and we can travel peacefully*" and "*peace means having the right to attend schools freely, go around freely, sell the things freely, farm freely*" (int. 68). Peace was therefore related to the ability to enact personal priorities.

Access to, Experiences and Perceptions of Formal Education

The presentation of the issues above identified by young people as constraining their opportunities for action provides a back drop within which to situate the current and potential roles of education as affecting youth agency. This section provides a more detailed discussion of engagement with and experiences relating to formal education as articulated by both education professionals and young people participating in the research. Particular attention is paid to the gendered dimensions of learning experiences as well as the lack of encounter with the formal, secondary education system. While it is recognised that the proposed education reforms seek to strengthen the capacity of education structures and improve learning experiences for future students, the issues raised here reveal the impacts of previous and existing education practices on young adults who have been affected by these experiences.

Accessibility and Absenteeism

The high level of absence and attrition from formal schooling amongst Myanmar's youth – otherwise known as a high school drop out rate – was perceived by many informants to be a major societal challenge in Myanmar. Indeed, it was referred to by one informant from an aid organisation as "*potentially a social bomb*" (int. 6), because of its role in jeopardising the prospects of the country's large youth demographic. This drop out of youth from schooling occurs at different stages and for different reasons, but is most pronounced at the early secondary level (Department of Population 2017). This was perceived by respondents to result in a large youth population that is unskilled and unprepared for labour market opportunities, as well as lacking recognised, formal educational qualifications.

Youth absenteeism was largely understood as a product of family poverty and financial pressures. The high costs of education prevented families, especially migrant workers, from sending their children to school (int. 31). Moreover, family pressures for youth to contribute to the family income by taking up low paid work or farming in rural areas also explained youth non-attendance. As one teacher working with out of school children and youth explained:

> The first priority is money, so the children can't go to school because it is their working time. If they come to school they have no money, so their parents don't like to send the children to school. (int. 15)

Within conditions of extreme precarity, where daily survival was the foremost challenge, the potential benefits of education for youth personal development were devalued and dismissed by many parents. As one informant put it:

> The most important thing is money and their family survival… for the villagers the financial is first and education is second … they don't want to be poor so they will do anything. (int. 6)[1]

In addition to economic explanations, lack of schools and teachers in rural areas and a general perception of inadequate educational provision was perceived to contribute to a lack of commitment amongst youth and their parents to education, resulting in high levels of absenteeism. One young woman in rural Mon State noted that *"even the headmaster has to teach because of a teacher shortage"* (int. 69). Moreover, long journeys to school, as well as security issues caused by a military presence in some areas, also rendered many youth disinclined to attend (int. 2). Such factors are also likely to particularly affect girls' attendance, as well as a lack of suitable options for girls to participate in schooling in remote areas (int. 23), with parents being more hesitant to send daughters on long journeys to school from remote areas:

> if there isn't a middle school in their village then they've got to go far and particularly for girls families don't like that. For any child it's tough, [but] particularly for girls, [parents are] uncomfortable with girls travelling very far or having to go to another village. (int. 4)

The risks of undertaking journeys for school are magnified in conflict areas, with one community education practitioner reflecting on the impact of militarisation on children that often goes unacknowledged:

> Another thing is if there is military in the areas, they feel it's not safe to go to school. For girls, many incidents, a lot of big experiences, unwritten stories, so they disappear in the air. (int. 22)

While it appears that in many areas enrolment rates for girls in school are reasonably high and that there is roughly gender parity in access to education (UNICEF 2012; Department of Population 2015, 2017), there continues to be a lack of accurate data from within schools to verify that this is actually the case in the classroom, as data collected on the basis of registration lists does not always reflect consistent participation in school. Regional variations are apparent in the data that does exist, with higher rates of enrolment for girls in some areas in the east compared with lower rates in the west (MoE 2013; Department of Population 2017). Where variations in participation are identified, the causes of school drop-out by boys or girls are also often under-researched. One international education practitioner consulted highlighted these gendered variations:

> We see different patterns in different parts of the country, so [in] some of the more traditional communities or some of the remote or ethnic communities it may be the boys who

[1] This association made by our youth informants between rural poverty and low rates of access to secondary education is also supported with evidence such as from the UNDP's Integrated Household Survey in Myanmar Poverty Profile for 2009–2010 (UNDP 2011).

> are brought out of school because they're needed to work or they're needed [for] the family income; in others it may be the girls because for social reasons or because the boys are considered more likely to be breadwinners, so the reasons vary. (int. 4)

A community education teacher working to support girls' access to education also identified cultural barriers and expectations that restrict education opportunities for girls:

> in the house, some parents think girls don't need education much, [because] they will be getting married one day and the husband will take care of the girls, so they think they don't want to invest in the girls' education. (int. 23)

Additionally, female students themselves identified factors including the lack of adequate WASH facilities in schools and having experienced body shaming especially during menstruation (ints. 23, 24 and 88) as contributing to their reluctance to attend school consistently. For example, one former student from Ayewaddy division recounted having missed school for several weeks after being shamed for having stained her *longyi* while menstruating and being too embarrassed to return to school (int. 125).

For those likely to be marginalised within society, education experiences were characterised as difficult at best. Disabled youth highlighted their frustration that "*most of children with disabilities in Myanmar have been still losing their right to access education as others*" (int. 116). Challenges experienced in attending school included:

> There are many inaccessible places and infrastructures for children with disabilities in mainstream schools in [the outskirts of Yangon]. They are muddy or unlevelled paths, classroom entrances, inaccessible toilets and classroom infrastructures. (int. 116)

During the same group discussion, teachers admitted their lack of knowledge and resources to adequately cater for disabled students which was driving young people with disabilities away from education:

> Almost all teachers in mainstream schools don't know how to teach children with disabilities. [Having] no knowledge about how to teach children with disabilities causes them not to be accepted in schools and become out of school. (int. 116)

As also highlighted below, there is an evident collective frustration for young people at a formal education system that they felt had not adequately served them and in many cases actively discriminated against them.

Relevance of Learning

The lack of relevance of the content of the formal school curriculum to youth economic, social and political aspirations was cited as a key cause of youth disaffection and alienation from current educational provision both amongst youth as well as national and international actors. Many informants critiqued a systemic failure of curriculum provision to respond to the needs of youth within their diverse contexts and situations and daily realities. Thus it was noted that:

> What is said in the textbooks and what the children are hearing and also observing in the outside world are quite different. This has a negative impact or influence on the children. (int. 4)

During a group discussion with youth respondents from Mon State, one young man commented that *"we need education that fits with the reality... Education should help with solving the problems you face now"* (int. 57). Youth also critiqued the lack of attention to civic and political education as well as opportunities to develop critical thinking skill (ints. 38 and 57) as undermining their capacity to exercise control over their lives. *"If they teach the children to think, they will think about their lives"* explained another young woman during the same group discussion (int. 57). Faced with abuses of power, *"we will think and know that it is because of some people who are using the authority in the wrong way"* (int. 57). Such comments underline the strength of youth feeling about the weaknesses of current curricula provision in undermining their agency across many dimensions of their lives.

There was also a general perception that the curriculum was not preparing youth with relevant skills, knowledges and competencies to enter into labour markets and lacked practical relevance to their economic aspirations (ints. 9, 6, 23, 38, 54, 57

Learning History in Government Schools in Mon State

In a series of discussion groups undertaken in Mon State with current and former students frustrations were reported with learning history in government schools. In particular, reinforcing findings discussed elsewhere in the chapter, they highlighted didactic, lecture-based approaches in which they were expected to take notes and memorise information. These experiences left no opportunities for them to ask questions, or to express their viewpoints, leaving many bored and uninterested (int. 54 and 55). As one young woman put it, *"the teacher needs to teach interestingly and give chance to ask questions of the students"* (int. 91). Such comments point to a disconnection between youth experiences of historical learning outside of school as emergent from community-based interaction and as encountered within the formal classroom through authoritarian pedagogical practices. Indeed, youth associated learning history through teacher-centred transmission of historical information with coercive student-teacher relationships resulting from the exercise of corporal punishment (int. 54 and 55).

The ethnic Mon students also expressed resentment at the selective content of the school history, which they perceived to be Bamar dominated and lacking recognition of or incorporation of the history of their ethnic group. This confirms recent research that has concluded that "space in school curricula for history other than that of the Burmese nation state is narrow" (McCormick 2014, 323). Youth perception of an exclusive historical narrative was understood as a mismatch between the content of government school history textbooks and the insights they had derived from their families. So one young man commented: *"One very interesting thing to me is that Mon history was*

(continued)

written by the Burmese government and its very different story or information from what my grandfather told me" (int. 71). These youth experienced this perceived manipulation of historical content by the state as a conspiracy to belittle their ethnic identity and historical memories and therefore as source of alienation, mistrust and conflict. In particular, this group of Mon students expressed a sense that such exclusions amounted to a failure to recognize the painful experiences suffered by their ethnic community at the hands of the Bamar (int. 71). In linking their investment in the subject with recognition of the distinctive experiences of their ethnic identity understood as under threat, these youth viewpoints reflect those held more broadly among Mon local historians as shown in the recent work of McCormick (2014).

Additionally, the students critiqued the dominance in the current curriculum of *"wars and fighting"* (int. 54), which they perceived as legitimising violence and warfare, and called for more relevant subject content oriented to their daily realities, interests and concerns. They wanted a greater focus on Myanmar's post-independence era as well as social and cultural history, which dealt with agriculture, religion and the history of science (int. 39 and 54). Finally, the students saw the potential of the subject to impact their own and others' peacebuilding behaviours through offering a reservoir of examples of exemplary ethical behaviours which they could refer to and imitate (int. 54).

and 117). As one informant noted with despair, *"what they have learned in school is no use to them... 11 years in schooling for nothing"* (int. 6). Lack of career guidance, relevant agricultural knowledge and more general life-skills support for youth were cited as particularly being absent within a system geared to rote learning for the final matriculation exam (int. 23). In relation to the perceived lack of links between education and the labour market, there was agreement on the importance of offering youth better and targeted vocational education, linked to labour market needs (int. 17, 86 and 119). The failure of the education system to valorise work related learning and to provide youth with qualifications linked to Myanmar's developing labour markets was perceived as a significant weakness, undermining youth capacity to exploit the benefits of increased foreign investment.

Additionally, the lack of sex education in state schools was also identified as failing to prepare young men and women for relationships which was perceived as exacerbating gender inequalities (ints. 23, 24 and 88). Young urban women interviewed particularly highlighted issues of sexual and reproductive health, abortion and trafficking as areas of concern for them, but which are entirely absent from formal school curricula (ints. 23, 24, 52 and 125). Other women in urban areas talked of the social hostility to their education and the paradox of obtaining qualifications (int. 114). While it is a mark of prestige and pride for the family for a daughter to receive a degree, actively using that education beyond clearly defined social roles is often not encouraged. Additionally, for many university courses, entrance grade requirements differ for men and women, with women requiring a higher grade than men to access courses including medicine and engineering. For some courses this has been justified as a quota system to encourage male enrolment (Maber 2014, 147), however it reinforces institutionalised gender inequalities, the association of certain subjects as more suitable for certain genders and perpetuates a climate of male privilege, as illustrated by one young man in a group discussion expressing: "*Men are better than girls. In the matriculation exam boys can attend good schools with lower marks than girls*" (int. 38).

Language of Instruction

Several youth respondents, particularly those in Mon State, emphasized that the lack of mother tongue instruction and the use of Burmese language as the only medium of instruction in state schools was leading to learning difficulties and educational underachievement of non-Bamar ethnic youth. This took the form of inability in the early years of schooling to understand lessons taught in an unfamiliar Burmese language, and a recourse therefore by ethnic students in government schools to rote learning rather than meaningful comprehension (ints. 29, 41, 44, 52 and 59). This initial inability to access the curriculum was deemed to result in subsequent underperformance in exams and in learning more broadly. One Pa-Oh youth explained:

> The challenge in the school is that we can't understand the lessons and can't catch all the information very well because of the language barrier. We don't get equal opportunities like others [who speak] Burmese. (int. 35)

Teachers similarly reported how ethnic minority children are *"struggling to understand the lessons and taking more time studying than Burmese [Bamar] children"* (int. 74). Others noted that being in a classroom for ethnic minority youth amounted to "*studying in a foreign country*" (int. 13). These observations on the linguistic impediments to learning faced by ethnic minority youth have been supported by in country research by the Nyein foundation and research into early grade reading abilities (Nyein Foundation 2012; Lo Bianco 2015, 13).

Youth participants in the research also perceived language-linked educational disadvantages to result in exclusions from broader economic and social opportunities for their empowerment and well-being. In this sense, the failure to maximize the educational opportunities of ethnic minority youth through addressing their linguistic disadvantage was for many symptomatic of structural economic and social inequities experienced by their ethnic community. Related by several informants to a broader issue of unequal (re)distribution in educational provision, the particular issue of language of instruction opened up into a broader critique of a centralized education system skewed in favour of securing the achievement of the dominant Bamar language groups. Articulating this perceived underlying inequity, a deputy education officer of the Karen Language Association pointed out that *"when the children go to school, it is kind of less opportunity than others"* (int. 37).

Finally, some youth were explicit on the potential of language of instruction reform to enhance peacebuilding dynamics within Myanmar through addressing what was perceived as a failure of cultural recognition that generated feelings of alienation and therefore conflict. One Pa-Oh youth pointed out that:

> We felt that we are forced to learn Burmese language…. So we feel angry and feel that we don't get full rights… if all ethnics are able to learn their own language, they will feel more confident and happier... so in my opinion it links to peacebuilding. (int. 35)

Youth saw multi-lingualism as a potential opportunity for improvement of their social, political and economic empowerment. A trilingual vision of complementary language acquisition was succinctly expressed by one Pa-Oh youth who pointed out that "*youth should learn Pa-Oh language first, Myanmar [Burmese] second and English third*" (int. 68). This linguistic repertoire was perceived to extend the possibilities for youth to communicate with different groups both national and international. In this way multiple language skills were deemed to play a pivotal role in expanding the social networks of communication and socialization for youth, therefore playing both an enabling and empowering role. The benefits of learning English as an international language which might facilitate access to information and communication outside of the country were also widely recognised (ints. 40 and 73). This finding confirms McCormick's (2014) conclusions about the reputation of English language use as a tool of empowerment and, indirectly of cultural validation amongst Mon communities. It also reflects youth concern to capitalize on the recent opening up of Myanmar to greater contact with the international community (ints. 57 and 73).

Pedagogy and Gendered Learning

Negative experiences of the curriculum were also linked to critiques of pedagogical practices which several of the youth respondents experienced as alienating. Youth pointed in particular to the dominance of rote learning methods within authoritarian instructional techniques and an exam-dominated approach to learning. One young man noted that *"we are afraid of the teachers at the schools and the teachers lecture and we memorise it"* (int. 38). Moreover, some youth regretted what they saw as poor relationships between teachers and students such that they felt *"unable to speak freely in the classroom"* (int. 57). The inability to ask teachers questions was perceived as a particular hindrance to their learning about civic and political issues (int. 57), as well as for ethnic minority students and students with visual or hearing impairments who expressed frustration at not being able to ask for clarification or assistance (ints. 116, 125 and 126).

Authoritarian practices within the classroom are seen to reproduce hierarchies of subordination and gender inequalities, a disadvantage particularly experienced by women and girls in contemporary Myanmar society (Maber and Han 2018). Even though teachers themselves may be women, the prominence of rote learning and the suppression of critical thinking skills in teaching practices has the gendered effect of not preparing girls to challenge the social inequalities which they face (Maber 2014, 146–7). This was also articulated by participants in the research as limiting girls' and women's opportunities to be prepared to access positions of leadership and take action against subordination (ints. 23, 53 and 57). One community teacher explained that schools were not doing enough to support girls to overcome these cultural expectations, also pointing to the intersections of disadvantage experienced by ethnic minority students:

> For the boys, they are coping [with] the difficulties, but for the girls, due to the culture, they are stopped in speaking out… So in school, they can't speak out. They are afraid that they become wrong. [And] the ethnic girls are facing the language barrier. (int. 23)

The same educator continued to highlight further ways that practices in the classroom are replicating cultural assumptions about gender and failing to prepare women to lead:

> Another thing is that they don't have a chance to be a classroom leader, group leader, because we don't have girl leaders in the school. Very few schools have girl leaders. From the girls' point in education, they don't know how to work with other people and how to lead others. If they lead, they don't know how to make decisions. Another point is sexual part – in the classroom, the girls are facing sexual abuse by the boys verbally or non-verbally. (int. 23)

The absence of a space for critical reflexivity within pedagogical practices also denies boys the opportunity to interrogate the patriarchal norms and assumptions which may frame their masculinity. Likewise, curriculum material that is dominated by representations of military men not only fail to provide girls with models of leadership, but also glorify and reinforce dominant associations of masculinity and violence for boys. As one community educator highlighted:

> In education, in our school curriculum, in history, Myanmar history, we have many women leaders, they don't put the women leaders in the curriculum. And also in history, it's really violent, so which king is how to fight to the enemy, how to do, how to revenge, so they don't put about how to negotiate. If they negotiate, which kings give their daughter to which kings. (int. 23)

As also reflected in the quote above, the intersections of gender and violence were commonly encountered. These intersections also combined with other experiences of disadvantage or discrimination including age, ethnicity, linguistic and cultural identity, socio-economic position, disability and sexual orientation, so that members of the LGBT community, disabled women and HIV positive youth were more frequently raising experiences of gender-based violence within education (ints. 24, 67, 88, 116 and 126).

Previous experiences in formal education have therefore frequently been problematic for young people and compounded a sense that the state education system has not been adequately supporting and preparing all youth for their futures. However, beyond the formal sector, a variety of non-formal learning initiatives aim to provide a counter-point to formal education practices and offer alternative spaces of learning. While such non-formal initiatives can vary widely in their scope and aims, below we draw attention to three case studies that prioritised varying dimensions of youth agency, including social, cultural and economic.

Non-formal Education Initiatives for Youth

During the course of the research undertaken between January and April 2015, the research team studied several non-formal education initiatives working with youth in Yangon Division and Mon State. The intention was not to set up an opposition between formal and non-formal education practices, but rather to uncover examples of initiatives that sought to support and advance differing dimensions of youth agency and explore their varying approaches to doing so. In line with our methodological approach outlined in Chap. 2, we aimed to maintain a balance between cultural (social), political and economic initiatives (CPE). Three of these case-studies of non-formal youth initiatives are presented here: the Human Drama Forum Theatre, based in Shwe Pyi Thar, Yangon Division; the Pa-Oh Youth Cultural and Literacy Society based in Mon State; and the Centre for Vocational Training in downtown Yangon.

Our analysis of how each intervention enhanced youth agency draws on interviews with youth participants and (youth or non-youth) staff of these initiatives. In each specific subsection that discusses one of the three cases, we focus firstly on the objectives and theories of change that underlies the design of the initiatives. We explore how and to what extent the initiatives take account of and address the particular contexts that shape and constrain youth possibilities for action. In doing so, we clarify the underlying assumptions of the initiatives about how best to impact and enhance youth agency – essentially teasing out their context-specific and constituency-specific theories of change. Of particular importance also is the extent to which the operation of initiatives themselves were constrained by the uncertain dynamics of Myanmar's transition during 2015. Secondly, we identify the processes through which the intervention impacts youth behaviours, attitudes, knowledges and skills. Thirdly, we reflect on participants' perceptions of the initiatives, noting how they understand its impact and benefits as well as the ongoing challenges they face. While mindful that youth agency may be broken down into various yet interconnected dimensions – political, economic, social and cultural – the analysis aims not to impose such categories on our findings too strongly. On the contrary, we are keen to respect and uncover the holistic ways in which youth horizons of action as well as constraints are frequently experienced within their day to day realities.

The Human Drama Forum Theatre

The Human Drama Forum Theatre is a peer led drama group based in Shwe Pyi Thar that is supported by FXB (François-Xavier Bagnond organisation) and the British Council, with initial training provided by Pan Intercultural Arts. FXB works with people living with HIV to support health awareness, and provide livelihood opportunities through vocational skills training and work in their product making and shop. The theatre group of twelve youth performers and two theatre troupe managers, working in the same location, are all young and marginalized in multiple ways. Many have dropped out of school for various reasons including family poverty and experiences of violence. Using a collaborative approach participants write and perform role plays and sketches in participation with community members in marginalized community areas. The group have been performing for 4 years and in this time have accomplished over 300 performances across the country as well as cascading their techniques to over 220 social and community activists. This study draws on data derived from interviews and group discussions with two support staff, three youth trainers and ten youth participants (three male and seven female).

The Human Drama Forum Theatre mobilises several approaches to effecting changes in the skills, attitudes and overall wellbeing of participants. Central to the ethos of the group is the close collaboration with communities. The group work with a given community, mostly in the industrial outskirts of Yangon but also across the country in Kachin, Mon, Kayin and Thaninthayi, to get to know the social issues that are concerning them. These have commonly included domestic violence, HIV/AIDS, drug use, human trafficking and sexual assault. They then spend a few weeks preparing a drama performance that will help share awareness and strategies to address these issues within the communities. During the drama performances, youth facilitators encourage the community audience members to participate and interact with the performance, in order to build greater connection with what is being shared. For example, when presented with a dramatized 'worst case scenario' audience members might be asked to indicate how the script can be rewritten to avoid these outcomes. As one facilitator reflected, "*the essence of Forum Theatre is encouraging the audience to participate in the theatrical performances to let them voice out and get involved actively*" (int. 24). Audience sizes tend to be of at least 50 community members across a range of ages. An additional success of the performances has been their ability to engage those who are most marginalised, particularly women, to share issues that are traditionally kept private, such as reproductive health, domestic abuse, sexual assault and child rape. Although both men and women participate in the performances, women have tended to outnumber men as audience members, adding to an environment in which individuals feel more comfortable in sharing their experiences.

By working in a creative and participatory medium, the group engages with community members who may be less enthusiastic about more traditional education means. By taking on this role of educator the young drama participants are placed in a position of leadership which is evidently valuable for their own self-confidence.

Drawing on the power of drama to catalyse discussion, the project positions young people in leadership roles as agents of awareness raising on issues which are not often talked about in their communities. Consequently, youth participants aim to *"facilitate the audience in the community to speak up [about] their feelings and find ways to solve their problems through dramas"* (int. 24). Through managing such collaborative and inter-generational reflection they could also become agents of behavioural and attitudinal changes. For instance, one trainer noted that:

> When some audience realize the effects of their bad behaviours, they even come and promise the drama group members that they would stop doing those bad things like drinking alcohol and so on. (int. 24)

Verifying the longevity of the behavioural change that might accompany such promises is challenging, however wherever possible the group maintain contact and return to the communities for follow-up visits, recounting that it is "*satisfying to see the reduction in discrimination in the community after their performance*" (int. 24). Supporting such follow-up activities would be a potentially promising space for more sustainable change in communities. Likewise, the youth trainers explained: "*we also give training to some people in the community so that they can run forum theatre performances on their own in their community*" (int. 24). Sustaining such multiplying initiatives has the possibility both to expand the reach and impact of the performances and could also support the development of the youth performers to take on further training responsibility.

Involvement in the writing and production of drama also provides an opportunity for young people to gain confidence as performers in public spaces as well as developing a range of social and communication skills. Peer trainers also underscored this satisfaction and sense of achievement *"upon finishing the training and being able to participate in the performances"* (int. 24). Connecting to the enhancement of youth agency, a feature of this programme is how it manages to turn young people's negative experiences in life including disadvantage, discrimination, and violence, into sources of transformative reflections and actions. When discussing their personal experiences through participating in the group, participants confided: *"I'm proud of being able to perform dramas about HIV*" and "*I feel pleased with being able to perform at the places where the people lack health education or knowledge*". (int. 24).

The project also supports youth to build on the social and communication skills developed through their involvement in drama productions by participating in youth forums which provide a related space for advocacy in relation to similar issues. Peer education and knowledge dissemination on the topics addressed by the dramas are also encouraged. Such collective and collaborative reflection by youth more broadly on social and economic issues which they prioritise are recognised by project participants as an important source of inspiration and empowerment. As one peer trainer put it, *"it's good to have forums among the youths. As we get to know more about other forums and organisations, we decide to work harder"* (int. 24). While currently small scale and community based, the Forum Theatre hopes to scale up its activities on a more national level and also to work with other youth organisations.

Focus for the coming years is also given to raising understanding of the rule of law and the changing legal environment as the country looks beyond elections. One key constraint on such activities is the need to seek permission from authorities before each performance process can begin. However, one youth trainer commented: "*we want the participation of the authority in our Human Drama group*" (int. 24), suggesting greater collaboration as the route forward to opening up further activities.

Pa-Oh Youth Cultural and Literacy Society

The Pa-Oh Youth Cultural and Literacy Society engages youth in educational and advocacy activities in relation to the preservation of one of Myanmar's ethnic languages and cultural traditions. The group works with youth from the Pa-Oh communities living in rural Mon State and is managed and supported by community elders. This study is based on interviews with the (youth) Chairman and Secretary of the Club, as well as focus group discussions, involving 11 youth participants (3 female and 8 male).

Underpinning the commitment of ethnic minority youth to the cultural activities organised by the association was a sense of the centrality of culture – language, literature and traditions – to their identity and self-definition and to the distinctiveness of their ethnic group. So one youth summarised the vision of the group in declaring that: "*everyone should value their own culture*" (int. 68). Comments such as "*literature is the life of each ethnic group*" and "*literacy is the heart of the people… if we do not know our language, we will be lost*" (int. 68) confirm their passionate commitment to the mission of the club. The youth club's appreciation of what they could learn from the group's cultural activities was also linked to a sense that they could function as agents of inter-generational cultural preservation and transmission, as one participant highlighted: "*We want to pass down our culture from generation to generation*" (int. 68). This was evident in their recognition that without their knowledge of their cultural traditions gained through their participation in the group, they would be unable to contribute to such endeavours, with the consequence that their particular culture may be destroyed (int. 68). One youth leader pointed out that "*if we lose our language and culture it will be like losing our tribe*" (int. 68). Involvement in such activities within the association thus symbolised for youth their participation in a larger project of cultural protection and renewal (int. 68).

The willingness of youth to invest so enthusiastically in the club's cultural activities – as a key dimension of their self-definition and expression – was driven by their perception of being situated within a particular socio-political context. On the one hand, in participating in such activities at all they recognised that they were enjoying a space of freedom unavailable during military junta rule; the youth leader of the club pointed out that attempts under the former regime to celebrate their ethnic day had resulted in arrest and imprisonment (int. 35). However their motivation for involvement in the club's vision was articulated as a response to a perceived lack of state recognition for their ethnic group, such that the pursuit of cultural activities were a means of self-valorisation. The sense of a culture and ethnicity under siege articulated by these youth was based on a fear and resentment at the prospect of cultural assimilation into Bamar majority customs and language. So the leader of the club explained:

> We want to preserve freely our literacy and culture, but we have no right to do it, so our ethnics feel angry and dissatisfied. From these problems, conflict can be caused. (int. 35)

Additionally, the youth club participants articulated their commitment to culture in relation to other pressing educational issues of inequality and injustice, including a lack of teachers that carry their customs and language in schools. They also mentioned how they feel forced to learn in languages other than their mother tongue (int. 68). In these ways, the youth's concern for cultural *recognition* intersected with a claim for a fair *redistribution* of educational resources, including adequate teachers, relevant curricula and language of instruction. This sense of unequal distribution of resources was connected to a broader concern to redress economic and political inequalities.

Hence, investment in cultural pride was also linked with political and socio-economic aspirations. In focus group discussions the youth linked cultural activities to the process of *"upgrading the living standards of our own ethnic people"* (int. 68). Work and livelihood opportunities were identified as urgently needed. As expressed by one youth participant as an invitation to both government and international actors:

> We would like the NGOs and organisations that work for development projects please do not leave us because we need support for health and transportation because we are behind others. (int. 68)

Moreover, the self-confidence provided by cultural recognition and awareness was also linked to aspirations to greater political representation and to equip youth to participate in the new democratic openings. One youth pointed out that:

> Now as we have democracy we need to be able to walk in[to] democratic parliament, only if we have representative[s] in parliament we can talk about our development and dangers upon us. (int. 68)

The club was perceived to also serve as a training ground for youth to learn about the political systems with a view to representing their ethnicity in the 2015 elections. Those elections have ultimately offered a sense of greater hope and opportunity for the Pa-Oh community as a Pa-Oh minister was inaugurated in 2016 who is viewed as active in support of improved education.

While the youth seemed to be aware that these beliefs can lead to sectarianism and intolerance, participants and (youth-led) staff of the club considered that knowledge of and pride in their own culture would strengthen their capacity for respect and tolerance of other ethnic groups, thereby contributing to peaceful coexistence and co-operation with other groups in society. They offered the logic that they needed to enjoy the self-esteem that awareness of their own cultural traditions would give them as the basis for respect for other groups. Thus the view was expressed that *"we will improve our own ethnic groups and also stay peacefully with other ethnic groups"* while avoiding becoming *"narrow-minded"* (int. 68). Indeed, an elderly community member who reflected on the work of the club, coming from the same ethnic background, confirmed that the club's strategy to strengthen cultural recognition was seen as *"a way to negotiate with the government without fighting"* (int. 68). The club expressed an interest in harnessing social media as well as radio to further their cause, but ran into practical constraints of a lack of online connectivity, especially in rural areas.

From a position of marginalisation, the struggle for recognition (representation and redistribution) of this ethnic youth club connects to a broader argument made in other contexts, such as the education reform for intra-and intercultural education in Bolivia (Lopes Cardozo 2011, 2013). On the other hand, the literature also points to potential warning signs of strong identification processes arising from a position of alienation, isolation, fear and humiliation, which according to Davies (2008) can in some cases lead to forms of radicalisation and 'othering', rather than a fostering of social cohesion. We view the youth in this club as being positioned in between a sense of solidarity with their elders, while at the same time expressing a wish to foster inter-ethnic understanding and mutuality in these changing and rather volatile times for the country.

Centre for Vocational Training (CVT)

The Centre for Vocational Training (CVT) works with young apprentices and companies in and around Yangon to provide training and support to young people in the workplace as well as also providing training to the hosting companies. Apprenticeships and vocational training courses offered cover five professions: furniture maker, metal worker, hotel and gastronomy assistant, commercial assistant, and electrician. While some international volunteers contribute their time to support the training and expertise of the centre, the organisation is largely staffed and managed by local trainers, managers and administrators. This study is based on interviews with two organisation directors and teachers, a focus group discussion with six alumni (three male and three female), informal discussions with students and graduates and participation in events associated with the organisation.

CVT takes an integrated approach to vocational training, seeing skills development as necessarily parallel to the needs of industrial and professional sectors. Drawing from a model of European vocational training to offer professional development through apprenticeships, they differ significantly from more transient approaches to skills training by developing sustained relationships with participating companies, with one of the managerial staff outlining: "*This education is a close co-operation with team work with companies and school*" (int. 17). In contrast to some more *ad hoc* approaches to vocational training, the organisation prioritises building relationships with industry, businesses and with Ministries, including the

Ministry of Labour, Immigration and Population, the Ministry of Natural Resources and Environmental Conservation, and the Ministry of Social Welfare, Relief and Resettlement, to improve working conditions for young people. The organisation therefore works in close collaboration with host companies and business to improve health and safety standards and contract arrangements (int. 119). Opportunities for young people's employment are seen as closely linked to Myanmar's transition, and therefore skills are aimed towards both versatile and expanding sectors including hospitality and electrical engineering. Responding to a shift in orientation amongst young workers, the aim is to position young people to benefit from the changes in Myanmar, which include more building and construction work, expansion of the hotel and tourist industry and increased international business. However, the organisation also aims to position young people not only to develop their skills to participate in the labour force, but also to participate more broadly in Myanmar's economic, social and political transition, as one manager underlined:

> Seven years ago, the students wanted to go to other countries. Now they are not very [keen] to go to other countries, but they want to get a good place, good salary [here]. [It's] slowly changing...Our objective is not only just a skilled labour but also to make them young leaders. (int. 17)

CVT accepts young apprentices to its professional courses, which last 3 years: "*usually our category is middle school dropouts, high school dropouts within the age of 17 to 22*" (int. 17). Vocational training was seen as a means of providing an alternative pathway for young people who have not always benefited from formal schooling environments: "*So I'm sure although they do not pass the middle school or high school, if they have a chance to learn, they also can develop*" (int. 17). In this way staff also acknowledged the need for different methods of learning to be available to youth:

> Some young people, instead of learning a lot of academic [subjects], they prefer to start working. We do not have a very good career counselling centre and program and approach in Myanmar. So sometimes young people are not sure where their interests are. (int. 17)

The professionalism of the organisation has contributed to its own reputation, in turn raising the reputation of its graduates. Professionally, the impact for students of training with the organisation was clear. Graduates reported being promoted and receiving an increase in salary, for some up to 80% (ints. 117 and 118). Likewise, the alumni interviewed were unanimous in attributing their subsequent professional success to their participation in the organisation. One young woman graduate of the Hotel and Gastronomy Assistance programme highlighted her career progression and further ambitions:

> I started my career as a waitress before joining Hotel and Gastronomy Assistance Class. I was promoted to bartender as soon as I joined CVT. I became a bar supervisor while I was a second year student. I want to be a General Manager at a five star hotel and I am still trying to get there. (int. 117)

Graduates also highlighted the inter-personal skills that they had developed during their studies and apprenticeships. These had benefitted their working practices recounting that they now had "*better interpersonal skills*", "*improved communication skills*" and were "*more understanding to others and the nature of their jobs and responsibilities*" (int. 117). However, at a more personal level these were also associated with improved well-being for the youth, who identified having "*become more conscientious*", "*become more mature*", "*[made] more friends*" and having "*more confidence*" (int. 117) through their engagement with the organisation.

For some, professional success had brought them "*less worries*" (int. 117). However, several alumni also highlighted the pressures they faced as young people trying to balance work and study commitments with family responsibilities and caring roles. Being unable to take a regular day off in some cases contributed to declining relationships or was associated with depression and health problems as a result of having "*no personal time and family time*" (int. 117). Others also highlighted the multiplication of pressures for less privileged youth, who had to travel long distances on public transport from their homes on the outskirts of the city to their work and study sites (int. 118). The prioritisation of professional obligations over well-being illustrates the personal dedication of these individual youth and also reflects the challenges many young people in our research articulated of balancing the competing demands on their time.

Conclusions

The issues highlighted by young men and women in the research revealed a diversity of priorities for individuals in being able to exercise their agency, and also indicated the central role that education is perceived as playing. Experiences within formal learning environments have therefore galvanized a dual characterization of education as simultaneously having contributed to young people's disempowerment while also being identified as potentially offering opportunity to improve their circumstances. The legacies of neglect and co-optation of the formal education sector to serve the agendas of the military governments have resulted in many young people's prior experiences of schooling being frequently negative and exclusionary, which has been exacerbated for socially marginalised groups including young women, ethnic and religious minorities and those with disabilities. These negative experiences were also presented as not only disempowering in the moment, but also subsequently through the denial of educational advancement, skills and opportunities for secure employment. Informed by these experiences, youth respondents continued to place emphasis on their desire to see advancements in the formal education sector and the contribution that greater inclusivity and improvements in educational practices could make to their agency and empowerment.

As a counterpoint, this chapter has presented three case studies of non-formal education initiatives that are offering alternative approaches to learning. These three initiatives engaged youth in a variety of ways through both peer learning and structured hierarchies and included drama, cultural and language activities, and vocational training. While non-formal initiatives may take varied forms motivated by diverse agendas, a strength of the selected initiatives was their connection with the daily realities and political, social, economic and cultural challenges experienced by young people. Varying degrees of political will and resource commitment, together with the legacies of a restrictive political economy context continue to pose challenges for such non-formal initiatives. However, the case studies indicate examples of ways in which programmes may draw on the pre-existing indigenous initiatives of young people and those that encourage inter-group peer networking, as well as opportunities to reformulate structured learning environments, with the intention of building the agency and empowerment of young people to contribute to improvements in their communities as well as their immediate circumstances.

References

Davies, L. (2008). Gender, education, extremism and security. *Compare, 38*(5), 611–625.

Department of Population. (2015). *The 2014 Myanmar population and housing census – the union report: Census report Volume 2*. Nay Pyi Taw: Department of Population, Ministry of Labour, Immigration and Population.

Department of Population. (2017). *The 2014 Myanmar population and housing census: Thematic report on education*. Nay Pyi Taw: Department of Population, Ministry of Labour, Immigration and Population.

Lo Bianco, J. (2015). *Myanmar country report. Language, education and social cohesion (LESC) initiative*. Unpublished report.

Lopes Cardozo, M. T. A. (2011). *Future teachers and social change in Bolivia: Between decolonisation and demonstration*. Netherlands: Uitgeverij Eburon.

Lopes Cardozo, M. T. A. (2013). A critical theoretical perspective on education and social change in Bolivia. In S. C. Motta & M. Cole (Eds.), *Education and social change in Latin America* (pp. 89–106). New York: Palgrave Macmillan.

Lukes, S. (1974). *Power: A radical view* (Vol. 1). London: Macmillan.

Maber, E. (2014). (In)Equality and action: The role of women's training initiatives in promoting women's leadership opportunities in Myanmar. *Gender and Development, 22*(1), 141–156.

Maber, E. J. T., & Han, P. L. (2018). Challenging gender inequalities through education and activism: Exploring the work of women's organisations in Myanmar's transition. In M. Najafizadeh & L. L. Lindsey (Eds.), *Women of Asia: Globalization, development, and social change*. New York: Taylor and Francis.

McCormick, P. (2014). Writing a singular past: Mon history and "Modern" historiography in Burma. *SOJOURN: Journal of Social Issues in Southeast Asia, 29*(2), 300–331.

Ministry of Education (MoE). (2013). *CESR rapid review of Myanmar basic education policy and proposed way forward. Phase 1*. Yangon: MoE.

Nyein Foundation. (2012). *Policy paper on language in primary education in the republic of the union in Myanmar*. Yangon: Nyein Foundation.

UNDP. (2011). *Integrated household living conditions survey in Myanmar (2009–2010) — Poverty profile*. Yangon: UNDP.

UNICEF. (2012). *Baseline study: Child-centred approaches and teaching and learning practices in selected primary schools in child-friendly school focused townships in Myanmar*. Yangon: UNICEF.

Chapter 11
Youth Experiences of Non-formal Education for Peacebuilding

Tabea Campbell Pauli and Kiymet Schipper

Introduction

In the context of reconstruction and reconciliation that forms Myanmar's peace process, education has been a key tool to which stakeholders, activists and policymakers look with enthusiasm. They see the possibilities of increasing the skills and knowledge of the youth population, as well as reconciling difference and building stable and peaceful relations in a diverse and often fragmented country. Indeed, there is an unmistakable point at which peace and education intersect, which is central to the nation-building exercise at the heart of the peace process. The case studies presented in this chapter explore this intersection, questioning how young people in Yangon try to engage in peacebuilding and political development projects during this time of transition, by seeking out opportunities to access training and learning in activism, advocacy, critical thinking and leadership skills. The first case study describes a political awareness training, and its influence on growing political agency in young adults, in the run-up to the 2015 elections. The data revealed that, as students participated in the training programmes, they were also adapting and appropriating these skills and knowledge to meet their own desires and intentions, beyond the expectations of the training providers. The second case study centres on a post-secondary programme in a civil society-led school, founded on the importance of ethnic diversity and inclusion in producing education of peacebuilding within the Myanmar context. Key findings revealed that the content and teaching style promoted at the school formed a curriculum which is unique in Myanmar, using practice, innovation and a focus on context to engage students with peacebuilding and also development. Simultaneously, some of the methods and materials used in the classroom forged strong links with international practices and systems, leading to questions around their suitability for the Myanmar context.

T. Campbell Pauli (✉) · K. Schipper
University of Amsterdam, Amsterdam, The Netherlands

M. T. A. Lopes Cardozo, E. J. T. Maber (eds.), *Sustainable Peacebuilding and Social Justice in Times of Transition*,
https://doi.org/10.1007/978-3-319-93812-7_11

Through the findings of these case studies, the role of non-formal education systems is analysed, as it builds young people's capacities for civic engagement and active roles in the political transitions and attempts to foster peace in Myanmar. The educational programmes are shown to supply critical skills and knowledge, but they also occupy a complex and often contested space in Myanmar's education landscape, as they are defined in opposition to the generally poor and outdated public education system in the country. This data connects with broader discussions around the various "faces" of education in conflict-affected settings (Bush and Saltarelli 2000), wherein differences in access and content between young people in Myanmar may be seen to have negative repercussions, by creating new divides or conflicts. The research also highlights the significant flexibility with which the young learners embrace and utilise their newly acquired competencies to respond to the complex and evolving context of political development, continued tensions and peacebuilding initiatives in Myanmar, in unexpected and unintended ways. Thus, the non-formal institutions also provide youth with the space to experience and incorporate unfamiliar ideas, which help to shape their perspectives on the context of conflict-to-peace transition, and the roles they could occupy in it. These case studies show that both education programmes that were provided often had unintended outcomes, which highlights the nonlinear nature of schooling.

Methodology

Research within the first case study on Myanmar Exitus[1] was conducted between August and December 2014, one year before the election that led to a historic victory for the National League for Democracy (NLD). Myanmar Exitus is a local organisation that has provided political awareness trainings in Yangon from 2006 onwards, and one of the first organisations to teach politics, which was remarkable at a time when discussing political issues was highly sensitive. The training programme and the organisation itself occupied ambiguous positions, due to their affiliations with the military-dominated government. However, they were permitted to operate because they were not deemed to be subversive. In contrast, the field site of the second case study, Kant Kaw Education Centre (KKEC), occupies a more contested space in the field of education services in Myanmar. The school was created and is run by local NGO Thabyay Education Foundation, and offers a uniquely diverse cohort of students a one-year programme in 'community leadership and social studies'. The school opened in 2009 in Thailand, but has since been able to move to Yangon, as relations between the Government and the civil society sector have evolved. In contrast to Myanmar Exitus, KKEC staff are a mixed group of national (Burmese and ethnic) and international (Southeast Asian and "Western") staff, which added to the difficulties it faced in establishing itself. Research for the

[1] All names of individuals and organisations have been altered unless express permission has been granted by them.

second case study took place between January and April 2016, in the period after the election and before the transfer of power to the new Government. Along with the unpredictable and shifting context, limited timeframes influenced the epistemological standpoints and determined the choice of data collection tools in both research projects. The case-study methodology is based on in-depth research with a relatively small pool of informants, to ensure that its findings are meaningful in the particular circumstances of the research. The value lies not in producing statistically generalizable data, but in generating intimate and holistic insights into the field site, a sort of "snapshot" of a specific time and place, allowing space for a real diversity of thoughts and ideas to be captured.

Both studies used anthropological techniques for data collection and analysis. Drawing from the overall methodological approach of the broader research project, we applied critical ethnography, which is epistemologically linked to critical realism (see Chap. 2 in this book). This allowed us to observe power structures and political purpose that reveal themselves in the study of Myanmar Exitus training. By trying to understand the points of view of participants, and to speak on their behalf – rather than for them – critical ethnographers attempt to use knowledge for social change (Thomas 1992, 3). In both case studies, contextual information and thick descriptions were used. Also, the thoughts and opinions of the young people were given authority, in order for them to be transforming in conflict. To capture and make sense of the large diversity in research participants at KKEC, a high degree of relativity during analysis was important. A unique approach to this research includes positioning the case study in relation to different paradigms than are usual for many western social scientific studies, such as indigenous and feminist-based perspectives. It was hoped that in this way greater prominence would be given to voices that may often be subdued in mainstream discussions, supporting the case study's overall focus on inclusion. Mixed methods approaches were taken in both case studies, with a combination of qualitative and quantitative tools used to generate data. These include participant observation, semi- or un-structured interviews, focus group discussions, but also surveys and questionnaires. While both studies are based on relatively small sample sizes (around sixty participants in each), the groups include gender and ethnic diversity. Due to the focus of both case studies on youth experiences, the majority of research participants belonged to the 20–30-year-old demographic.

Conceptual Discussion

In contexts of conflict, education often plays a central role, with schools varyingly seen as safe spaces for families affected by violence and displacement, or as targets and tools for symbolic or physical attacks against civilians (Davies 2010; Lopes Cardozo 2008; UNESCO 2011). Indeed, far from relegating schooling to a neutral service function, it is important to understand how curricula can be designed with varying degrees of bias or agenda in them. This links to Bush and Saltarelli's notion of the different "faces" of education (Bush and Saltarelli 2000). In the context of this research topic, the *negative* face corresponds to the promotion of conflict in schooling, through authoritarian teaching styles, physical violence or militarism in the classroom, and the perpetuation of harmful social and political discourses. The *positive* face sees the cultivation of tolerant and respectful attitudes, with an emphasis on critical thinking and mediation (Hilker 2011; Davies 2005). This 'positive face' can be carried into discussion of critical pedagogy, and how education is used for social change. Giroux argues that schooling is "implicated in the construction and organisation of knowledge, desires, values and social practices" through pedagogy's role in the production of meaning (Jackson 1997). A useful framework for exploring the critical change theory for peacebuilding is Novelli et al.'s "4Rs" model (also introduced in Chap. 2 in this book). Expanding on Fraser's (1998) three Rs – redistribution, recognition and representation – the fourth R is reconciliation, linking social justice theory to contexts of conflict-to-peace transitions. In this framework, the emphasis is on social development as a tool for peacebuilding:

> Political, economic, social and cultural transformation is needed in conflict-affected societies to support positive peace, and to address rather than reproduce or sustain the injustice and inequality that largely drive conflicts. (Novelli et al. 2017, 5)

When applied to the case studies presented in this chapter, the framework helps to understand the ways in which education can be transformative.

The training offered by Myanmar Exitus supports young people to participate in the country's political sphere, to reveal their individual agency in a complex and shifting context. This is an illustration of the "representation" dimension of the framework, which investigates "the extent to which education policy/reforms involve stakeholders participation". By supporting the increased inclusion of young people in the political realm, this training increases their political awareness. KKEC's emphasis on ethnic and diversity and inclusion in the classroom links to the "recognition" dimension, which calls for "recognition of cultural diversity through curriculum" and "citizenship and civic education as a means of state-building". In addition, elements of KKEC's curriculum target conflict resolution and nation-building, such as the Peace and Conflict class, which connects with the "reconciliation" dimension by "addressing historic and contemporary economic, political and cultural injustice", as well as analysing "how education strengthens/weakens social cohesion" (Novelli et al. 2017, 22). At the core of KKEC's programming is the desire for students to learn about peace and conflict through each other's experiences, and how they can come together to participate in peacebuilding. Despite the fact that within these case studies the main focus has been on "representation" and "recognition" it remains important to mention that essentially the 4Rs are always interconnected and hence analysed in conjunction.

As follows from our application of the 4Rs framework, *peacebuilding* is a core theoretical concept at the heart of these case studies. In both, peacebuilding is connected specifically to themes of democracy, citizenship and nation-building. Indeed, conflict in Myanmar is rooted in issues including, but not limited to, self-determination and power-sharing. Considering the astonishing number of ethno-linguistic and religious communities involved in struggles over territory, resources and representation, rebuilding of the nation is a core pillar of the formal peace process. Salem-Gervais and Metro define nation-building as the "process of constructing or structuring a national identity using the power of the state" (2012, 27). In creating a national identity that corresponds to a defined territory, state structures are put in place which turn individuals into citizens, whose role is dismantling conflict and preventing it in the future. The success of peacebuilding hinges on the success of citizenship work, which is where citizenship education becomes important, in its most critical and ideal form teaching people to "act politically, to advocate both individually and collectively for themselves and for other marginalised people" (Sleeter 1996, 246). In recent history, Myanmar's population has accessed only a reduced form of citizenship under military government, making the political encounter, and participation, a key dimension of any citizenship education. *Encounter* refers to the recognition of political and social diversity in the citizenry, and facilitating relationships between communities, essential in the process of guaranteeing civic rights (Gutmann in Osler and Starkey 2005). *Participation* sees the number and diversity of individuals and communities expressing themselves politically increasing, which may include previously marginalised or minority groups (Lall and Win 2012).

The training delivered by Myanmar Exitus was designed to build the capacity of young people to participate in the country's political sphere, albeit with the aim of increasing sympathy for the military-backed USDP Government at the time. However, as is explained below, the research revealed that a significant unintended outcome was that the training facilitated the encounter of many young people from different backgrounds, and with diverse ideas and opinions. This encounter links with the theory outlined above, in which peacebuilding occurs with the coming together of diverse groups and perspectives, within a system of citizenship work through participation in the political sphere. In contrast, KKEC's programming is designed with peacebuilding as an explicit goal. Diverse groups of young people are brought together to develop skills in active citizenship and conflict resolution, among other fields. KKEC even supplies a particular vision of peacebuilding in the Myanmar context by emphasising locally-informed, bottom-up social development and community engagement as key strategies for the conflict-to-peace transition, further explained below.

The research at KKEC centres on the concept of inclusive education, connected to education discourses around human rights and capabilities, with a broad definition provided by Block et al.:

> An inclusive learning environment is one that provides a curriculum that caters to a diverse range of students and accommodates diverse voices and perspectives so that all children feel they belong and can contribute. (2014, 1340)

Increased attention to inclusive education in international conventions and treaties (see e.g. UDHR 1948; CRC 1989; UNESCO 2009) underlines the determination of some of the international community to make education open and accessible to a wide range of social groups, and responsive to their needs, from students with disabilities or special needs, to other identity markers, such as cultural background of ethnicity. Research in this field (Sleeter 1996; Osler and Starkey 2005) suggests that this style of education is important, not only for students' personal growth, but also for "building social cohesion" in a wider context (Taylor and Sidhu 2012, 54) by fostering feelings of belonging within other social groups, such as nationality. This is particularly important in contexts with a high rate of cultural or ethnic diversity. Inclusivity in classrooms can be strengthened through attention to issues of voice, representation and justice (Junne and Verkoren 2005; Apple 1990; Sanchez and Rognvik 2012).

In the context of KKEC's work in Myanmar, this approach to inclusion in the classroom connects to the concept of peace education, or peacebuilding education. A concise definition is missing, although core elements include creating a desire for peace between rivals, building knowledge about conflicts and their contexts, promoting behavioural and attitudinal changes toward inclusion, non-violence and conflict resolution, and addressing structures that produce inequality and injustice (Fountain 1999; Bush and Saltarelli 2000; Harris and Synott 2002; Lopes Cardozo 2008; Lopes Cardozo and May 2009; Berghof Foundation 2012). What is critical in the implementation of peacebuilding education is attention to the wider contexts and individual characteristics of conflicts, rather than applying one-size solutions. Ideally, it would form part of a larger process of peacebuilding that goes beyond the classroom, exerting "political influence" into wider social structures (Lopes Cardozo 2008; Berghof Foundation 2012). This amorphous field lacks straightforward agreement around purpose, form and methods, with some critiques levelled against the use of "peace education" as a strategy for pacification, rather than a more constructive or transformative process than is often understood by "peacebuilding education" (see Novelli et al. 2017).

Case Study Myanmar Exitus: Youth Strategies for Enhanced Political Agency

This case study analyzes the influence of political awareness training by an organization called Myanmar Exitus, on the political agency (see Chap. 2 for an elaborate definition of political agency) of youth in Yangon. The time of the research was exciting and tense for many, as new elections were planned for November 2015. In countries with a history of military dictatorship, such as Myanmar, there is often limited attention – or space – for political awareness education. After the transition to the USDP Government in 2011 however, there seemed to be increased opportunities for youth in Myanmar to engage in discussions about politics and to explore their rights and duties in relation to their fellow citizens and the state (Matelski 2013, 160). Although the formal education system does not include political education, there were more and more non-formal institutes providing variations of political awareness education. This is confirmed in the second case study below in which the rise of private non-profit schools in Yangon is noted.

In this case study, the multi-scalar relationships between education and youth political agency are analysed, taking into account the strategic, selective context of Myanmar, building on the overall methodology discussed in Chap. 2. The research explores the question of how and to what extent the democratic governance training of Myanmar Exitus influences political agency of youth, and how this influences their perceived ability to contribute to the political transitions in the country. Political agency of youth is defined in this study as:

> the space for manoeuvre youth have, to develop (un)conscious strategies to influence political decisions and transform social relations that support or hinder the political transitions in their society. (Novelli et al. 2017, see also Chapter 2)

To unravel this "space for manoeuvre", the concept of agency was broken down into motivations – underlying reasons and interests of youth to participate in the political transitions, and perceptions – the way youth perceive the political situation and their ability to contribute to this, which leads to the development of (un)intended strategies – adopted by youth to participate in politics that hinder or support the transitions, in order to challenge or reproduce the status quo. By critically assessing this concept, the study aimed to increase understanding on if and how education can contribute to a more equitable, peaceful and socially just society (Shah and Lopes Cardozo 2015, 182).

This research showed that young people in Yangon were generally uninterested in participating in the political transition due to a culture of fear. A small group of youth did seem motivated to use the dynamic situation to be engaged in the political field. Their motivation was often related to the fact that they saw a role for themselves in changing the political situation in the country. These young people found ways in which they felt they had an influence, for example as political trainers. During in-depth interviews with students from Myanmar Exitus, they explained that the training motivated them to play a role in the political transitions, and provided them with guidance around ways to participate. This was illustrated by one respondent as an alumnus and trainer noted:

> I think Myanmar Exitus at least provides ideas about the political transition, in which the youth can participate. Otherwise youth think 'we are so afraid, the political field is not related with us'. But Myanmar Exitus changes their mind: 'The politics [is a field in which] you have to participate.' That is [the] key point in which Exitus has good successes in Myanmar.

It is interesting that Myanmar Exitus motivated youth to participate in the political transitions and also guided them in doing so, despite their purported aim of preventing youth from challenging the status quo. Providing political awareness education meant there was space created for an unintended outcome, as youth may be trained who will use these skills to challenge the status quo, which would counter their initial objective. This indicates that education is not a linear process, which will be elaborated on below.

The most important findings concerning youth perceptions showed that most respondents were sceptical about the political situation, while they did acknowledge some reform had taken place in recent years. They were often aware of the fact that changes generally benefited a small number of people, leaving the rest of society largely unaffected. Although most youth felt the influence they could have was limited due to age hierarchies and a history of military dictatorship, some were still motivated to make a change in their society. The negative perceptions they had of the political situation, regarding the many forms of injustice, led them to be intrinsically motivated to participate in the transitions. One respondent illustrated this by saying:

> I know everything, but I'm only one [person] and I'm a very small. [The government] control everything. I try to learn and I try to break their power. But this needs time. I will try to break the power, little, by little, by little. Trust building [between youth and the government] and then a little grow, little grow, little grow. After that we are the big group and they are the small.

The case study revealed that Myanmar Exitus did try to influence youth perceptions to prevent them from challenging the status quo. However, due to their many varying perceptions, the ways in which these they influenced young people varied. In the sample of this case study, three different archetypes – *the independent*, *the changed* and *the changers* – were established. It is important to note that while these categorizations are useful in guiding the analysis, agency is more complicated in reality, as the strategic spaces for manoeuvre can overlap and co-exist. Therefore, the separation implied by the archetypes does not do justice to the complexity of the positions of youth and might neglect the plurality of their strategies, and changes over time. Youth might move from one archetype to the other, and not all respondents would fit in one of these categories as they often take up different roles in a variety of times and spaces. Nevertheless, the three archetypes are useful examples to show the different ways in which the perceptions and strategies of youth were influenced by the political awareness training at Myanmar Exitus. *The independent* are those who had pre-formulated ideas about politics and were motivated to participate in the political field anyway, yet still wanted to join the training for various different reasons. *The changed* are less familiar with politics. They were most often introduced to the training by family or friends and did not yet have strong political opinions. This group seemed to be motivated to participate in the political transitions through the training. However, they were also easily influenced in their thinking. *The changers* also did not have much background knowledge about politics upon entering the training. This group seemed to become motivated, although they were generally more reflexive about the information they received than the second archetype. Therefore, they were not easily influenced, and often did not agree with the approach of Myanmar Exitus.

Because of the different perceptions youth held, they also adopted different strategies by making choices about the political field they would work in. Youth made strategic use of contacts in different networks and also moved between these fields. They seemed to do this in order to increase their influence while also ensuring their own survival. Reflecting on the archetypes described above, *the independent* was seldom influenced by the teaching of Myanmar Exitus and therefore decided for themselves in which political field they wanted to work. *The changed* tended to work for the government or for government-affiliated organisations, while *the changers* were generally engaged in civil society organisations and other bodies opposing the Government. The strategies of *the changed* were perhaps favoured over the other two archetypes, because these fit with the hegemonic culture present in the training programme. For example, one student with connections to the government lived in a very spacious apartment in the city centre of Yangon arranged by his contacts, which he would otherwise not be able to afford. Interestingly, this did not seem to discourage the other archetypes. They looked for other opportunities with, for example, (international) civil society organisations.

Acknowledging that it is difficult to influence decision-making, the research shows that youth did try to find other ways to exercise their agency, for example by being political trainers and teaching the younger generation. Myo, a participant in the research, adopted a myriad of strategies and could belong to the archetype *changed*, as he would not oppose the Government and would often mention that it was important to understand their point of view. Despite this, he enjoyed good relationships with NLD as well as ethnic party-members. Working as a political trainer he would provide trainings to the USDP, NLD and ethnic political parties. Through his own background as a Muslim, he was well-connected into that community, but also beyond it. He claimed to be a "*broker*" himself, using his contacts to create opportunities for different actors to meet. This gave him the feeling that he was able to make a difference in his society. Considering his own political affiliation, it was interesting that Myo would claim he did not want to work for Government, because it becomes more complicated to work in other fields. On the other hand, when there were demonstrations against the Government, he would make sure not to be around because he did not want to be affiliated with the opposition. Overall, he seemed comfortable in this ambiguous position, which afforded him convenience, and hence, he did not seem to be willing to challenge the status quo. This myriad of actions and plans is interesting because it shows how young people like Myo can strategically move between different networks. Apart from aiming to change or keep the status quo, it also became clear that for a lot of young people securing their own survival was an important aspect of the strategies they choose.

Case Study Kant Kaw Education Centre: Ethnically Inclusive Education for Peacebuilding

Reflecting the particularities of Myanmar's social, political and cultural characteristics, the findings show that the specific nature of the country's conflict shapes how education for peacebuilding is understood and delivered in this specific case. The cornerstone of KKEC's programme is its commitment to reflect Myanmar's social diversity in the staff and student body. Students are recruited primarily in the country's seven ethnic states, through the school managers' own personal and professional networks, and supported through scholarships to live and study together in Yangon for the length of the programme. This first contact between students in each new cohort is a critical moment where many of them may meet youth of other ethnicities and religions for the first time, gain knowledge about other communities, break down prejudices and build understanding about each other. One student contended that "*my ideas are probably a bit part of my ethnic [background], but here after I arrived, month by month, I understand [the other students]*". Another noted that "*some class*mates*' idea[s] are completely different. But it makes me to see from [the] other side*". Faced with the challenge of diversity, KKEC is tasked with creating an inclusive environment in which the differences between individuals do not inhibit their capacity to interact and learn, but open a learning space for all voices to be heard, and for positive experiences to take place. Building on the discussion of the 4Rs framework, this case study explores the intersection of peace, inclusion and education further, in the ways that staff and students at KKEC understand and experience what this research calls "ethnically-inclusive peace education".

The programme is built along two key lines: a progressive curriculum informed by international good practice and a degree of experimentation, while directly confronting some of the key issues at the heart of Myanmar's conflict, in the classroom. Conflict analysis, peacebuilding theory and civic education, based on cases in Myanmar and beyond, have students connect their own experiences to global examples. Communication skills are developed, to aid them in articulating different views effectively, and discussing more controversial or difficult topics in a constructive manner, with teachers encouraging group work and open debate as a way to explore ideas and negotiate differences. The school's programme director, a member of Myanmar's Karen ethnic community, described this process of interaction:

> At first [they] maybe [think] 'Kachin people are not good, Karen people are not good, Kayah people are not good'. But by letting them sit together in the classroom, it's also in a way teaching each other. These lessons, in a way, [are a] kind of peace education. You need to understand, [in] each group you have differences and similarities.

At the time of research, the first democratic elections had taken place, but the transfer of power to the NLD government had not yet. Many students confirmed that the country's history of political oppression and lack of freedoms continued to influence attitudes in their communities, and speaking openly about these issues in school was unfamiliar territory. As they became more comfortable engaging with these issues throughout the school year, it became clear that some students were concerned that their knowledge and skill level in civic and political education seemed to impose a kind of responsibility on them to confront these issues. As well as opening students up to new knowledge and empowering them to act, it could be said that the KKEC programme highlighted the low levels of information and understanding around the peace process amongst its students, perhaps reflecting much of Myanmar's population. This gives the impression of KKEC being a sort of "bubble" of knowledge, power and opportunity, and also responsibility, making students a new generation of active citizens in peacebuilding, as they may possess more of the key knowledge and skills than previous generations.

KKEC's particular vision of peacebuilding is to put peace education skills and experiences into practice, for students to be able to become effective community leaders, in their own local areas and other parts of the country. The emphasis on community-led change is also addressed on a practical level. Students learn career-oriented skills such as leadership and project management, and are encouraged to build their CVs through volunteering and internship opportunities. An example of this is the curriculum's 'service learning' element, in which academic and practical learning are combined around civic engagement and community service. Its aim is threefold: to encourage students' 'spirit of volunteerism' and awareness of community-driven change opportunities; to help students to give their academic skills and knowledge a practical basis; and to let students discover new and different parts of Myanmar and enter into a sharing and learning relationship with their host communities. In one group discussion with students, four out of five said that the most important experience they had at KKEC was service learning. This is summed up by the school's director of programmes:

> [One student] was assigned to stay in a remote village in area where there is no electricity, no running water, something like that. So when the night comes, you sleep. And water, you get it from the river. [He] started to learn how [to ride] a tractor, teaching the kids. I think it touched his heart, knowing the villages, and the daily experiences of the villagers. So after graduation, he wanted to teach. He wanted to serve the under-served children. So he went to work somewhere, teaching the children. Then, later, he got a job with World Vision in Mon State, to be coordinator for children's education programmes.

In this example, the student combined this 'experiential' learning with the theoretical background and skills acquired at KKEC, applying them in a development position with an INGO, after graduating from the programme. For many thinkers in the field of peacebuilding education, such "experiential" learning is a central component of it. There must be recognition and analysis of conflicts in order to learn about de-escalation and prevention (Berghof Foundation 2012). Simultaneously, students of peace education must learn to actively resolve conflicts and promote peaceful social environments (Lopes Cardozo and May 2009).

The programme encourages in students a multi-scalar way of thinking around peacebuilding and development. By capitalising on students' prior interests and any experience in civil society networks, the programme promotes a community-driven approach, teaching skills that would allow students to work with different groups across Myanmar, such as communication and mediation. Simultaneously, examples and theory from the rest of world are tied into discussion of conflict and peace processes. Finally, the use of English in the classroom, and the inclusion of career-oriented skills and experiences in the programme, are thought to enable graduates to work in English-speaking environments, with knowledge of how international labour and higher education markets function. This is exemplified in one student's answer to the survey question of what they hope to do upon leaving KKEC:

> First, I want to work [as] a volunteer in [a] NGO. Then, I want to apply [for a] scholarship to [study] abroad. My dream [is] to make business opportunities for my people from Rakhine and to help children who can't go to school.

Here, the student seems to bring together the different threads within the KKEC curriculum, from service learning, to development skills, and university entrance preparation. This multiplicity also leads to a tension around the (un)intended outcomes of this education. As an unaccredited, private school, KKEC already operates somewhat removed from the national education system. On top of this, through its curriculum, teaching and the opportunities it gives students, KKEC provides channels for engaging in change and development systems that are outside of the current public sphere. It is possible that this form of organisation contributes to the bypassing of state institutions, for example in so-called "NGOisation" (the rise of NGOs that take charge of services traditionally provided by governments). This is problematic as it may undermine national education and labour systems by promoting decentralised and privatised institutions, jeopardising the capabilities of public institutions to respond to and address issues of conflict resolution, peacebuilding and youth leadership in comprehensive and nationally-owned ways.

Following October 2015's elections, great changes were anticipated with the transition of power, and many young people in particular were impatiently waiting for chances to shape their futures in new ways. Democratic government has the potential to lead Myanmar to occupy a greater position on the international stage, rapidly bringing globalisation and all of its properties into the country, which have been largely absent until now. It is hoped by many in Myanmar that these changes will extend into the national education system through reform, expansion of access and improved quality. The question that KKEC should be asking itself for now is how far its curriculum enables students to enter this 'new world' in the changing country, and take an active position in effecting system change, on different levels. In other words, are students able to implement the skills and knowledge they have learned, to effectively contribute to peacebuilding and social, political and economic development in Myanmar, even as the context continues to evolve? For many students, the experience of learning in a multicultural and diverse environment was itself personally transformative, as described by KKEC's school manager:

> After this one year [students] develop friendship and understanding, understanding about different cultures. You will see [a] student, a Mon student for example, and now they are wearing [a] Karen outfit, something like that.

This, in a context where historical isolation has caused fragmented relationships between many communities, is perhaps one of the most important triumphs of KKEC's programme.

Discussion

The two programmes outlined in the case studies above are very different. Myanmar Exitus provides political awareness training, given by local teachers, while KKEC focuses on community leadership and social studies, and is taught largely by an internationally-oriented staff. Both institutions offer independently-developed and time-bound programmes, which can be seen to contribute to the creation of an internal "bubble". In both programmes, controversial and sensitive topics are discussed. It is important to recognise this, as it may be challenging for students to transfer the knowledge they gain within these courses, to situations and contexts outside of these environments.

In both case studies, it became clear that the participants in the programmes often already have connections to the organisation because they are familiar with the network of civil society actors in Myanmar. Respondents at Myanmar Exitus indicated that the same people are regularly invited for workshops or trainings, most of them living in or near Yangon. However, the inclusion of marginalised and remote-living youth is critical for any kind of movement for change in Myanmar, as politics and civic engagement are often centralised in Yangon. For change to be sustainable and far-reaching there has to be outreach to the full spectrum of diversity in the country's communities. KKEC's students generally represent this diversity, although they are recruited primarily through the civil society network, which the school and its managers belong to. This means that there is an inherent bias in the students who apply for and attend the programme every year, excluding other marginalised young people. Opportunities are thus unequal and might lead to increased injustices. It is therefore important to pay attention to the equal distribution of opportunities for youth to enjoy this kind of education. This connects to the "redistribution" element in the 4Rs framework, as outlined in Chap. 2, which points out that in order to work towards sustainable peacebuilding opportunities, access to education should be equal for everyone.

In terms of the "reconciliation" element, and the ways in which education contributes to either integration and segregation, it remains interesting to see that the two programmes have differing intentions, yet the outcomes overlap. The main focus of Myanmar Exitus is political education while they are not subversive, and training has different outcomes depending on what young people take from it. In that sense, Myanmar Exitus divides the youth community, who end up with very different thoughts and opinions, perhaps contributing to segregation more than integration. On the contrary, KKEC focuses on recognition and reconciliation, as their vision of inclusive development and peacebuilding for Myanmar can be seen as a response to the particularity of this country's conflict. This is understood to stem from historic, political oppression, as well as ethnic and religious difference, which is addressed in KKEC's "peace curriculum". Through citizenship education, students are given knowledge and skills to engage in civic processes, to advocate for rights and freedoms, and to participate in the country's political sphere. Simultaneously, the school places a strong emphasis on addressing and embracing the nation's cultural diversity in the classroom, encouraging young people from many different communities to come together, to learn together and about each other. Community is seen as the core social entity for understanding conflict, bringing about change, peace and development. The school makes a case for national peacebuilding to be a bottom-up, locally-informed exercise, as a way to address the particular context effectively. This is embodied in the emphasis on experiential learning and practical skills in the curriculum. That emphasis connects to peace education theory which demands strong attention to "various social, political, economic, historical and cultural contexts", to be able to respond to realities on the ground (Berghof Foundation 2012). Although it is not an explicit aim of its programme, Myanmar Exitus, in contrast, may unconsciously create spaces for people with different opinions to engage and communicate with each other. In the case study of KKEC, that space is created more consciously, as this is a key objective of the school. Thus, both programmes bring young people together, thereby creating new spaces in which young people can learn with and from each other.

This shows that both education programmes often had unintended outcomes, which underscores the unpredictability and non-linear nature of schooling. It is therefore important that programmatic interventions and policies in this sector are implemented with great sensitivity toward the social, political and economic context in which it is embedded, so as to avoid contributing to indoctrination, segregation and conflict. It is essential to critically question and assess the broader strategically selective context of Myanmar, especially considering the many actors adopting different political agendas. A key finding of both case studies is the importance of analysing who decides what is desired from education, as this might have critical implications for the consequences of education.

The case study of KKEC showed that education can have unintended results which are important to reflect upon. An example of the challenge this presents is in language of instruction. Bearing in mind that Myanmar is made up of 135 ethnolinguistic groups, English was originally selected by the school as a neutral option, which lent itself to the discussion of politically sensitive and controversial topics, including conflict, history but also gender studies. The research revealed that the use of English in the classroom further contributed to the removal of KKEC's curriculum from mainstream education in Myanmar, emphasising the "bubble" mentioned above. This bubble was also created within Myanmar Exitus, as this remained a place where generally sensitive political topics could be discussed. The language of instruction at Myanmar Exitus was mainly Burmese, which could have made it more difficult for young people from other states to join the programme.

While the case of KKEC in many ways corroborates and adds to existing ideas around peacebuilding education, the research found that the programme goes beyond just addressing peace and conflict. The focus on civic engagement, community experience and global issues, along with teaching language and career-oriented skills, contributes to "widening the gaze" of students and showing them different opportunities for their own lives. This is also the case for Myanmar Exitus. Although most young people did feel excluded from formal decision-making mechanisms, there were also those who sought opportunities to work as conflict transformers with other young people. They chose to contribute directly to their peer group in ways that appeal to them. These strategies and activities often seemed to go largely un-rewarded and unseen, although they need to be recognized, rewarded and fostered in order for youth to have a meaningful contribution to the political transitions in Myanmar.

Myanmar Exitus and KKEC can both be seen as unconventional providers of knowledge and skills that fall outside the scope of Myanmar's public education system, with a particular agenda around peacebuilding and political activism in the transitioning context. It remains important to point out that these parallel education systems that are emerging in Myanmar offer opportunities and can add subjects that are not covered in the formal curriculum. This highlights the general deficiency of Myanmar's public education sector, which may prompt young people to engage in alternative systems of schooling and employment, outside of the mainstream, which could lead to a bifurcation of civil society initiatives for peacebuilding and reconciliation, potentially causing new exclusions, inequalities or conflicts.

Findings of this research thus illustrate that education can have "multiple faces". In the first case study, Myanmar Exitus was able to motivate youth to participate in the political transitions while it was used as a political tool to diffuse the hegemonic state ideology (Lall 2014). Because the programme influenced some students but not others, it divided the youth community who ended up with different perspectives. In the second case study tension between local and international spheres is tangible, rendering uncertain which areas students feel prepared or inspired to work in. The predilection toward Western pedagogy and best practice in the programme resulted from a lack of home-grown solutions in Myanmar, since the opening of the school in 2009. In order for it to remain relevant and useful for the diverse group of students who join the programme, KKEC must continue to adapt in response to social and political developments in Myanmar, as well as the evolution of the peace process. Both case studies thus highlighted the positive/negative duality that is often seen in education research (see e.g. Shah and Lopes Cardozo 2014).

Conclusion

The core argument of this chapter is that policies and programmatic interventions should aim to provide youth with circumstances to realize the positive contributions in the transitions the country is going through. It remains interesting to see to what extent non-formal education initiatives, such as Myanmar Exitus and KKEC, meet the demands of the economic and political landscape facing graduates, in their communities in Myanmar, and how students recognise the opportunities that are made available to them, and understand and experience the benefits of such programmes within larger movements of political development and peacebuilding.

These case studies show that where such education providers provide spaces for youth to learn and engage, the outcomes may be unpredictable and perhaps unintended. This is illustrated by KKEC students' expressions of their future plans, post-graduation, which demonstrate an inclination toward further study abroad, and entering an international workplace. In the case study of Myanmar Exitus, this was shown by the fact that through the programme young people with different opinions were able to meet and learn from each other. In contrast to the stated objective of Myanmar Exitus, some of them even used this new knowledge and experience to work towards challenging the status quo.

Generally, youth should not be seen as disengaged political subjects, but should not be generalized and over-idealised as actors for progressive change either. Without putting too much emphasis on their youth-status, they should be provided with tools and opportunities to use their energy and agency in constructive ways, while taking into account the complex conflict-affected society they belong to. Perhaps the best way that can be done is to offer Myanmar's young people the widest possible range in knowledge, skills and experiences, and provide spaces for them to explore the possibilities and opportunities that can come from these, at home and beyond.

References

Apple, M. (1990). Is there a curriculum voice to reclaim? *Phi Delta Kappan, 71*(1), 474–477.

Berghof Foundation. (2012). *Peace education in Berghof Foundation, Berghof glossary on conflict transformation*. Berlin: Berghof Foundation.

Block, K., Cross, S., Riggs, E., & Gibbs, L. (2014). Supporting schools to create an inclusive environment for refugee students. *International Journal of Inclusive Education, 18*(12), 1337–1355.

Bush, K. D., & Saltarelli, D. (2000). *The two faces of education in ethnic conflict*. Florence: The Innocenti Research Centre.

Davies, L. (2005). School and war: Urgent agendas for comparative and international education. *Compare: A Journal for Comparative and International Education, 35*(4), 357–371.

Davies, L. (2010). The different faces of education in conflict. *Development, 53*(4), 491–497.

Fountain, S. (1999). *Peace education in UNICEF*. New York: UNICEF.

Fraser, N. (1998). *Social justice in the age of identity politics: Redistribution, recognition, participation*. Berlin: WZB Discussion Paper.

Harris, I., & Synott, J. (2002). Peace education for a new century. *Social Alternatives, 21*, 3–6.

Hilker, L. M. (2011). The role of education in driving conflict and building peace: The case of Rwanda. *PRO, 41*, 267–282.

Jackson, S. (1997). Crossing borders and changing pedagogies: From Giroux and Freire to feminist theories of education. *Gender and Education, 9*(4), 457–467.

Junne, G., & Verkoren, W. (2005). *Postconflict development: Meeting new challenges*. Boulder: Lynne Reiner Publishers.

Lall, M. (2014). Engaging the youth – citizenship and political participation in Pakistan. *Commonwealth & Comparative Politics, 52*(4), 535–562.

Lall, M., & Win, H. H. (2012). Perceptions of the state and citizenship in light of the 2010 Myanmar elections. In N. Cheesman, M. Skidmore, & T. Wilson (Eds.), *Myanmar's transition: Openings, obstacles, and opportunities*. Myanmar: Institute of Southeast Asian Studies.

Lopes Cardozo, M. T. (2008). Sri Lanka: In peace or in pieces? A critical approach to education in Sri Lanka. *Research in Comparative and International Education, 3*(1), 19–35.

Lopes Cardozo, M. T., & May, A. (2009). Teaching for peace – Overcoming division? Peace education in reconciliation processes in Sri Lanka and Uganda. In S. Nicolai (Ed.), *Opportunities for change: Education, innovation and reform during and after conflict*. Paris: UNESCO.

Matelski, M. (2013). Civil society and expectations of democratisation from below: The case of Myanmar. *Thammasat Review, 16*, 153–166.

Novelli, M., Lopes Cardozo, M. T. A., & Smith, A. (2017). The 4Rs framework: Analyzing education's contribution to sustainable peacebuilding with social justice in conflict-affected contexts. *Journal on Education in Emergencies, 3*(1), 14–43.

Osler, A., & Starkey, H. (2005). *Changing citizenship*. London: McGraw-Hill Education.

Salem-Gervais, N., & Metro, R. (2012). A textbook case of nation-building: The evolution of history curricula in Myanmar. *Journal of Burma Studies, 16*(1), 27–78.

Sanchez, E., & Rognvik, S. (2012). *Building just societies: Reconciliation in transitional settings.* Ghana: United Nations.

Shah, R. & Lopes Cardozo, M. T. A. (2014, September 8). *The fruit caught between two stones: The conflicted position of teachers during and after the conflict.* Conference paper, BAICE, Bath University.

Shah, R. A., & Lopes Cardozo, M. T. A. (2015). The politics of education in emergencies and conflict. In T. McCowan & E. Unterhalter (Eds.), *Education and international development: An introduction.* London: Bloomsbury Academic.

Sleeter, C. (1996). Multicultural education as a social movement. *Theory Into Practice, 35*, 239–247.

Taylor, S., & Sidhu, R. K. (2012). Supporting refugee students in schools: What constitutes inclusive education? *International Journal of Inclusive Education, 16*(1), 39–56.

Thomas, J. (1992). *Doing critical ethnography.* DeKalb/Newbury Park: Northern Illinois University/Sage.

UNESCO. (2009). *Policy guidelines on inclusion in education.* Paris: UNESCO.

UNESCO. (2011). *The hidden crisis: Armed conflict and education.* Paris: UNESCO.

United Nations. (1948). *Universal Declaration of Human Rights (UDHR).*

United Nations. (1989). *Convention on the Rights of the Child (CRC).*

Youniss, J. (2002). Youth civic engagement in the twenty-first century. *Journal of Research on Adolescence, 12*(1), 121–148.

Chapter 12
Drawing Conclusions: The Role of Education in Moving Towards Sustainable Peace in Myanmar

Elizabeth J. T. Maber, Mieke Lopes Cardozo, and Sean Higgins

Introduction

Given the persistence of conflicts in multiple regions of the country, the increase in violence in Rakhine State, the continuing accounts of atrocities and human rights abuses, and the hundreds of thousands who remain displaced both within and across Myanmar's borders, it may seem somewhat optimistic to speak of achieving sustainable peace in the country at present. However, the intention of this work has been to indicate the potential role for education to support efforts to move towards peace and the pitfalls that exist that may undermine peacebuilding efforts. The research presented in this collection has focused on areas of the country – Mon State and the broader Yangon area – that may be considered closer to a post-conflict context, precisely in order to examine the opportunities and the challenges that education initiatives encounter in the aftermath of conflicts and as political transitions are negotiated.

This concluding chapter aims to draw together reflections on the findings of the chapters and indicate potential ways to move forward. Towards the end of our period of data collection for the research in January 2016 members of the Amsterdam and Myanmar-based team facilitated a series of workshops in both Yangon and Mawlamyine. The intention of these workshops was to share initial findings of the research and to work collaboratively with research participants and other key stakeholders to develop some suggestions for ways forward. The results of these discussions are presented here in relation to the three main thematic areas of the research: (1) integrating education reforms and peacebuilding at the level of policy formation

E. J. T. Maber (✉)
University of Cambridge, Cambridge, UK
e-mail: ejtm2@cam.ac.uk

M. L. Cardozo · S. Higgins
University of Amsterdam, Amsterdam, The Netherlands

M. T. A. Lopes Cardozo, E. J. T. Maber (eds.), *Sustainable Peacebuilding and Social Justice in Times of Transition*,
https://doi.org/10.1007/978-3-319-93812-7_12

and implementation; (2) supporting teachers to foster teaching and learning environments conducive to building peace; and (3) supporting the socio-cultural, political and economic agency of youth in peacebuilding. While these reflections emerged from a time of political uncertainty about the process of transition in the wake of the NLD's election victory, they continue to hold resonance as peace processes and education reform processes have gradually advanced, yet remain unresolved.

The chapter then reflects on the application of the '4R' framework that has supported the analysis across the chapters. The potential opportunities to address root causes of inequalities and social injustices in education are summarised in relation Redistribution, Recognition, Representation and Reconciliation, emphasising the interconnections between these dimensions and the importance of complimentary efforts to ensure greater equality and ultimately contribute to a more sustainable peace. A strength of the findings of all chapters is their emergence from research partnerships developed between "northern" and Myanmar researchers at each stage of the research process, from joint decision making on data collection through to analysis, writing and dissemination. This edited collection therefore has greatly benefitted from the scholarly collaboration and distinctive form of knowledge production resulting from the participation of all the contributors to the research. Constrained by a historically restrictive environment for research, such collaborations have been difficult until quite recently, and it is hoped that opportunities will continue to expand to promote increased scholarly partnerships.

Consolidating Findings and Ways Forward

In Yangon two workshops were held: the first was conducted in the UNICEF country office with 27 participants and representatives from civil society organisations, education practitioners, policymakers and activist groups, national and international NGOs, UN agencies and other international agencies. The second was held with 13 youth respondents who participated in the case studies included in the research and programme facilitators working with these initiatives. In Mawlamyine, 2 workshops were held, 1 with 30 teachers and township education officers from across Mon State, and the second with 16 youth respondents and programme facilitators that participated in the Mon-based case studies.

The aim of each workshop was twofold. One was to validate the findings from the draft country report, and in particular how viewpoints and programmes were represented. The second was to co-construct ideas on ways forward from these findings, if the goal is to achieve a sustainable peace for the country. To do this, youth and teachers were asked to visually represent (in small groups) the types of changes that needed to happen at a number of different scales/levels, and who would be responsible for these changes – starting from the individual (self) and moving outwards to the international. With the policymakers' workshop hosted by the UNICEF country office in Yangon, similar questions were asked but responses were individually written on a feedback form. From this, discussions were held where participants were asked to identify where education in particular might figure as part of transformation processes. Both the activities and the subsequent discussions helped to shape the ideas noted below.

It is important to note that in these workshops and within the discussions presented here the research team has steered away from using the term "recommendations". What is provided below are ideas on how an agenda for building a sustainable peace within and through education could be better realised. This list is neither exhaustive nor definitive, and should be taken as areas for consideration rather than prescribed steps for change.

Considering the Role of Education in and Within Peacebuilding Processes

It is acknowledged that education reform since 2011 has taken place in a highly politicised arena driven by various and competing interests. Nonetheless, this resulted in peacebuilding principles being notably absent from key reforms, such as the CESR, the National Education Law (2014), and the NESP which was in draft form at the time. Following the 2015 parliamentary elections, new opportunities have emerged to make inclusion, conflict sensitivity and peacebuilding central pillars for further reform. However, there remain uncertainties about the prospects of capitalising on this opportunity, as significant political constraints remain (as detailed in Chaps. 4 and 5). There has been a stark divide between the national peace process and the process of education reform, and this appears to be continuing despite a more recent renewal of peacebuilding rhetoric (addressed in Chap. 3). This leads to a lack of understanding, particularly amongst those involved in the education sector, of the important grievances held by a wide range of non-state actors on matters of recognition and representation within and through education. The result has been a focus on redistribution as a primary broker for building a peace dividend as part of reform. As ways forward:

(a) Educational actors need to better understand the key grievances of the multitude of non-state actors and civil society to formulate appropriate policy responses.
(b) On the side of the (inter-)national peacebuilding community, there needs to be greater acknowledgement of the foundational importance of equitable social service delivery, in arenas such as education and health, that is both quantitatively and qualitatively supporting the construction of a sustainable peace.
(c) For both the international community and the national government, there is a need to move education reform beyond the modernisation – and economically focused – paradigm, and to situate it with a process of building a citizenry that is inclusive and reconciliatory (in the long-run).

To date, despite claims that educational policymaking processes have been made more transparent and representative of a variety of viewpoints, there remains a strong sense that such consultation is tokenistic in nature and exclusionary. Many continue to feel alienated and/or ignored in their claims for change, and resulting in widespread protests, as was evidenced following passage of the National Education Law in 2014. Venues for more effective engagement and participation in processes of education reform need to be considered, to avoid the creation of new grievances, as was highlighted in Chap. 5.

As also discussed further below, the gendered experiences and outcomes of schooling for boys and girls must be better considered at all levels of education reform and implementation. Quantitative data on gender parity and participation rates continues to mask significant inequities when it comes to how boys and girls are treated and valued in the classroom and their communities. Current education practices do not prepare girls to take on positions of leadership or to challenge traditional gender roles and inequalities. While women's participation in politics and policymaking, and representation in parliament and within the Ministries, has increased with the 2015 election, it continues to be low at roughly 10%[1] (Macgregor 2015) and remains a priority for women's rights activists and civil society leaders to ensure gender inequalities are addressed within reform initiatives. To ensure the adequate representation and recognition of women's voices in administrative and policy-making roles in education, avenues for the promotion of women into key decision-making roles in the education sector need to be strengthened. Likewise, more could be done to uptake principles of positive masculinity and address the myriad forms of gender violence that persist in the country.

Finally, ongoing developments in the policy for language of instruction in classrooms are crucial. Language is seen as central to the identity of various ethnic groups within the country, and the inability for children to learn and use their mother tongues in schooling has been a long-standing grievance of these groups. In early 2016 reforms had only moved as far as supporting an additive model of language policy (i.e. teaching of ethnic language as an additional subject) which may do little to better support children's learning and acknowledge past grievances. Ultimately it is critical that children across the country are able to enter into school and gain literacy in their mother tongue first.

Supporting the Role of Teachers, and Teaching/Learning to Foster Peacebuilding

The fragmented, piecemeal nature of teacher training provision (pre and in-service) to date has the potential to cause or exacerbate inequalities in terms of qualifications of those entering into the various sectors, career prospects, and the pedagogical

[1] This figure takes into account the 25% of parliamentary seats reserved for Military appointees, amongst which there are two female appointees. The number of women rises to 14.5% of MPs elected to the Union Parliament, and 12.5% of MPs elected to State and Regional Parliaments when excluding the non-elected Military appointees (Ninh 2016).

knowledge they are equipped with during their careers. From a peacebuilding perspective, particularly in regards to redistribution and recognition, teacher education could benefit from greater coherence and logic, with particular attention to the constraints within which teachers work.

Opportunities to bring teachers together across the various sectors could be increased. As outlined in Chap. 7, programmes like SITE and Head Teacher Training in Mon State have opened spaces for dialogue between educators working in the state, ethnic and monastic systems, and increased understanding of the shared challenges and dilemmas teachers within both systems face. However, such encounters need to be carefully managed, as they will bring to bear ongoing inequities which exist within the current system. As revealed in Chaps. 7 and 8, teachers are acutely aware of the inequalities that exist in terms of the resourcing and distribution of learning materials (such as textbooks or school uniforms). This forms a significant grievance. Positive steps, such as the training of township education officers and head teachers in Mon State, are working to raise awareness of this issue, and potentially serve to rectify the situation. This is dependent on state resources being made freely available to township education officers to redirect to schools and sectors that have been previously neglected. It is critical from a peacebuilding standpoint therefore, that promises of change are followed by meaningful action.

Similarly, the recent decision to increase salaries of state teachers has the potential to improve the status and self-worth of the teaching profession. There are, however, some important unintended negative consequences which could create new grievances. For one, it appears to be creating a greater divide in the status of state versus non-state educators. Additionally, it may also drain non-state schools of their most qualified and/or experienced teachers, as teachers are attracted towards the state sector. It is suggested that policies that aim to redistribute resources related to teaching and learning (such as the so called 'Quick Wins' discussed in Chap. 5) better consider consequences in terms of equity within and across the various education sectors.

There is also perhaps a danger that in the urge to draw on so-called international best practice from OECD countries in the content of teacher trainings and teacher education reform, the valuable, contextual knowledge and practical wisdom of current teachers working in diverse communities within the country may be side-lined. Given the distinctive challenges faced by the country's teachers, the development of teacher education curricula, while drawing on cross-national insights, should also build directly on local teacher knowledge, experience and examples of good practice. Crucially, teachers' agency should be respected and honoured in the new curriculum that is devised. Examples emerged in the research, as explored in Chap. 6, of how teachers are presently mediating content they perceive as divisive and exclusionary. Ideally, curriculum reform should provide teachers with a greater sense of autonomy to contextualise content to reflect their students' backgrounds and needs. Simultaneously, the reform process should provide sufficient guidance and support through resources and training, to effectively incorporate principles of peacebuilding – namely reducing inequality, accepting diversity, meaningful participation and building trust/cooperation (i.e. the 4Rs) – across all areas of the curriculum, rather than as a separate content area. It will also necessitate reform of the examination-based assessment system, and the consolidation of an overcrowded curriculum.

Significant issues remain in how teachers are deployed and managed within the state system and at the school level. This leads to concerns in terms of the distribution of qualified and appropriate personnel, and recognition and representation of community demographics and demands. Specific to initial deployment, greater consideration must be given to the needs of particular communities, as well as the qualifications, experience, background, and obligations (such as family) of individual teachers. Schools and townships across the country should maintain a standard *teacher:student* ratio that needs to be regularly monitored, with processes of deployment/redeployment responding to changes in enrolment numbers. This needs to be done in a transparent fashion. Likewise, important consideration must be given to the ability of teachers to instruct in the mother tongue(s) represented in the school.

As the research collected here indicates, there are attempts to centralise aspects of teacher management, particularly on matters such as the competency frameworks and qualification standards. At the same time, there are concerns that bridging the parallel systems and offering greater standardisation may not acknowledge the particular needs, challenges and expected roles of teachers vis a vis their communities. In the validation workshop in Mon State, teachers identified that aspects such as teacher accountability might be better managed within the profession itself, and ideally at the level of the school or township. At the school level itself, school leaders and township education officers should (be made able to) ensure that teachers' time and skill levels are being efficiently and effectively utilised across all grades.

Finally, appropriate school facilities, specifically adequate and clean toilets/running water, child-appropriate learning spaces, sports/recreation areas, should be made available to all students and teachers in Myanmar, even more for those outside the state system. There are currently significant challenges in terms of making schooling accessible to all, which exacerbates inequalities from a redistribution standpoint and fails to recognise the needs of students and teachers to feel safe in their learning environments. The school mapping exercise undertaken by the government in coordination with its development partners is a positive first step, particularly if it is able to cover the entire country and maps schools within and across the various sectors. This will need to be followed by the appropriation of adequate resourcing to areas of greatest need, irrespective of sector or locale.

Supporting the Socio-cultural, Political and Economic Agency of Youth in Peacebuilding

Policy and practice must move beyond considering youth as a singular entity, and better acknowledge the distinctive, contrasting priorities of various youth constituencies whose lived realities are rooted in families and communities. In responding to diverse needs and demands, care should be taken to carefully examine if and how some constituencies might be privileged, or how some peacebuilding agency dimensions (e.g. enhancing economic or civic participation) might be prioritised over others, despite the desire of some youth for the strengthening of socio-cultural agency, or inter-cultural cohesion.

Similarly, there is a strong desire and need for increased physical and virtual spaces available for youth to learn and connect both formally and informally. Such spaces can provide opportunities for young people to come together, build bridges and foster mutual understanding. However, the creation of these spaces – such as youth centres, libraries, community meeting places, and online forums – can be problematic and should be sensitive to the dangers of over-privileging one group over another. Merely increasing access or redistributing access to such spaces may not serve (i.e. represent) the needs of all youth actors. Consideration should be given to who is perceived to be directing and/or funding such initiatives, which voices are dominant and which youth may feel excluded.

There is a need for greater representation of diverse youth voices in political processes at multiple scales and this is accompanied by a need for greater policy development for youth related issues. At the national political level, youth have a history of and continued desire to engage in political activity – which has often been marginalized or violently obstructed. Moving forward, youth expressed a need for policy-makers to recognize and act upon their demands and grievances in non-violent, democratic and meaningful ways, an observation that was similarly reflected in a report by Paung Sie Facility (2017). The developments of the NLD government in formulating a National Youth Policy and inviting youth representatives to participate in renewed peacebuilding dialogues are positive steps to engage young people in addressing the issues that concern them (Phyo 2016; PSF 2017). Youth participation in these consultation processes have also further underlined the prioritisation of education amongst young people's concerns (Phyo 2016). The historic absence of inclusion of youth within reform processes, however, remains a concern for the enactment of education reforms such as the NESP. Additionally, it remains critical that such efforts are representative of diverse youth voices and that consultation processes are followed up with actions that address the concerns raised (Min 2016). At the community-level, youth engagement in community decision-making mechanisms, and within the diverse spaces and contexts they occupy in community structures, must be enhanced if their potential agency is to be fully realised. Likewise, the findings presented in Chaps. 9, 10 and 11 illustrate how (formal and non-formal) education can contribute to youth political empowerment by equipping them with knowledge and understanding of political processes. However, existing social norms and intergenerational hierarchies can limit the extent to which youth participation is able to move beyond a tokenistic role. There is a need to provide youth with the adequate tools to participate, and create open, meaningful, and effective avenues for their perspectives to be heard and authentically considered at the national as well as community levels.

In the reform of the formal education systems, attention needs to be paid to the need to ensure relevance of both content and learning experiences. Youth respondents expressed a strong desire for a system that equips them for broad engagement with life and work, would include critical thinking skills, civic, political and media literacy, and that was responsive to their daily realities and challenges. There was also a desire for conflict resolution skills to be integrated into educational provision. The need for education to provide youth with skills for work, linked to labour market opportunities was also emphasised. Ethnic minority youth expressed a strong concern for the need to have their cultural and linguistic identities recognised and protected. Language of instruction and the teaching of history were key aspects of the curriculum in which this could be taken up. Additionally, the impact of gender, sexual orientation and sexual health and reproductive rights require greater consideration within and throughout education experiences and interventions. Education systems are not equipping girls and other marginalised groups of youth with leadership and critical thinking skills to address and interrogate social and cultural hierarchies and prejudices. This undermines their participation in the peace processes and political leadership. The system also currently fails to equip boys with critical thinking to enable them to question patriarchal norms that may condition their behaviour.

There is a need for a greater variety of flexible and continued learning opportunities responding to the diverse needs of different youth constituencies. Recognising the different positions, experiences and educational trajectories of youth, there should be greater opportunities for non-formal vocational education, continuing opportunities to reskill, and routes back into (formal) learning for those with interrupted learning trajectories. Such diverse provision would also require state support for systematic recognition and accreditation. Particular strengths exist in non-formal educational initiatives for youth which could be built upon by both the formal and non-formal system. These strengths include their recognition of pre-existing youth agency and experiences, and their ability to attend and respond to their diverse contexts and challenges. Nevertheless, non-formal education initiatives are not a panacea or alternative to reforms of formal schooling, considering its more inclusive reach amongst a wider, and more diverse range of youth consistencies in the future.

Reflecting on Applying the 4Rs in Myanmar

As various stakeholders and research participants were familiarised with the 4Rs framework in Myanmar, it became apparent that many saw it as a useful heuristic tool for conceptualising the various domains by which peacebuilding could be viewed. Applied to education specifically, many could make clear links to issues of redistribution, representation, recognition and reconciliation and ways that the sector had or could respond to these imperatives. Building on Fig. 2.2 that visualised the various connected relations between the 4Rs in a pyramid shape (Chap. 2), we now provide some concrete reflections on the ways in which choosing to prioritise one R over another could lead to unintentional consequences and unforeseen trade-offs.

As an example, the Quick Wins programme has stressed the redistributive side of peacebuilding, and in particular sought to secure peace dividends by expanding service delivery. Yet, in doing so, and deploying new teachers to some of the more conflict-affected and remote areas of the country, it may signal a lack of recognition of the historical grievances held by ethnic groups regarding issues such as the inclusion of cultural identity in schooling. Such a policy also lacks in representation by failing to ensure that the teachers deployed reflect the background and aspirations of the communities they serve, and instead, places the teachers themselves in vulnerable positions.

Likewise, the desire for rapid visible changes (driven by a focus on supporting redistribution through more effective and equitable education service delivery) sits uneasily with desires to make current reforms representative of diverse stakeholders' viewpoints and aspirations for education. The pace of reform, particularly during the Thein Sein presidency, resulted in consultation processes being judged by many as symbolic rather than substantive, and created a public perception that not all viewpoints are equally valued. Many groups continue to feel "unrecognised" in the new reforms, despite their promise of representing a broader range of the country than before, which (unintentionally) carries the danger of undermining rather than supporting processes of trust-building and reconciling past and present grievances.

Myanmar has been following a liberal peacebuilding thesis, one which presupposes that by redistributing opportunity (i.e. improving educational access), faith in the state can be restored. This assumes that it is matters of redistribution which matter most to the country's citizenry. What was heard from stakeholders we engaged with, however, was that issues of representation and recognition were equally if not more important to them as needing immediate addressing. In particular, concerns about the irrelevance of the current education system to the needs of its stakeholders, the lack of responsiveness of the state to constituency demands, and the lack of perceived control over key decisions in education, were voiced quite vocally in the various workshops held in January. Without acknowledging this, processes of meaningful reconciliation remain absent from the peace being built in the country.

In sum, a clear dialogue needs to occur between the various 4R's dimensions for them to effectively inform the design and implementation of approaches towards supporting and sustaining peace in the country at present. Attention must be paid to where matters of representation, recognition, redistribution and reconciliation can be worked on concurrently in all four moments of education (Robertson and Dale 2015 – as introduced in Chap. 2), and in relation to the broader cultural political economy context, rather than isolating or focusing on one R only – or the education sector as an isolated arena. The table below (Table 12.1) therefore presents further opportunities for changes within the education system to reduce inequalities, understanding that actions are complimentary, and if taken independently may fail to adequately address injustices.

These opportunities for avenues to address social justice within education structures indicate the deeply political nature of education provision. Likewise the analysis indicates the need to reconceptualise the relationship between education and the realm of the political, moving beyond a presentation of "politics" as confined to ministerial processes of reform or, within the classroom, to teaching subjects such as civics. Rather, the research has revealed the impact and infusion of politics across education settings, grounded in local realities that are varied and evolving, and

Table 12.1 Applying the 4Rs

Applying the 4Rs: potential opportunities to address root causes of inequalities and social injustices in education	
Redistribution (addressing inequalities)	Decentralised teacher deployment, responding to the needs of communities, schools, students and teachers
	Adequate salaries for all teachers, reducing disparity between schools
	Equitable distribution of resources in schools, such as teaching materials and facilities, including sanitation and hygiene facilities
	Access and resources for disabled students and staff in schools
	Equitable learning outcomes for students across and with the different schooling systems
	Equal opportunities for promotion within education structures, including for women, ethnic and religious minorities
Recognition (respecting difference)	Opportunities for learning in mother tongue and managed transition to national language
	Analytical skills and critical thinking rather than rote learning and memorisation
	Inclusive pedagogy and varied teaching approaches to accommodate diverse learning styles
	Equal entrance grade requirements for women and men in tertiary education
	Availability of sex education and information on healthy sexual practice, including recognition of sexual orientation and gender identity expressions
	Absence of gender, religious and cultural bias, including through practices in schools and acknowledging diversity within the curriculum – in particular reducing the glorification of male military violence and heroism in the curriculum
Representation (encouraging participation)	Removing barriers to meaningful participation by focusing on:
	Political representation of diverse women and men across levels of government and ministerial departments
	Participation of diverse women and men, including female and male teachers, in education policy formation and consultation processes
	Representative school-based management and avenues for involvement in decision-making processes, including for teachers, parents and students
Reconciliation (building trust and cooperation)	Promoting non-violent classroom management and addressing bullying and violence within schools, whether committed by students, teachers or administrative staff
	Building vertical and horizontal trust within the school community, including through teaching practices and curricula that promote discussion, inclusion and respect between identity-based groups
	Using history teaching as an opportunity to learn about the past, its relevance for the present and new imaginaries of the future, and to understand differing viewpoints
	Creating spaces for peer learning, amongst students and amongst teachers and administrators in different school settings
	Trust building in reform process that is gender sensitive and inclusive

suggests a more micro-level awareness of where politics is enacted and experienced. Of vital importance is confronting education's role in addressing prejudice and processes of othering across these levels of interaction. Historic and current conflicts have been deeply motivated by fear and hostility towards different identity-based groups, and counterbalancing such pervasive mistrust necessitates sustained efforts across the dimensions of inequalities.

The wide array of findings presented in the chapters of this edited volume paint a complex picture, not only with regards to how we could further explore the multiple dimensions of education's potential positive and negative contributions to peacebuilding processes at multiple levels, yet also in terms of the complexity of possible responses and approaches that are constructive, inclusive and geared towards a creative imagining of a more socially just future. We have steered away consciously from all too prescriptive "recommendations" as highlighted above, yet in doing so, we do hope that the level of detail and range of voices represented in this volume might contribute to continued informed debates about Myanmar's future. We see a crucial need to view education as an indispensable and holistic part and parcel of any peacebuilding intervention, be it at micro, meso or macro levels of discussion and action. Here lies a crucial role for continuous research being undertaken by and in collaboration with young female and male students, teachers and Myanmar researchers with a stake and needed expertise in the various education systems. Serious investments in such studies, to inform and shape policies and practice, is needed in order to ensure addressing and limiting the unintended negative consequences of unequal and exclusive educational processes, while rather enabling the potential of education for peacebuilding to support Myanmar towards a more socially just and peaceful future.

References

Macgregor, F. (2015, December 1). Woman MPs up, but hluttaw still 90% male. *The Myanmar Times.* http://www.mmtimes.com/index.php/national-news/17910-woman-mps-up-but-hluttaw-still-90-male.html. Accessed 1 Apr 2017.

Min, A. K. (2016, October 20). Youth policy held back to allow for more inclusion. *The Myanmar Times.* https://www.mmtimes.com/national-news/23192-youth-policy-held-back-to-allow-for-more-inclusion.html. Accessed 15 Dec 2017.

Ninh, K. (2016, March 2). Myanmar elections Usher in unprecedented number of women parliamentarians. *The Asia Foundation.* https://asiafoundation.org/2016/03/02/myanmar-elections-usher-in-unprecedented-number-of-women-parliamentarians/. Accessed 14 Nov 2017.

Paung Sie Facility (PSF). (2017). *Youth and everyday peace in Myanmar: Fostering the untapped potential of Myanmar's youth.* PSF. http://www.paungsiefacility.org/uploads/3/0/1/8/30181835/youth_paper_english.pdf

Phyo, P. T. (2016, June 13). Youth policy draft slated for October. *The Myanmar Times.* https://www.mmtimes.com/national-news/20819-youth-policy-draft-slated-for-october.html. Accessed 15 Dec 2017.

Robertson, S. L., & Dale, R. (2015). Towards a 'critical cultural political economy' account of the globalising of education. *Globalisation, Societies and Education, 13*(1), 149–170.

Appendices

Appendix I: Table on Gender Dimensions to Consider in RAs 1–3

Applies to:	Some key gender dimensions to consider
Cross-cutting analysis (all sections)	Ensure gender-informed analysis when considering 4Rs framework: male/female dimensions of *redistribution, recognition and representation* (e.g. salaries/educational and (un) paid job opportunities/"obligations" (joining the army/caring for the family)/voice/decision-making power etc.) and *reconciliation,* dealing with gender specific legacies and atrocities of the past
	Intersections of gender dynamics with various forms of violence, including:
	Roles of men/women in violence
	Binarism: male as perpetrators, female as victim; Rape as a weapon of war; Discrimination and exclusion
	Roles of men/women in PB – issues of impunity/trauma/healing
	4As of the right to education applied to gender (*accessibility, adaptability, acceptability, availability*: Tomasevski 2003)
	Gendered language (classrooms, society, policy)
	Effects of natural and men-made disasters/emergencies on the gender landscape + gendered effects of migration
	Impact of religious discourses on gender relations
RA1	Education as sector to transform/reproduce gendered behaviours
	Presence/absence of specific policies for e.g. women, girls, LGBT, economic/labour gender parity, etc.
	Role of women's movements in policy influence and legislation formation (ED and PB)
	Gender (mis-)representation and political participation (national, local, SBM) and gendered nature of sectors and ministries
	Gender (in-)equality in entrance grade requirements
	(Mis-)recognition of gender needs in education

M. T. A. Lopes Cardozo, E. J. T. Maber (eds.), *Sustainable Peacebuilding and Social Justice in Times of Transition*,
https://doi.org/10.1007/978-3-319-93812-7

Applies to:	Some key gender dimensions to consider
RA2	Gender specific risks for teachers (e.g. single women in remote areas, military violence)
	Gender dimensions of teacher deployment, employment opportunities and promotion (e.g. remote duty stations required for promotion which female teachers are less willing to undertake)
	Gendered nature of (school) codes of conduct/policy
	Text books (representation and roles of men/women)
	Classroom practices, including:
	Teacher responses to or acts of gendered behavior/GBV/peer violence
	Corporal punishment
	Teachers expectations of girl/boy performance
	Gendered nature of the teaching profession – dominance of female/male teachers in specific educational functions and levels
RA3	Peer violence: boy-to-boy; girl-to-girl; boy-to-girl/girl-to-boy
	Gendered aspects of students/young people's voice and agency and perceived gendered treatment by teachers
	Gender dimensions of participation, including:
	Relevance of initiatives for male/female youth
	Who participates? (e.g. class and gender intersections)
	Segregation and interaction in the classroom
	Gendered reasons for school drop-out (income potential, family division of labour, school violence, unsafe journeys to school, education provision, trafficking of girls and forced military recruitment of boys), relating to the 4As
	Impact of gendered nature of textbooks (e.g. dominance of male (military) heroes, few female role models etc.)
	Sex and sexuality education
	Body shaming and inadequate WASH facilities
	Issues for young mothers/fathers and early marriage

Appendix II: Table on Violence Dimensions to Consider in RAs 1–3

Applies to:	Some key violence dimensions to consider
Cross-cutting analysis (all sections)	Reflect on the relationships between direct and indirect violence across all thematic areas (direct vs. structural, symbolic forms of violence)
	Reflect on the relationship between broader forms of violence and gender based violence
	Reflect on the way different stakeholders conceptualise violence, the causes of violence and the solutions (addressing root causes versus symptoms)
	Reflect on the way violence related to the 'drivers of conflict' is addressed versus violence related to the 'legacies of conflict'
RA1	Reflect on policy and reform that addresses or reinforces modes of overt and covert forms of violence
	Explore ways in which the policy process reflects forms of indirect violence: cultural, symbolic, structural
	Explore ways in which the policy process reflects or redresses forms of direct violence
RA2	Explore the relationship between direct violence against teachers and indirect forms of violence
	Explore direct violent attacks on teachers, teachers on students, students on teachers
	Explore in-direct forms of violence on teachers, teachers on students, students on teachers
	Explore stakeholders conceptualisations of violence in relation to teacher policy, programming and practice
	Explore gendered dimensions of violence in all of the above
RA3	Explore the relationship between direct violence against youth and indirect forms of violence and vice-versa
	Explore direct violent attacks on youth
	Explore in-direct forms of violence on youth
	Explore stakeholders conceptualisations of violence in relation to youth policy, programming and practice

MIX
Papier aus verantwortungsvollen Quellen
Paper from responsible sources
FSC® C105338

If you have any concerns about our products,
you can contact us on
ProductSafety@springernature.com

In case Publisher is established outside the EU,
the EU authorized representative is:
Springer Nature Customer Service Center GmbH
Europaplatz 3, 69115 Heidelberg, Germany

Printed by Libri Plureos GmbH
in Hamburg, Germany